Caribbean Literary Discourse

Caribbean Literary Discourse

Voice and Cultural Identity in the Anglophone Caribbean

Barbara Lalla,

Jean D'Costa,

and Velma Pollard

THE UNIVERSITY OF ALABAMA PRESS
Tuscaloosa

The University of Alabama Press
Tuscaloosa, Alabama 35487-0380

Manufactured in the United States of America

Typeface: Caslon

Cover design: *Jamie Buttram*

∞

The paper on which this book is printed meets the minimum requirements of American National Standard for Information Sciences—Permanence of Paper for Printed Library Materials, ANSI Z39.48-1984.

Library of Congress Cataloging-in-Publication Data

Caribbean literary discourse : voice and cultural identity in the Anglophone Caribbean / Barbara Lalla, Jean D'Costa, and Velma Pollard.
pages cm
Includes bibliographical references and index.
ISBN 978-0-8173-1807-9 (trade cloth : alk. paper) — ISBN 978-0-8173-8702-0 (e book)
1. Caribbean literature (English)—History and criticism. 2. Discourse analysis, Literary—Caribbean Area. 3. National characteristics, Caribbean, in literature. I. Lalla, Barbara, 1949– II. D'Costa, Jean. III. Pollard, Velma.
PR9210.C35 2014
810.9'9729—dc23

2013017503

you cannot tear my song
from my throat

you cannot erase the memory
of my story

you cannot catch
my rhythm

(for you have to born
with that)

—Olive Senior, "Meditation on Yellow"

Contents

List of Tables

Acknowledgments

The authors thank the University of the West Indies and the Government of Trinidad and Tobago for the funding that supported this project. We are also grateful to Ryan Durgasingh for his assistance with sorting and preparing material for this collection.

This volume includes content that has appeared elsewhere in published form or has been presented at conferences. In part I, chapter 1, "Songs in the Silence: Literary Craft as Survival in Eighteenth-Century Jamaica" by Jean D'Costa includes material from an earlier article, "Oral Literature, Formal Literature: The Formation of Genre in Eighteenth Century Jamaica," *Eighteenth-Century Studies* 27, no. 4 (1994): 663–676. Some material in chapter 2, "Black Wholes: Phases in the Development of Jamaican Literary Discourse," and chapter 5, "Creole and Respec': Authority and Identity in the Development of Caribbean Literary Discourse," both by Barbara Lalla, appeared earlier in "Creole and Respec' in the Development of Jamaican Literary Discourse," *Journal of Pidgin and Creole Languages* 20, no. 1 (2005): 53–84, following on three presentations (two at the Conference of the Society for Pidgin and Creole Linguistics: "Creole Dimensions of Development in Caribbean Literary Discourse," plenary address, and "Caribbean Creole and Respec' in Literary Discourse," panel presentation, University of Hawaii, Honolulu, August 14–17, 2003; one at the Third Cultural Studies Conference, "Black Wholes: Creole Dimensions of Development in Caribbean Literary Discourse," plenary address, the University of the West Indies, St. Augustine, Trinidad and Tobago, January 2004).

Chapter 3, "The Caribbean Novelist and Language: A Search for a Literary Medium," by Jean D'Costa, combines and develops content previously discussed in two articles: "The West Indian Novelist and Language: A Search for a Literary Medium," in *Studies in Caribbean Language*, ed. Lawrence D. Carrington in collaboration with Dennis Craig and Ramon Todd Dandaré (St. Augustine, Trinidad and Tobago: Society for Caribbean Linguistics, University of the West Indies, 1983), 252–265; and Jean D'Costa, "Expression and Communication: Literary Challenges to the Caribbean Polydialectal Writer," *Journal of Commonwealth Literature* 19, no. 1 (1984): 123–141. Chapter 4, "*To Us, All Flowers Are Roses:* Writing Ourselves into the Literature of the Caribbean," by Velma Pollard, is reproduced from *Centre of Remembrance: Memory and Caribbean Women's Literature,* edited by Joan Anim-Addo (London: Mango Publishing, 2002), with permission.

In part II, chapter 6, "Bra Rabbit Meets Peter Rabbit: Genre, Audience, and the Artistic Imagination—Problems in Writing Children's Fiction," by Jean D'Costa, first appeared in Selwyn R. Cudjoe, ed., *Caribbean Women Writers: Essays from the First International Conference* (Wellesley, MA: Calaloux Publications, 1990), 254–262, and appear here (revised) with permission. Chapter 7, "'The Dust': A Tribute to the Folk," by Velma Pollard, appeared in *Caribbean Quarterly* 26, nos. 1–2 (1980): 41–48, and is reproduced with permission. Chapter 8, "Collapsing Certainty and the Discourse of Re-Memberment in the Novels of Merle Hodge," by Barbara Lalla, incorporates and expands on two conference presentations ("The Validity of Cross-Disciplinary Analysis: The Language of Collapsing Certainty in the Novels of Merle Hodge," presented at the Seventeenth Conference of West Indian Literature, the University of the West Indies, Mona, Jamaica, April 5–9, 1998; and "Gender, Identity, and Nationhood in Diaspora Literature: The Novels of Merle Hodge," presented at the Centre for Gender and Development Studies Round Table for the Fiftieth Anniversary Distinguished Lecture Series, the University of the West Indies, Hugh Wooding Law School, April 2, 1998). Chapter 9, "Cultural Connections in Paule Marshall's *Praise Song for the Widow,*" by Velma Pollard, appeared in *World Literature Written in in English* 25, no. 2 (1985), 285–298, and is reproduced with permission.

Chapter 10, "Louise Bennett's Dialect Poetry: Language Variation in a Literary Text," by Jean D'Costa, builds on an earlier work: "Louise Bennett's Dialect Poetry: Problems of Variation along a Creole Continuum in a Literary Text," in *Studies in Language Ecology,* edited by Werner Enninger and Lilith Haynes, 135–158 (Wiesbaden, Germany: Franz Steiner Verlag GMBH, 1984). Chapter 11, "Conceptual Perspectives on Time and Timelessness in Martin Carter's 'University of Hunger,'" by Barbara Lalla, draws on material in an essay, "Conceptual Perspectives on Time and Timelessness in Martin Carter's 'University of Hunger,'" in *All Are Involved: The Art of Martin Carter,* ed. Stewart Brown (Leeds: Peepal Tree Press, 1997), 106–114 (and before that from a presentation at the Sixteenth Annual West Indian Literature Conference, the University of Miami, Florida, April 1–4, 1997), but it is considerably reworked. Chapter 12, "Mixing Codes and Mixing Voices: Language in Earl Lovelace's *Salt,*" by Velma Pollard, appeared in *Changing English* 6, no. 1 (1999): 93–101, and is reproduced with permission. Chapter 13, "Opening *Salt*: The Oral-Scribal Continuum in Caribbean Narrative," by Barbara Lalla, is developed from a presentation at a conference in honor of Gordon Rohlehr on his retirement, at the University of the West Indies, St. Augustine, Trinidad and Tobago, October 4–6, 2007. Chapter 14, "Mothertongue Voices in the Writing of Olive Senior and Lorna Goodison," by Velma Pollard, appeared in *Motherlands: Black Women's Writing from Africa, the Caribbean, and South Asia,* edited by S. Nasta (London: Women's Press, 1991), 239–245, and is reproduced with permission. Chapter 15, "The Facetiness Factor: Theorizing Caribbean Space in Narrative," by Barbara Lalla, has evolved from a keynote address at the Twenty-Ninth Conference on West Indian Literature, University of the West Indies, Mona, Jamaica, April 29–May 1, 2010.

The authors also thank Olive Senior for permission to reproduce lines from her poem "Meditation on Yellow" (in *Gardening in the Tropics* [Toronto: McClelland and Stewart, 1994], 17).

Caribbean Literary Discourse

Introduction

Caribbean discourse—in literature and in oral performance alike—has attracted international attention as much for its inherent richness and diversity as for its strange and unique origins. With an eye to discourse from the wildly popular to the erudite and formal, a wide range of audiences increasingly looks to the Caribbean as a vital source of new insights into what it is to be caught up in the crosscurrents of history. Once deemed the antithesis of civilization and the high arts, Caribbean culture today offers the discourse of artists, critics, and scholars of Caribbean literature and cultural studies, work that swells the holdings of major university libraries worldwide. The works of Derek Walcott, Bob Marley, Edwidge Danticat, V. S. Naipaul, Louise Bennett, Stuart Hall, and so many others engage an ever-widening public through academic journals and popular magazines, the Internet, the press, on stage, and on YouTube, exerting a global influence that could never have been foreseen a few decades ago.

Most significantly, the mere existence of such literary creations was utterly unimaginable to the generations of exiles and descendants of exiles whose lives—whatever they were centuries ago—fashioned this culture and its discourse.

However unlooked-for internationally, in the Caribbean, this explosion of verbal art was neither new nor sudden; the intricate mutual involvement of scribal and oral in this developing literary discourse has—like a force of nature—proceeded irresistibly for centuries. Caribbean writers and readers (in particular) have a growing appetite for their own words and their own voices. Nothing less can represent the complexities of their experience and their cultures. The study that follows considers this engagement with the Caribbean voice and—especially—the consequent inscribing of the voice, and it investigates the way in which discourse constructs and mediates Caribbean culture even as the development of Caribbean literary discourse itself illuminates wider, more global movements.

Many of the studies (especially those in part I) focus on Jamaica, but the volume deals with literature from other territories as well, notably Guyana, Trinidad and Tobago, and beyond to the Caribbean Diaspora. Multicultural, multilingual, hybrid, and creolized, the Caribbean is characterized by its very complexity, its multiplicity of origins, its elusive boundaries, and its defiance of fixity. Nowhere is this chaotic essence more obvious than in discourse.

Therefore, this book addresses itself equally to Caribbean scholars and to international scholars of Caribbean discourse, as well as to those readers with wider interests in such matters as the nature of cultural interface; language contact and change; and literary history, together with the relationship between discourse and identity. A wide range of scholarly programs and projects should benefit from a volume devoted to literary discourse and language in the Caribbean. The international academic market has begun to address the historicity of cultural evolution in the light of contact situations, while interest in diasporic relations expands. So too has the sharing of ideas between and among the former colonial countries of the era of European expansionism, especially in the matter of language as a symbol and as a living cultural tool. This work therefore is addressed to college- and university-level audiences interested in the cultural history and development of postcolonial societies as well as in literature and language. Its focus lies in the politics of language choice and usage confronting speakers and writers in such situations of complex loyalties and tensions. In this sense, the work is directly relevant to creative writers interrogating the mechanisms and purposiveness of verbal artistry.

By focusing attention on Caribbean discourse, the study advances the discipline of linguistics by expanding the frontiers of literary linguistics, stylistics, and narrative theory. Caribbean linguistics has so far paid relatively limited attention to linguistic issues in literary discourse. Discourse analysis (and critical discourse analysis of Caribbean material) has, up to now, mainly dealt with nonliterary texts. Caribbean linguists have carried out extensive conversational analysis: recent work such as Valerie Youssef's[1] has been directed to journalistic and legal material. Gender analyses of language and discourse have been directed specifically at either the operations of language or literary interpretation, but in the investigations that follow, the authors address the role of linguistic contact and of a creole language situation in the development of a vernacular literature; the implications of code-switching and of language continua for identity in a postcolonial literature; the operation of intertextuality in postcolonial and diasporic literature; and the linguistic issues involved in the representation of a multilingual and multivocal culture and in the representation of what Gordon Rohlehr has termed an oral-scribal continuum.[2] Beneath these matters lie issues of political choice and national identity.

This volume also advances Caribbean criticism by articulating the characteristics of the literary medium, the linguistic and discursive features of fiction and narrative, and the linguistic dimension of poetics in the context of our Caribbean culture. It proposes a theorizing of Caribbean literature that draws heavily on references to the Caribbean voice and on the interplay between oral and scribal cultures. Literary and cultural studies have in recent years become increasingly interconnected. Several essays in the study (whether or not they pursue technical description or analysis of language) explore the mutually constructive relationship between literature and cultural history, and the book engages directly with those linguistic choices that confront the artist.

Because an important thrust of the work is historical, it investigates the development of Caribbean literature in relation to changes in language culture and in relation to the interface of oral and scribal traditions. The significance of the language situation and, in particular, the ongoing dynamic of interaction between Anglophone Creole and the official language stands central to the study. Evolving language attitudes directly affect the emergence of a recognizably Caribbean literature. The study thus begins with discussion of how literary discourse has emerged and operates within the sociocultural framework of one specific territory (part I), then proceeds to address the discourse of individual texts (part II). In keeping with the volume's historical approach, most (though not all) texts chosen for analysis come from the work of authors born in or before the first half of the twentieth century. A further limitation, urged by constraints of space, has been one of genre. Much of the analysis focuses on fiction rather than verse, and drama has not been undertaken. Many of our conclusions, however, seem likely to apply across the genres.

As this literature is, throughout the study, discussed as discourse, the use of this term warrants consideration here. Discourse, like text, constitutes an integrated structure made up not only of components such as sentences but also of those binding mechanisms that, fastening sentences together, produce *cohesion*. More than this, however, discourse being language in use and social practice, each text stands contextualized, filtered through particular voices or angled from a particular point of view, and, in crucial ways, in its very nature determined by social forces. Narrative discourse, for example, functions as a means of organizing experience, preserving and shaping memory (often along definitive pathways), transmitting beliefs, and (as Herman suggests) constructing models of reality.[3] The content plane of the narrative—that which we call *story*—is (as Chatman has long pointed out) delivered through an expression plane we call *discourse*.[4]

Various approaches to discourse analysis are therefore applicable. Critical discourse analysis, for example, being quite eclectic, is as useful for analyzing literary discourse as any other type, mediating between linguistic issues and the imagined social frameworks that creative writers produce. The manipulation of language and discourse being a crucial vehicle for exercising power, literary discourse projects ideology and perpetuates or challenges distributions of power that discourse analysis can then interrogate. The current study operates on the principle that systematic investigation of patterns governing and defining the language and discourse of creative writers (poetics) and, in particular, the considerations underlying their linguistic choices and the effects of these choices remains of crucial interpretive value. It is, as Fabb says, possible to generalize about the operations of language in literature,[5] but we believe it is also possible and useful to propose generalizations on the use of language in Caribbean literature.

The fact that discourse comprises language in use, text contextualized, means that the study of discourse involves us in discerning ways of seeing and of projecting and perpetuating these ways, as well as in interrogating them; of tracking discursive constructions of self and identity; of describing operations of narrative in revealing coherence or rupture in experience and self formation. Thought and speech representation in literature involve linguistic and discursive choices of code that are of vital significance in our region, as are interactions not only of many voices but of many texts. Our writers operate out of a literary context in which the discourse of the colonizer remains acutely influential; nevertheless, other traditions in our heritage, some long suppressed yet insistent, gain increasing prominence. In this situation of interfacing and interacting discourses and of linguistic choices set in circumstances of intense language attitudes, our writers sometimes reflect explicitly on conscious decisions that they make. Indeed, a favorite topic among our creative writers is creative writing, so both intertextual and metadiscursive elements of the literature call for consideration.

The range and variety of literary discourse across the Anglophone Caribbean and its diaspora is so vast that the current volume cannot—without sacrificing depth of attention to developmental issues—represent it in terms of texts selected for analysis. This reason alone decided our limitation to texts drawn mainly from Jamaica, Barbados, Trinidad, Guyana, and the diaspora. In any case, however, the authors' experience of and expertise in language and discourse in Jamaica has made Jamaican discourse their natural choice for focus on development in a particular territory, and such focus is essential to discussion of the connections between discourse and identity. Despite the crucial parallels in the evolution of Caribbean language in territories across the region, and despite the cultural interactions that have led to the emergence of Caribbean literature, developments in discourse have also come about territory by territory in relation to an imperial discourse.

In the British Caribbean, metropolitan English at first formed the written usage of the literate few. Seventeenth-century documents show few variations from Standard English save in private papers. Metropolitan English adorns the notebooks of overseers from Wales, Lancashire, and Somerset—men who understood that spoken and written style had parted company forever. Ships' logs of the period show similar standardization. British colonials of the Caribbean recorded neither their own dialects nor the contemporary Caribbean, African, and pidginized languages, nor the Anglophone Creoles that, eventually, almost everyone spoke.

In the metropole, variant forms such as "stage Irish" added specks of local color, satire, or comic effects to popular British literature. Eighteenth-century writers who could have demonstrated otherwise fitted their style into metropolitan norms. Olaudah Equiano wrote in metropolitan English; Francis Williams, the black Jamaican graduate of Cambridge University, wrote ornate Latin verse.[6]

As the romantic movement and the cult of the innocent savage focused on peoples beyond the metropolitan pale, European writers such as Rousseau, Burns, and the brothers Grimm raised new literary goals. Yet only a stereotypical pidgin availed to represent any nonmetropolitan culture "from Greenland's icy mountains / To India's coral strand."[7] In the Americas, European languages simply extended the metropole, despite the myriad languages surrounding white colonials. Black writers such as Frederick Douglass wrote in standard American English, the established language of literature. Captain Mayne Reid (1818–1883) shows some skill in black speech of the Americas, but no writers spoke from within Caribbean creole culture itself.[8]

After 1776, European power entered its long decline in the Americas, and whites in America gradually began to hear new voices in such experiments as Mark Twain's *Huckleberry Finn*, published in England in 1884 and in its homeland in 1885. But even before this, *Tom Cringle's Log* had appeared in 1833, written by a once-popular but now largely forgotten Jamaican-by-adoption, Michael Scott.[9] Both novels record the nonstandard speech of whites and blacks; both have been accused of racism; both display the language behavior of their own and later times.

Tom Cringle's Log, with its graphic creole comedy, demonstrates why the earliest Anglophone Caribbean poets chose literary English. In Scott's time, Creole language signifies ignorance, backwardness, and distance from the metropole. Its tones fall short of traditional requirements of lyric and tragedy such that genre appears to conflict openly with language. Yet those who write about the Caribbean, whatever their descent, have always felt the pressure of the languages around them. Most have responded simultaneously to the pressure of Creole and to that of metropolitan English, the official language of legal documents, textbooks, and formal public usage, even as Anglophone Creole and English have continued to coexist with other languages such as Bhojpuri, French Creole, or Spanish.

In the extended relationship between English and Creole, syntactic contrast (along with other structural differences of word formation, vocabulary, and pronunciation) establishes the Anglophone Creoles as systemically alien to English itself, even though much of their lexicon is of English stock. Consequently, Caribbean speakers have available to them not only two ranges of vocabulary, but two ranges of grammatical expressiveness, permitting rich and complex rhetorical effects as writers and speakers code-switch between the levels of the continuum. This same bilingual complexity requires teaching strategies in schools that few Caribbean educational systems have yet perfected. The Creole forms of individual territories also tend to be strange to speakers from other areas: Standard English is a powerful means of international communication, and publishers have been cautious about issuing texts that stray far from that norm.

At the same time, to varying extents, the Anglophone Caribbean writer has, typically, grown up among dialects and variant language forms. In nineteenth-century Trinidad, for example, French and French Creole held sway alongside English, Creole English, Spanish, and various African and Indian languages. In this setting, every child came in contact with more than one dialect or language. The same was true to a lesser extent in all of the other English colonies. Folk songs and tales today include traces of this complex linguistic past while even novels from two generations ago, like Vic Reid's *The Jamaicans* (1976), have attempted to re-create the cultural crosscurrents of history by invoking linguistic features from many sources.[10]

In the later twentieth century, the forces of standardization (books, movies, television) have come directly into conflict with the demands of the Creole language. English stands as a prestigious international language but Creole exerts a growing pressure on linguistic choices, mutating and expanding vigorously because it exists free from the constraints of standardization. It is alive—and problematic—in ways long denied the standardized languages. Caribbean writers—aware of the power of their varied past and sensitive to the vitality of the present—mingle Creole and Standard English in poetry, prose fiction, and (most of all) in writing for the theater. Once despised as "broken English," these varieties of Creole and nonstandard English dialectal forms now constitute a vital asset to the creative genius of the Caribbean literary imagination.

Most twentieth-century Caribbean writers have depended on a standardized English as their staple while interpolating dialectal, Creole, or other linguistic material (such as Twi in Brathwaite's *The Arrivants*) to meet the needs of setting, dialogue, or narrative voice. Satirists such as Louise Bennett (Jamaica) or Sam Selvon (Trinidad) use Creole or a Creole-based dialect extensively, foregrounding their usage against the felt presence of the standard language. For each writer, language presents a series of choices that determines the shape and purpose of a work. These choices are far more critical than is the case in monolingual communities. Language variation defines the variant paths of the Caribbean present and mirrors the imagery and tone of Caribbean life itself.

Increasingly in the twentieth to twenty-first centuries, the Anglophone Caribbean community code-switches: topic, audience, and speaker interact to produce an appropriate linguistic code, whether Creole or Standard English. Thus any speech act, however simple-seeming, carries in its linguistic form crucial information about situation and speakers. Similar complexities of language exist in all other areas that share our colonial past.[11] Each colony bred its peculiar opportunities for the re-creation of experience through linguistic experimentation.

Early twentieth-century portrayals of original Caribbean experience[12] attempted a linguistic realism found in few predecessors. Henry Garland Murray, whose dramatic monologues in the mid-nineteenth century blended Creole and Standard English, created and performed his narratives without any established models for such a genre (a point taken up in chapter 1).[13] Unlike Scott's generic association of "creole and comedy," Murray's *Tom Kittle's Wake* movingly describes the death and funerary rites of a fisherman. Dialogue and inner monologue are Creole forms, and the narrative is Standard English. Tone shifts across language lines. Genre hesitates. Within a few generations, Rhys, Harris, Kincaid, Brodber, and others proceeded to break old rules to shape new literary forms.

New language cultures create new genres and demand new linguistic experiments. For each Caribbean writer, language presents a series of choices that determines the shape and purpose of a work.[14]

Recent and contemporary scholarship has hardly addressed these considerations so pivotal to the definition of Caribbean writing. So far, research in this dynamic area of literary discourse in the Caribbean includes linguistic analyses directed at understanding how Caribbean language operates in literature (with little interest in literary interpretive value), and literary studies that refer to the crucial role of Caribbean language in defining the literature (with little linguistic or discourse analysis). There are crucial studies by critics such as Mervyn Morris and Evelyn O'Callaghan, and by linguists such as Susanne Mühleisen,[15] and there are now more and more essays and journal articles employing literary linguistics.[16] Hitherto, however, no book-length study or collection has to our knowledge analyzed Caribbean discourse by fusing literary interpretation with linguistic or discourse analysis.[17]

Yet the concept of a specifically Caribbean literary discourse is deeply grounded in Caribbean poetics. In referring to a medium for Caribbean creative expression, Edward Kamau Brathwaite adopted the term *nation language* with special (but not exclusive) reference to the African dimension of the Caribbean voice, hitherto submerged.[18] His usage of the term does not suggest that it is synonymous with Creole, and it is used in both literary and linguistic Caribbean commentary on the language of creative expression, but without precise definition. Elsewhere, Barbara Lalla has attempted to demystify the use of the term *nation language* in relation to creative discourse; to relate it to (but also distinguish it from) another, more widely used term, *postcolonial discourse;* and to consider its regional significance.[19]

Brathwaite's usage of *nation language* as a descriptor for the region's creative discourse proposes that this discourse belongs essentially to a group defined by shared heritage,[20] and the term appears in Caribbean criticism first in reference to a creative discourse that conveys a Caribbean (especially an Afro-Caribbean) voice. Torres-Saillant evaluates Brathwaite's tireless pursuit of cultural authenticity as cohering around the effort to bring visibility to a genuinely Caribbean language;[21] yet, at the same time, Brathwaite's explanation of nation language remains linguistically vague, partly because he is operating by introspection,[22] but also partly because nation language, as he describes it, is highly dynamic in Caribbean discourse. Other scholarly viewpoints offer a widening set of possible approaches to a language form that has arisen from exile, fracture, amnesiac memory, and essential creative powers.

In discussing Caribbean language history, Maureen Warner-Lewis notes the limitations of hierarchical models of linguistic development and creolization in the Caribbean and bases her preference for a model of convergence on the sustained contact and persistent survival of African forms too prevalent and hardy to be represented as substrate.[23] Similarly, our creative language in writing results not only from cultural survival and integration of submerged and discontinuous fragments but also from accommodation and transformation of the non-African dimension.

Our literary discourse has emerged in a multilingual context involving regional and social distinctions and interactions between an international code and one or more local codes. The background includes a physical context of geographical separation between parent and offspring language communities. These also exist, historically, in a locked relationship of at least implicit comparison and contrast with each other. That is, the metropolitan standard language exerts constant pressure on the Creole language even while the other contributing languages of the past retain little place in living memory. At the same time, the circumstances have consisted of more than mere passive experience of interaction; they have constituted an active gathering of forces. Caribbean literary discourse provides the vehicle for expressing and claiming this social capital (Caribbean culture) in whatever code or set of codes may be available to the speaker. Contextual dimensions are not only sociohistorical but socioeconomic. The speakers and writers of our discourse share not only a background of contact and colonization but also a foreground of rigid social structure, of economic disparity in a developing country with its characteristic social conditions. These speakers and writers are not only involved in but have advanced in a movement to self-sovereignty and affirmation of identity.

Caribbean discourse, sited as it is in our region, is centered discourse, in contrast to marginalized discourse. That is, the speaker's orientation in physical and conceptual space is such that the Caribbean speaker occupies the center rather than the periphery of action, attention, experience, and intention. Indeed in interactions between Caribbean and imperial discourse, imperial discourse *is* Other. We can define our discourse not only on the basis of the statable circumstances under which it occurs but also by the functions for which it is employed. One function serves to effect an ideological perspective, an attitudinal orientation, as indicated in reference to centered discourse.

Social mores, literary traditions, and other forces of imperial and neocolonial culture wield an authority that Caribbean discourse may choose not only to resist but also to ignore as it exerts its own authority in developing its own canons. The implied presence of the Other as imperial, or as neocolonial, privileges interactivity and intertextuality, but the speakers of our discourse function as agents rather than as patients. They initiate rather than react.

Caribbean literary discourse, then, cannot be homogeneous but must function as a composite of linguistic options and of pragmatic rules for choosing, switching, shifting, or mixing; its language is not a single code, but a spectrum of linguistic opportunities for self-definition. However, Creole representation has its limitations,[24] and much literary discourse is clearly Caribbean without demonstrating extensive evidence of Creole structures (the matter of navigating between Standard English and Jamaican Creole is discussed in chapter 3). Caribbean writers—themselves entrenched between exclusively oral Creole and written and oral Standard English—are never monolingual Creole speakers, so the norm consists of a representation rather than a consistent use of Creole, an alternation of codes or a selection of diction indicative of the Caribbean. Caribbean discourse appears to be an abstraction comprising the full set of alternating discourses available in Caribbean creative discourse (in Creole, local standard varieties and their intermediate forms and through oral and scribal media) intercepting each other according to a system intrinsic to the community.

In addition to its significance as representative of the Caribbean creative voice (a regional significance), Caribbean literary discourse projects its language beyond the region, reinforcing its regional autonomy, its independence from linguistic imperialism.[25] Rather than resisting authority, the discourse becomes the expression system for the newly centered voice of authority, authorizing, naming, and imposing control that is locally sited. Any description of

Caribbean literary discourse must account for the current ability of our creative writing to address an international readership and to convey a Caribbean voice while retaining comprehension through precise, limited, and selective representations of the voice. The concept must also account for the simultaneous comprehension by the Caribbean reader of additional layers of meaning and form implicated by shared competence in Creole.

Caribbean literary discourse, then, is characterized by a privileging of unofficial status. It symbolizes national, ethnonationalistic, and regional identity, authenticating the voice as Caribbean in literary/creative circles. It is both a unifying and a separatist device. It does not actually comprise, but it does *represent* the speech of ordinary conversation. It exhibits wide currency among both educated and noneducated citizens, however controversial its educational value. According to proponents, it is widely understood and easy to teach (though teaching may be unnecessary), while other views insist on the difficulty of learning unstandardized language (especially for purposes of writing and reading) without adequate teaching resources. Creole is not a school subject. At the same time, its perceived value for wider communication has changed as local and regional literary and oral culture travels worldwide in language that includes Creole to varying extents. This current work looks at the nature and texture of this complex discourse.

Included among the chapters that follow are some that develop arguments worked out over decades or that present—afresh—earlier papers that we believe to be significant to a growing understanding of Caribbean literary discourse. Our concern has been to bring together existing and relevant but scattered scholarship on the subject with current thought.

The study consists of two parts, the first ("Fusing Forms and Languages: The Jamaican Experience") focusing mainly on the development of the discourse. Jean D'Costa opens this section by considering the sociohistorical underpinnings of genre and narrative in eighteenth-century Jamaica, in "Songs in the Silence: Literary Craft as Survival in Eighteenth-Century Jamaica."

She identifies, in even the earliest written material, the interplay between informal and formal and the blending of oral and scribal expression that characterizes Caribbean literature today. In "Black Wholes: Phases in the Development of Jamaican Literary Discourse," Barbara Lalla traces stages in the evolution of the literature in terms of its writers' representation of the Creole voice in a widening range of functions, and she theorizes a range of reader-engagement with the Creole language in the text.

In the third chapter, "The Caribbean Novelist and Language: A Search for a Literary Medium," Jean D'Costa reflects on the individual writer's engagement with the complex language situation as a dimension of the creative process itself. Velma Pollard then rolls out a broader canvas of creative writers' approaches to Caribbean expression: "*To Us, All Flowers Are Roses:* Writing Ourselves into the Literature of the Caribbean." The fact that the growing significance of Creole is not only acceptable in but definitive of Caribbean literature forms the focus of the last chapter in part I, Barbara Lalla's "Creole and Respec': Authority and Identity in the Development of Caribbean Literary Discourse."

The second part of the study, "Language and Discourse in Caribbean Literatary Texts," addresses the cultural context of linguistic and literary development and of their mutual interplay in both child and adult experience, as well as the language of specific authors. In "Bra Rabbit Meets Peter Rabbit: Genre, Audience, and the Artistic Imagination—Problems in Writing Children's Fiction," Jean D'Costa reconciles the genres of high and low cultures in children's literature, demonstrating the need for writers to bridge this gap so as to prepare a readership of primary school children for both sets of literature. Also focusing on folk elements, Velma Pollard analyzes "The Dust" in the ensuing chapter, "'The Dust': A Tribute to the Folk," but she examines these elements in terms of their contribution to intimacy, to a sense of community, and to concreteness in the work. She points out the mingling of scribal and oral traditions in biblical reference and identifies the integration of voices that she describes as essential to Caribbean literary and language culture.

Fragmentation and integration are also considered in the chapter that follows, Barbara Lalla's "Collapsing Certainty and the Discourse of Re-Memberment in the Novels of Merle Hodge." Here, the dislocated child experiences not only separation but an undermining of confidence conveyed, for example, through modality. The experience of the child reflects that of the developing nation—a recurrent trope in the literature of the later twentieth century. In chapter 9, Velma Pollard's "Cultural Connections in Paule Marshall's *Praise Song for the Widow*" explores parallels and intersections between peoples of the black diaspora who come to recognize both linguistic and cultural interconnections.

Jean D'Costa's "Louise Bennett's Dialect Poetry: Language Variation in a Literary Text" (chapter 10) surveys the occurrence of Creole language features and the variant forms used by Bennett. Consistency and variation are weighed for acceptability of Creole to a wide range of audiences, and the significance of Creole evaluated for signaling politeness, mockery, and implied shifts of meaning. In chapter 11, Barbara Lalla's "Conceptual Perspectives on Time and Timelessness in Martin Carter's 'University of Hunger'" analyzes Carter's poem, as English and as Creole, especially through investigation of tense and aspect in both codes. The multiple perspectives and voices produce a reconceptualization of history as timeless and continuous.

Velma Pollard's "Mixing Codes and Mixing Voices: Language in Earl Lovelace's *Salt*" (chapter 12) tracks the shifting of the narrative voice between Trinidad Creole and English, linking this manipulation of language to Lovelace's representation of cultural complexity. In "Opening *Salt*: The Oral-Scribal Continuum in Caribbean Narrative" (chapter 13), Barbara Lalla probes the interlocking continua of the Creole and English languages, of oral and scribal discourses, of direct and indirect speech, and of historical and fictional narrative in relation to cultural transmission and disruption. Next, Velma Pollard's "Mothertongue Voices in the Writing of Olive Senior and Lorna Goodison" (chapter 14) discusses how these writers convey characterization and establish Caribbean identity through their linguistic choices. Finally, in chapter 15, Barbara Lalla's "The Facetiness Factor: Theorizing Caribbean Space in Narrative" explores the mechanisms by which Nalo Hopkinson integrates folk memory with futuristic technology in rewriting diaspora as space travel and, in the process, mapping the inner space of the Caribbean consciousness.

From one angle or another, every chapter addresses the language culture of the Caribbean. The essays highlight the linguistic tensions associated with literary representation of a complex language situation and probe the writer's need to maintain an international audience while being true to the Caribbean voice.

These essays came to be written (and in many cases re-explored) because all three authors have had to contend personally with every aspect of the challenges described here. We have wrestled with the problems of language choice and genre, of language choice and audience, of language choice and the possibility of not being published anywhere, of having no readership. As teachers of literature and linguistics and as workers in the field of primary, secondary, and tertiary education, we have had daily, weekly, and yearly experience of the challenges posed by Caribbean language culture. These educational challenges are further influenced by our personal engagement with the creative arts of language as writers, as readers, and as audience. Such are the issues that shape the intellectual, imaginative, and emotional lives of Caribbean writers, scholars, and artists alike. This collection seeks to explore the many-storied, ever-branching constructions of the Caribbean's literary domain as it opens onto new worlds.

Notes

1. For example in Valerie Youssef's "Working Out Conversational Roles through Questioning Strategies," in *Due Respect: Papers on English and English-Related Creoles in the Caribbean in Honour of Professor Robert Le Page* (Kingston: University of the West Indies Press, 2001), 219–246.

2. "Literature and the Folk," in *My Strangled City and Other Essays* (Port-of-Spain,

Trinidad and Tobago: Longman, 1992), 68. We have made a distinction throughout this book between the use of "Creole" (with a capital C) versus "creole" (with a lowercase c). With a few exceptions, the term is capitalized when referring to the language or an aspect of the culture that has a linguistic connection ("Jamaican Creole poetry"; "Creole proverbs," etc.) but lowercased when referring to people ("creoles living in town") and also when used in most adjectival (but nonlinguistic) contexts ("creole cuisine," "creole music," etc.)

3. David Herman, *Story Logic: Problems and Possibilities of Narrative* (Lincoln: University of Nebraska Press, 2002), 17.

4. Seymour Chatman, *Story and Discourse: Narrative Structure in Fiction and Film* (Ithaca, NY: Cornell University Press, 1978), 146.

5. Nigel Fabb, *Linguistics and Literature: Language in the Verbal Arts of the World* (Oxford: Blackwell, 1997), 1–21.

6. Olaudah Equiano, *The Interesting Narrative of the Life of Olaudah Equiano, or Gustavus Vassa, the African* (London: n.p., 1789); Edward Long, *The History of Jamaica* (London: T. Lowndes, 1774), 2:476. For further information on forms of English writing forged through early colonial contact, see also Raymond Hickey, ed. *Varieties of English in Writing: The Written Word as Linguistic Evidence* (Amsterdam: Benjamins, 2010).

7. A popular missionary hymn by Reginald Heber, 1819.

8. Capt. Mayne Reid, *The Maroon,* 3 vols. (London: Hurst and Blackett, 1862).

9. Michael Scott, *Tom Cringle's Log,* 2 vols. (Edinburgh: Blackwood, 1834; London: Gibbings, 1894; London: Picador, 1999).

10. Vic Reid, *The Jamaicans* (1976; repr., Kingston: Institute of Jamaica, 1978).

11. Bill Ashcroft, Gareth Griffiths, and Helen Tiffin, *The Empire Writes Back: Theory and Practice in Post-Colonial Literatures* (London: Routledge, 1989).

12. Claude McKay published *Songs of Jamaica* by 1912 (Kingston: A. W. Gardner and Co.), and Alfred Mendes, *The Wages of Sin and Other Poems* by 1925 (Port-of-Spain, Trinidad: Yuille's Printer).

13. Henry Garland Murray, *Manners and Customs of the Country a Generation Ago: Tom Kittle's Wake* (Kingston: Jordan, 1877).

14. See chapter 3 and Jean D'Costa, "Expression and Communication: Literary Challenges to the Caribbean Polydialectal Writer," *Journal of Commonwealth Literature* 19, no. 1 (1984): 123–141.

15. Mervyn Morris, *"Is English We Speaking" and Other Essays* (Kingston: Ian Randle, 1999); Evelyn O'Callaghan, *Woman Version: Theoretical Approaches to West Indian Fiction by Women* (London: Macmillan Caribbean, 1993); Susanne Mühleisen, "Introduction—Creole Languages in Creole Literatures: Status and Standardization," special issue, *Journal of Pidgin and Creole Languages* 20 (2005).

16. Merle Hodge, "A Study of Language in Trinidad and Tobago Prose Fiction of the Twentieth Century with Special Reference to the Works of Earl Lovelace" (PhD diss., University of the West Indies, 2007); Maureen Warner Lewis, "Samuel Selvon's Linguistic Extravaganza: *Moses Ascending,*" in *Something Rich and Strange: Selected Essays on Sam Selvon,* ed. Martin Zehnder (Leeds, England: Peepal Tree Press, 2003), 65–76.

17. For example, Lee M. Jenkins, *The Language of Caribbean Poetry: Boundaries of*

Expression (Gainesville: University Press of Florida, 2004) is a valuable work, but essentially literary in its analysis and theoretical framework. While it refers to code-shifting, orality, and intertextuality in the verse, it rarely analyzes the linguistic or discursive operations themselves.

18. Edward Kamau Brathwaite, *History of the Voice: The Development of Nation Language in Anglophone Caribbean Poetry* (London: New Beacon Books, 1984).

19. Barbara Lalla, "Nation Language and Caribbean Discourse" (presentation, Conference of the Society of Caribbean Linguistics, University of the West Indies, Mona, Jamaica, August 2000).

20. Ronald Wardhaugh associates ethnonationalism with "the continuing power of primordial attachments" and with a "revival of a felt historical identity" that has been intensified by social pressure to conformity, resulting in the impersonal treatment of individuals. This ethnonationalism seems more pertinent to our understanding of *nation language* (as used currently by literary critics) than the sociolinguistic use of *nationism*. See Ronald Wardhaugh, *Languages in Competition: Dominance, Diversity, and Decline* (Oxford: Blackwell, 1987), 40–41.

21. Silvio Torres-Saillant, *Caribbean Poetics: Towards an Aesthetic of West Indian Literature* (Cambridge: Cambridge University Press, 1997), 140.

22. Ralph Fasold points out that the introspective reporter is analyzing behavior that is automatic and largely below the level of consciousness. See *The Sociolinguistics of Language* (Oxford: Blackwell, 1990), 48–49.

23. Warner-Lewis, "Samuel Selvon's Linguistic Extravaganza."

24. Barbara Lalla, "A Sociolinguistic Approach to Critical Analysis in the Caribbean," in *Studies in Caribbean Language 2*, eds. Pauline Christie, Barbara Lalla, Velma Pollard, and Lawrence Carrington (St. Augustine, Trinidad and Tobago: Society for Caribbean Linguistics, 1999), 112–127; and Barbara Lalla, "Virtual Realism and the Inscriber's Dilemma: Representing the Caribbean Voice" (Occasional Paper 32, Society for Caribbean Linguistics, University of the West Indies, St. Augustine, Trinidad and Tobago, 2005).

25. Robert Phillipson defines *linguistic imperialism* (with particular reference to English) as "the dominance of English asserted and maintained by the establishment and continuous reconstitution of structural and cultural inequalities between English and other languages." Phillipson further identifies English linguistic imperialism as a subtype of *linguicism*, or "ideologies, structures, and practices which are used to legitimate, effectuate, and reproduce an unequal division of power and resources (both material and immaterial) between groups which are defined on the basis of language." See *Linguistic Imperialism* (Oxford: Oxford University Press, 1992), 47.

I
FUSING FORMS AND LANGUAGES: THE JAMAICAN EXPERIENCE

1
Songs in the Silence

Literary Craft as Survival in Eighteenth-Century Jamaica

Jean D'Costa

Exiles created Jamaica's literature.[1] Transcending loss of home and culture, they endured wars, forced migrations, captivity, transshipment, enslavement, and desperate loneliness, and yet they kept memory and instinctive genius alive despite all odds. Such were the ancestors whose amnesiac memories together brought forth Jamaica's visions and founded our literary heritage. Their story is not unique in its sorrow and triumph. It is unique in that our literature is characteristically Jamaican and Caribbean; that it is at once singular and universal; and it was shaped in the severest conditions during the last three and a half centuries. In eighteenth-century Jamaica, the plantation economy built on slavery and sugar forced a new culture into existence. Literature had no place there; language served the meanest purposes. Yet, strangely, out of its inhumanity came these most deeply human attributes: a literature fashioned in its own language.

Because these origins are so veiled in fragmented memory, so shaped by the discontinuities of history and mortality, critics such as M. Keith Booker and Dubravka Juraga place the beginnings of Caribbean literature only at the start of the twentieth century.[2] This view relegates to silence many voices of significance in the development of both oral and written discourse. It also denies the influence of patterns of resistance and survival devised by the generations who created this culture, and it fails to acknowledge the nature of the genres and discourse embedded in this language culture. Édouard Glissant notes the ambiguity with which discourse on the plantation was fraught, reaching as it did toward naming the forbidden, the proscribed aspects of domination and control. Alienation in these conditions becomes not only an outcome of deracination and domination, but it could be adopted as disguise, as a mask behind which forgetting and remembering could happen in relative safety, a place where language itself might be constantly remade in response to an ever-changing, always dangerous world.[3] Concealment and masked disclosure served the purposes of survival and left their stamp on the literature they formed.

In the fused yet divided world of the Caribbean plantation, a world as alienated from its own products as from its cultural origins, literature of any kind once seemed strangely out of place. Indeed, the experience of many Caribbean thinkers suggests that a profound antipathy to the life of the mind lay at the center of eighteenth-century Caribbean culture, to be handed down in the nineteenth and twentieth centuries as an alienated view of art and letters and a deeper alienation from its own lived experience, the "amnesia" of Derek Walcott's *Another Life*. In this spiritual and artistic autobiography, Walcott presents the "divided child" of the Caribbean striving for coherence, for a rooted life of the mind. The "divided child," cut off from its past, "hears nothing." Yet, engulfed by that past, the child also "hears everything / that the historian cannot hear, the howls / Of all the races that crossed the water."[4]

By hearing "nothing," the child cannot speak to its experience. Comparing itself to the European or American, the child sees itself with nothing to match the imported books, machines, and goods of the "real" world up north. Since the dawn of its exile culture in the late seventeenth century, the child has been told, again and again, that its language, rituals, and ideas have no value. Among exiles, the child artist is an exile twice over, for what value has art against money?

So deep was the alienation even in my lifetime that Jamaicans with literary aspirations expected to live in exile in order to pursue literary careers. In his early twenties, Claude McKay (1889–1948) moved to the United States; the novelist John Hearne (1926–1994) began his career in England; in 1963, Mervyn Morris (1937–) told a group of high school students that he might have to leave Jamaica in order to develop as a poet. Yet the "divided child" does hear everything while hearing nothing. The proof of that "everything" lies in the shapes and forms, the styles and registers of Caribbean literature today. In this present time, partly because of the privilege of distance and partly because the process of fusion has taken fuller effect, we can recognize the genres forged during the years in which forgetting and invention resembled each other, and, worst of all, art seemed nothing more than broken fragments of languages and lives.

In the latter twentieth century, these broken fragments have yielded a literature that ranges from the novels of Naipaul and Rhys; to the poetry and drama of Derek Walcott; to the reggae of Bob Marley and the dub recitatives of scores of singers; and to the fiction writers, poets, and playwrights of today. Its genres appear to fall within the usual European classifications: the novel, the short story, the short lyric poem, the long narrative, plays of various lengths, and the essay. The resemblance to metropolitan genres is, however, both real and profoundly misleading. Even readers acquainted with the voices in Jean

Rhys's *Letters 1931–1966*[5] are often ill-prepared for the dominance of viewpoint and voice that can so compellingly disarrange the shape of a Rhys novel. Many of her works seem strangely plotless yet compellingly whole, as the story "I Used to Live Here Once" demonstrates in its two-page evocation of a transcendental moment.[6] Even Caribbean readers—all nourished on the same canonical models as their metropolitan counterparts—have found their own literature strange, disturbing, and yet haunting, sometimes frighteningly so.

In Erna Brodber's prose poem *Jane and Louisa Will Soon Come Home,*[7] the generic pattern of expectations connecting reader to speaker does not account for the movement and shape of the prose. Instead, the voices of young girls and older women form the connective life of a family and a village. "[Brodber's] first novel—revolutionary in its structure—celebrates aspects of the life of a small Jamaican village" and possesses the ability to create not only the vivid life of the individual mind as well as that of shared experience, but also to summon up such scenes as "an extraordinary evocation of two people dancing at a country fair" in which music and song merge with dialogue and interior monologue.[8] The voices possess auditory assault. One hears them all too clearly in one's mind. And while one expects such generic directness in calypso and dub, one does not dream that the genres of oral literature could really reshape those powerful written models taken from Europe.

Nevertheless, those models have been the grist of a patient, little-known mill in and around the very plantations where no one imagined art or letters to have a place. The voices that created new forms began their shaping long ago. In the writing of today, the child who remembers nothing and everything speaks through the dramatic rhetoric of the tea-meeting,[9] the wake,[10] the satiric narrative ballad, the *kasakasa* (Twi for a dispute) and the cussing match, the storytelling, and then breaks off to sing the rejoinder with the audience grouped around. Retelling stories from Ireland, Scotland, or Yorkshire; memorizing the missionaries' Bible stories; reading school editions of Scott, Dickens, and Macaulay; and reciting Shakespeare, Longfellow, and Tennyson, the child has worked patiently on everything brought to the mill of its mind. When it writes its own stories, the deepest influence of all comes from the oral models, creating a voice that engages directly and reshapes the way in which fiction must be cast.[11]

One hears this voice in Naipaul, Selvon, Mais, and Rhys. One hears it yet more provocatively in latter twentieth-century Jamaican authors such as Anthony Winkler, Olive Senior, Lorna Goodison, Erna Brodber, Martin Mordecai, and Velma Pollard.[12] Even when these voices do not speak a Caribbean dialect (or pretend not to), one hears them so well that they seem to provoke replies, a dialogue, or some kind of living response. When the speaker uses Creole, the dynamic effect of the speaking voice shapes the story along the lines of a back verandah gossip session. Olive Senior's "Ascot"[13] captures the quality of what I must name the *gossip-narrative,* there being nothing generically akin to this deeply Caribbean literary mode in our store of written models.

In a typical story by Senior, the voice (whether in first or third person) interacts with the reader, sometimes by overt cues such as questions or exclamations, but more often by subtler, underlying modes of address inferring intimacy and direct connection to the audience. In other words, the reader is truly an *audiens*, one who listens to the speaker on equal terms, as a member of the speaker's group. This connection appears in the autobiographic narratives in *Lionheart Gal: Life Stories of Jamaican Women*, tales based on the documentary theater of the acting group Sistren.[14] Here one can trace the influence of performance (using that term to include the action of storytelling as well as that of conventional theater): strongly marked beginnings join the reader to the speaker, and endings give the firm moral closure of gossip-narrative. Many stories have the underlying form of an explanation of a problem, and many conceal a didactic element. All insist on the utter uniqueness of the main characters. This is our life, they say: this happened only to us.

The distinctiveness of Caribbean genres appears most clearly in drama. Here the influence of *carnival* (the best term that Europeans could give to the rituals and celebrations of the Afro-creoles) has bred a theater that invites participation rather than passive watching. Based on African rites that once expressed and established the union of material and spiritual worlds, such celebrations as carnival, John Canoe, and other seemingly secular entertainments generate a quality of participation and audience enthusiasm that go beyond the mood of European carnival. Behind these stand such religious survivals as Haitian *vodun*, Trinidadian *shango*, and Jamaican *cumina*. Each of these religions insists on the union of participant and ritual, not unlike that of the earliest Christian drama. One observes such involvement between audience and production in many of Derek Walcott's plays, as in *Dream on Monkey Mountain* with its choruses and dancers, and *Ti-Jean and His Brothers* with its griot, the Bird, and its chorus of demons and animals.[15] Very clear examples of remade genres may be found in Jamaican pantomime (a creole blend of English and African traditions) and in the work of Caribbean playwrights such as Zeno Obi Constance (*The Ritual*) and Kendal Hippolyte (*The Drum Maker*).[16] In his notes on staging these plays, Keith Noel shows how "the tension that existed in the arts between the folk and European forms mirrored the tension that existed between the ways of life of the folk and those of the educated middle-class."[17]

It is from this tension, dating back to the founding of the present Caribbean societies in the seventeenth and eighteenth centuries, that the genres of Caribbean art and literature draw their individuality and their vitality. In Jamaica, cultural mixing began in the very earliest stages of English colonial occupation and has been extensively documented by scholars.[18] Although precious little survives from the seventeenth century, the records of visitors such as Sir Hans Sloane point to the songs and dances of the Africans and other non-European peoples as a major feature of Jamaican life.

Song becomes action in ritual: the secret religions of the Africans and the carnivals, the "mummings," and the other public ceremonies enabled exiled Africans to re-enact their connections to their homeland and to their kin. Many gestures now known as dance steps once had invocational and symbolic power; many drumming styles denote gods or the spirits of ancestors or the yet-to-be-born. Invocational, ritual language must have been among the very earliest literary genres implanted in the Caribbean psyche. Whether one was a participant or a distant listener, one could not have resisted the power of ritual singing, whether it was as simple as a digging song or as haunting as a burial chant. The child who remembers nothing and everything therefore has an instinctive sense of action as inherent in the genre "song." Poetic words, whether sung or spoken, suggest invocational action and response as part of their style and generic symbolism.

Exponents of this purely Caribbean genre include the Jamaican Creole satirist, Louise Bennett (see chapter 10), the Barbadian Edward Kamau Brathwaite (especially in *The Arrivants*),[19] and, in a very direct way, the dub poets. One must also include aspects of Walcott's drama in which song becomes action, as at the climactic moment when the child-hero, Ti-Jean, triumphs over the Devil.[20] Roger Mais's novel *Brother Man*, set in the slums of Kingston, makes explicit formal use of choric voices, chanting, questioning, as well as ritually intertwined dialogue and monologue.[21] Other oral genres of the seventeenth and eighteenth centuries included the songs and ring-games played by English, Irish, and Scottish sailors, settlers, and soldiers, all of whom contributed directly to the culture of exile. The new genres included also the "cuss-cuss" or "tracing," a formalized cursing match, in which the Scots "flyting" fused with the Asante ritual (in Twi, *kasakasa*) to emerge in the poems of Louise Bennett and the calypsos of Sparrow as another poetic genre: the monologue—or dialogue—of invective as a form of satiric art. Ned Ward, a scurrilous English journalist who briefly tried his luck in Jamaica in 1698, and John Atkins, a surgeon who visited in 1722, attest to the vivid and comprehensive skill in cursing displayed by the Jamaican creoles, both white and black.[22]

It is in the eighteenth century, however, that the clearest evidence of cultural remaking begins to appear. This period would mark the onset of that deep amnesia of which Walcott speaks: Thousands and thousands of captive exiles moved into Jamaican life. Mortality rates far exceeded birthrates. A multilingual, multicultural community of adults adjusted to constant loss and constant accommodation to strangers, while the tiny but growing group of native-born began to evolve a uniquely Jamaican ethnicity. After the rebellion of 1760, other changes made the black population more creolized and less African.[23] The small numbers of creoles, of whatever color, lived among Africans and Europeans and—of all three groups—enjoyed the best mortality rates. These creoles passed down their language culture to the nation they created.

According to Silvio Torres-Saillant, "Caribbean poetics comes into being primarily as an exploration of language. Language in Caribbean Literature is not merely a medium that makes the art possible, nor is it a neutral channel to convey ideas and sensations. It is a strenuous vehicle of communication, a means of ontological positioning with respect to the environment, and a constant object of reflection."[24] The evidence of Jamaica's past shows that the processes of literary creation began as soon as groups of people came here. New experience fused with memory, giving rise to unusual modes of depicting the world. Planes of irony, of dramatic narrative, of compressed imagery marked out new visions of experience: in a word, new genres.

As Jamaica's seventeenth-century exiles established alien communities and deployed various means of communication among themselves, languages and literature rose and fed the minds of the thousands who constantly arrived, labored, and died, while adding their part to a uniquely Jamaican literature—and all of this activity in spite of and beyond the understanding of an imperial language-culture, that of Jamaica's English masters, the owners of lands and slaves. Power marked the uses of languages, creating attitudes and behaviors now entrenched in Jamaican language and literature.

There is another consideration. Those who were *not* slaves, those who governed the lives of captives in Jamaica, were less than concerned with high, civilized arts. In plantation Jamaica, books were mostly estate accounts and lists of goods, monies, human chattels, and animal livestock. Many whites were illiterate or semiliterate. The scattered groups of Scots, Irish, and English people (mostly men) who controlled the captive workforce were themselves exiles living among a majority of Africans with whom they had very little in common. Family life scarcely existed for the free or for the captive. Education hardly existed. The kinds of human groupings that encourage what we like to call "civilization" were denied by the structure of the society as well as by early and frequent deaths from disease and hardship among both Africans and Europeans.

The critical period lies between 1660 (when the English invaders finally expelled the few Spanish colonials) and the early eighteenth century (when the infant English colony fought African Maroons on land and hunted Spanish merchant ships at sea). English Jamaica divided its activities between planting and piracy. African Jamaica had its share in both concerns but concentrated on survival, escape, and resistance.

To the tiny official world of governors, army officers, and wealthy planters, there was no such thing as African literature, let alone Jamaican literature. For that matter, they knew almost as little about Celtic languages and literatures, despising the Irish and Welsh workers almost as much as they despised Africans. As far as the masters were concerned, English was paramount. They had forgotten their own servile past and the three centuries they endured as serfs using a debased language, medieval English. Just as the colonized and disenfranchised English serfs dragged the language of their Norman French overlords into their world and remade it in their image,[25] so too did Jamaica's African exiles use English along with their own languages to make new shapes and vehicles of meaning.

Jamaica in the seventeenth and eighteenth centuries was a very African society. If Guinea Coast Creole English was spoken by some African captives, both this and Twi were connected to a wider-ranging African pidgin used by Jamaica's captive people to make themselves understood by newly arrived Africans. As Edward Long complains, "the language of the Creoles is bad English, larded with the Guiney dialect, owing to their adopting the African words, in order to make themselves understood by the imported slaves; which they find much easier than teaching these strangers to learn English."[26] We have no way of knowing how widespread these contact languages may have been, nor how many came and went over time. We know only that the making of new languages formed a major feature of life in the Caribbean and in Jamaica in the early decades of English colonization and African captivity.

At this time, English planters from the eastern Caribbean (notably Barbados and Montserrat) brought entire households and gangs of workers to Jamaica where sugar was beginning to take hold as the moneymaking crop. With these immigrants came more language forms: even more African and European languages, dialects of English as well as Creole languages and pidgins that arose in trade and among laborers. Jamaica was highly multilingual. Between 1660 and 1700, it is possible that several African languages merged to form new pidgins in Jamaica. Speakers would reserve these languages for special uses. The new Africans meanwhile were also taking in the English dialects of the English and Irish bond-laborers who worked beside them in field and factory, along with the English-based Creole of Barbados and Nevis-Montserrat, a complex process resulting in the formation of Jamaican Creole. Deep in these language cultures were the oral literatures of many peoples.

Before attempting to explain how Jamaican literature came into being, and what it embraces, let me remind the reader of some of our expectations and attitudes to literature today. In novels and in most printed matter, most Jamaican readers expect certain conventions of language usage. For example, a novel should be told in Standard English (or at least, in Standard Jamaican English).

This authoritative narrative voice must "speak" in the language of established power. The dialogue within the narrative, however, may switch between varying kinds of Jamaican usage according to the characters' social standing, their situation, their behavior, and the topic of the moment. An omniscient narrator speaking Creole perplexes—unless the narrator is telling his or her own story, in the freedom of first-person narrative. In such situations, readers expect a social register representative of that speaker, from a Rasta to a minister of religion. In some recent works, writers such as Olive Senior have insisted on an omniscient narrator whose worldview demands Creole.

The same expectations, constraints, and freedoms hold true for drama, whether on stage, radio, or television: character and action require their culturally determined language. In music, Jamaican expectations shift even further and go deeper into the oral literary tradition created here so long ago. Unless the songs come from an official metropolitan source (such as hymnal or prayer book), their language is that of the oral culture. When song and drama work together, the result demands Creole and audience interaction, as in dub, in the poems of Louise Bennett, and in the liturgical music of Father Richard Ho Lung. Certain attitudes, prejudices, tastes, expectations, experiments, and reactions arose between the 1660s and 1700, bringing Jamaican literature into being.

In seventeenth-century Jamaica, groups and communities were small, no more than ten, twenty, or a few hundred people except in flamboyant Port Royal or Spanish Town (the capital). At Guanaboa Vale (deep in the island almost midway between Old Harbour and Worthy Park), an English planter, Francis Price "was the head of a community that consisted of one white woman and four children (presumably his own family), fifty-five adult and three child slaves, and seven 'servants.'"[27] Isolation fosters loneliness; loneliness compels intimacy. Everyone knew everyone else. We have no way of telling what were the daily relationships between masters, white indentured servants, and captive labor (which was mostly, but not wholly, African). The few records that survive do insist, however, on the fact that songs, tale acting, dancing, and drumming characterized the lives of Africans who, by 1700, had attained demographic superiority. Lacking most forms of self-realization, captive and controlled, African Jamaica nevertheless gained a significant cultural weapon: majority status. More voices spoke those African languages and recalled the African past than any others.

By the 1720s, the white children born on rural plantations were said to be as African in their speech, customs, and manners as the Africans who, in many cases, had brought them up and who outnumbered them twenty to one.[28] In this world, the only book a child might see was an account book, and the only uses of writing were to record and calculate the running of the plantation and the sale of its produce. Yet strangely, many of these white Jamaicans identified fiercely with their birthplace and defiantly kept their fluency in slave speech,[29] both in Jamaican Creole and in the relevant languages of Africa, so unlike those of Europe in sound and structure. Thanks to some curiosity on the part of a few English people regarding the captive labor force spreading through Jamaica, the first tiny images of literature appear in written records.

Visiting Jamaica in 1689, Sir Hans Sloane, the famous botanist, took down two brief African lyrics: one is from Ghana and the other from Angola. The Ghanaian song (the only one so far translated) represents a genre outside European experience. A version of this song survives in modern Twi as a children's play-song: one sings, mimes, and dances its words. "Meri Bonbo mich langa meri wa langa" survives in modern Twi as "Michi langa / Kofi so langa." The child claps in time to the tune, dancing a kick-shuffle step to go with the words, "I am coming / Kofi is coming." In Sloane's version, most of the elements are repetitions of nonsense words typical of play-songs. "Such a song would by its very nature survive in the memories of exiled Africans when the more complex and sophisticated knowledge of adult life perished."[30]

We know, from many statements made in those times, that the languages and the fragmented cultures of Africans survived in Jamaica for generations. By 1700, white Jamaica had taken note of the frequent use of songs among their captives. The nature of the songs differed widely. Few non-Africans would have taken this children's song as any kind of threat to the arrangements of power. Yet even a nursery rhyme or a lullaby asserts the cultural identity of the singer and audience: inevitably, both are more closely bound together. Thus, the song can become the bearer of desires and intentions never stated openly.

African chants and songs fulfilled, however, deeper and more complex purposes, as white authority would gradually learn, though dimly. Songs, chants, and dances-to-singing formed the daily and weekly actions of the captives. They sprang to life in the rituals of funerals, and African funerals involved very strange activity (to the eyes of outsiders), much of it in the form of songs and chants. Drumming was an important feature of these rituals and was gradually restricted as it began to dawn on white society that such ceremonies often foreshadowed rebellions or active kinds of resistance. Such activities fortified Walcott's divided child as it strove to create a habitable world: "this child . . . without history, without knowledge of its / pre-world" exists simultaneously in a state of alienation and of creative invention.[31]

The restoring of the child's sanity and selfhood arises in its remaking of a whole world through the agencies of language formation and literary creation. The divided child hears not only "the howls / of all the races that crossed the water,"[32] but it brings those ancestors alive in the transcendental process of creation. Cleansed by amnesia, fortified by memory, the child creates a new world seen for the first time through its eyes. Such is the force and energy of the songs, tales, and dramatic monologues created during six generations of enslavement in which Jamaican culture came into being.

The most apparently harmless kinds of songs were the work-songs (surviving to later times as digging songs and songs to urge on gangs of stone-breakers or load-bearers). The form of these songs involved a leader and a choric response. So, too, did the chants honoring the divine aspects of existence, and these were many, springing up in the midst of what would have seemed to be common work to any but African eyes: "The slave owner had no qualms about having even the most magnificent [sacred] cotton tree felled without a word of thanks or explanation to the spirit of that tree though his ancient forebears would have thought differently. Before carrying out such an order, the African [enslaved] immigrant, and later his Jamaican descendant, would sing and make peace with the life, the spirit of the tree about to be destroyed. A song used in that context up to the 1940s was: 'A noh me, a bahss say' ('Don't blame me, it's the boss's order')."[33] Most outstanding among the literary genres that grew and dominated Jamaican consciousness from the seventeenth to the nineteenth centuries are the following: songs and lyrics, many of them working songs, some drilling songs, others humorous, sardonic, or mournful; proverbs and wise sayings; ritual chants; elaborate ritual cursings (the best invented not by Africans but by whites); war cries; dramatic ritual ceremonies enacted through dance, gestures, music, and verbal exchanges; storytelling (often interactive); narratives (in verse or prose) satirizing and mocking the master class; other narratives describing atrocities and terrible experiences; and, once Christianity began to be spread by African Jamaicans, moral tales, sermons, and prayers, as well as hymns.

Song marked the culture of exiled Africans in the Americas. Every experience could be rendered in song, or accompanied by song, or preserved by song. Many Europeans noted the powerful tendency among Africans and Afro-creoles to create narrative, descriptive, satiric, elegiac, and expressive lyrics and to keep these songs alive over long periods of time. Songs embodied protest then, and they do so still. Sometimes they lend us an identity that offers comforting familial associations: "Jane and Louisa will soon come home," for Jane and Louisa could be ship-sisters, cousins created by fate, not blood. Sometimes, the songs simply remind us of who we are, even if our true names and identities are lost. Sometimes, as in Jean Rhys's famous "Let Them Call It Jazz," the song embodies the essence of Caribbean selfhood and of hope in an alien world.[34]

Given the complicated and culturally fragmented details of Jamaica's past, we must ask ourselves what were the thoughts, the memories, the reflections on experience, as well as the many languages brought to the Americas on the ships of the Atlantic slave trade? What literary forms did these speakers bring?

Did Asante warriors sometimes chant the praise-songs of their lost kings? How did tales of the spider-god, Ananse, transform into satiric stories of cunning and survival? How did those distant Africans make a new, common language that could express their ideas, both the old and the new? The exiles' languages did not disappear. They were spoken here for centuries, in varying forms, mixing and changing. Archaic dialects of England, Scotland, and Ireland mingled with these languages such that the tales, songs, and sayings of Britain and West Africa fell together: "Man born fe heng cyaan drown"; "When Puss gaan, Rat take house"; "Circumstances alter cases: shorter trousers, longer braces."

By the latter half of the eighteenth century, more visitors and local writers began to record (and comment on) what they heard around them.[35] The following poem (or song) captures the mythologizing process by which things afar became transmuted into things Jamaican, features both of imagination and of experience, fused into a unified vision by the pain of exile:

If me want for go in a Ebo,
Me can't go there!
Since dem tief me from a Guinea,
Me can't go there!

If me want for go in a Congo,
Me can't go there!
Since dem tief me from my tatta,
Me can't go there!

If me want for go in a Kingston,
Me can't go there!
Since massa go in a England,
Me can't go there!

Kingston, Congo, England, and the Ibo homeland in Nigeria become a single domain of loss: such was the telling insight into unfolding experience among Jamaica's enslaved people.

The recorder of this song, J. B. Moreton, worked as a bookkeeper on a plantation in Jamaica and published *West India Customs and Manners* in 1790. Moreton also records "Me Know No Law, Me Know No Sin," a lyrical exploration of a life lost between the brutal injustices of slavery and the speaker's defenseless state. Another version of it appears over forty years later in Michael Scott's highly popular novel, *Tom Cringle's Log* (1834). In both versions, the speaker is Jamaican-born, black, and female. Her life consists of prostitution, blame, punishment, rape, and despair.[36]

Altho' a slave me is born and bred,
My skin is black, not yellow:
I often sold my maidenhead
To many a handsome fellow.

Kept for a while by massa, she produces a black infant, gets a whipping for so doing and is banished to work in the field gang. Then along comes the overseer, and she bears a child "almost as white as missess." It is now the turn of her jealous missess to flog her, or "fum" in the language of the time:

Me fum'd when me no condescend;
Me fum'd too if me do it;
Me no have no one for 'tand my friend,
So me am forc'd to do it.

Me know no law, me know no sin,
Me is just what ebba them make me;
This is the way dem bring me in;
So God nor devil take me!

It makes one pause to realize that *this song* stayed well-known and popular from the 1770s until the 1830s. One wonders how much of its bitter critique of the speaker's social world crept into the minds of those who wrote it down. Did they even sniff the odor of protest and resistance layered in these verses?

The song shows us some of the fusing of languages and literary genres taking place at the time, using verse form and rhymes similar to those of English songs. Its style has clear marks of upper-class English but in linguistic terms, its deep structure is based in Jamaican Creole. Such sanitizing of Jamaican Creole texts was inevitable when the recorders were English speakers writing down this new language and regarding it as a deformed version of English. Thanks to this attitude, very little was set down in Jamaican Creole until the period of the missionary and abolitionist movements in the late eighteenth and early nineteenth centuries.

This legacy of shame regarding our own words lives on too. Even today, writing for the metropolitan world of London and New York presents many difficult choices and inhibiting shackles for the Jamaican writer, even if that writer's imagination roams free (see chapter 2). Experiencing in one language, we instantly, unconsciously transfer into another as we aim at different audiences (see chapter 3). It is the audience rather than the topic that decides our linguistic medium, but topic has its own power, as we shall see.

Tale and narrative song formed close ties in eighteenth- and nineteenth-century Jamaica. The latter served as a kind of newspaper devoted to recounting scandals and horror stories such as is captured in the popular song "Carry Im Along." Based on a notorious incident in 1788, the song appears in Matthew G. Lewis's memoir of his visit to Jamaica in 1815. It was a favorite of the slaves on his plantation. Another version appears in an Anancy story recorded late in the nineteenth century but clearly connected to the atrocities practiced by Mr. Bedward of Spring Garden, the speaker in the poem who orders a dying slave to be thrown in a gully, stripped naked, and left to die:[37]

"Take him to the Gulley! Take him to the Gulley!
 But bringee back the frock and board!"—
"Oh! massa, massa! me no deadee yet!"—
"Take him to the Gulley! Take him to the Gulley!
 Carry him along!"

The song, short as it is, invokes the terrible drama of an evil man and his murdered victims set in a world that permits such abuse. Contemporary sources tell us that the pleading man was, however, the last slave to suffer at Bedward's hands. Secretly tended by his fellow slaves and helped to escape to Kingston, the man made good until, some while later, Bedward recognized him in Kingston and tried to seize him. The man's outcry brought support from the onlookers whose anger at Bedward drove him from Kingston, forcing him to abandon his so-called property. The tale must have taken many forms in the telling: It lingered until the late nineteenth century when it became part of a folktale, "Dry Bone." This Anancy tale of greed and inescapable burdens ends with a version of the 1788 song, invoking abandonment and death:

Carry him go 'long,
Anancy say so,
Me'll pay fe cock,
Carry him go 'long.[38]

Eighteenth-century Jamaica presents us, however, with the interesting case of a black, Jamaican-born poet whose life and work seem remote from the victims of Mr. Bedward or the anti-heroine of "Me Know No Law." Unlike the latter, this man traveled freely. A foundational member of that black Jamaica which laid down its cultural structures in this period, this schoolmaster represents Jamaica's assimilation of the culture of the metropole. A double cultural transplant, he joins those Jamaican children who found themselves exiled to schools in English from a very early age, returning after a decade or more to a half-forgotten birthplace.[39] For some, Jamaica became a new exile; for others, it was the bedrock of identity. We cannot speak for Jamaica's first classicist, Francis Williams, a free black Jamaican, an intellectual, and probably the first person of African origin to receive a British university education. New connections were being laid down between African Jamaica and English Jamaica.

Francis Williams (ca. 1700–1770) was the freeborn son of John and Dorothy Williams, and Jamaica's first classically educated writer. Francis was educated in England from the age of ten as an experiment to test the assumed intellectual inferiority of blacks. Williams studied Latin and Greek, as well as mathematics. His life and work must be traced mainly from the biased account given by Edward Long.[40] What little of Williams's writing survives shows no trace of his Jamaican background. Racial justifications for slavery were, however, to become less secure in the face of Williams's achievements.

Yet his writing and the school he founded indicate how imitation works as one aspect of cultural integration. In 1759, Williams penned a Latin ode in praise of the new governor of Jamaica, George Haldane. The style of the Latin is florid and overwrought, following the elaborate rhetoric fashionable in university schools of the time.[41] Williams's highly derivative style and his ethnic self-hatred ("Show me a Negro and I'll show you a thief") illustrate the nature of alienated imitation through which new cultures pass. Long's English translation captures the florid style of Williams's original only too well:

Oh! Muse of blackest tint, why shrinks thy breast,
Why fears t' approach the *Caesar* of the *West!*
Dispel thy doubts, with confidence ascend
The regal dome, and hail him for thy friend:
Nor blush, altho' in garb funereal drest,
Thy body's white, tho' clad in sable vest.[42]

Using the classical allusions, metaphors, and ornament of European high style, Williams's poetry shows no evidence whatsoever of his Jamaican background except for his self-destructive racism. In the only other poem ascribed to Williams, the same kind of derivative form and rhetoric appear:

What was it made great Alexander
Weep at his unfriendly fate
twas because he cou'd not Wander
beyond the World's strong Prison Gate
For the World is also bounded

by the heavens and Stars above
Why shoud We then be confounded
Since there's nothing free but Jove.[43]

In this popular song ("Welcome, Welcome Brother Debtor"), the imagery and diction, the connotative and suggestive aspects of the language all fall within the accepted style of eighteenth-century English. Nothing marks this work as that of a Jamaican.

Jove might reign in the poetry of Francis Williams, but a very different and more influential deity, Ananse, had taken up residence in the Jamaican psyche during this period. The African spider-god became the cunning hero of survival in the tales of creole society. References to an extensive body of tales occur in the early nineteenth century, pointing to a considerable depth (both in time and in usage) for this genre.[44] The West African genre became remade so as to depict Jamaican experience. Its dramatic and interactive nature remained, but its characters mirrored plantation slavery and it even developed a special ironic formula ("Jack Mandora, me no choose none") used to mark the end of a tale and the narrator's self-conscious rejection of responsibility for the actions of the hero (often self-serving, cunning, and unscrupulous). The Anancy story went beyond entertainment, for it was also a vehicle for moral and psychological insights: "a moral is always an indispensable part of a Nancy story," writes Matthew G. Lewis in 1817,[45] commenting on tales, songs, sayings, and other literary genres in Jamaica.

While Francis Williams was composing in Latin and trying to forget his African culture, others were creating poetry as vivid as anything written in Latin. Dated to the late eighteenth or early nineteenth century by its mingling of archaic Ewe, Twi, Fante, and Ga, the following chant survived in the parish of St. Thomas as a kumina ritual performance. By the mid-twentieth century, the meanings of the words had been lost, but the purpose of the words and the chant itself survived as powerful vehicles of religious belief. Recorded by Joseph G. Moore, an American anthropologist, it was translated and explained by two native speakers of Ewe in 1989. The entire text and translation, with the Odamttens' glosses and comments, can be found in Lalla and D'Costa, *Language in Exile* (1990). Here are the first four lines, in Moore's phonetic spelling, followed by Vincent Odamtten's translation:

Tangɛ langɛ Jɛni dı Gəl ɛvə
Di lɔ cumorti pangɛ le
Gəl Im wɔto pangɛ mama le
Di le kuwidi pangɛ le

On the other side of the river, the great Lange,
Demands the beautiful one comes willingly
Pange, the reincarnation god, demands devotion
In this place of death
Great grandmother of Pange creates legends in this manner
Pange demands you willingly search in this death-dawning.

Notice that the ritual itself calls for the creation of legends, of poetic forms to take the participants "on the other side of the river" where "I shall eat in panic of the Lady," the river goddess, Pange, giver of love and death.

Song marked the culture of exiled Africans in the Americas. Every experience could be rendered in song, or accompanied by song, or preserved by song. Many Europeans noted the powerful tendency among Africans and Afro-creoles to create narrative, descriptive, satiric, and expressive lyrics and to keep these songs alive over long periods of time.

Other oral genres of the seventeenth and eighteenth centuries included the songs and ring-games played by English, Irish, and Scottish sailors, settlers, and soldiers, all of whom contributed directly to the culture of exile: "There's a brown gyal in dah ring" who will "skip across the ocean" unlike Moreton's captive women. Songs such as these appear in Rhys's fiction as allusive emblems of time, place, and a shared viewpoint. In *Wide Sargasso Sea,* Antoinette Rochester Cosway sings of "Charlie over the water," a creole song about a Stuart prince. Here the lost Stuart cause expresses the universal theme of exile: "Grandpappy [pass] his glass over the water decanter and the tears [run] down his face for all the friends dead and gone, whom he would never see again. That has nothing to do with England, I said."[46] Set in Jamaica in the 1840s, *Wide Sargasso Sea* captures that mythologizing process by which lost worlds become transmuted into a creole world, creations of imagination sustained by echoes of exile.

At the same time, languages unknown to European masters invariably worked to preserve identity and the hope of freedom, as the fleeting appearance of Arabic demonstrates. Preserved as much for its religious meaning as for its value as a writing system, written Arabic might have had a profound effect on the unfolding of the diaspora. Speakers and writers of Arabic would have been brought to the Americas at any point in the eighteenth century. In Brazil, their literacy furnished them with the perfect means to plan the great slave rebellion of 1835. Yet what can matter more than a letter from a friend, a letter speaking of a long lost home, and especially in one's own language? We do not know how many people literate in Arabic came to Jamaica, but we do know that such people existed, shown here in this letter by Edward Donlan, whose real name was Abu Bakr al-Siddiq:[47]

From Edward Donlan to Robert Tuffit.
Kingston, Jamaica, October 18, 1834.

Dear Countryman,
I now answer your last letter, my name, in Arabic, is Abon Becr Sadiki, and, in Christian language, Edward Donlan, I born in Timbuctoo, and brought up in Geneh; I finished read the Coran in the country of Gounah, which place I was taken captive in war. My master's name in this country is Alexander Anderson. Now, my countryman, God hath given me a faithful man, a just and a good master; he made me free and I know truly he has shown mercy to every poor soul under him.
. . . .
Whenever you wish to send me a letter, write it in Arabic language; then I will understand it properly.

I am, dear Sir,
Your obedient servant,
Edward Donlan.

To Mr Robert Tuffit, Manchester.

Abu Bakr/Edward Donlan was born about 1790 and, caught up by chance in the Asante wars, was captured and sold in 1805 to an English slave ship. In Jamaica, he became a storekeeper and kept his records in Arabic. The letter is a model of its kind. Many Jamaicans and Africans of the early nineteenth century would have had cause to compose such messages, orally or in writing, just as they composed sermons, prayers, and formal speeches in all of the languages the country could provide. As more and more Jamaican-born people enlarged the population, the processes of cultural fusion picked up speed, establishing a Jamaican literature that we can recognize.

Tales and narratives (generically called Nancy stories, according to Matthew G. Lewis) filled the lives of captives as the island became more and more native-born, more Jamaican. An excellent example of this developing literature comes down to us in Henry Garland Murray's little-known (but vividly entertaining) work, *Manners and Customs of the Country a Generation Ago: Tom Kittle's Wake*, published in 1869 and claiming to describe Jamaican life in the 1840s and 1850s. The depth of memory actually predates emancipation, so one may safely take it that Murray was recalling a Jamaica belonging to the first decades of the nineteenth century, or even earlier. The main narrative language is Standard English, while all of the dialogue (and this carries the expected Jamaican vividness) is written in Jamaican Creole. Murray was a man of the theater and a dramatic performer of his writings. Unfortunately, only *Tom Kittle's Wake* has come down to us from what was probably a considerable body of oral-based, dramatic narratives and expositions of character composed by Murray and his two sons.[48]

Tom Kittle's Wake tells the story of a humble Montego Bay fisherman, Tom Kittle, who inherits a fishing boat and his own freedom on the death of his master, "an old brown man named John Marshall. He and Tom had grown side by side together in life. For over fifty years . . . he and Tom had frequently looked in danger's face in the waters . . . between Montego Bay and Lucea . . . and Falmouth." Murray describes the deep bond between the two, their exploits on the sea (especially in shark hunting), and the much loved canoe with its inscription "I jan masshal beter an beholin, mantega bay, river bay." Old Marshall dies, and then in time, Tom himself lies dying. The rest of the story presents the moving and at times comic events surrounding Tom's last instructions to his somewhat shady grandson, Sam; Tom's death; his wake; the question of how to pay for the wake; and Sam's meditations on the correct way to handle "dead-lef." Murray highlights Tom's quiet death, "the dull low cooing of the partridge . . .—an old African omen of death," and Tom's very last words to Sam regarding Tom's doves: "Mass Sammy when I ded let go de bud!"[49]

The following description of the wake itself tells us much about how and where our literature took form:

> [In] the inner yard the people had spread themselves about in every direction, and gaiety and merriment were the order of the day, or rather of the night. They sang, they danced, they ate, they drank. Some played marbles in the moonlight, some gambled with grains of corn blackened on one side; others with pieces of broken ware [crockery]. Tales went around of all kinds: tales of horse racing, tales of cock-fighting, stories of ghosts, and especially they all opened their eyes and ears with amaze [at the words of] Old Peter Brown, on the terrible evils that are ever attendant on the act of leaving a wake after midnight. The women shook their heads, and uttered that "click, click," peculiar to them at such times—made by a rapid contraction of the muscles of the throat—while the little children clung close to their mothers' sides as old Brown told of the troubles he endured one night under Mr. Morris's cotton tree, on his way homeward, having left a wake after twelve o'clock; and how he went off in a fit at length, when after braving and escaping all danger from without, he found on entering his bedroom that the dead man whose wake he had deserted, was sitting on the side of his bed![50]

The pull of our past affected other writers of the nineteenth century. Herbert G. de Lisser (1878–1944) gave us some of the most exact and insightful portrayals of impoverished, working-class Jamaican women. In 1912, his first novel was serialized in the *Daily Gleaner* under the title *Jane: A Story of Jamaica.* Later published as *Jane's Career*, the novel tells the story of a young servant girl from the country, new to Kingston, and the object of much exploitation and harassment. It says much for de Lisser's literary skill and for the unconscious, unadmitted empathy of his *Gleaner* readership that such a life could be the focus of a novel, and a well-received novel at that. Walter Jekyll (1849–1929) recorded many of the folktales created by our ancestors or brought here from Africa. Jekyll took special pride in recording the stories in the exact language used by his informants, so that language and literary form fuse together as one, with no sense of phony translations or sanitizings shaded in for an overseas audience. The sermons and prayers and later the speeches made by Jamaicans asserting their independence were made in formal Jamaican Creole. Many such oral statements were documented by missionaries, with one example taken down verbatim on Friday, August 1, 1834: "O Lord, our gracious saviour, what we is meet togeder for dis mornin' when we don't usual to do so dis day of de week? We is come to bless and to magnify dy great and holy name dat dou has done dis great blessin' unto us, to bring us out of de house of bondage dis day. . . . Dy word tell we dat king and prophet wish to see de tings dat we see, and to hear de tings dat we hear, an die widout de sight."[51] Reverend Phillippo, the Baptist minister who recorded this prayer, would have been anxious to show off the speaker's skill in formal English. Like other missionaries, he disapproved of things African and saw a command of English as proof that his people were worthy of their freedom.

Once despised, oral histories have preserved much of Jamaica's vivid and painful past in families, villages, and closely knit groups. The shapes of these oral histories (as well as their content and form) have laid their mark on Jamaican literature. All such histories offer the narrative structure of true literary art: clearly defined characters, a plot involving conflict, and after a crisis, resolution. Each displays the classic beginning, middle, and ending. Aristotle would recognize these genres.

Three examples must suffice.[52] The first originates from Lucea in Hanover, ca. 1835: "My great-great grandmother, they say, was suddenly charged with a debt by the man who owned her and her children. She had very little money, but she could have perhaps worked off the debt over a long time. If, instead, she refused to pay him, he would send her to the workhouse where she would have to dance the treadmill (a dreadful punishment), but the debt would go clear and she could use her small savings to buy her children's freedom. She went to the workhouse. She danced the treadmill. They say it cut up her feet and legs, it beat her up, but she paid off the debt, and used her money to buy her children." The next comes from Glengoffe in the St. Catherine hills and dates from ca. 1760 to 1834: "An Irishman named John Crary had a place with about a hundred or more acres and a lot of slaves. It was in the eighteenth century, some such time. He never married but he had children with the African women on the estate, we called it Creary's Road. When he died, years passed but nobody came after the land or the people, so we lived same place until emancipation time, and then some of us left and went to Port Maria. All of us black people from up there are of the Ashanti." The third is from Westmoreland, in about 1840 to 1850:

> They say the white man up in the great house saw her: she was very pretty, people say, just a young girl. Black skin but hair long down to her waist. So he sent down the headman and dem took her up to the great house and big massa had her up there until she got with baby. She went home to her family and had the baby boy. The big man let her keep him until im reach two, then he take away the little boy to the great house and say she not to come see him. Never tell the boy who the mother is. Boy soon forget. Keep him up there living in de stable an raise him as stableboy, then coachman. Well, dem used to give de people Sunday off, sometimes, and when de boy turn sixteen, him aks de white man why im cyaan go out go visit on a Sunday? Him did hear who him mother is, and him want to see har, but him no tell him father so. Well, Sunday come, him dress good, an him walk the so-so two mile go a im mother yard. When im reach, im find say she married to one black man, dem have must be five pickney, all a dem dress fe go a church wid Bible in dem han. So dem glad to take him too. An when dem reach inside, an service start, im see all to de littlest one a him bredda an sister da open bible an hymn book, da start fe read an sing, and him never yet see book before in all him life. Im cyaan read not one blind word. One vexation tek im same time, him vex, im vex, im head full a fire! An from dat day, im never go back up a im fada place, and im never lay eyes pan dat white man again. Dem say him leave go a Panama.

All the elements of irony, tragedy, satire, comedy, and pathos lie open to view here. In some ways, Jamaican life offers experiences and models almost too rich and numerous for the fiction writer to manage.

In the eighteenth and nineteenth centuries, the Jamaican-born children of exiles would have absorbed the tales of white servants and black slaves, heard the chants and drums in the distance as nine-nights celebrated the passing of an African to the land of belonging, and they would have helped to make Bluebeard into a Jamaican planter and the spider-god Anancy into a survivor, witty, "longheaded," and cunning. Before radio, urban migration, and other forces for change had altered Jamaican life still further, the countryside offered the seemingly divided child a wealth of oral narratives, dramatic monologues, ritual performances, proverbs, songs, and chants. In these genres and in the everyday talk of people lies also an immense range of ironic, satiric, parodic, pathetic, and melodramatic language in which metaphor and word-games flourish.

The country folk of my childhood stand in direct descent from the old Jamaican man portrayed two hundred years ago in the anonymous travelogue *A Short Journey in the West Indies* (1790): "[Cudjoe] speaks his mind, and advancing years have had their wonted effect upon his tongue. He loves to talk, and I love to hear him talk. Our colloquies would divert you, could I remember them verbatim, for his remarks are often proverbial, and his allusions keen and novel. . . . The language of the negroes is more expressive than I could have supposed, and conveys their ideas most forcibly. Cudjoe has gained experience, and he tells stories with humour."[53] Even today, few Jamaicans can conceive of their language as serving any purposes save those of comedy, irony, and parody. A profound belief in the anti-intellectualism of Jamaican Creole (and all that exists within it) has prevailed since the eighteenth century among all classes of Jamaicans. For many, this distrust of their mothertongue has bred a tragic alienation, an alienation widely encouraged by many Jamaicans.

Both black and white creoles underwent a rejection of their parents' origins while retaining a nostalgia for both Africa and Europe. If this statement sounds like paradox, then let it be clear that paradox forms the underpinning of the creole worldview. Thanks to this alienation, and to our paradox-laden skills as imitators and creators, Jamaicans remain intensely aware of language as a value system, as a group marker, as topic and situation centered, as a form of identifying behavior, and as a highly variable instrument. Writers such as Anthony Winkler, Kei Miller, Olive Senior, and Louise Bennett use this cultural sensitivity to capture the essence of the Jamaican voice, whether in poetry or in prose. Such writers use the ranges of Jamaican language—from Creole to Standard Jamaican English—to express action, viewpoint, irony, and shifts of character and to intensify moments of climactic joy, high comedy, or tragic recognition.

While few other Jamaican writers possess Bennett's skill in composing in Creole (see chapter 10 of this volume), all of us recognize the truth of Derek Walcott's claims regarding the Creole sources of our art. In the prefatory essay, "What the Twilight Says: An Ouverture," Walcott introduces *Dream on Monkey Mountain and Other Plays* (1970) in terms of the richness of oral expression in the Caribbean imagination. What he says applies as much to Jamaica as to any other island. All of us know the streets with their "theatre of degeneracy" enacted by the lost souls of every community, the insane, the drunkards, the "derelicts who mimed their tragedies, [and] . . . improvised absurd monodramas."[54] Tales in bars and backyards invoke the vivid presences of the dead and the inhuman spirits of forest, river, and desolate land. Recalling the songs he heard ("a strange croaking of Christian and African songs") and the tales of the strong brother and the foolish brother, Walcott notes that in the Caribbean mind all of these genres "sank like a stain. And taught us symmetry. The true folktale concealed a structure as universal as the skeleton, the one armature from Br'er Anancy to King Lear."[55] With perfect Aristotelian balance, the form of these tales moves from the classic beginning that states its unique problem and demands an expansion into a crucial middle ground from which arises a third and final stage, the moral and emotional resolution of the essential question. Every Caribbean child has grown up sensing the power and existential rightness of this fundamental form: to Walcott, "the apparent conservatism of West Indian fiction . . . is not an imitative respect for moulds" but an inbred, inculcated "memory of that form."[56]

And so the eighteenth century filters through the Caribbean imagination even when we have no comprehensive written histories nor even exact oral recollections of the period. Neither European nor African, the great-great-great-grandchildren of the exiles now pass beyond the imitativeness of Francis Williams, of the nineteenth-century missionary school and the twentieth-century university in Europe or the United States, to create our literature out of the nothing we remember and the everything that escapes both scholar and critic so as to live on in our fictive art.

For there was and is no real division, no clash between tales heard and tales read, between officially approved literature and the stories told to us or read to us. Contrast there will be: the human mind plays and surmounts such division, having created it in the first place. The divided child holds all worlds in its power, for the child itself is not divided. The language forms have no real boundaries: Creole and English extend one another, give color and texture, life and energy to expressing the world around us, the legacy of Jamaica's past, of exile and survival and renewal.

Jack Mandora, me no choose none.

Notes

1. Part of the material in this chapter appeared in an earlier essay: Jean D'Costa, "Oral Literature, Formal Literature: The Formation of Genre in Eighteenth Century Jamaica," *Eighteenth-Century Studies* 27, no. 4 (1994): 663–676.

2. M. Keith Booker and Dubravka Juraga, *The Caribbean Novel in English: An Introduction* (London: Heinemann, 2001), 5.

3. Édouard Glissant, *Caribbean Discourse: Selected Essays,* trans. and introduced by J. Michael Dash (Charlottesville: University Press of Virginia, 1992).

4. Derek Walcott, *Another Life* (London: Jonathan Cape, 1972), 143.

5. Edited by Francis Wyndham and Diana Melly (London: André Deutsch, 1984).

6. In *Tigers Are Better-Looking* (New York: Popular Library, 1976), 175–176. Note that Rhys's tribute to song appears in "Let Them Call It Jazz" (ibid.).

7. London: New Beacon Press, 1980.

8. See Pamela Mordecai and Betty Wilson, eds., *Her True True Name* (Kingston: Heinemann Caribbean, 1989), 42.

9. An informal concert organized to provide entertainment and to raise money. Uniquely Jamaican, tea-meetings feature songs, speech-making, much humor, and bidding by the audience to stop a performer or to cause the "queen" of the evening to unveil (Olive Senior, *Encyclopedia of Jamaican Heritage* [Kingston: Twin Guinep, 2003], 479–480). Improvised song and speeches formed the core of Caribbean folk entertainments at weddings, funerals, and indeed all celebrations. Note the singing Scrubbers of Barbados whose Christmas caroling involves ad hominem humor, fund-raising, and much improvisation of words and music (Sean Carrington, Henry Fraser, and John Gilmore, eds., *A–Z of Barbadian Heritage* [Kingston: Heinemann Caribbean, 1990], 157).

10. For an excellent account of a nineteenth-century wake, see Henry Garland Murray, *Manners and Customs of the Country a Generation Ago: Tom Kittle's Wake* (Kingston: Jordan 1877). It is reprinted in Jean D'Costa and Barbara Lalla, eds., *Voices in Exile: Jamaican Texts of the 18th and 19th Centuries* (Tuscaloosa: University of Alabama Press, 1989), 88–110.

11. For Jamaican folk literature, see Walter Jekyll, ed., *Jamaican Song and Story* (1907; repr., New York: Dove, 1966); Laura Tanna, *Jamaican Folk Tales and Oral Histories* (Kingston: Institute of Jamaica, 1984); and Daryl Cumber Dance, *Folklore from Contemporary Jamaicans* (Knoxville: University of Tennessee Press, 1980).

12. Many of these authors appear in Mordecai and Wilson's anthology (see n. 8) and in Daryl Cumber Dance, *Fifty Caribbean Writers* (Westport, CT: Greenwood Press, 1986).

13. In *Summer Lightning and Other Stories* (Harlow, England: Longman Caribbean, 1986), 26–35.

14. Sistren, with Honor Ford-Smith, *Lionheart Gal* (London: Women's Press, 1986). Sistren, a theater group of working-class women directed by Ford-Smith of the School of Drama, Kingston, Jamaica, produced scenes from their life stories as theater. The group has been highly successful on its tours in the Caribbean, North America, and elsewhere.

15. In *Dream on Monkey Mountain and Other Plays* (New York: Farrar, Straus, and Giroux, 1970).

16. See Keith Noel, ed., *Caribbean Plays for Schools* (Portsmouth, NH: Heinemann Educational Books Ltd., 1985).

17. Ibid., 6.

18. F. G. Cassidy, *Jamaica Talk* (London: MacMillan, 1971); R. B. Le Page and David DeCamp, *Jamaican Creole* (London: MacMillan, 1960). H. Orlando Patterson, *The Sociology of Slavery* (London: MacGibbon and Kee, 1967), and Michael Craton, *Searching for the Invisible Man: Slaves and Plantation Life in Jamaica* (Cambridge: Harvard

University Press, 1978); as well as Barbara Lalla and Jean D'Costa. *Language in Exile: Three Hundred Years of Jamaican Creole* (Tuscaloosa: The University of Alabama Press, 1990).

19. Edward Kamau Brathwaite, *The Arrivants: A New World Trilogy*. London: Oxford University Press, 1973.

20. Walcott, *Dream on Monkey Mountain,* 162.

21. Roger Mais, *Brother Man* (London: Cape, 1954; reprint, London: Heinemann, 1974).

22. [Edward Ward], *A Trip to Jamaica, with a True Character of the People and the Island* (London: n.p., 1698); (Bodleian Library ref. Mason 1.1. 147); John Atkins, *A Voyage to Guinea, Brasil, and the West Indies* (London: Cesar Ward and Richard Chandler, 1736).

23. Craton, *Searching for the Invisible Man,* 55.

24. Silvio Torres-Saillant, *Caribbean Poetics: Toward an Aesthetic of West Indian Literature* (Cambridge: Cambridge University Press, 1997), 77.

25. This matter forms the body of Barbara Lalla's extensive study of medieval English language and literature, viewed as a process of postcolonial adjustment and change. See Barbara Lalla, *Postcolonialisms: Caribbean Rereading of Medieval English Discourse* (Kingston: University of the West Indies Press, 2008).

26. Edward Long, *The History of Jamaica* (London: T. Lowndes, 1774), 2:426–427.

27. Craton, *Searching for the Invisible Man,* 12. Peter Roberts describes the language situation at this time in the Caribbean as a whole, in *From Oral to Literate Culture: Colonial Experience in the English West Indies* (Kingston: University of the West Indies Press, 1997).

28. Atkins, *Voyage to Guinea,* 245; also Le Page and DeCamp, *Jamaican Creole,* 36, 80–83, 91.

29. Lalla and D'Costa, *Language in Exile,* 86–87, 90–91, 131.

30. For the original material, see Sir Hans Sloane, *A Voyage to the Islands Madera, Barbados, Nieves, S. Christophers and Jamaica: With the Natural History . . . of the Last of Those Islands; to Which Is Prefix'd an Introduction, wherein Is an Account of the Inhabitants, Air, Waters, Diseases, Trade, &c. . . . Illustrated with the Figures of the Things Describ'd.*, 2 vols. (London: British Museum for the Author, 1707–1725). This incident appears in volume 2, 1. For a fuller discussion of Sloane's records, see Lalla and D'Costa, *Language in Exile,* 127–28.

31. Walcott, *Another Life,* 143.

32. Ibid.

33. Olive Lewin, *Rock It Come Over: The Folk Music of Jamaica* (Kingston: University of the West Indies Press, 2000), 25, from the chapter, "Old Souls in a New World."

34. In *Tigers Are Better-Looking,* 49–72.

35. Both of the songs that follow appear in J. B. Moreton, *West India Customs and Manners* (1790; repr., London: Parsons, 1793), 153–155.

36. For a fuller discussion, see D'Costa and Lalla, *Voices in Exile,* 12–17, notes, 130–131; the original song appears in Moreton, *West India Customs and Manners,* 153. Michael Scott's highly popular novel, *Tom Cringle's Log*, 2 vols. (1833; repr., Edinburgh: Black-

wood, 1834), presents Jamaican life at the turn of the eighteenth century. The late Professor John J. Figueroa praised it for its faithful rendition of Jamaican Creole. It was popular among Mico Teachers College students as late as the 1930s (personal communications from the late Professor John J. Figueroa and the late Rev. George L. Creary, my father).

37. Matthew G. Lewis, *Journal of a West India Proprietor* (London: Murray, 1834), 323.

38. "The Tale of Dry Bone," in D'Costa and Lalla, *Voices in Exile,* 28–30, also 133n8.

39. For overseas education in eighteenth century Jamaica, see Lalla and D'Costa, *Voices in Exile,* 23.

40. Long, *The History of Jamaica,* 2:475–485.

41. D'Costa and Lalla, *Voices in Exile*, 9–11 and 130n4.

42. Long *History of Jamaica*, 2:483.

43. D'Costa and Lalla, *Voices in Exile,* 130n5 explains this fragment: "The single surviving copy of this song in the National Library of Jamaica shows . . . [a] handwritten text . . . in poor condition. . . . The only identification . . . reads: 'francis Williams negre de la Jamaique Voyez Histoire de cette isle par Édouard Long et'" followed by "Paris, Arsenal., Mss. Fr. 6339."

44. See Lalla and D'Costa, *Language in Exile,* 40–41.

45. Matthew G. Lewis (an English novelist also known as "Monk" Lewis) visited his Jamaican estates in 1815 and again in 1817. More humane than most owners and an opponent of the "execrable" slave trade, he made careful observations of the people on his plantations, noting that Africans who came on the same slave ship adopted one another as close kin, passing this bond on to their children. Lewis died in 1817; his journals were published decades later. See *Journal of a West India Proprietor,* 255. Other versions appeared in 1845 and 1861.

46. Jean Rhys, *Wide Sargasso Sea* (Harmondsworth, England: Penguin, 1980), 122.

47. See a full discussion in D'Costa and Lalla, *Voices in Exile,* 68, 138.

48. Ibid., 81–111.

49. Ibid., 93–94.

50. Ibid., 102–103.

51. Ibid., 61.

52. The Hanover history is based on personal communication by M. P. Patterson to the author, November 2010; the St. Catherine story of John Crary was told me by my father, George Creary; and the third (set in Westmorcland) I ovcrhcard at age six when my mother and uncle were discussing their grandparents' lives.

53. *A Short Journey to the West Indies* (London: Murray and Forbes, 1790), 1:72; Lalla and D'Costa, *Language in Exile,* 130–131; Walcott, *Dream on Monkey Mountain,* 23.

54. Walcott, *Dream on Monkey Mountain,* 23.

55. Ibid.

56. Ibid., 24.

2
Black Wholes

Phases in the Development of Jamaican Literary Discourse

Barbara Lalla

Caribbean Creole has participated fundamentally in the evolution of literary discourse in the Anglophone Caribbean. Among the linguistic choices available, the choice of Creole for literary discourse was, traditionally, severely constrained, yet this unprestigious, indeed stigmatized language evolved to the extent that it is increasingly represented as a mechanism for conveying Caribbean perspective in literature. At the same time, literary discourse in the Caribbean also evolved, shaped by competing forces: linguistic choices that involve appropriation of a prestige code and linguistic choices that resist pressure to conform to this privileged code.

Because this chapter focuses on the intersection of literary and linguistic analysis, the ensuing discussion requires an interdisciplinary framework, combining the methodologies of language history and literary history with those of what has come to be termed literary linguistics. Literary linguistics is eclectic in similar ways to critical linguistics, except that critical linguistics offers a wider application to (often nonliterary) scribal material. Critical linguistics also provides an interdisciplinary approach to language study that brings together different methodologies and meshes various theoretical frameworks comparable to the mesh of frameworks employed in critical discourse analysis. Such analysis—particularly of power relationships that are discursively constituted, entrenched, or resisted—explores mechanisms for encoding perspective, and perspective (particularly on the ideological plane) is a useful tool to apply in analyzing the significance of Creole in literary discourse. Perceptual perspective (encoded, for example, through deixis) is normally distinguished from psychological orientation (encoded, for example, through person) and ideological orientation. Ideological orientation is not only encoded through modality, transitivity, and so forth,[1] but it is also conveyed through code-shifting.

Through code-shifting from English to Jamaican Creole, writers have encoded Jamaican perspectives throughout the history of Jamaican scribal discourse. The crucial significance of perspective emerges when we reflect that rather than merely signifying the angle from which a story is told, *perspective* is now increasingly being applied to "the totality of the world- and belief-models of the story world."[2] Thus, although Gerald Prince distinguishes narrative voice from perspective in terms of who speaks, as distinct from who sees, and (along with Genette) explains voice in terms of a set of signs characterizing the narrator,[3] voice in narrative discourse also mediates between the narrator and those speakers that the narrator represents. Representations of narrative voice, of thoughts of the central consciousness, and of the voices and thoughts of characters are essential world-creating properties, such as Herman discusses,[4] because fictional worlds based on our real-world experience model not only characteristics of our actual physical world (such as persons, states, events, motivations, and so on), but also discourse characteristics such as varieties of communicative behavior, discourse situations, registers, and code choice.

In exploring the significance of Creole language representation to the development of literary discourse, this chapter incorporates references to and examples from a range of representative literary texts spanning three centuries, and these texts are drawn both from Jamaican literature and from literature set in Jamaica though not authored by Jamaicans.[5]

Caribbean literature, of which Jamaican is one national variety, is widely defined in connection with the Caribbean voice and perspective represented in the discourse; yet Caribbean linguistics (even in discussing the status of Caribbean Creoles[6]) has up to recently focused little on Creole in the literary discourse even when commenting on the history of literary activity in the Caribbean.[7] The circumstances and mechanisms through which Caribbean language maintains a pivotal role in encoding Caribbean perspective in the literary discourse and thus in defining the literature therefore remain a fertile area of enquiry. Work on Creole in Caribbean literary discourse has mainly comprised analyses of language in individual texts and of issues associated with representation. Less has been said about the role of Creole in the growth of indigenous literature or about the significance of Creole in sociohistorical development of literary discourse, although Mühleisen has taken a decidedly diachronic approach to her analysis of prestige in Caribbean Creole discourse, approaching Caribbean Creole as a regional discourse.[8]

My own approach is to focus on the literature of one territory. In selecting a few authors, such as Alfred H. Mendes, V. S. Naipaul, Earl Lovelace, and Patricia Powell, as Mühleisen does, we may overlook contextual differences (national, ethnic, gendered, and so forth) that may account for contrasts, and we may then go on to confuse such differences with changes. It would be instructive, for example, to compare changes in the discourse of a writer like Lovelace over decades with those of other writers in his own territory, such as Selvon.[9] Indeed, through detailed analyses of single texts—analyses like that of Schneider (2002)—data is provided for further refinement of observations such as mine and Mühleisen's. Because Jamaican is best known to me—a knowledge strengthened by my familiarity with texts in which Creole is inscribed from the earliest documentary evidence—but also because it provides a more consistent frame of reference than a wider regional spectrum, I draw most of the evidence from the discussion that follows from Jamaican literary discourse.

The Evolution of Creole Participation in the Literature

Creole participation in Jamaican literature has proceeded through a number of stages. Inscribing the Jamaican voice in literary discourse through anything resembling code-shifting has fragile roots in the eighteenth to nineteenth centuries, but tracing it earlier than the twentieth century poses challenges associated with the circumstances of representation. Essentially, the earliest inscribers of Creole were inventing or, at best, documenting the discourse rather than expressing a local viewpoint. Indeed, it would have been thought that there was little to represent. Walter Ong associates with oral society an interactive communication that is supported by a verbal culture, and Roberts therefore distinguishes the formative period of West Indian vernaculars as "pre-oral," as not yet sustaining the type of interaction that Ong describes.[10]

Nineteenth-century records of interaction in Jamaican reflect an oral society. For example, Henry Garland Murray represents exchanges at a wake in anecdote, song, commentary, and extended story.[11] Murray's record preserves an English account scattered with numerous Jamaican references and containing dialogue broadly representing Creole voices. Some of these speakers shift into anecdote in which Creole is more closely represented. One recounts a folktale, and this embedded discourse is basilectal—preserving Creole language features now encountered only in the most conservative speech and, indeed, some features that have now disappeared. Within the folktale, a song fragment comprises features no longer comprehensible.

The Murray text preserves discourses embedded in each other, and the deeper the observer progresses through one embedded discourse into the next, the older each seems. Inscribing the Jamaican voice even in this single text produces such historical complexity (even in the earliest phase of literary activity pertaining to Jamaica) that it is difficult to apply a straightforward chronological account of development to the literary discourse. Nevertheless, major patterns of development emerge in the creative representation of Creole.

Well before Murray's latter nineteenth-century record, dialogue in scribal discourse incorporated Creole features. Some of this material predates the literary discourse generally recognized as Jamaican literature. A clear set of criteria governed the selection of appropriate discourses from this early phase of the evolving literature:

- The material should be literary and creative.
- The speakers must be represented as Jamaican.
- The material should convey contrasts in code choice.
- The setting of the material should be Caribbean and, in this instance, specifically Jamaican (unless the intention was to compare material from Jamaican and other settings).
- The context of the material should display an interest in Jamaican life, circumstances, or worldview.
- The material should, cumulatively, represent a chronological range from the earliest to the most recent extant textual material.

In specific circumstances, the requirement of creative writing might be relaxed. Extended samples of appropriate creative writing might, for instance, be difficult to find in the eighteenth century. To discover the earliest roots of Creole representation in literary discourse, it was necessary to take into account mixed genres in pre-twentieth-century material. Literary journals and books of domestic manners, while generally documentary, include anecdotes and record folk material including tales, and such sources yielded up dialogue in circumstances other than that of objective transcription.[12]

Much eighteenth- and nineteenth-century Jamaican discourse that includes Creole is naïve with regard to any viewpoint but British adventuring and exploratory perspective: clueless voyeur or reporter types of writing, in which Creole exoticizes the literature. Even now, Maryse Condé points out that the Creole can function as a means of exoticizing the Caribbean for European readers.[13] Eighteenth- and nineteenth-century scribal discourse that represents Jamaican reality actually functions as a support for imperial perspective and tends to be limited in linguistic accuracy. In various senses, then, a curious continuum exists between fiction and nonfiction. The polemic, the book of domestic manners, the travelogue, and the novel of adventure shade imperceptibly into each other. In these genres occur representations of speech that I would describe as *ventriloquist dialogue*, speech (by the British author) on behalf of the silenced Caribbean voice.[14] This rendering of Caribbean speech is in many instances invented (and in this sense fictional) rather than objectively transcribed. It is characteristically brief because it does not function as an opportunity for local expression. It is also characteristically English with occasional but indiscriminately applied Jamaican Creole characteristics. Consider, for example, *The Importance of Jamaica to Great Britain*, a mid-eighteenth-century argument by an anonymous author: "Why should they leave goodee Master, and goodee

Mistress, where every Thing is provided for them, to meet with Troubles and starvee starvee about the Streets."[15] The rare page that includes Creole may represent it through one phonological feature, as in the final vowel of *goodee* ("good"), and one morphological feature, like reduplication, as in *starvee starvee.* Another page signals Creole through one syntactic feature, the insertion of *no* (without auxiliary) before the main verb, *no know one another.*[16] Not only is the book's ideological perspective clearly reflected in its title (*The Importance of Jamaica to Great Britain*) but the third person is used for reference to the speaker even within direct speech, further marginalizing the creole consciousness. The content of this book strengthens the likelihood that the "reported" discourse presented as direct speech is invented. It is reported for the purpose of legitimizing imperial power, and its other deictic elements are oriented in relation to the locus of power. What is *presented* as dialogue must be an authorial construction of the black speaker's largely unknown discourse.

Longer representations of Creole dialogue come with development in the characterization of the Creole language speaker beyond what has been little more than a dimension of setting, but there is as yet no real Caribbean voice. In the early nineteenth century, the anonymous author of *Marly,* possibly a Scot, slides between creative writing and report, producing an argument pretending to be a novel.[17] While it reflects more of Jamaican Creole than does *The Importance of Jamaica,* the language, clearly, has still not been acquired by its author: "Him Joseph's broders hab be much angry at dis, and him Joseph habing be on de penn, and much far away from him's puppa's house, him's broders catch him Joseph, and sell him to de buckras who hab be in de want of neger; for de house neger."[18] English characteristics (like possessive -s) persist alongside a thin scattering of select Creole characteristics, such as Jamaican [b] replacing English [v], and Jamaican [d] versus English [đ]. Elsewhere too there are occasional non-English words and grammatical forms, such as *savvy* and *nyam,* and the negative in *him no savvy.*[19] An important Creole characteristic in *Marly,* and prominent in the preceding quotation, is *him* for third person animate and inanimate, male and female, and for subject and object reference. However, *Marly* also includes *hims* as possessive (although elsewhere *him* functions rightly as possessive). Moreover, indiscriminate application that occurs in the case of *him* also occurs in some other items, like *hab. Marly* is followed by more competent fiction (such as novels by Michael Scott, William George Hamley, and Capt. Mayne Reid) and there are literary records of oral narrative, for example, by Charles Rampini.[20] However, Creole speech in nineteenth-century literary discourse continues to be represented by the nonspeaker. Indeed, apart from the local and perhaps colored Henry Murray, there is little evidence of local literary discourse that includes Creole.

Within this ventriloquist phase, the official code provides the point of departure for representing Jamaican Creole language. Standard English structures overwhelm the representation or, at least, constitute the norms for deviant forms. Peter Roberts considers literary activity in the seventeenth- to nineteenth-century Caribbean as essentially English and identifies drama as the genre that best fitted the society that was, essentially, nonliterate. He concludes that "there was not a level of literacy and other intellectual activity in the plantation slave society to promote and validate a literate variety of West Indian English, distinguishable in itself."[21] To this observation, we can add that at this stage there is not as yet an ideological orientation to permit a sustained Creole-speaking center of consciousness.

In the second half of the century, parallel to an emerging awareness of a discourse of the Other, there develops a new, metadiscursive movement. Thomas Russell produces a record, titled *The Etymology of Jamaica Grammar,* just before J. J. Thomas's description of Creole in Trinidad.[22] Thomas's far better-known record ends by translating biblical and classical texts (English, French, Latin, and Greek) into Creole—a step too progressive for Russell. According to Faith Smith, Thomas writes in a context in which "Creole designates insider versus outsider in relation to complex and not necessarily consistent notions of nationalism, ethnicity, respectability, and authenticity, as well as to phenotype and complexion."[23] Unlike Thomas, Russell offers his work for entertainment and warns playfully that extended analysis, especially of syntax, may end in madness. Thomas, however, is serious. Smith remarks, "In making sense out of chaos Thomas captures and even honors the noise, but he also helps to regulate and reduce it."[24] Whatever sense of chaos may have dogged both commentators, they shared a recognition of describable form, Russell insisting that "every corruption resolves itself into certain fixed rules."[25]

Russell's fledgling linguistic description that at once distinguishes Creole but evaluates it as distorting emerges at the very same time that literary representation of Jamaican Creole grows less inventive and more mimetic. At about the same time, latter nineteenth-century fiction admits substantial dialogue in Creole rather than through illustrative fragments. Nevertheless, the sense of distortion continues to support the comic, even when the mimetic impulse is moving representation beyond the level of deviant English.

In general, even within the ventriloquist phase, Creole attributes come to be displayed for an increasing variety of purposes, but they are being *displayed.* Natalie Schilling-Estes discusses "self-conscious" speech, what she terms *performance speech,* as that register associated with a "speaker's attempt to display for others a certain language or language variety, whether their own or that of another speech community."[26] Spurred no doubt by curiosity about the exotic, the non-Creole-speaking writers of Creole seize on the most obvious (often basilectal) fragments of Creole with which to construct the Other voice.

In addition, they imply the Other by simply altering Standard English. Non-Creole speakers produced the eighteenth- to nineteenth-century scribal discourse that includes what purports to be Jamaican. Not surprisingly, most of this creative writing functions as a support for imperial perspective. This ventriloquist discourse is not only characteristically brief but (especially at first) is limited in accuracy and precision. It offers no opportunity for local expression.

It could be argued that even dialogue that merely departs from Standard English replaces silence. This departure is achieved however, by selecting minimal characteristics of Creole language and applying them inexactly. The writer then places the invented discourse in the mouth of a particular type of speaker: the character-as-attribute-of-setting. A writer can apply selected features of Creole language regardless of verisimilitude where there is no awareness of the local speech as rule-governed and—significantly—no sense of a local point of departure.

The discourse of the time shows only the point of departure associated with the center of power. In these circumstances, not only is Creole dialogue deviant text, but deviant text constitutes Creole dialogue.

In the latter nineteenth century, both the quantity and the quality of Creole language representation increased, and by the early twentieth century, there is marked development both in length and in precision. The earliest local narrative found is by Cyrus Perkins (1911), the resident and perhaps native author of *Busha's Mistress*.[27] In this fiction, a female character, Catherine Brown, begins as a Creole speaker and later becomes a focal consciousness, but to begin with we do not enter her thoughts. The narrator can only speculate on them: "Miss Brown now rose from her seat, took a survey of the staircase and the yard, apparently to ascertain that the coast was clear. She then resumed her seat and said: 'You is a newcomer, sir, and you don't know nothing yet. If Busha hear you ask me anything, he will be vex. Bockra-sah on the estates never allowed to talk to the Negroes; if Busha knows of such a thing he always send them away,' replied Miss Brown." Educated in Standard English, Catherine is fluent: "'Had he been in good circumstances,' said Catherine, 'I should not have gone to look after him, but as it is, I am willing to suffer any hardship if I can but see him again in a decent situation. Perhaps had I remained with him, he would never have come to what he has.'" Only then, as an English speaker, does she become a consciousness that the reader may enter: "Poor Catherine's heart sickened as she rode amidst all this hurry-scurry and thought how slender her chance was of meeting with Jackson."[28]

In the characteristically English discourse with its occasional but indiscriminately applied elements of Creole language, the Creole dialogue occurs as fragments because it *cannot* be sustained (not having been acquired). More importantly, the Creole dialogue is fragmentary because it *need not* be sustained, being merely a signal of the Other. Indeed, the Creole "dialogue" is not yet in fact dialogue, but snippets purporting to represent black speakers in the Caribbean: it is a variation in the imperial monologue—a sporadic kink in the standard.

Even as it enters a new phase of involvement in literature, the Creole language remains *functionally* separate from English and fixed in association with the social class of characters who speak it, so the language of the text is diglossic. Cooper and Devonish point out that Herbert de Lisser "faithfully documents Jane's speech as a kind of curiosity—local colour" in *Jane's Career,* so even the insider's presentation of Jamaican Creole is distanced at this stage by attitudinal positioning.[29] Similarly, J. Downing Thompson notes that although de Lisser includes local expression in his work "in a fashion that is not entirely mocking nor entirely demeaning," this inclusion of local language "is certainly not celebratory."[30] De Lisser himself reminds us that Jamaican Creole is "rude dialect, hardly intelligible to the stranger and scarcely to be rendered by the written word" in his author's note to *Jane's Career.*[31]

So in this new phase, which I distinguish as a *censorship phase,* local artists find themselves torn between strong oral traditions of the folk culture on the one hand and dominant imperial scribal conventions on the other, as they maneuver between restricted functions of Creole in written discourse. The local writer represents Creole with greater accuracy but strictly confines its use.

Creole discourse functions as *marked* discourse in written texts of both these early phases. Indeed, it is this marking itself that is actually offered—a signal that the voice changes to that of a Creole language speaker. Writers limit Creole language characteristics to the quantum a reader requires in order to comprehend that the shift has taken place. Creole marking alienates the text from the exclusively Standard English speaker—an effect that writers avoid proliferating. In addition, given the temper of the times, there would be a sense among Caribbean writers that to assign Creole to the Caribbean consciousness would be to further chain and marginalize this consciousness. In literary discourse in the first half of the twentieth century, therefore, the voice of the Creole speaker signals its existence and then effaces itself.

At the same time, creative representations of unsuccessful efforts to write Creole throw light on developments in ideological perspective associated with code choice. In *Banana Bottom,* which appeared in 1933, Claude McKay's main characters are Standard English speakers, but the limited Creole dialogue that exists is not a distancing strategy nor an element of ridicule but part of serious characterization. Anty Nommy, whose voice is represented in the following extract, is a serious and sensible character:

> Bita, although taken entirely unawares by the promptness of Anty Nommy's decision and confused, said she was ready to be married immediately. But Hopping Dick was trapped and squirming in his place.

> "I can't get married now," he said. "I don't hab no house."
>
> "Then when can you?" demanded Anty Nommy. "Bita har spile harse'f. Becausen a disayah trouble she cyant stay yah any longer. She hab to liebe yah. Will you promise fer marry har in 'bouten a month?"
>
> Hopping Dick had never thought that his little philandering would have carried to such a crisis.[32]

In the same novel, however, written discourse that departs from Standard English invites ridicule, as in a letter to Bita, the educated Jamaican heroine, from an untutored admirer whom she has rejected: "I beg to apolojoys for trying to mek a little pleasantry wid you as a genelman and you not a lady as big to apreachiate it. I not just a fool country naygur not know nothing, but I is a pusson traveled far abroad jest lik yousef an I is acquented wid all the etykwets. That is why I wait until you was all alone by youself to get a good introduction to you. I is sorry you did tek it in such a bad way and insult me lak a dawg but I is willing to forgive you and even be a frien to you ef you will tek that back."[33]

McKay selects and maintains for the rejected suitor a register that aims unsuccessfully at impressing. In part, McKay conveys this tactic through the spelling errors that reveal deviations from accepted English pronunciation, as well as departures from expected Creole pronunciation. For example, *apolojoys* self-consciously distances the fictional writer from the [oj] > [aj] Jamaican Creole pronunciation in terms like English *spoil* > Creole [spajl] or [spwajl]. Alongside this appear circumlocutions like *mek a little pleasantry wid you* and pluralization of abstract nouns as in *etykwets*. Jamaican Creole persists clearly at the phonological level (*wid, mek, tek, dawg, frien,* and *pusson*) and at the syntactic level (*I wait*), but these genuine Creole elements are not the elements that invite ridicule. The comic effect of the letter reflects the status of its writer (who is clearly distinguished in value from other Creole-speaking characters) and reflects the status of a discourse that falls between two available codes. Here, comedy resides in affectations and the failure to master the written standard. Here arises a residual ambivalence regarding the Creole voice, an ambivalence consistent with Paul Jay's recognition of McKay's novel as critiquing absolutist discourse grounded on race, nationalism, and ethnicity, yet somehow operating in terms that "reinforce the ideology he seeks to displace."[34] Referring to Paul Gilroy's concept of the double consciousness that foregrounds the role of commercial institutions associated with slavery and colonialism,[35] Jay concludes that Bita has no real identity with which to connect: McKay's ironic complicity with the positions he seems to counter in his liberal language is itself disrupted by dominant ideology.

In *Banana Bottom,* McKay does indeed move Creole discourse beyond functioning as an attribute of setting to becoming a dimension of characterization.

This is representation not by a curious outsider (an observer that perceives him- or herself as centered in "civilization" and gazing at the Other-and-marginal) but by an observer with insider perspective. The discourse is not yet a vehicle for expression assigned to a central consciousness, but it can be the medium of sensible communication—intuitively sensible rather than informed or trained. In this censorship phase, limited use of Creole appears in serious speech by characters of limited education and social standing. Scribal discourse can encode orality seriously, but (within the fictional world) serious representation of the literary must be English.

When language choice in literary discourse truly becomes an issue we are passing to a new stage, the *alternation phase.* At this stage, native speakers are inscribing the Caribbean voice, and Creole is represented knowledgably and with attention to accuracy. By this time, some freedom of movement between the codes has become possible in literature; the function of these codes remains to some extent distinct, but with the growing seriousness extended to Creole discourse, there arises some overlap in the circumstances in which Creole or English are selected. Creative writers, especially those who are also performers, select Creole for substantial stretches of text:

> Sun a-shine an pot a-bile, but
> Tings noh bright, bickle noh nuff!
> Rain a-fall, river dah-flood, but
> Wata scarce an dutty tuff![36]

Creole features selected are often those that compare (sometimes superficially) with Standard English forms. To the uninitiated, for example, the Creole imperfective *a* loosely resembles archaic English *a-* ("lords a-leaping"). Twi *dutty* is widely interpreted as English *dirty* (see Cassidy and Le Page, *dutty* from Twi dɔté, "soil, clay, earth, mud"). Also favored are intermediate forms like *noh,* rather than Creole *nah* or English *not,* and mixtures like *tings*—Creole in its phonology but English in its plural marking. As a performer, Bennett projects the oral language; as a writer, she engages with the challenges of inscription (see chapter 10).

In this phase, Creole serves as an occasional vehicle dedicated to marking the viewpoint from which to deliver sociopolitical commentary and intellectual speculation, as in Bennett's "Colonisation in Reverse."[37] As artists like Bennett ponder the creative vitality of Creole language, metadiscourse becomes part of artistic performance. Nevertheless, in the mid-twentieth century, critical attention focuses first on the choice of Creole for serious artistic endeavor rather than on the issues of inscribing it. In his 1966 introduction to the work of Louise Bennett, Rex Nettleford remarks: "She has carved designs out of the shapeless and unruly substance that is the Jamaica dialect—the language which most of the Jamaican people speak most of the time." Nettleford further describes this process as "an artist's struggles to shape an idiom whose limitations as a bastard tongue are all too evident."[38] The metaphor of disobedience is *positively* applied in anticolonial and postcolonial commentaries of the sort for which Nettleford himself has been a notable pioneer, and the limitations he ascribes to Creole at this stage refer at least in part to its lack of orthographical convention. Nevertheless, it is felt necessary to justify linguistic analysis of a Creole language: "There has developed genuine academic interest in the Jamaican dialect, which has been carefully studied by reputable scholars."[39]

The alternation phase demonstrates substantial progress beyond earlier dismissive or derisive evaluations of Creole, and beyond more serious but uninformed and even fanciful interpretations of Creole such as characterize the censorship phase. It also facilitates more extensive and more thoughtful representation, as Jean D'Costa demonstrates in chapter 10.

Mid-twentieth-century choices to convey the Jamaican voice through selected Creole characteristics affect considerable stretches of dialogue and involve increasing interaction between official and vernacular codes in writing. Moreover, in the alternation stage, the relationship between Jamaican Creole and English has moved from strict functional specialization. In contrast to the censorship phase, which shows a diglossic association of Creole with oral and performance, and Standard English with scribal discourse, alternation permits (in a limited sense) some competition between the codes. This development signals a sustainable literature that is identifiably Caribbean. The alternation phase accommodates negotiation for authority in the sense that Creole comes to be privileged for functions that extend beyond authenticating setting and beyond establishing characterization that is rigidly bound to social class. In this sense, serious social commentary in the Creole speaking voice can be inscribed in the literature.

Moving from the alternation phase, the relationship between Creole and Standard English evolves toward equilibrium. Like the spoken language, literary discourse contributes to the construction of social identity, which, in the Caribbean, is hybrid, shifting, and contradictory, ever renegotiating the locus of power. Representing the Creole voice over extended stretches requires conscious attention to the language and produces gradual codification in the sense that patterns of selection, some individual consistency, and more frequent metadiscourse begin to develop in the written Creole.

In the current situation, the expansion phase, the discourse is open to a wider range of influences. The indigenous voice occupies more if not all of the literary work and is drawn on to assert a local perspective in rewriting imperial texts. This expansion does not necessarily mean "more Creole," although it tends to encompass a wide range of local usage (including the local standard). Expansion enables a fluid, often unflagged movement between Creole, Jamaican Standard English, and intermediate varieties.[40]

In the expansion phase, extensive code-shifting contributes to a hybrid discourse comprising plural and often dissonant voices among characters and even within a single character (note Jean D'Costa's discussion of the polydialectal society in chapter 3). Within the history of the literature, the privileging of Creole language, even in a dilute literary form, constitutes a perspectival shift that relocates the Caribbean consciousness to the center (rather than margin) of a valorized discourse, which then becomes an instrument of identity construction. Even if it is not represented in detail, the voice of the Creole speaker is increasingly "evoked" in literature of the Anglophone Caribbean.

In the creative discourse of Jamaican writers in the latter twentieth century, the quantum of Creole discourse has become more substantial and the shifts between codes and varieties more complex. The following example from a collection of stories by Velma Pollard maintains English narrative with Creole dialogue. The extract is a conversation at a funeral, overheard by the daughter of the deceased:

> "A didn know ar but a sih dih face; is fat kill ar noh?" (My mother was rather busty but that was as far as the fat went.) She didn't wait for an answer but continued: "A nevva sih wan of dese deds that come back from England yet." (No one had taken the trouble to tell her it was America not England.)
>
> "But de reason why a come to see ar is becaaz I was dere meself an a always seh ef a ded, dey mus sen mih back. Is now a sih ow a woulda look! But tengad a lucky a come back pon me own steam . . . . An you sih dis big finneral shi have? She wouldn't get it in Englan' you know. Since one o'clock she woulda gaan an' if they cremate ar, while we drinking a cuppa tea, she bunnin'."
>
> "Wat?" asked her audience at last. "Deh gives tea?"[41]

Pollard has selected a form of representation that for the most part avoids apostrophe except in regular Standard English use (as in *didn't*). The Standard English plural in *dese deds* may reflect a register designed to impress, as the content suggests. The inclination to impress also draws some hypercorrection from "audience" (*dey gives*). Several basilectal forms, like *me* subject, are noticeably absent—no doubt authentically so in view of the register. Pollard comments on the variation between *I* and *a* (the former being more emphatic) in an afterword.

Pollard adds this brief afterword (on Jamaican Creole in fiction) with a glossary of eight items, explaining, "I have simply written as I speak when I use JC." She also locates her effort to represent the Creole speaking voice as part of a comparatively new trend, versus earlier reliance on readers to "select the intonation as they read, from their knowledge of the character."[42] Despite the acknowledged fluctuation, her representation is relatively systematic, as in the case of *sih, dih, mih*. However, English orthography intervenes. Pollard's stated adherence to how she speaks when she uses Jamaican Creole accounts at least in part for the tendency to intermediate forms like *ar* versus *im* for third person, singular, object, feminine reference, and *I* or *a* versus *me* for first person, singular, subject reference, as Pollard probably does not fall naturally into basilectal Creole.

The tendency to intermediate forms is significant in the recent development of the discourse. Because centers of consciousness in current literary works can be Creole speakers, Creole may be represented in extensive passages, even whole novels. Apart from the quantity of discourse represented as Creole, however, Creole occupies crucial areas of the literary work. For this reason, considerations of legibility[43] increasingly constrain representation. The greater the space allocated to Creole discourse, the greater the challenge to wide audience comprehension, and so Creole representation remains (necessarily) dilute. In the expansion phase, Creole operates multifunctionally, and in the literary discourse (as in Pamela Mordecai's *de Man*[44]) shifts may be fluid and seamless.

How much Creole we discern in Caribbean literature has much to do with what we mean by *Creole,* with whether we associate intermediate language varieties in the Anglophone Caribbean as much with Creole as with English. Mühleisen usefully explores the concept of *Creole* in linguistic and discourse analysis, and in another helpful study, Carolyn Allen examines the sliding meaning of *Creole* in discussions of Caribbean culture.[45] Such ambivalence is magnified when literary and linguistic uses of the term interrogate each other. What has Creole linguistics to do with creolization in interdisciplinary usage and with such concepts as postcolonialism? For the purposes of this current study, *creolization* includes the construction of an indigenous literary discourse through cultural confrontation and the persistence of dissonance.

In the expansion phase, code-switching in the literary discourse is differently motivated than it was in the earlier history of the literature. No longer governed by desire for authentic atmosphere that included setting and even characterization, and no longer constrained by the perspective of an essentially non-Creole speaker, Caribbean discourse comprises expression of an indigenous voice. Code-switching becomes a mechanism for laying claim to discourse, and literary Creole constitutes a mechanism of resistance.

In the face of these developments, the persistent assumption that Creole discourse remains inherently oral rather than literary is simplistic and somewhat paternalistic—a view betraying a colonial mindset even within academia itself. This is a mindset that so maps orality into our understanding of Creole as to obscure the extent to which Creole participates in literary discourse. This mindset is a perpetuation of the ventriloquist stage in which Creole is viewed as a receding language, and Caribbean discourse is evolving inevitably toward English through decreolization. On the contrary, reconstructive work demonstrates that a range of varieties between Creole and Standard English, as recorded by non-Creole speakers, was alive and well and living in Jamaica in the nineteenth century as in the twenty-first.[46]

Where eighteenth- and nineteenth-century writers played with deviations from English, in the current phase of literary development there are Creole-speaking writers who play with deviations from Creole. Winer points out deliberate distortions that produce forms neither English nor Creole and make sense only to the Creole reader. Winer concludes that the English reader must "be aware and suspicious of the underlying language of the text."[47]

Such duality emerges in Pamela Modecai's *de Man*, a narrative poem that rewrites the Crucifixion in local terms, through which a mesh of code ambiguity supports the meaning of the poem. In reference to Christ's baptism (he "mek de Baptist dip him"), *Baptist* (singular) refers to John the Baptist, but also to a general understanding of *Baptist* (plural) in Jamaica, members of a denomination that practices baptism by full adult immersion, traditionally at a riverbank or shore, an immersion called *dipping*. The total effect is to localize the action, making it more immediate, without wholly sacrificing comprehension by the non-Creole reader.

Indeed, the whole event is framed by the opening exclamation, "*Oonu see mi dyin trial!*" The exclamation idiomatically expresses outrage in Jamaican Creole, but it also reverberates with an actual trial (that will lead to capital punishment, a *dying*) as well as the connection between the death of the Savior and judgment of mortal (*dying*) humanity (including the speaker). The observers (and humanity at large) display *ignorance* in terms of their lack of understanding and knowledge (the Standard English sense) but also in terms of unreasonable aggressiveness (the Creole sense), both of which contribute to the unfolding violence:

So dem send some old
Criminal fi drape him up . . . .

In English, *drape* conveys a limp object hanging, and so, through prolepsis, refers to the Crucifixion. In Creole, *drape* means "arrest," and arrest by the criminal reflects the central theology of the punishment of the innocent by the sinner. And so on.

So Creole and English not only persist side by side in this poem, but are drawn on simultaneously, while a Creole speaker's perspective dominates the discourse. Indeed it is the voice of the Creole speaker that is interrupted by code-switching when the speaker (a servant of Pilate's wife) breaks into English to relay the words of her mistress, then returns to the voice of the people:

> . . . . Me hear
> Her tell de Pilate one
> "You let him die and you
> Will have no peace." She seh. . . .

At this point, English might be identified as the marked code—in the loose sense of the foregrounded form.[48] In examining the concept of markedness in Creole languages, Alain Kihm rejects the concept of Creole grammars as globally unmarked, interrogating Ian Roberts's proposal of the unmarked nature of Creoles in comparison to Derek Bickerton's sense of the default (the obligatorily chosen form unless there is a reason not to choose it). Alain settles for the concept of default settings, with an array of nondefault settings available for acquisition.[49] My own use of the term, in the context of interfacing codes in literary discourse, more closely pertains to the sense of oppositional pairs in which the English would traditionally have been the default setting in a literary environment and in which the rules of literary engagement have radically changed.

In its current phase of development, the multilingual Caribbean enables its writers to play a variety of linguistic games, one involving simultaneity: a manipulation of discourse to facilitate both English and Creole readings. In the scribal representation of an oral discourse, English and Creole interweave for the meanings in the different codes to interrogate each other. (See table 2.1.)

Black Whole: The Expanding Universe of Caribbean Discourse

In the expanding universe of Caribbean literary discourse—through all its history of encounter, fragmentation, re-memberment, and growth—its writers have adjusted points of departure, have shifted perspective, reorganized structure, reconceived meaning, redefined genre, and—most impudently of all—recodified expression. The *universe of discourse,* a term originating in mathematical theories of logic and probabilities to refer to the sum of all entities, is sometimes also referred to as the *domain* and can also more generally apply to any world in which something exists along with everything tacitly or explicitly present in or relevant to that world. In terms of literary and language history, how has a Caribbean world of letters come into being?

Table 2.1. Phases in the development of Creole representation in Caribbean literary discourse: A summary

Ventriloquism	Censorship	Alternation	Expansion
Representation: fragmentary and infrequent	Representation: brief and occasional	Representation: varied length and more frequent	Representation: varied length and more frequent
Occasional Creole characteristics	Limited but more numerous	Varied quantity, may be extensive	Varied quantity, may be extensive
Few levels of linguistic description indicated	More levels represented	Most levels represented	Most levels represented
Inaccurate, imprecise	More accurate, imprecise	Accurate, relatively precise	Accurate, relatively precise
Characterized mainly by deviance from Standard English	Characterized as Creole but as functionally restricted	Increase in functions	Further increase in functions
Creole barely recognizable	Creole becoming describable, representable	Identification with Creole voice possible	Creole a marker of social identity
Perspective: external, imperial	Perspective: internal, colonial	Perspective: internal, (post)colonial, immigrant/diasporic	Perspective: internal, postcolonial, diasporic/national/regional
Anecdote/tale in travel narrative, in Caribbean setting	Mainly fiction in Caribbean setting	All genres in Caribbean/diasporic setting	All genres in Caribbean/diasporic setting
Dialogue only, minor character	Dialogue only, wider characterization	Dialogue including center of consciousness	Dialogue including center of consciousness and narrative
Standard English and Creole discourse kept clearly separate. Creole restricted to specific "limited" characters	Standard English and Creole kept clearly separate. Different characters use different codes, but Creole speakers allowed more dialogue than in previous phase	Standard English and Creole distinguished but characters may shift between them	Free shifting between Standard English and Creole. Ambiguity may reinforce plurality of meaning

Caribbean literary discourse has evolved to a point at which partial representation of the Caribbean voice in writing can evoke a whole discourse—in English, in Creole, or in an intermediate variety—dependent on the audience of the particular work. This multivalency is tied to a development in perceptions of the discourse: in particular, to a development from the perception of a void—almost a hole in reality—to the perception of a whole, a coherent structure.

At first, in its earliest inception (which was contextualized by intercultural insensitivity), Caribbean discourse was conceived in relation to lacunae—gaps not only in humanity, intelligence, and refinement but also in communicative ability. Assumptions regarding "lack of language," regarding muteness, no doubt increased a sense of the *unrepresentability* of Creole speech. In addition, the loss of ancestral languages, the processes of language death that might be in progress at different rates in that earlier linguistic environment could only have reinforced an imperial perception of the Caribbean as a linguistic void. Framing this perception was a view conveyed in the mid-eighteenth to nineteenth century: that of the Caribbean as a space from which to draw resources, from which to return to Britain, and from which to send children "home."[50] Governing assumptions in eighteenth-century ideology converged to produce a view of the Caribbean as a hole continually attracting and emptying, inherently vacuous.

Inaccurate representation of Creole in pre-twentieth-century writing is unsurprising in the context of these perceptions. Approaches to representing Creole reinforce the impression of gaps. In part, this reinforcement results from a selection of Creole features such as the following:

- consonant cluster simplification, as in [st] > [t] and [nd] > [d] in Creole *tan* for English "stand"
- consonant shifts that surface in spelling as an omission of a letter, as in [ŋ] "ng" > [n] "n"
- adjective predication understood as omission of the copula

Such choices of Creole attributes, divorced from any concept of the language as structured, reinforce a sense of incompleteness. Assumptions of muteness, structural incompleteness, and receding language cumulate to an overall implication of linguistic void and permeate representation and metadiscourse regarding Creole up to and into the twentieth century.

Current literature, in privileging Creole language even in a dilute literary form, effects a perspectival shift that relocates the Caribbean speaker to the center rather than the margin of the area in view and, in this sense, the discourse operates as an instrument of identity construction. The shift also valorizes the voice of the Creole speaker, correcting the perception of a linguistic void. By negotiating such adjustments in attitudinal orientation, Caribbean writers since the mid-twentieth century have, increasingly, encoded new and incorrigibly disobedient identities while projecting a Caribbean voice in the place of silence and hitherto presumed emptiness. Conscious negotiation of oral and scribal characteristics in Caribbean discourse turns the gaze inward, reorienting the Caribbean consciousness to the center of our universe of discourse.

At the core of the resulting dynamic stands a dialectic of fragmentation and wholeness.

Any discussion of diaspora, for example, implies some sense of periphery, which hinges on location of center. Once the Caribbean speaker or writer becomes central to the universe of discourse, the periphery must then be defined on such bases as nonindigeneity. However, does this development apply to expatriate, resident, or emigrant writing about the Caribbean? How long must one be away to be diasporic, and what of a diaspora within the Caribbean, such as the dispersal of Guyanese? Elsewhere, in discussing constructions of Caribbeanness, I argue that the Caribbean voice is fabricated as a dimension of a fictional world. In doing so, I draw on Doležel's understanding of a universe of discourse that is not restricted to the actual world but spread "over uncountable possible, non-actualised worlds."[51] Development of a Caribbean literary discourse and Caribbean constructions of Caribbeanness have been interdependent.

In any case, now that the Caribbean perceives its own diaspora, Caribbean discourse can be defined to take into account spatial and ideological outposts. Discussing Caribbean diasporic writing (and so conceptualizing diaspora from a location historically perceived as, itself, diasporic) invites a mental collapse of boundaries.

Fraught with a politics of intellectual territorialism along with the almost nihilistic denial of boundaries, the discourse both absorbs and resists the influence of imperial, canonical discourse. These centrifugal and centripetal forces make the discourse, increasingly, an irresistible site of inquiry from within and beyond the Caribbean. Indeed, the very notion of a Caribbean literary canon implies a transformation of epic proportions. The site of emptiness (from which all meaning was excluded, all value sucked) has become a site of ancestral and new resources and energy, and this phenomenal change in scope and influence of Caribbean discourse has comprised a fundamental aspect of its expansion.

Crucial to the current capacity of Caribbean creative writing to address an international readership and to convey a Caribbean voice is an ability to retain comprehension, across codes, through precise, limited, and selective representations of the voice. How is this possible?

In part, the international currency of literature infused with the Caribbean voice rests on our writers' negotiation of linguistic and pragmatic boundaries. Ironically, Caribbean discourse first institutionalizes informality by frequent selection of Creole and then goes on to dissolve pragmatic rules governing the use of Creole in written texts. With decreasing constraints on the use of Creole in literature, representations of Creole appear in indirect as well as in direct speech, and boundary maintenance becomes optional. Fairclough views boundary maintenance as partly a matter of choice between direct and indirect discourse representation.[52] Such a concept of optional boundary maintenance may well account for the different degrees of comprehension by the non-Caribbean reader and by the Caribbean reader, who each experience Caribbean discourse simultaneously: the Caribbean reader enjoying (through competence in Creole) additional layers of meaning that are shared with the writer.

In other words, as code shifts occur in the discourse, and as the functional divide between official and unofficial codes (between Standard English and Creole) becomes increasingly permeable, individual utterances may not only be differently understood by Creole and non-Creole speakers but may even privilege plural meaning. On the one hand, an international audience can be approached through the official, written form of the language and be alerted to the Caribbean voice by specific linguistic pointers. On the other, these pointers may trigger for the Caribbean reader more comprehensive and nuanced understandings. The international and regional currency of the discourse rests on an antipathy to boundaries.

Caribbean literary discourse is multivalent precisely because it comprises components that are overtly Caribbean and implies others that are *understood* to be Caribbean. In any text the speaker actually produces limited explicit matter, and the rest is assumed, and this potential also applies to attributes of Caribbean language. The Caribbean voice effaces itself in giving way to English orthography but also inserts itself into the text through restricted representation to produce a strategically split discourse. Currently, this composite but split discourse maintains a relationship between its different codes even as it moves toward the disintegration of linguistic boundaries. In doing so, the discourse conveys multiple and dissonant voices as is appropriate to Caribbean language culture.

It is generally recognized that readers bring to written work sets of understandings through which (rather than exclusively through the information of the text itself) a world takes shape in the reader's mind, a gestalt. Hockett early drew on the concept of gestalt perception, but as a strategy for construing words in another code by building up a holistic pattern from a more limited set of familiar characteristics,[53] and Winer brings a comparable concept to bear on language in Caribbean discourse, exploring it as resonance.[54] Current narrative theory regarding the construction and narrative comprehension of fictional worlds probes comparable operations in narrative discourse.[55] I suggest that gestalt perception is pivotal to the comprehension of much literary discourse in the Caribbean as Creole discourse, where wide readership depends on the writer retaining the non-Creole speaker's comprehension while fully engaging the Creole speaker. And, as Winer has demonstrated, comprehension of Creole discourse by a nonspeaker (even at its best) is quite distinct from the comprehension of Creole discourse by a Creole speaker. Optimum comprehension rests on a balance to be achieved in the split discourse, and it is in this context that gestalt perception lies at the heart of Caribbean discursive practice associated with Creole representation in literature. Gestalt theory proposes that we see whole organized and cohesive objects (in this case, for example, Creole discourse) rather than discrete, chaotic components (such as limited characteristics of Creole, often arbitrarily chosen). Such perception accounts for how readers of Caribbean literature have come to interpret stretches of discourse as *Caribbean* and even specifically *Creole* rather than *English,* by collecting characteristics on the basis of proximity, symmetry, complementation (closure), mutual influence, and other bases of gestalt perception.

In expression as well as in content, the reader draws heavily on prior knowledge, applying what is known (through personal experience and other such frames of reference) in filling the gaps in representation of the Creole voice. The necessary schemata comprise linguistic information (actual Creole language structure); cultural information (circumstances in which speakers operate and which influence linguistic choices and attitudes); and textual information (regular or expected patterns in the mapping of the story that prompt readers to anticipate or react along established lines). Such textual information would provide bases for the persuasive impact of Creole language or English in relation to setting or characterization, for example, or in relation to the role of code choice and code shift in assisting a reader to arrive at an acceptable model of a fictional world. Readers of different competencies, however, generate different sets of inferences in keeping with their primary linguistic competencies.

In the case of Caribbean literature that represents Creole speech, the nonspeaker may recognize representative Creole discourse as a *signal* and depend on those parts of the discourse that are English as distinct from Creole, or, English as well as Creole. The nonspeaker builds up from these parts an English discourse to stand in place of the Creole discourse that is understood to be ongoing—and this process has no doubt been at work from very early writing about the Caribbean. On the other hand, there is the Creole speaker who is more comfortable with English as the written language and who may well speak a variety of Creole other than that of the text. Such a reader comprehends the Creole and builds up an English discourse with some embedded Creole or, perhaps, a Creole discourse in his/her own variety. Finally, the Creole speaker who is comfortable in the variety represented may go further and extend the Creole language actually represented on the page to a reading that is structurally complete either as Creole or as an intermediate variety. This range of possibilities for building a Creole reading of a literary discourse belongs only to a relatively recent stage in development, a stage at which a Creole-competent readership has become substantial.

In "The Carpenter's Complaint," by Edward Baugh, fewer than one-third of the words in the passage are marked as Creole, about 66 of 222.[56] (That is to say, these terms convey some indication of phonological, lexical, morphological, syntactic, or semantic characteristics of Jamaican Creole.) Read by a Jamaican Creole speaker, however, over two-thirds of the passage may be Creole. This outcome may or may not be what the poet intends. The carpenter may well (being on his dignity and in a state of righteous indignation) be using an intermediate variety. The issue is that the Creole component of most Caribbean texts is practically impossible to quantify once it remains on the page.

Indeed, how much Creole should be understood in Caribbean literary representation has much to do with what we mean by Creole, with whether we associate the intermediate varieties as much with Creole as with English. Within the discipline of Caribbean linguistics itself, however, the involvement of Creole language in literary discourse remains underexplored. Such neglect hinges, perhaps, on a notion that Creole lacks a literary discourse, and the perception of a linguistic void persisting in the most unlikely of all contexts.

Meanwhile, Caribbean writers actually play with deviations from Creole. The multilingual Caribbean enables its writers to indulge in a variety of linguistic games, one involving simultaneity—a manipulation of discourse to facilitate both English and Creole readings (for example, of the word *dread*). Lexical meanings in English and Creole interrogate each other in Lorna Goodison's coinage, *edenism* (which would overlap with Jamaican pronunciation of *hedonism*), to intercept a sense of "heedless pleasure" with that of "paradise" lost through unholy violence in Jamaica.[57]

Caribbean discourse now absorbs oral and scribal resources, imperial and submerged cultures, and facilitates the construction of whole discourses (in alternating or simultaneous codes). Expanded to a flexible and multivocal discourse, Caribbean creative writing projects the unofficial code through selected characteristics as one of a range of voices in their complex relations—which are neither coherent nor harmonious. Indeed, once the Caribbean center of consciousness is ascribed to a voice that may be *read* as Creole or as English, as the situation demands, the accessibility of Caribbean discourse increases and, with this, the sheer quantum of indigenous literature has been enlarged, projecting a Caribbean voice not through chaotic fragmentation but as a *perceptibly* complete and coherent entity.

Notes

1. Following on the work of Roger Fowler and others, this issue is discussed by Gerald Prince, and Paul Simpson expands on the various planes of perspective with particular attention to ideology. See Roger Fowler, *Linguistic Criticism,* 2nd ed. (Oxford: Oxford University Press, 1996); Gerald Prince, *Narratology: The Form and Functioning of Discourse* (Berlin: Mouton, 1982), and *Dictionary of Narratology* (Lincoln: University of Nebraska Press, 1987); Paul Simpson, *Language, Ideology and Point of View* (London: Routledge, 1993).

2. Carol Surkamp's entry in David Herman, Manfred Jahn, and Marie Laure-Ryan, eds., *Routledge Encyclopedia of Narrative Theory* (London: Routledge, 2005), 423. Surkamp's assessment is based on such work as that of Marie Laure-Ryan, David Herman, and many others. See Marie Laure-Ryan, *Possible Worlds, Artificial Intelligence and Narrative Theory* (Bloomington: Indiana University Press, 1991); David Herman, *Story Logic: Problems and Possibilities of Narrative* (Lincoln: University of Nebraska Press, 2002).

3. See Prince, *Narratology* and *Dictionary,* and Gérard Genette, *Narrative Discourse: An Essay in Method,* trans. by J. E. Lewin (Ithaca, NY: Cornell University Press, 1980).

4. Herman, *Story Logic,* 4, but see also Catherine Emmott, *Narrative Comprehension: A Discourse Perspective* (Oxford: Oxford University Press, 1997).

5. Records of the earliest scribal discourse have been collected by Jean D'Costa and Barbara Lalla in *Voices in Exile: Jamaican Texts of the 18th and 19th Centuries* (Tuscaloosa: University of Alabama Press, 1989) and subjected to linguistic analysis and reconstruction by the same authors (Lalla and D'Costa, *Language in Exile: Three Hundred Years of Jamaican Creole* [Tuscaloosa: University of Alabama Press, 1990]). For the development of a Jamaican perspective in fiction pertaining to Jamaica, see Barbara Lalla, *Defining Jamaican Fiction: Marronage and the Discourse of Survival* (Tuscaloosa: University of Alabama Press, 1996).

6. For example, by Lawrence Carrington, "The Status of Creole in the Caribbean," in *Due Respect: Papers on English and English Related Creoles in the Caribbean in Honour of Professor Robert Le Page,* ed. Pauline Christie (Kingston: University of the West Indies Press, 2001), 24–36.

7. As does Peter Roberts in *From Oral to Literate Culture: Colonial Experience in the English West Indies* (Kingston: University of the West Indies Press, 1997). Nevertheless, Susanne Mühleisen notes that "writing is one of the most important sociocultural domains in determining language prestige" (*Creole Discourse: Exploring Prestige Formation and Change across Caribbean English-Lexicon Creoles* [Amsterdam: John Benjamins, 2002], 184). Although Édouard Glissant connects Caribbean literature to Creole language in distinguishing this literature from a forced poetics of the European languages, he suggests that the sociohistorical circumstances of (French) Creole have left it unready to play a definitive role in the development of the literature, and his arguments do not involve extended linguistic analysis, (*Caribbean Discourses: Selected Essays,* trans. and introduced by J. Michael Dash [Charlottesville: University Press of Virginia, 1992], 105, 121).

8. Robert Le Page remarked on it early in "Dialect in West Indian Literature,"

Journal of Commonwealth Literature 7 (1969): 1–7, and linguistic studies have become progressively more probing, as in Edgar W. Schneider, "Investigating Variation and Change in Written Documents," in *The Handbook of Language Variation and Change,* ed. J. K. Chambers, Peter Trudgill, and Natalie Schilling-Estes (Oxford: Blackwell, 2002), 67–96; Lise Winer, "Comprehension and Resonance: English Readers and English Creole Texts," in *Creole Genesis, Attitudes and Discourse: Studies Celebrating Charlene J. Sato,* ed. John Rickford and Suzanne Romaine (Amsterdam: John Benjamins, 1999; Kingston: University of the West Indies Press, 1999), 391–406. Interdisciplinary approaches that apply both literary and linguistic criticism have further expanded our understanding, notably Maureen Warner-Lewis, "Samuel Selvon's Linguistic Extravaganza: *Moses Ascending,*" in *Something Rich and Strange: Selected Essays on Sam Selvon,* ed. Martin Zehnder (Leeds, England: Peepal Tree Press, 2003), 65–76; Merle Hodge, "Dialogue and Narrative Voice in *The Schoolmaster,*" *Journal of West Indian Literature* 8, no. 1 (1998): 56–72; and several studies by the authors of the present volume, referenced in these notes and listed in the bibliography.

9. Merle Hodge addresses historical development in "A Study of Language in Trinidad and Tobago Prose Fiction of the Twentieth Century with Special Reference to the Works of Earl Lovelace (PhD, University of the West Indies, 2007). Substantial work on Selvon by Karen Mah-Chamberlain is now underway, but focusing on discourse genre and metanarrative rather than on historical development (PhD diss., in progress, University of the West Indies, St. Augustine).

10. Walter Ong, *Orality and Literacy: The Technologizing of the Word* (London: Methuen, 1982), 34; Roberts, *From Oral to Literate Culture,* 107.

11. Henry Garland Murray, *Manners and Customs of the Country a Generation Ago: Tom Kittle's Wake* (Kingston: Jordan, 1877).

12. For example Lady Maria Nugent, *Lady Nugent's Journal of Her Residence in Jamaica, from 1801 to 1805,* ed. Philip Wright (Kingston: Institute of Jamaica, 1966); E. L. Joseph, *Warner Arundell, Adventures of a Creole,* ed. Lise Winer, Bridget Brereton, Rhonda Cobham, and Mary Rimmer (1838; repr., Kingston: University of the West Indies Press, 2001).

13. Maryse Condé, "On the Apparent Carnivalization of Literature from the French Caribbean," in *Representations of Blackness and the Performance of Identities,* ed. Jean Muteba Rahier (Westport, CT: Bergin and Garvey, 1999), 95.

14. The term is adopted and reapplied from Verene Shepherd's description of early historical writing in "The Ranking Game: Discourses of Belonging in Jamaican History" (inaugural professorial lecture, University of the West Indies, Mona, Jamaica, April 12, 2002).

15. *The Importance of Jamaica to Great Britain Consider'd in a Letter to a Gentleman* (London: Dodd, 1740), 18.

16. Ibid.

17. *Marly, or, the Life of a Planter in Jamaica,* 2nd ed. (Glasgow: Printed by R. Griffin, 1828), republished, ed. Karina Williamson (Oxford: Macmillan Caribbean, 2005).

18. Ibid., 134.

19. Ibid., 210–211.

20. Michael Scott, *Tom Cringle's Log,* 2 vols. (1833; repr., Edinburgh: Blackwood, 1834; republished, London: Picador, 1999); Col. William G. Hamley, *Captain Clutterbuck's Champagne: A West Indian Reminiscence,* 4 vols. (Edinburgh: Blackwood, 1862); Captain Mayne Reid, *The Maroon,* 3 vols. (London: Hurst and Blackett, 1862); Charles Rampini, *Letters from Jamaica, the Land of Wood and Streams* (Edinburgh: Edmonston and Douglas, 1873). See also Cynric Williams, *A Tour through the Island of Jamaica from the Western to the Eastern End, in the Year 1823* (London: Hunt and Clarke, 1826).

21. Roberts, *From Oral to Literate Culture,* 190–191.

22. Thomas Russell, *The Etymology of Jamaican Grammar, by a Young Gentleman* (Kingston: M. De Cordova, MacDougall, 1868); J. J. Thomas, *The Theory and Practice of Creole Grammar* (Port of Spain, Trinidad and Tobago: Chronicle Publishing Office, 1869; London: New Beacon Books, 1969).

23. Faith Smith, *Creole Recitations: John Jacob Thomas and Colonial Formation in the Late Nineteenth-Century Caribbean* (Charlottesville: University of Virginia Press, 2002), 4.

24. Ibid., 97.

25. Russell, introduction to *Etymology of Jamaican Grammar,* xiii; see also Lalla and D'Costa, *Language in Exile,* 186.

26. Natalie Schilling-Estes, "Investigating 'Self-Conscious' Speech: The Performance Register in Ocracoke English," *Language in Society* 27 (1998): 53–83.

27. Cyrus Francis Perkins, *Busha's Mistress, or, Catherine the Fugitive: A Stirring Romance of the Days of Slavery in Jamaica,* ed. Paul E. Lovejoy, Verene A. Shepherd, and David V. Trotman (1911; repr., Kingston, Jamaica: Ian Randle, 2003).

28. Ibid., 45, 132–133.

29. Herbert G. de Lisser, *Jane's Career: A Story of Jamaica* (London: Methuen, 1914; repr., London: Heinemann, 1972); Carolyn Cooper and Hubert Devonish, "A Tale of Two States: Language, Lit/orature and the Two Jamaicas," in *The Pressures of the Text: Orality, Texts and the Telling of Tales,* ed. Stewart Brown (Birmingham, England: Center of West African Studies, 1995) 60–74.

30. "The Novel before 1950," in *A History of Literature in the Caribbean: English- and Dutch-Speaking Caribbean,* ed. Albert James Arnold (Amsterdam: John Benjamins, 2001), 2:119.

31. De Lisser, *Jane's Career,* 4.

32. Claude McKay, *Banana Bottom* (1933; repr., London: Pluto, 1986), 223.

33. Ibid., 131.

34. "Hybridity, Identity and Cultural Commerce in Claude McKay's *Banana Bottom,*" *Callaloo* 22, no. 1 (1999): 176–194.

35. *The Black Atlantic: Modernity and the Double Consciousness* (Cambridge: Harvard University Press, 1993), 2.

36. Louise Bennett, *Jamaica Labrish,* ed. Rex Nettleford (1966; repr., Kingston, Jamaica: Sangster's Bookstores, 1972), 120.

37. Ibid., 179; see also Louise Bennett, *Aunty Roachy Seh,* ed. Mervyn Morris (Kingston, Jamaica: Sangster's Bookstores, 1993), 1.

38. Rex Nettleford, introduction to *Jamaica Labrish,* 9, 10.

39. Despite widespread recognition of Louise Bennett's role in the development of literary discourse not only in Jamaica but also in the Caribbean as a whole, close technical linguistic analysis has been rare but a number of important literary analyses have included sensitive commentaries on language (Nettleford, introduction, 23). See Mervyn Morris, "*Is English We Speaking" and Other Essays* (Kingston, Jamaica: Ian Randle, 1999); Carolyn Cooper, *Noises in the Blood: Orality, Gender and the "Vulgar" Body of Jamaican Popular Culture* (London: Macmillan, 1993), 47–67.

40. See Barbara Lalla, "Registering Woman: Senior's Zigzag Discourse, and Code-Switching in Jamaican Narrative," *Review of International English Literature* 29, no. 4 (1998): 83–98; "Virtual Realism and the Inscriber's Dilemma: Representing the Caribbean Voice" (Occasional Paper 32, Society for Caribbean Linguistics, St. Augustine, Trinidad and Tobago, 2005).

41. Velma Pollard, *Considering Woman* (London: Women's Press, 1989), 32–33.

42. Ibid., 74–75.

43. Prince, *Narratology.*

44. Pamela Mordecai, *de Man* (Toronto: Sister Vision, 1995).

45. Mühleisen, *Creole Discourse;* Carolyn Allen, "Creole: The Problem of Definition," in *Questioning Creole: Creole Discourses in Caribbean Culture,* ed. Verene Shepherd and Glen Richards (Kingston, Jamaica: Ian Randle, 2002; Oxford: James Curry, 2002), 47–63.

46. See Lalla and D'Costa, *Language in Exile,* 79–98.

47. Winer, "Comprehension and Resonance," 401–402.

48. Nigel Fabb uses it thus in relation to verse, in *Linguistics and Literature: Language in the Verbal Arts of the World* (Oxford: Blackwell, 1997), 13. See also Barbara Lalla, "Conceptual Perspectives on Time and Timelessness in Martin Carter's 'University of Hunger,'" chapter 11 of this volume.

49. Alain Kihm argues this point in "Creoles, Markedness and Default Settings: An Appraisal," in *The Handbook of Pidgin and Creole Studies,* ed. Silvia Kouwenberg and John Victor Singler (Oxford: John Wiley and Sons, 2009), 411–439. Ian Roberts bases his position on a number of properties, formed by regular (though extreme) language change, in "Verb Movement and Markedness" in *Language Creation and Language Change: Creolisation, Diachrony and Development,* ed. M. DeGraff (Cambridge: MIT Press, 1999), 304–307. See also Derek Bickerton, "How to Acquire Language without Positive Evidence," in *Language Creation and Language Change,* 49–74. However, the discussion of markedness by Creolists has focused on grammatical systems, while in the context of literary linguistics the term is more broadly applied (to a foregrounded form or nondefault setting) and is being extended in my argument to contrasting codes.

50. Orlando Patterson, *The Sociology of Slavery: An Analysis of the Origins, Development and Structure of Negro Slave Society in Jamaica* (Kingston, Jamaica: Sangster's Bookstores, 1973), 35.

51. Barbara Lalla, "Possible Caribbeans: Assembling the Fictional Voice," in *Reassembling the Fragments: Voice and Identity in Caribbean Literary Discourse* (Kingston, Jamaica: University of the West Indies Press, forthcoming); Lubomír Doležel, *Heterocosmica: Fiction and Possible Worlds* (Baltimore: Johns Hopkins University Press, 1998), 13.

52. Norman Fairclough, *Discourse and Social Change* (Cambridge: Polity, 1992), 119.

53. Charles Francis Hockett, *Refurbishing Our Foundations: Elementary Linguistics from an Advanced Point of View* (Amsterdam: John Benjamins, 1987), 41.

54. Winer, "Comprehension and Resonance," 391–406.

55. Catherine Emmott examines the role of the narrative text as a series of cues that requires the reader's input, drawing on the reader's prior knowledge but also on text-specific knowledge that is supported by cooperation between producer and receiver such as H. P. Grice describes—in other words on how inference-making enables text and reader to interact (although Emmott focuses on chains of reference, especially through pronouns, that establish textual coherence). See Emmott, *Narrative Comprehension;* H. P. Grice, "Logic and Conversation," in *Syntax and Semantics,* ed. P. Cole and J. Morgan (New York: Academic Press, 1975), 3:41—58; and "Further Notes on Logic and Conversation," in *Syntax and Semantics,* 9:113–127; Michael F. Dahlstrom, "The Role of Causality in Information Acceptance of Narratives: An Example from Science Communication," *Communication Research* 37 (2010): 857–875. http://crx.sagepub.com/content/37/6/857.

56. Edward Baugh, *It Was the Singing* (Toronto: Sandberry Press, 2000), 36.

57. Lorna Goodison, "Jamaica 1980," in *Selected Poems* (Ann Arbor: University of Michigan Press, 1992), 38.

3
The Caribbean Novelist and Language

A Search for a Literary Medium

Jean D'Costa

The Caribbean writer operates within a polydialectal community with a Creole language base. The relationship between Jamaican Creole and other oral and written varieties of English exemplifies this direct challenge to the fiction writer.[1] The medium—written language—belongs to the sphere of standardized language that exerts pressure within the writer's own language community while embracing the wide audiences of international standard Englishes. If writers are to satisfy themselves, their local audience, and that wider international audience, they must evolve a literary dialect that will meet the following: the pressure for authentic representation of their immediate language culture and the demands for acceptability within and without their own community. Writers must reconcile these multiple and partially opposing aims and devise for them an orthography that goes beyond playing with spelling systems, phonetic or otherwise, by creating orthographic signals that assist in expression and communication and that can reach both local and international audiences.

In this chapter, I use my experiences as a writer of children's fiction to explore some of the difficulties faced by writers placed in this kind of linguistic environment. I do not claim to have solved satisfactorily any or all of the major language problems encountered while writing *Sprat Morrison* (1972), *Escape to Last Man Peak* (1975), *Voice in the Wind* (1978), and a failed historical novel, *Evening, Morning* (unpublished, 1980) that foundered on linguistic problems. The audience receiving the literary work alone can decide whether the work *does* provide a solution, or not.

My exploration of the choices faced by Caribbean writers begins by describing something of the process of creative ideation leading to the selection of graphic signs on the written page. Caribbean writers setting out to express in written form those mental events that they desire to communicate to audiences both inside and beyond their immediate speech communities face at once a range of necessary acts of selection before a single word can appear on paper.

Writers must confront in their own minds the array of possible language forms that arise at the bidding of any single notion to be expressed and communicated. At this partially conscious level we must sift the mental events, emotions, and patterns of association, each of which may surface in more than one variant lect of a total "language competence."[2]

At this level, the simplest ideas—leaving a room, recognizing a sound or color—make simultaneous claims upon more than one lect in the writer's language competence. For those whose receptive and productive abilities are widely separated, the claim may be made upon forms that the individual knows but would never use in her own performance. The presence of the whole system or set of systems is always a felt reality, whatever the final selection may be.

This process suggests a kind of language competence on the part of Caribbean people in which variation, minimal shifting, and code-switching form a complete internalized reality that should be seen as a whole structure rather than as discrete systems realizing themselves in different surface structures. The treatment of variation and of minimal shifting would seem to bear this out. I make the claim therefore from the objective evidence of language usage in the Caribbean of a range of language varieties reaching from basilect to acrolect, from deep Creole to Standard English. This situation is characterized also by the ability of speakers to code-switch—to choose features of Caribbean Creole or Standard English in response to certain kinds of stimuli. Scholars working in the field since the 1950s have explored these aspects of Caribbean language culture.

I make the claim also from the subjective experience of a native speaker of Jamaican language: I have internalized certain varieties and elements within the Jamaican continuum, and, even as I compose this sentence, I find myself responding to the pressure of alternative codes within the continuum that disturb and influence the nature of the message I wish to convey. I also find that these varieties and elements (for want of a better name) seem to form an integrated structure within my mind. Such problems of expression as exist in the operations of my own mind become apparent to me only when I move into *communication*.

This problem stretches beyond the well-known business of organizing a spoken into a written form or the simple difficulty of operating well or badly in a well-defined literary standard. For me, a writer striving to express *and* communicate experience from the complex Jamaican language situation to an international English-speaking audience whose own language cultures partially overlap with the system to which I belong, the formulation of any message is fraught with choices that may radically alter the idea that is awaiting verbal form. This situation complicates the traditional Saussurean distinction of *langue* and *parole,* in that the classical structuralist view of langue makes no accommodation for those users of language whose competence consists of a set of overlapping, partly conflicting, exchangeable, intersecting, and partly integrating systems and subsystems—and all in flux.

A single language event is capable of definition according to its dialect or diatype—its mode, tenor, and field, which represent in terms of register "the varieties according to use of which a text may be regarded as an instance."[3] Thus any standard has the means of providing varieties of usage arising from and responding to different contexts and situations. In Halliday's terms, a register is "a configuration of semantic resources that the member of a culture typically associates with a situation type. It is the *meaning potential* that is deployed in a given social context. It thus represents the semantic options . . . that are 'at risk' under particular environmental conditions."[4]

Thus it is the meaning potential that is most important in any and all social situations, and the user of the language must survey the range of semantic resources at her disposal to select expression and deploy communication, knowing that these processes may be at odds. Variation works far more strangely in language communities such as the Caribbean than in (other) bi- or multilingual communities. Some lexical items have overlapping meanings in Creole and in English, or, they may appear to be the same, yet diverge such that quite different sets of meaning may be invoked by what seem to be ordinary, well-formed sentences in both English and standardized Creole. Consider the following: (1) *He is an ignorant man;* (2) *She is a big woman now.* In Jamaican semantics, the first example signifies that "he" is an irritable, loudly quarrelsome person, while the second indicates that "she" is no longer a child under authority but has now reached sexual maturity and adulthood. These examples are far from being few or unimportant.

From my own experience as a user of language in general, and as a writer in particular, I am driven to conclude that meaning potential resides in what is loosely called *style,* and that the essence of the literary problems facing me and other Caribbean writers could most effectively be studied through the semantic and semiotic aspects of language culture. Concepts of the role of situation and register all seem to point toward the ultimate fulfilling of meaning potential. My failings in expression and communication have been tied to failures of meaning potential, or else of using symbols, signs, and signals (whether by allusion or metaphor) that have not given adequate expression or communicativeness to a given notion.

Studies of the role of semantics and semiotics in literary criticism cannot account fully for the subtlety or the complexities of language choice and interpretation available to the writer. Both disciplines attempt, however, to chart the large open-ended domain of human culture and to go beyond lexical meaning into the interrelationships of perception, of cultural conditioning, of aesthetics, and of language as system and as social interaction. The usefulness and limitations of both semantics and semiotics in the study of literary art were early indicated by Umberto Eco and Jonathan Culler in their discussions of meaning, language, and literature, and as Culler points out, each audience brings to any literary work knowledge and responses that, so far, are quite beyond the reach of linguistic analysis, even though these are as much a feature of language-as-literature as sound is a feature of language-as-speech.[5] Culler explains the task of linguistics as not one of revealing what sentences mean but rather one of explaining how the speakers determine meaning in these sentences.

With all these warnings in mind, I propose that it is the pursuit of meaning through language that is the writer's real endeavor. To understand how meaning operates in language, and how language forms affect the transmission of meaning (communication), must be the major part of a writer's technical and intuitive equipment. I suggest too that a language continuum is likely to operate semantically and semiotically in rather different ways from other kinds of language situations. "Shifting along the continuum" may require certain kinds of semantic and semiotic adjustments quite unlike those available to a bilingual speaker, let alone a monolingual one.

While acknowledging the fraught nature of continuum theory, I take particular note of Valerie Youssef's concept of varilingualism.[6] For the speaker within the continuum, far more may be at risk than the configuration of semantic resources by which Halliday defines the notion register. The severe linguistic insecurity and inhibitions of Caribbean children in the middle grades of primary schools suggest that a whole range of learning and cognitive skills are affected when the teaching of structures takes precedence over the teaching of meaning.

My work as a writer of fiction has brought me sharply up against this aspect of my language culture, and in this chapter, I consider how this central problem of Caribbean language has affected my own writing.

Our complex Caribbean language situation, as opposed to monolingual, diglossic, or even bilingual situations, offers the native speaker a multiplicity of contrasting, interrelated, or closely related choices for the expression and communication of any given meaning potential arising within her environment. Variation is richer and subtler than anything that operates within the clear boundaries of diglossia and bilingual situations, and it is wider in scope than the choices available in the monolingual community.

I will not repeat here what has been put forward by others on the nature of code-switching or shifting in continuum situations. Attention has centered mostly on the formal features of variation, or on the sociolinguistic aspects of the continuum, rather than on the semantic and semiotic aspects of usage in a continuum. Only recently have linguists begun to discuss in any depth the implications of these for literary style beyond what is suggested by studies of interference in written and spoken styles.

To the writer, however, the nature of the linguistic choices available in a continuum situation makes clear demands both on the meaning potential to be conveyed and on possible literary modes. As meaning has the power to elicit more than one language form, so too these variant forms nuance meaning. Shifts along the continuum may appear to be interchangeable, but in fact are found to alter the attitudes of addresser or addressee, or of both. These attitudinal changes in turn can be tested and found to carry small but discernible changes of meaning easily identified by native speakers. In other words, each language event carries with it attitudinal, behavioral, emotional, and social information that affect meaning. For example, the sentence "He is an ignorant man" is affected formally and stylistically by the speaker's place in the continuum, by her relationship to the person addressed, and by her intentions and motives toward the addressee and the immediate situation. By choosing any other variant form, the speaker at once alters the relationship between herself and the addressee, as well as her perceived attitudes to the possibly uninformed or possibly angry man, revealing which of these two semantic cores should be targeted. Such problems often arose in my fictive writing.

Forms of variation natural to the Caribbean language situation are of deeper significance than as behavioral or as sociolinguistic signals. Variation involves not simply lexical and morphosyntactic contrasts but semantic and semiotic contrasts also. Each variant can be traced as leading to some different end, possessing some shade of meaning or teleological bias, which together form a challenge to the Caribbean writer. Each minimal shift seems tied to delicately but firmly differentiated associations, behavioral patterns, interpretations of social situations, chains of meaning, or eruptions of insight or of misunderstanding.

If this were not so, there would be no "problem" about writing and communicating in the Caribbean communities; no quarrels about usage; no uncertainty about language norms; little or no interference of one part of the continuum with other parts. The continuum would possess a magical one-to-one correspondence with the whole experiential range of life, generating without doubt or conflict all of the registers relating to "any given social context." All that a writer would have to do is to choose the appropriate register, secure in the knowledge that genre and rhetoric would follow the dictates of a semantically unified whole.

My usage of and interaction with the language continuum of Jamaica involves my written codes in numerous and difficult acts of semantic and semiotic differentiation. What may appear to be surface structure or interference problems of morphophonemics, syntax, and lexis, in fact turn on deeper problems of meaning and purpose. I therefore raise the question as to whether the continuum, by its very nature, may not exist as an interrelated set of semantic-semiotic systems, reflecting and carrying interrelated cultural sets, and manifesting itself in variant surface structures derived from differentiated but co-existent deep structures, forming a total grammar of Jamaican culture.

Put directly, it appears to me that the Jamaican language continuum operates as a single "hypercode" (to use Umberto Eco's term, which includes in itself "a complex network of subcodes"),[7] and that these have the means of generating all of the meaning potential by which I, as a Jamaican writer, perceive and interpret my environment.

Our situation is hardly unique. In *Writing Degree Zero,* Roland Barthes points to the example of French in the early seventeenth century when linguistic variety and linguistic insecurity worked together in the times before standardization, a phenomenon which we take too much for granted nowadays: "[Until] around 1650, French literature had not yet gone further than the problematics of the language . . . and . . . it was as yet unaware of modes of writing. For as long as a tongue is still uncertain about its very structure, an ethics of language is impossible; modes of language appear only when the language, being established on a national scale, becomes a kind of negativity, a line which separates what is forbidden from what is allowed, without asking itself any more questions about its origins or the justifications for such taboo."[8] In the Jamaican situation, Standard Jamaican English—itself beset by the pressure of British English and haunted by features of American English—provides one of the poles of the continuum and lacks authority to establish for Jamaican culture the literary standard that the French grammarians devised for French in the classical period.

Standardization is not, however, conferred on a language community by scholars. The successes of the French Academy of the eighteenth century arose from the desires of a ruling class (and the assent of other classes) to establish a language code that would perform as a prestige model for the entire community. Efforts by generations of teachers and community leaders to do the same for Jamaica have met with little success, for the dominant group is itself divided about aims and means, and does not always support its officially stated policies. The existence of such a standard would at once confer generic order and curb the ability of the continuum to explore and express shades of meaning. Louise Bennett, Jamaica's classic Creole poet, would have resisted such constraints (see chapter 10).

Here one might usefully glance at an analogous situation, that of medieval England. In *Postcolonialisms: Caribbean Rereading of Medieval English Discourse,* Barbara Lalla describes and analyzes the shape and significance of first the

Norse conquest and then the establishment of Norman and later of Angevin hegemony in England, with the many consequences for governance, religion, land tenure, trade, social life, and language.[9]

During two or more centuries of political and cultural oppression, the language of the majority, English, lost all cultural value or functional standardization. A Cornishman, John of Trevisa (ca. 1340–1402) describes the resulting dismemberment of English, outlining a situation of language contact, language diversity, and class divisions along language lines. Not only are the regional dialects so diverse as to be almost mutually unintelligible, but the presence of French adds to the difficulties of choosing proper usage for speech and writing. He notes that children learn better when taught in their first language (English), although upward mobility requires some kind of French. Curiously, Norman French seems to operate as a single standard speech form in England, says Trevisa, even though "ther is as meny dyuers maner Frensch yn the rem of Fraunce as ys dyvers manere Englysch in the rem of Engelond."[10]

Trevisa speaks *as a* writer and a native speaker, from within the confines of medieval language culture. He offers no prescriptions, though he does attempt some explanations that fit closely with current dialectology, sociolinguistics, and creolization theories. He takes pains to explain the causes of language variation (especially in the case of contact situations between unrelated languages). He is concerned most of all with *communication:* communication across dialect boundaries and communication on an international level.

Then, as now, writers who seek to communicate from the center of a linguistically diversified situation such that they are understood within that community and also on an international level must accept certain conditions. The writer must recognize that an externally imposed set of norms (Standard British English, Standard American English, or even Standard Jamaican English) will be incapable of meeting the full meaning potential of her language culture. Her outer audiences will lose as much as her own community will. She must try to resolve the conflicts between what is *permitted* (as distinct from what is *understood*) both by members of her community and by the audiences outside. The interacting "ethics of language" (whereby British audiences accept the dialects of *Huckleberry Finn* and Americans come to terms with Scott and Dickens) had not yet encompassed the Caribbean four decades ago and (though beginning to come into play) are not yet entrenched. Notable achievements have been made by Trinidadian writers such as Selvon and Naipaul, but the language situation of Trinidad differs from that of Jamaica: the distance between basilect and acrolect is narrower in that country. Traditions of rhetoric are also different: Trinidadian calypsonians draw heavily on Standard English for their word play. The same is not true of reggae lyrics or traditional Jamaican folk song.

The Jamaican fiction writer has to face the fact that the use of literary Standard English presents as much benefit and threat as the use of Creole does. Each may falsify and change the meaning of what she has to say. Each is "wrong" in certain situations. Yet each has a function in expressing so diversified a culture, and each has a semantic-semiotic task in the attempt to establish and maintain a connection with her audience.

These issues, more than the glaring aspects of phonology and lexis, constitute the "problematics of language" in the Caribbean situation, for which only time and an evolving literary tradition are likely to offer solutions. I will now turn to my own attempts to deal with the problematics of Jamaican language and to show how my first four novels became distinct and separate experiments in usage and communication.

The Novels: A Series of Linguistic Experiments

I began writing my first children's novel, *Sprat Morrison,* in 1968.[11] It follows certain stylistic and structural formulae that I had worked out before I began writing: the register, Standard Jamaican English, should be an area of the Jamaican continuum that could be accepted as natural by Jamaican children of all classes and backgrounds.

- The audience to which the work was primarily directed was the ten- to twelve-year-old age group in Jamaica, including all who could read or be read to.
- The mode and style of the story had to be such that the narrator could enter and stay in communication with this audience, while avoiding the disapproval of the parent, teacher, and educator groups.
- Children of the same age in the rest of the English-speaking world formed a natural extension of this audience.
- The main character was to be male because of the low motivation of the average Jamaican boy to acquire reading skills or to develop a liking for the world of books. Girls of the same age possess higher skills and motivation and do not seem to need strong role models of their own gender.
- The book was to bring enjoyment and pleasure to the child audience. It was not a school text but a sample of the storyteller's art.

These conditions may seem quite simple to the uninitiated. However, the background of the sixties in Jamaica shows up the pitfalls and problems of such a literary program.

The use of a Standard Jamaican English register necessitated drastic structural organization of the plot and action to eliminate many kinds of dramatic, intimate, informal, and out-of-doors incidents. These incidents (street, market, playground, backyard, back-fence, and joke-telling episodes) could have been the liveliest and most attractive aspects of such a novel. If the book was to pass the censorship of the Ministry of Education, the teaching profession, and the parent group, then there could be no overt trace of Creole or dialect anywhere in it. Senior education officers whom I consulted in 1969 laid down these rules. *The ministry would not introduce any text containing the smallest trace of nonstandard into any classroom or school library.*

The dialogue of the hero and his friends thus fell within narrow linguistic constraints. A heroine's usage might have been credibly more standardized than a hero's usage, the oral style of boys in informal situations being (at least at that time) more heavily biased toward basilectal and mesolectal patterns. To get around this possibly gender-related feature, I made the hero an only child, used to solitude though friendly with other children. Much of the action turns on his learning to deal with loneliness, or surviving difficult situations on his own, or receiving active, nonverbal aid from others, his thoughts and reflections forming the only verbalization of the action. He spends much of his time with adults, often working with them but not talking to them. In the Jamaican society of the time, this was not unusual. Children were still to be seen and not heard, especially in the lower-middle-class suburban group to which my hero belongs. His personality too is that of a reflective, inquisitive antihero, an individualist, neither groupie nor leader.

I also very much wanted the story to go directly to its Jamaican child audience: school life offered mainly boredom and drudgery to children, with little enjoyment associated with work. Meanwhile, I had to contend with the language attitudes of teachers in particular and Jamaican adults in general. These were the same as those of the senior staff of the Ministry of Education; in the fifties and sixties, many an educational battle was fought as "on a darkling plain / Swept with confused alarms of struggle and flight, / Where ignorant armies clash by night." Matthew Arnold's ignorant armies all too well symbolize our debates on language.[12]

The linguistic research of the late fifties (by Cassidy, Le Page, Loftman-Bailey, DeCamp, Craig, Jones, and others) was misunderstood by most teachers and by the community at large. One of the chief symptoms of the "struggle and flight" of the "ignorant armies" was the failure in those days of Jamaican teachers of English to form professional associations concerned with their subject. The breaking point was always the same: languages. No one would admit that there was a learning problem bound up with language varieties. Few would admit publicly to a knowledge and use of Creole. Not until the early 1970s were teachers willing to admit that they lived and worked in a language continuum situation with which they had to come to terms *as teachers.*

Sprat Morrison evaded the armies and crossed the darkling plain to its audience of eleven-year-olds by the following means:

- Relying both on the instinct of a native speaker and on a conscious observation of informal Standard Jamaican English registers, I selected a range that lay within the *receptive* ability of the child audience.
- I sought contact with groups of children in schools (first forms, grade sevens) to test the *acceptability* of this range in the context of storytelling.

The contacts were unstructured and unscientific. I was not making a linguistic study so much as reinforcing in myself the role of storyteller while noting the reactions of the audience. What I learned in this way is borne out by the comments of Joseph E. Grimes, a dialectologist writing on the nature of communication across dialect boundaries. Even though the Jamaican continuum includes a grammatical boundary separating Creole from Standard Jamaican English, its graduated nature permits speakers to move along it receptively and productively. This insight matches closely Grimes's findings on intelligibility tests between dialects: "Intelligibility tests between dialects give results with three characteristics that need to be taken into account in their interpretation: asymmetry, sensitivity to changes in threshold, and incompleteness."[13] Thus the threshold of awareness in my audience would vary according to situation and function within Jamaican language culture. In Grimes's words, "intelligibility is calibrated with reference to different threshold levels for different purposes of communication."[14] My purpose of communication had to be such that it would generate a Standard Jamaican English register acceptable to an audience whose usage represents every stage along the Jamaican language continuum.

The purpose of communication in *Sprat Morrison* resides in the authorial narrated experiences of a ten-year-old Jamaican schoolboy, covering his last year in primary school. The omniscient voice reports on Sprat's comings and goings, his everyday life, and the people and events that make up this critical year. Using this voice as a filter, I screened out the basilectal and mesolectal codes that would otherwise have been obligatory. Using certain child viewpoints, I screened out those adult Standard English codes unacceptable to my audience.

The opening paragraph of the novel uses a Standard Jamaican English register that places the narrator in a certain relationship to the child audience: that of empathetic authority figure/teacher-as-friend/in-group user of an informal standardized code. The direct, anecdotal narrative implies certain attitudes on the part of the omniscient author, which in turn trigger acceptance and involvement on the part of the audience: "He was late for school again. He was a fat, untidy little boy known to most people as Sprat. One day at the

Papine primary school Sprat Morrison ate forty cents' worth of sprats: his lunch, Alvin Barrett's lunch, Desmond Harris's lunch, and Desmond's sister's lunch. It was the result of an elaborate bet as to who would get to sit at the back of Miss Watkins's health science lesson."[15]

The narrative voice's in-group relationship is set up by the absence of pejoration of "he": Sprat will not be blamed for being late because the narrator clearly approves of him. This attitude balances the negative image ("fat, untidy, little") with a positive reference, "known to most people." Informal Standard Jamaican English of the storytelling mode assures the child audience that the authorial voice is not operating as a hostile force, nor as an alienating control, two of the social roles most often associated with Standard Jamaican English or any other Standard English.

The lexical items on the opening page fall within the range known to the child audience from everyday school life, from the mass media, and from other situations associated with Standard Jamaican. The novelty of hearing child-centered experience expressed in what is usually an adult code for most Jamaican children is mitigated by the manipulation of character and plot: "who would get to sit at the back of Miss Watkins's health science lesson."

More importantly, throughout the novel there are many verbal signs and other cues that act as in-group markers to the child audience. Many of these are directed to the entire child audience, Jamaican and otherwise. Some conceal signals that can be picked up only by a Jamaican or a Caribbean audience. On the first page of the novel, the following appear:

1. a caning was handed out to all
2. getting mixed up in bad boys' games
3. this morning was a shortcut morning
4. diving under a fence
5. sliding on your behind
6. where the Papine goats spent a lot of their spare time.

These are definitely not features of Jamaican Creole. They are Standard Jamaican English signaling common experiences shared by Jamaicans and appealing to the outlook and experience of schoolchildren in all times and places.

These phrases, however, point to experiences that are normally cued to Creole usage in Jamaican language behavior. A comparison of the meaning potential of these phrases and their Creole versions is revealing:

1. Hot lick fe every one a dem
2. get mix up inna rudie-bway game
3. a short-cut maanin dis

4. cut t'rough fence
5. siddung slide pan im batty
6. whe de Papine goat go breeze-off dem self.

Taken in turn, the meaning potential undergoes the following shifts:

1. From school-associated punishment of a particular kind (echoes of *Tom Brown's Schooldays*, *Jane Eyre*, and *David Copperfield*) to a peculiarly Caribbean style of punishment that is not confined to school situations.
2. *Rudie-bway* carries more than *bad boys,* touching on a subculture of rebellion, active sexuality, delinquency, and associations with reggae and Rastafarianism.
3. A shift from the merely habitual to an elevated, sharpened, axiomatic prominence with strong associations of crisis, tension, and escape.
4. A shift akin to the preceding item, (3), related to the proverbial "Cut t'rough bush," a cue signaling practiced evasions, escapes, and cunning avoidances of authority.
5. A richer, actualized image of the action.
6. A complete shift of image and associations, showing the nonequivalence of the two versions in semantic terms. Each is acceptable in terms of plot and character, but each has quite different semantic content and semiotic cues.

Educators such as Craig have noted the habit of mothertongue Creole speakers to translate standard into Creole while reading standard texts. This pattern has been observed in the first three years of school, where children faced with a sentence such as "She is at home" read instead "Him at home." This act implies not merely translation but a shift of perception and cultural response.

Using English to evoke Creole language culture opens complex possibilities. The audiences will respond according to their abilities: asymmetrically, incompletely, and with shifting changes of threshold, to use Grimes's terms. Outer audiences will perceive a thinner world of meaning in *Sprat Morrison* than will Jamaican and Caribbean audiences. Standard Jamaican English speakers with a resistance to Jamaican Creole will share this thinner insight. On the other hand, these outer audiences respond to literary cues and other signals that might almost certainly elude the young Jamaican audience.

Caribbean language cultures offer a rich testing ground for the interaction and conflict of fields of meaning. Linked as they are to the cultures of the north, and at the same time preserving and evolving their own culture, Caribbean language situations necessarily present semantic and semiotic patterns very different from those of a classical monoculture.

Thanks to the work of lexicographers such as Cassidy, Le Page, Allsopp,

Winer,[16] and others, we now have a body of material that gives clear guidelines to semantic contrast and shift at the lexical level. The writer has to pay special attention to such sensitive items as *rude, ignorant, mash, coward,* and *lazy*—to name but a few of the lexical items whose meanings differ in Standard English and Jamaican Creole. These have to be used in a framework of allusion, action, characterization, metaphor, or symbolism such that the network of meanings is made functionally clear to the audiences. It is as easy to adhere to the standard semantic pattern and lose the Jamaican Creole audience as it is to use the Jamaican Creole meanings and fail the international audience. An attempt to meet the demands of both audiences may be seen in the examinations episode of *Sprat Morrison,* where the class dunce Junjo writes an essay on "My Best Friend": "He started writing about Alvin, and then couldn't find anything to say after the first sentence, which ran, 'My best friend is the rudist boy I kno.' Somehow that did not seem quite the right opening, so he crossed it out and spoilt the page."[17]

An element of mischievous ambiguity enters here for the Jamaican Creole audience, who will glean both the standard meaning of "rude/rudest" and the Creole meaning of "very aggressive sexually" as given by Cassidy and Le Page in the *Dictionary of Jamaican English.* The verbal cue *rudist* operates successfully in two quite different cultural and semantic fields.

In addition to such semantic/semiotic cues, I also used a number of purely literary strategies. *Sprat* is a novel of reported thought and action in which the filter of the omniscient narrator alternates with a child consciousness. The following passage shows how the adult, authorial voice mingles with and counterpoints the child's: "Easter came in with dry, windy days and clouds of dust (AUTHOR). There were fewer lilies in the vendors' baskets by the roadside (AUTHOR). . . . Water was rationed, and Sprat wondered how Mischief was getting on, if grass was running short (CHILD). . . . Tempers were short (CHILD)."[18] The authorial voice acts mostly as a mediator between the Jamaican and Caribbean audiences on the one hand and the international Standard English audiences on the other, while the child voice uses more markedly Standard Jamaican English features in reported and direct speech in which are usually embedded the semiotic and semantic cues directed to the Jamaican child audience.

The Standard Jamaican English registers used in the novel did more than limit action and structure. They acted as a perfect inhibition against certain kinds of situation, viewpoint, and diction common enough in international Standard English literature, especially as part of the genre "children's story set in exotic country." Not even at a metaphorical or allusive level could occur any of the "quaint" native customs, the sentimentalized landscapes, and alien curiosities that characterize traditional Standard English literature looking outside of its immediate language culture. The Standard Jamaican English registers forced a tone and treatment as matter-of-fact and as realistic as any ethnocentric work of Britain or North America. *Sprat Morrison* puts its non-Caribbean audiences in the center of its world, emphasizing the shared reality of a complex but common civilization. This possibility convinced me that there is a literary via media, through Standard Jamaican English, but the price paid for taking that route is high.

Escape to Last Man Peak (1975)[19] was an attempt to put into literary form the full range of Jamaican language behavior, making use of code-switching as a formal device in characterization, plot development, tone, and contrasts of scene and action. The characters are defined as much by their language behavior as by their nonverbal acts and physical appearance. I felt it most important to "get their speech right," and there lies the essence of the style of this novel.

The characters of *Escape* are very different from those of *Sprat*. The novel deals with ten children from an orphanage: working-class and peasant children with different levels of education, maturation, and sophistication. Their language behavior had to show this reality in all its complexity. At the same time, I still had to cater for the audiences beyond Jamaican Creole and Standard Jamaican English. Following the model of the conventional novel, I used standard *literary* English as the language of narrative, reported speech, and inner consciousness, a kind of recitativo. This device gave me all of the codes and registers (written and spoken) of my own language competence. Structurally, this mode was easy to put into practice, for the novel is a first-person narrative, with all of the action seen through the eyes of an eleven-year-old girl, Nellie. Yet in spite of this, the dialogue was not easy. Certain features of Creole morphosyntax and lexis made heavy demands on the interpretive English framework. I evolved a system whereby the occurrence of Creole lexis or syntax is matched with the use of English orthography, and vice versa: "I jus' hope it *better* quick," said Pauline. "I don' know what to do if it *turn out*."

Better and *turn out* (verbs "to heal" and "to become infected") are Creole forms. Normally they would appear in a frame of Jamaican Creole syntax and phonology, such as, "Me dis 'ope i' betta quick. Me nah know wha fe do ef i' tun out." This version would have been more fitting in that the words occur as part of a very frightening incident, and Creole usage is situationally linked to stress. However, the cultural form "novel" allows for the use of conventions and deviations of many kinds, which different audiences are likely to accept simply because of a shifted threshold of awareness.

The expectations linked to the novel form include standardized literary language for Caribbean readers as for other peoples in the English-speaking world. This receptivity enables the Jamaican audience to use the few Creole cues in Pauline's speech to re-create the kind of atmosphere that would have generated basilectal forms in real life. At the same time, the standardization helps the non-Jamaican audience to grasp the situation quickly. As with *Sprat,* the non-Caribbean audience must inevitably miss certain fields of meaning that exist only in Jamaican language culture, though I used other literary strategies to compensate for this imbalance.

The diction of the narrative passages constitutes one of the means used to communicate with the outer audiences. In their journey across the island, the children have many adventures, one of which is the discovery of an abandoned house whose owners have died in the epidemic from which the children are fleeing: "[Quite] suddenly the trees opened out before us, and we found ourselves looking at a wide, untidy, sunlit garden. In the midst of it was set a very dilapidated, oldfashioned house. I saw at once why Jimmy was sure it was empty. Many of the french windows that opened on the shaggy lawn were swinging loose, some of their panes broken. Ragged curtains showed at the windows upstairs. A huge rice-and-peas vine spread its dark leaves and rich purple flowers all along the upstairs verandah, and it had grown right across the front door itself. A drift of red and purple blossom lay on the weeds and grass that sprouted on the low front steps."[20]

This is the language of science fiction, of traditional adventure stories, and, further back still, of elegy and lyric. The plot of the novel is modeled on the archetypal patterns of epic and saga, and all of these form part of the "additional experience" that enables communication between writer and audience. The fact that the action concerns the fate of a close-knit group of children also allows the writer certain liberties of diction that would be denied if the novel was concentrated on one or two characters, as is the case in *Sprat.*

Thus, in *Escape,* the plot, diction, characters, and setting are themselves semiotic cues that draw the Jamaican cultural material and that of other Standard English cultures into a synthesis. This novel is the most popular of all my books; it has been widely used in Jamaican schools, and teachers and parents report that it is read avidly. Letters from young readers also bear this out. From no one has there been a hint that the language is in any way wrong, difficult, inauthentic, or strange.

The linguistic strategies of *Escape* may be summarized as follows:

1. Representation of authentic Jamaican language features (especially situationally related code-switching) in an orthography that is faithful to Jamaican Creole morphophonemics, *but of only a limited number of items of high frequency or usage* (e.g., *mek* for English "make" or "let"; *gwaan* for English "go on"; *dem* for English "them"; *bway* for English "boy," and the Jamaican Creole pronoun *unnu* for English "you" plural).
2. For items less frequent in usage and closer to English, the use of a standardized orthography to aid the non-Caribbean audiences. Thus [wãã] is represented as "want," [haaks] as "ask," and [kỹãã] as "can't."

3. Use of code-switching to aid the non-Caribbean audience, in what almost amounts to the double-glossing of medieval English writers faced with a similar problem.
4. Use of a first-person narrator whose inner consciousness reports in Standard English, though she herself moves along the continuum in dialogue.
5. Provision of a short glossary of twenty items, perhaps the least useful feature of the book.

In *Escape,* I felt fairly satisfied that I had managed a literary union of Jamaican language varieties and Standard English literary modes. There must be many aspects of the language of this novel that others are better equipped to comment on, but as its writer I feel that I have fulfilled my primary artistic aim: to use Jamaican language behavior as a *literary* tool. I was very encouraged by the editors' attitudes to these language experiments, richly borne out by responses from children and teachers.

Escape was written in 1972 and revised in 1973 after various cuttings and minor changes, none of which concerned language. In December 1973, I started *Voice in the Wind,*[21] another novel for the same age group and audience. I worked on the manuscript for about two years, and shortly after, my interpretation of the laissez-faire editorial policy underwent a strange illumination. I discovered that *Escape* was to be marketed only in the Caribbean, indeed, only in Jamaica. The Longman sales manager replied to my query that such literature would find no reception outside of Jamaica; that even the immigrant Caribbean communities in Britain would reject such writing on linguistic grounds; that the children of such communities were totally acculturated to their new homeland; and that Caribbean culture would be as meaningless to them as to the other non-Caribbean audiences with which I imagined myself to be communicating.

As *Voice* was to be part of the same series as *Escape* when it came out, I no longer found it strange that the editors had said nothing about dialect and Creole usage in either case. As for the views expressed by the sales manager, those had the effect of sending me on a tour of twenty middle schools in Birmingham, Coventry, and London in 1977. From this experience, I learned that these audiences did indeed crave Caribbean literature, and, far from having given up their Caribbean culture, were using Jamaican Creole as a common in-group language. Their teachers remained in blissful ignorance of the Caribbean Creole language culture shared by their middle-school pupils, both black and—quite often—white as well. Shortly after this visit, the Longman marketing policies were revised and both books became available in Africa, but never in Britain.

This experience was valuable in that it obliged me to confront the cultural block that always faces artists who attempt to take an art form across cultural boundaries. A straight imitation of *Little Women* with Jamaican faces and places would have been wholly acceptable; a reworking of an adventure in wholly Jamaican terms was not. Yet language was the means by which the literary work could become representative of Jamaican and Caribbean culture.

Fortunately I had almost completed work on *Voice* when I heard the sales manager's views, and these did not affect my handling of *Voice*. In this novel, I was interested in a different use of language from that of *Escape*. On the surface it might appear to fit in with stereotyped views of "ideal" language usage in Jamaica, in that the novel is clearly bilingual. One alone of the main characters, and one of the minor characters speak Creole; no one else does, not even the three children who form the center of the action. The children are receptive in Jamaican Creole, and very close emotionally to the two Creole-speaking characters, yet their own dialogue—even in private and in moments of danger and stress—is always in Standard Jamaican English.

Voice gives a picture of Jamaican language behavior in a different time and a different social setting from those of *Escape*. The world of *Voice* is that of rural middle-class Jamaica of the late colonial period, in the years 1940–1942. Class and language lines were much more rigid in that period than in the latter twentieth-century setting of *Escape*. Mesolectal forms were less frequent; movement along the continuum was marked by complete shifts of morphosyntax and lexis, rather than by the minimal shifting of the mesolectal speaker. Oratory in both Standard English and Creole was prized, and each felt to have its own appropriate "genius," to borrow a nineteenth-century term.

Moreover, much more than is the case with *Sprat*, the world of *Voice* is based on my own experience of language and society in the 1940s. The plot and characters are fictional, but their language, their values, their social attitudes, and their concerns are firmly rooted in my past. The bilingualism of the novel was a social reality. I have detected traces of this now archaic usage in other writers such as Andrew Salkey and C. Everard Palmer. It can be a danger in that it is *of a period* and that writers may unconsciously model contemporary fiction on the patterns of their childhood. This is not to say that bilingualism has disappeared from Jamaica but that it no longer exists in the clear stratification across class and occupational lines as in the generation before radio and television.

The language usage of *Voice* may be summarized as follows:

1. Standard Jamaican English forms the principal mode of discourse for all of the major characters save one. It is the variety used for authorial comment, narrative reported speech, and action.
2. In the descriptive and narrative passages, the Standard Jamaican English elements merge directly into literary Standard English.

3. Changes of register occur within Creole or English, thus there is no code-switching from one to the other. This pattern differs from the usage of *Escape.*
4. The Creole usage is set against the Standard Jamaican English backdrop and is of prime importance in the unfolding of plot and character. It is thus of great structural and stylistic importance.
5. The language behavior of the characters is consistent throughout the novel, defining roles and relationships.

In following these rules, I was trying to be faithful to the social and behavioral patterns of a certain period in Jamaican history.

Whereas I felt constrained in *Sprat* to keep the authorial voice within literary Standard English, I felt no such obligation in *Voice*. On the contrary, Standard Jamaican English and literary Standard English mingle without distinction in the narrative passages, creating what is in effect a Jamaican literary standard. In *Escape,* this fact was disguised by the role of the first-person narrator, Nellie. The highlighting (or foregrounding) of Creole is also an important feature of the book. The interaction of Standard Jamaican English and Jamaican Creole can be seen in the following episode involving ten-year-old Annabell and old Maud, one of the most critical passages in terms of plot and character:

> Annabell passed spoons, washed knives . . . and waited. . . . At last she had her reward. The yabba, covered tightly with a cloth, was dragged into the bottom of the kitchen safe. . . . Annabell did the dragging, so that Maud would not have to bend her old back. She asked,
>
> "Maud, please, what was it that Uncle Edwin saw on the night of the 1907 earthquake?"
>
> Maud . . . seemed amused at some private joke.
>
> "You h'uncle h'Edwin? Dat fool-fool bway, call 'imseif h'engineer?" she chuckled, wiping her hands on her apron. "Come sweep off 'ere for me!"
>
> Annabell fetched the broom . . . and began sweeping slowly, one eye on Maud. . . . "Well, me ironin' sit down all dis while doin' nottn', Saviour know is only two hand me got." [Maud] rose from the armchair . . . [then] she winked at Annabell.

This passage occurs when Peter, Annabell, and Dennis are trying to unravel the meaning of the appearances of the family ghost. Old Maud, cook, authority figure, and family retainer, forms the link between present and past, between generations, between social classes, between a materialistic environment and a transcendent, ineffable cosmos. Maud is a Creole speaker, using a form usually associated with social inferiority. Yet her usage forms the focus of the most important revelations of the plot. Although it is the children who see and hear the ghost of their great-aunt—the voice in the wind—it is Maud who acts as interpreter and guide.

Maud's role (impossible to express in anything other than Creole) is a kind of artistic foregrounding such as Jan Mukarovsky describes in his essay "Standard Language and Poetic Language."[22] Arguing the relationship of poetic (that is, literary) language and standard language, Mukarovsky claims that the interaction of dialect and standard expands the aesthetic and functional ranges of language:

> Poetic language is . . . not a brand of the standard. This is not to deny the close connection between the two, which consists of the fact that, for poetry, the standard language is the background against which is reflected the esthetically intentional violation of the norm of the standard. . . .
>
> The violation of the norm of the standard, its systematic violation, is what makes possible the poetic utilization of language; without this possibility there would be no poetry.[23]

Mukarovsky contends that the foregrounding occurs through dialect shifts that contrast normative (standard) language and the traditional canon. Further, he argues that the mutual relationship of foregrounded (dialect) and unforegrounded (standard) features make up the dynamic structure of the literary work, each component of which has value through its relationship to the whole. This dynamic structure exists in *Escape* and *Voice,* and, to a lesser degree, in *Sprat*. Even more important to the Caribbean writer is Mukarovsky's argument that the subject matter of a literary work is its largest semantic unit and resides in the sum total of its language usage,[24] so that change in the interest of correct language inevitably interferes with the essence of the work.

The place of language variation in the semantic wholeness of a literary work is plain in *Sprat, Escape,* and *Voice*. In the fourth full-length novel, a historical novel intended for age group fourteen to fifteen and titled *Evening, Morning,* the use of standardized features became, in the end, a fatal problem. Set in the 1770s, the novel concerns the fortunes and friendship of two thirteen-year-old girls, one white, one black, both in bondage. They grow up together on a small estate owned and run by an elderly English spinster; at the start of the action they are suddenly taken to the establishment of a Spanish Town moneylender as part payment for their mistress's debts.

The semantic and semiological field of this novel includes eighteenth-century languages, social customs, attitudes, values, and experience both in terms of historical events (the colonial wars and Maroon wars) and social institutions: plantations, slave markets, monetary systems, trade, and the curious social hierarchy developing around these.

A representative from a distinguished British publishing house contacted me in 1977, keen to work with the writer of *Sprat Morrison*. After lengthy discussions with this eager new editor (who saw the work as being addressed primarily to an international Standard English audience), I agreed to the following linguistic strategies:

1. No attempt would be made to represent archaic Creole or eighteenth-century English dialects. Other languages would not appear.
2. Language variety should be suggested by lexical and metaphorical means. Specimens should be few and their meanings made clear by context.
3. Phonetic spellings were to be avoided totally.
4. Idioms, proverbs, and idiosyncratic features of archaic Creole were to be represented through translation *or* transliteration.

As I worked on the novel, I found it more and more difficult to keep within these limits. This Jamaica was a multilingual community. Some characters were Africans for whom pidgin or Creole was a second language; very few were mothertongue Creole speakers; others commanded Creole and some variety of English; still others commanded more than one English dialect and some Creole; others commanded some English, some Creole, and one or more other languages, which might be African or European, or both. These people might be white, black, or anything in between. Such were the facts of life in that world. The two heroines are at the center of it. Plot, action, character, setting, conflict, and the resolution of the plot all depend upon different varieties of language for their very being. For example, language is the main marker of social distance or of intimacy between protagonists. To have them all using a version of literary Standard English would be to "deny the essence of the work," in truth. More than anything else, language defines each character's cultural history and social standing, and his or her relationship to all of the other characters, as well as his or her self-image.

The many disputes on usage ("not suitable for an international audience . . . incomprehensible terms like *ship-sister, ship-brother, mulatto,* and *quadroon*") forced on me once more the problem of communication from Caribbean language culture to the outer Standard English audiences. The editors tried to help: They advised me to stick to "speech rhythms" and forget grammar, in blissful ignorance of the fact that Creole word order *is* Creole grammar, for the most part. Phonetic spellings made them desperate.

The problems finally concentrated themselves into strange lexical items, weird morphosyntax, and phonetic spellings. I tried to resolve these as follows.

As far as vocabulary was concerned, instead of discarding important Creole or eighteenth-century terms, I worked each into a dynamic of action, social reference, and character reference such that its web of meaning stretched through the whole novel. This is most clear in the case of racist terminology such as *mulatto,* but it applies equally to *laudanum* and *pepperpot,* terms that carry important meaning patterns of eighteenth-century life in Jamaica. Such terms were selected for their semantic value in relation to the plot and setting. Their occurrence in varying contexts builds up and reinforces their meaning associations. Some, such as the snatches of Latin prayers uttered by one of the heroines, are highly foregrounded features evoking cultural associations over and beyond the lexical value of the word or phrase. For instance, the word *paternoster* carries a wealth of meaning and behavioral response beyond its literal value.

Morphosyntax was, as usual, much harder to handle. I kept word order as the pattern for Jamaican Creole, but in many cases (as in the speech of upper servants), I rendered the words in standardized spellings.

In the speech of certain characters, a few Jamaican Creole items (verbs and pronouns) are consistently used even when the rest of their usage is standardized. Often these items are double-glossed. The number of these items is low but their frequency of usage is high. The number of such items is lower than in *Escape* and *Voice,* but their foregrounding is stronger and more consistent.

The same rigid selection applied to phonetic spellings, and I tried to use those that seemed absolutely essential [gal], [de], [dem], [ol]. These signs were associated with particular characters and limited to their usage. In many cases where the word order marked the utterance as Jamaican Creole, I used standardized spellings. I also made use of non–Standard English forms such as the present participle /-in/ for *-ing* and the nonphonemic initial /h/ of Cockney and Jamaican Creole.

These were all seemingly rational compromises. Yet again and again I was haunted by the sense that I could not *hear* the voices of my people, my characters; that I had betrayed them and their world by washing out their own true words; that I could see them—as if through a glassy window—but their voices were cut off and silenced. I was shut out by the conditions laid on me by my kind and helpful editors. Worst of all, no representation of West African languages appeared anywhere. The majority of the speakers in this world were rendered voiceless. Perhaps what happened next was a blessing in disguise.

In 1980, the new publisher accepted the final draft, a contract was signed, an advance paid, but within a year, major financial losses caused the closure of half of the children's literature department and the departure of several editors, including mine. At the same time, I remained very uneasy about the semantic and semiotic wholeness of this work. When after two years no response came from the survivors of the now tiny department, I returned the advance fee and reclaimed the draft manuscript. It has never been published.

In the following years, I tried to work out the reasons for this failure and have concluded that without adequate representation of the complex language culture of that world, "its largest semantic unit," the words on the page simply did not give life to the world of characters.

These linguistic restraints had not changed the plot or the characters. They had not caused scenes to be deleted or included or viewpoints rearranged. Instead they had deprived the entire work of any life whatsoever. By reducing and subverting language, I had diminished a whole world and, at great cost, I learned the peril of letting anyone—however well-intentioned—dictate the language of a writer's visionary worlds.

I have tried to give an account of how I dealt with the problem of language varieties in the first four children's novels that I have written.[25] In all of them, I have had to make compromises between my own instincts and experience, on the one hand, and the expectations and attitudes of editors, educators, and members of the standard language audience on the other. My task has been as much to educate that audience as it has been to entertain my young audience, and the former had to be carried out with much tact and subtlety. Such response as I have had to the first three novels encourages me to feel that language need not be a problem per se. Rather it is the whole context of meaning and association revealed by the work that permits interpretation of the linguistic sign and assigns value to both the work and the individual signs.

Seen from another angle, "we should not speak of the stylistic function of a linguistic item but, instead, of its precise function; nor of the style of a piece of language, but instead of its precise meaning and effect."[26] Although J. M. Ellis directs these words to linguists and literary critics, writers might do well to ponder them. In the same essay, Ellis emphasizes the fact that analyzing the function of any linguistic attribute in a text amounts to analyzing its relation to all the other elements in that text.[27] Thus it is the combinative rather than the individual aspects of language that best serve the semantic and communicative effectiveness of any literary work. The selection of linguistic features in a literary work must be carried out with this single purpose in mind.

Art involves synthesis and the integration of many complex systems; these must be felt to work together meaningfully in order to form that coherent whole recognized as novel or poem within the language culture. Let the writer remember that it is meaning that determines what is loosely called style by most and precise function by rigorous analysts. As writers struggle with this medium (and editors too, although it is the medium that gives the real trouble), let them be guided by the demands made upon them by meaning and by the communication of meaning. Only then may they examine the variant lects at their disposal. In the difficult task of selection, the writer may well come to agree with J. M. Ellis's early conclusion that there perhaps is no such thing as *free* variation,[28] and that for the Caribbean writer, the kinds of variation open to her are all tied firmly to meaning and culture. This view is reinforced by Youssef's concept of varilingualism.[29]

The delicate interrelationship of the individual linguistic parts of a work to the meaningful whole of that same work is demonstrated by a discussion of *Finnegans Wake,* in which Culler comments on Stephen Heath's treatment of James Joyce: "The unreadability, the violent ambivalence of the work is not an obstacle to be overcome by judicious translation into an interpretive language but rather the mark of a thematic project which determines the practice of writing. The work undertakes a 'theatralisation' of language,' a foregrounding of the word in the network of its potential differential relations. The signifier is no longer a transparent form through which one accedes to meaning; *it is displayed as an object in its own right.*"[30] The discussion goes on to reveal how Joyce's purpose was to create a linguistic play that evades conventions of language and communication so as to produce indeterminacy through dislocation and contradiction. Thus, what is commonly perceived as the difficulty of Joyce's style turns finally on his treatment of meaning and language itself.

Like Joyce, the Caribbean writer works from a rich and complicated language culture that offers great opportunities for inventiveness and innovation. Far from perceiving our language situation in the Caribbean in terms of problematic, we should see this condition as the very means whereby we may explore and communicate the essence of our culture and its many links, past and present, with other language cultures. We must mediate between the forces of artistic convention, audience expectations, spoken and written forms, as well as differentiated but interlocking cultures. We must also recognize that each work of literary art alters, in however small a way, the language culture into which the new work enters.

That, as linguists know, is how literary standard languages are created, and reshaped, and created anew.

Notes

1. Previously discussed in two articles: Jean D'Costa, "The West Indian Novelist and Language: A Search for a Literary Medium," in *Studies in Caribbean Language,* ed. Lawrence D. Carrington in collaboration with Dennis Craig and Ramon Todd Dandaré (St. Augustine, Trinidad and Tobago: Society for Caribbean Linguistics, University of the West Indies, 1983), 252–265; and Jean D'Costa, "Expression and Communication: Literary Challenges to the Caribbean Polydialectal Writer," *Journal of Commonwealth Literature* 19, no. 1 (1984): 123–141.

2. M. A. K. Halliday, *Language as Social Semiotic: The Social Interpretation of Language and Meaning* (London: Edward Arnold, 1978), 111. In *A Dictionary of Linguistics and Phonetics* (Oxford: Blackwell, 1985), David Crystal defines "lect" as "a collection of linguistic phenomena which has a functional identity within a speech community," different levels being recognized within the variety continuum.

3. Halliday, Ibid., 8.

4. Ibid., 111.

5. Jonathan Culler, *Structuralist Poetics: Structuralism, Linguistics and the Study of Literature* (London: Routledge and Kegan Paul, 1975); Umberto Eco, *A Theory of Semiotics* (Bloomington: Indiana University Press, 1976).

6. Valerie Youssef, "Varilingualism: A Discrete Sub-Type of Language Competence," *Journal of Multilingual Communication Disorders* 3, no. 3 (November 2005): 216–226.

7. Eco, *Theory of Semiotics,* 125.

8. Roland Barthes, *Writing Degree Zero,* trans. Annette Lavers and Colin Smith (1953; repr., New York: Hill and Wang, 1968), 56.

9. Barbara Lalla, *Postcolonialisms: Caribbean Rereading of Medieval English Discourse* (Kingston, Jamaica: University of the West Indies Press, 2008), 12–19.

10. John of Trevisa was a fellow of Exeter College, Oxford (1362–1365) and translator of two major works: Ranulph Higden's *Polychronicon* (a history of the world from Creation to the year 1352); and the then-definitive encyclopedia of natural science, *Bartolomeus de Proprietatibus Rerum*, completed in 1398. See Ranulph Higden, "*Polychronicon Ranulphi Higden, Monachi Cestrensis," Together with the English Translation of John of Trevisa and an Unknown Writer of the Fifteenth Century,* ed. Churchill Babington and Joseph Rawson Lumby, Rolls Series 41, 9 vols. (London: Longman, Roberts, and Green, 1865–1886). For a discussion of Trevisa's usage and his descriptions of fourteenth-century English dialects, see Kenneth Sisam, ed., *Fourteenth Century Verse and Prose* (Oxford: Clarendon Press, 1955), 145–150, 251–253.

11. Jean D'Costa, *Sprat Morrison* (Kingston, Jamaica: Ministry of Education and Collins-Sangster, 1972; London: Longman, 1990).

12. Matthew Arnold's famous despairing poem, "On Dover Beach"(first published in 1867) captures the angst that affected many in the latter nineteenth century, a time of great change as new nations (Germany and then Italy) came into being. Matthew Arnold, *Lyric, Dramatic and Elegiac Poems* (Oxford: Hall and Stacy, 1881), 65.

13. Joseph E. Grimes, "Dialects as Optimal Communications Networks," *Language* 50, no. 2. (1974): 260.

14. Ibid., 260.

15. D'Costa, *Sprat Morrison,* 7.

16. F. G. Cassidy and R. B. Le Page, *Dictionary of Jamaican English* (Cambridge: Cambridge University Press, 1967); Richard Allsopp, *Dictionary of Caribbean English Usage* (Oxford: Oxford University Press, 1996); Lise Winer, *Dictionary of the English/Creole of Trinidad and Tobago* (Montreal: McGill-Queen's University Press, 2009).

17. D'Costa, *Sprat Morrison,* 88.

18. Ibid., 181.

19. Jean D'Costa, *Escape to Last Man Peak* (Harlow, England: Longman, Blue Mountain Library Series, 1975; London: Longman, Horizon Series, 1980).

20. Ibid., 91–92.

21. Jean D'Costa, *Voice in the Wind* (London: Longman, 1978).

22. Jan Mukarovsky, "Standard Language and Poetic Language," in *Linguistics and Literary Style,* ed. Donald C. Freeman, trans. Paul L. Garvin (New York: Holt, Rinehart, and Winston, 1970), 40–56.

23. Ibid., 42.

24. Ibid., 48.

25. My other books for seven- to nine-year-olds are dedicated works for class. Consequently, they use Standard Jamaican English: *Duppy Tales* (Harlow, England: Addison, Wesley, Longman, 1992); *Caesar and the Three Robbers* (Harlow, England: Addison, Wesley, Longman, 1996); *Jenny and the General* (Kingston, Jamaica: Carlong, 2006). The stories in *Over Our Way* (a collection by many authors coedited with Velma Pollard [Harlow, England: Longman, (1980) 1993]) make use of differing levels of Creole, Caribbean Standard English, and levels between.

26. J. M. Ellis, "Linguistics, Literature, and the Concept of Style," *Word* 26, no. 1 (April 1970): 65–78.

27. Ibid., 75.

28. Ibid., 76.

29. Youssef, "Varilingualism," 216–226.

30. Culler, *Structuralist Poetics,* 124.

4
To Us, All Flowers Are Roses
Writing Ourselves into the Literature of the Caribbean

Velma Pollard

The language of the earliest written creative efforts of colonized peoples the world over has tended to be the language of the colonizer, which is the language of education and of all official transactions in these societies. In the former British West Indies, that language has been English. The very act of writing in another language, during the fledgling years, was revolutionary in a situation where *literature* invariably meant English (or at least British) literature. In schools in the Caribbean as in other British colonies, children were taught British and European history and studied English novels, poems, and plays. Merle Hodge in her 1970 novel *Crick Crack, Monkey* dramatizes and satirizes this situation.[1] Olive Senior's now famous words describe it succinctly: "There was nothing about us at all."

> Studying History Ancient and Modern
> Kings and Queens of England
> Steppes of Russia
> Wheatfields of Canada
> There was nothing of our landscape there
> Nothing about us at all.[2]

When writers began to react negatively to being written out of the literature and to being represented entirely by English, the language of their formal but not of their intimate motions, they sought ways of including the sound of a local and authentic voice in what they wrote.

Different writers achieved this in different ways. Very few chose to write exclusively in the Creoles, popular languages born of the interaction between the African languages of the slaves and the European languages of the planters. Louise Bennett of Jamaica, among the women, stands out for having written in Jamaican Creole from the forties, when she began, and for the rest of her days. Today Bennett tends to be regarded as a "performance" poet, which means that her verse is meant to be performed, spoken before an audience, not read in a quiet interchange between reader and text.

Other writers have written predominantly in English but have used varying means to achieve a satisfactory Jamaican Creole flavor. This chapter illustrates how Lorna Goodison and Olive Senior, Jamaican women writing predominantly in English, write themselves, their culture, and their identity into their work by exploiting the dual linguistic heritage.

One of the advantages of writing in an environment where the official language is related to the popular Creole is the possibility of using the same word or the same phrase with different meanings because the closest relationship between the languages is at the level of lexicon. So, for example, the title of this chapter, "*To Us, All Flowers Are Roses,*" which is the title of Lorna Goodison's 1995 collection of poems, means in English (at a metaphorical level) that all flowers are as valuable as roses are, but in Jamaican Creole it means (at a very literal level) that the term *rose* may be used to describe all flowers.[3] So that a rose garden need not have any roses at all. The following quotation from a farewell speech on the campus of a tertiary institution supports the point made in Goodison's line. The worker who was chosen to give the gift to the outgoing principal's wife said, "Through as we know Miss L . . . like roses we give ar this Orchid," which translates: "Because we know that Mrs. L . . . likes flowers we are presenting her with this orchid." The title of one of my own collections of short fiction is *Considering Woman,* which in English has woman as object to be considered, that is, thought about.[4] In Jamaican Creole, she is subject and the present participle/adjective "considering" describes her attitude. So "Considering Woman" becomes "Woman, a thinking (considering) person." The reader who does not understand Jamaican Creole has access to one meaning, the bilingual reader has access to at least two.

What is important here is that the Creole speaker is continually being identified as a vital (and vibrant) part of the Jamaican man/woman scape although the writing is mostly in English. The breach, which Senior's poem quoted at the beginning of this paper identifies, is being constantly repaired in the new writing. As an example, let us examine briefly the opening lines of an exquisite short Goodison poem "O Love You so Fear the Dark":

O love, you so fear the dark
you so accustomed to fighting. . . .[5]

The second line might be read in English with a stress on "you," making it a repetition of the form in the first line. But it might also be read as a Jamaican Creole line with a shortened "you" and a shortened "so." It then becomes "you so accustom(ed) to fighting." The phonological change carries with it not only a change of rhythm but a change of grammar. Each language represents a different persona. The overlap of identities is signified by the overlap of linguistic systems.

The Caribbean (in this case Jamaican) language situation is complex. The relationship that sociolinguistics identifies between language and class in the situation is sometimes too simple and imprecise. The "high" language, English, is often said to be the language of the upper and middle classes, while the "low" language, Jamaican Creole, is said to be the language of the Other. But there is nothing cut and dried about it. Jamaican Creole speakers speak "up" in certain formal situations. Not all of them achieve English; some achieve a code somewhere between the Creole and English, and all classes tend to relax in Creole. Code-switching, code-sliding, and code-mixing are part of the reality of day-to-day Jamaican life. The super/subordinate relationship between English and Jamaican Creole, however, allows class distinctions to be made in writing, through the manipulation of the languages.

When this complex language situation is represented effectively, several Jamaican selves may be identified, each using a code that is different in some respects from the others. Later in this collection, in the chapter "Mothertongue Voices in the Writing of Olive Senior and Lorna Goodison," I discuss at length code-switching in Goodison's "Ocho Rios II," pointing out that "the rendering of complex behaviours and the sound of complex voices in a single statement by the deft manipulation of lexicon and syntax is . . . Goodison's major contribution to Caribbean literature."[6] I still consider that poem the finest example of the representation of the complex language situation. There the voice of the Rastaman is distinct from the voice of the peasant farmer, which in turn is distinct from that of the first person (middle-class?) narrator. The same mixing of languages is accomplished if somewhat less dramatically in one of Senior's earlier poems. "City Poem" recalls an inner-city street where a middle-class young woman walks with some terror as young men call out to her: "*hello hello. miss psst psst.*"[7] The first-person narrative voice comments,

> but I cannot answer: The Age of Anxiety alas, is still very much
> alive.

In parenthesis there is the comment,

> (And if you taught me to speak
> with your words would I touch
> could I reach beyond the collapse
> of garbage cans in hungry streets?)

The next movement in that poem describes a terrible day in the lives of the very citizens who people the hungry streets. A bulldozer came to destroy homes (shacks to outsiders) to facilitate the building of lower-income houses. A woman describes her own reaction and the more extreme reaction of her friend Mavis:

Wen de bulldoza come a back-a-wall
we jus pickup all we have an all
we have is chilren an we leave
Mavis doan wan leave Mavis aksin
why why why A seh Mavis
move fus aks question las
di ting out dere biggern yu
an it caan talk . . .

The poem continues in English asking the rhetorical question:

Why
did you damage
the statue
of the National hero?
and responds,
—Because I have plenty damage
inside me.[8]

All the selves represented here are female (except for the male calling "psst psst"). English, however, represents the concerned middle-class; Creole, the suffering female self.

The use of Caribbean Creoles has received some attention in literary commentary on Caribbean writing. But it remains true that English is the more widely used language in the creative work issuing from the region. However, the judicious use of the Creole word or phrase continually ensures a Caribbean sense in any piece. The Creole flavor of a whole poem, for example, may rest in a single word.

Let me identify two of the Creole grammatical features, which frequently appear in these predominantly "English" literary environments. The verb *to be,* perhaps the most commonly used verb in English, does not always have an equivalent in Jamaican Creole. See, for example, /mi kwol/ "I am cold," /mi veks / "I am angry," /yu tuu fuul/ "you are too stupid," where the predicate adjective translates the English verb *to be* + adjective. But that "absence" (sometimes described as zero copula) does not get in the way of comprehension of the intended meaning by the speaker of English who does not also speak Creole. So, for example, the persona in Senior's "Meditation on Yellow," speaking for the historically conscious local "I" serving tourists (modern Columbuses) at that time but due to move from "kitchen to front verandah," one day comments wryly:

So I serving them
coffee
tea
cock-soup
rum
Red Stripe beer
Sensimilla[9]

and says of her/himself, "I not quarrelsome . . . I tired now." Later the "I" suggests that tourists cannot catch the Caribbean rhythm: "(for you have to born with that)."

Perhaps the most outstanding grammatical feature of all Creole languages is the unmarked verb. The base form of the verb (used in English with *to* for the infinitive) is the commonly used form. No tense indication is contained there. The form is the same for yesterday, today, and tomorrow. But while the use of this feature ensures the creole presence, it does not affect comprehension by the non-Creole speaker.

Note how in the poem "To Us, All Flowers Are Roses," Goodison mixes an English verb marked for tense with a Creole unmarked verb in a characteristic sentence. Writing about the names of flowers she mentions

A strong young breeze that just takes
these names like blossoms and waltz
them around turn and wheel them on the tongue[10]

After the initial marked verb "takes," all others are unmarked. Reinforcing the Creole sensibility in this instance is the fact that "wheel and turn" is a phrase from a local folksong that asks, "Wha mek yu da wiil an tun mi?" ("Why are you wheeling and turning me?"). Later in the same poem, Goodison writes that a cargo of slaves landed free because

somebody sign a paper even as
they rode as cargo shackled on the high seas [11]

Ensuring the presence of the Creole speaker while writing in English is Goodison's special skill. I have written elsewhere that Goodison is a great manager of the code-mixing that is commonplace in Jamaican speech. Other critics have commented on the extraordinary manipulation of language in this poetry.[12] What I want to highlight at this point is her skill in using a single word to invoke the creole sensibility.

Goodison's "My Will" is a poem written entirely in English.[13] It is a catalog of wishes from a mother for important spiritual (nonmaterial) good things for a son. Near the end of the third of five stanzas she writes: "may you never know *hungry*" (my emphasis). It is easy to miss the fact that the expected abstract noun "hunger" is replaced by the adjective "hungry." In Jamaican Creole, the form used for the adjective in English does the function of both adjective and adverb. The substitution of that one word for the expected other immediately raises the wish to the level of a benediction from an old and wise woman in a traditional community. And this is in keeping with the image of the lines immediately before it when she wishes for her son inter alia,

> . . . the right to call
> all older than you
> Miss, mister or mistress
> in the layered love of our
> simplest ways[14]

Let us revisit the title poem of the 1995 collection from which I have taken the title of this essay. It is unashamedly an "insider" poem—a poem for people of a particular cultural and linguistic community. Yet it is written in such a way that the reader from outside can understand it. After all, the language is English. It begins by proclaiming the Akan ancestry to which many Jamaicans are heir: "Accompong is Ashanti." Accompong is the name of a place, a maroon settlement, as the poem goes on to tell:

> . . . maroons dwell in dense places
> deep mountainous, well-sealed
> strangers unwelcome. Me no send you no come.[15]

That last is a place name too: "Me no send you no come." It means the same thing as "strangers unwelcome" of the preceding sentence. At least the sense is the same, for it translates "If I don't send for you, do not come." The one who is inside will determine when the other, who is outside, should arrive: "Do not come until I send for you." And everywhere in this poem insider information is interspersed with general information, the former indicated by carefully selected heavily weighted Jamaican Creole sounds.

In a catalog of Jamaican place names, in an environment of English, an alternative pronunciation is suggested for just one name: "hola Mount Zion" as opposed to the more conventional "Holy Mount Zion." This single item invokes, for those who recognize it, not simply Jamaican Creole but the drums of Rastafari:

> It is Holy here, Mount Moses dew falls upon Mount Nebo south of
> Jordan Mount Nebo, rises here too hola Mount Zion high.[16]

(The "hola" is written in lower case suggesting that a pun on it is possibly intended. The English "whole of" does become "hola" in Jamaican Creole). That "hola Mount Zion" is a line from a rendition of Rastafari chanting and allows the inclusion of that other theology in a string of place names invoking the Christian religion.

The final and personal affirmation of that poem introduces within an English sentence a Jamaican word whose meaning is highly specific. If you know it you understand the pride in being a Jamaican that these words proclaim, in this case a free woman, a daughter of slaves from Jamaica:

> . . . I was born at Lineen—
> Jubilee!—on the anniversary of Emancipation Day
> I recite these names in a rosary, speak them
> when I pray, for Heartease, my Mecca, aye Jamaica[17]

The public maternity hospital in Kingston, the Victoria Jubilee, named for that queen, is lovingly called Lineen in a euphonious pronunciation of "lying-in," which is the state of a woman waiting to give birth. The "I" of the poem was born in that place on the anniversary of the emancipation of slaves—the first of August. She prays for peace, which here, as in many other Goodison poems, is located in a physical/literal and metaphorical place "Heartease," a place as highly valued as Mecca was in early world history. This is an insider poem, but it allows any outsider who can read English to enter it at a certain level.

In the chapter, "Re-Membering the Marooned Consciousness" of the critical work *Defining Jamaican Fiction: Marronage and the Discourse of Survival*, Barbara Lalla writes of the "secret encoding of Creole epistemes under guise of conformity (and with all the advantages of international 'legibility')" and labels it "the most subtle of the linguistic transgressions that constitute the verbal dimension of marronage."[18] This is one way of describing the doublespeak that is contained throughout this particular Goodison poem:

> "To us, all flowers are ROses"
> "To us all flowers are roSES"

The stress in the first version falls on the first syllable of the word "roses," giving it a Jamaican English pronunciation. In the second version, it falls on the second syllable giving it a Jamaican Creole pronunciation.

Jennifer Rahim, discussing representations of the tropics in Senior's *Gardening in the Tropics* and Goodison's *To Us, All Flowers Are Roses,* writes: "The idea that Caribbean poetry is an enterprise of the recovery and, therefore the re-presentation of the people and the spaces they inhabit, remain pertinent given the ongoing dialogue of Caribbean literature with history and identity."[19]

It is in this kind of manipulation of language that the cause to which Rahim refers, is most effectively served.

Notes

1. Merle Hodge, *Crick Crack, Monkey* (London: André Deutsch, 1970).

2. Olive Senior, *Talking of Trees* (Kingston, Jamaica: Calabash Publishers, 1985), 26.

3. Lorna Goodison, *To Us, All Flowers Are Roses* (Urbana: University of Illinois Press, 1995).

4. Velma Pollard, *Considering Woman* (London: Women's Press, 1989).

5. Lorna Goodison, *Heartease* (London: New Beacon Books, 1988), 48.

6. Lorna Goodison, *Tamarind Season* (Kingston: Institute of Jamaica, 1980); *Selected Poems* (Ann Arbor: University of Michigan Press, 1992); and note Velma Pollard, "Mothertongue Voices in the Writing of Olive Senior and Lorna Goodison," chapter 14 of this volume.

7. Senior, "City Poem," *Talking of Trees*, 65.

8. Senior, "City Poem," 66.

9. Olive Senior, *Gardening in the Tropics* (Toronto: McClelland and Stewart, 1994), 15.

10. Goodison, "To Us, All Flowers Are Roses," in *To Us, All Flowers Are Roses,* 69.

11. Ibid., 70.

12. See, for example, Pamela Mordecai, "Wooing with Words: Some Comments on the Poetry of Lorna Goodison," *Jamaica Journal* 45 (1981): 38–40; Edward Baugh, "Goodison on the Road to Heartease," *Journal of West Indian Literature* 1, no. 1 (1986): 13–26; J. Edward Chamberlin, *Come Back to Me My Language: Poetry and the West Indies* (Toronto: McClelland and Stewart, 1993).

13. Lorna Goodison, *I Am Becoming My Mother* (London: New Beacon Books, 1986).

14. Goodison, "My Will," in *I Am Becoming My Mother,* 19.

15. Goodison, "To Us, All Flowers Are Roses," 69.

16. Ibid., 70–71.

17. Ibid., 71.

18. Barbara Lalla, *Defining Jamaican Fiction: Marronage and the Discourse of Survival* (Tuscaloosa: University of Alabama Press, 1996).

19. Jennifer Rahim, "From Archaeology to Iconography: The Tropics in Senior's *Gardening in the Tropics* and Goodison's *To Us, All Flowers Are Roses,*" *Journal of West Indian Literature* 8, no. 2 (1999): 69.

5
Creole and Respec'
Authority and Identity in the Development of Caribbean Literary Discourse

Barbara Lalla

Recognition, acceptability, and prestige of a language are closely associated with (indeed consequent on) its distinctiveness, on recognizable norms associated with it, on its standardization, and on the social status of its users.[1] The inclusion of Caribbean Creole in Anglophone Caribbean literature, described in chapter 2, has affected the growth of the literature in varied and often contradictory ways. In the evolution of a Caribbean literary canon and of the national literatures this canon includes, Creole language has been profoundly significant in authenticating Caribbeanness. In this intertwined literary and linguistic history, the Creole voice authorizes the literary text even as literary use elevates the social standing of Creole.

In the first place, distinctiveness—pivotal as it is to recognition of a discourse—has been at least to some extent at issue on the level of general language awareness in the Anglophone Caribbean. To begin with, much of the vocabulary of this Creole is derived from English. Then, our writers' employment of extensive code-shifting and widespread use of intermediate forms problematize (for the nonlinguist) sharp distinctions between Creole and English. The fact that Creole is rendered through English orthographical practices further blurs distinctiveness. The relation between scribal representation of Anglophone Creole language and the language itself is fraught not only with the inexact fit between English and its own archaic orthography but also with the awkwardness of orthography carried over from the language for which it was developed to another language of quite different phonological structure. More than this, the orthography must represent a range of varieties between the two. Under these circumstances, the spelling system worked out by F. G. Cassidy, based on Jamaican Creole phonemes, is not applicable to Jamaican language (Jamaican) across the continuum.[2]

Pauline Christie points out the persistence, even among linguists, in stereotyping Creole "as an entity distinct from another entity . . . not withstanding the linguistic complexity which is the reality."[3] Perhaps this stereotyping relates to the concern, evident from the 1960s, to establish Creoles as autonomous structures. Yet the experience of speakers runs counter to this insistence on boundaries. Winer points out how difficult it often is for Creole speakers "to determine the exact boundaries between Creole and English, and between different varieties and registers of metropolitan English,"[4] and she goes on to argue a link between the haziness of such distinctions on the one hand, and on distorted comprehension of Creole texts by English readers on the other.

The degree to which Jamaican and English are linguistically distinct continues to vary today in the perception of readers and perhaps of writers. Prescriptivity favors Standard English, and Creole maintains its nonofficial status, but the growing recognition of Caribbean culture privileges and even favors Creole as the popular medium. Meanwhile, the tendency to select intermediate forms for literary representation, together with growing freedom to code-shift in an increasing range of social contexts, increases general ambivalence about distinctiveness.

Like distinctiveness, norms contribute significantly to the prestige of a language, and the extent to which norms exist and are recognized in Caribbean discourse relates to the extent of acceptance and respect accorded to the language. The establishment of norms is a fundamental issue in lexicographical decisions such as Allsopp discusses: "What is the right/wrong *national* way to speak? May local or regional usage be *formally* written? By what criteria is *acceptability* judged, and acceptability to whom—Britain, North America, the 'international' community, other Caribbean states, teachers?"[5]

This concept of norms is particularly important to literary representation, and lexicographical work often provides a reference point for providing such norms. As distinct from Cassidy and Le Page, whose work on lexicography reaches into every area and level of Jamaican speech, Allsopp confines his collection to usage in upper and intermediate speech, to norms in a version of English rather than of Creole. In the Caribbean, discussion of norms even by a Caribbean lexicographer relates essentially to English.[6] Nevertheless, written documentation of the Creole contributes to a sense of the normative in the Creole. As Creole discourse becomes familiar in writing, associated language attitudes grow increasingly contradictory. Departures from the norms of English, often (though not always) in the direction of Creole, are an important subject of complaint in Caribbean metadiscourse. Milroy and Milroy have pointed out the importance of language complaints in maintaining Standard English, noting the connection between attacks on points of usage to (often increasingly implied) superiority of one language system over another.[7] At the same time, in Caribbean literature, such evaluations exist in tension with the Creole's function as a mechanism for resistance.

The specifically Caribbean language that is represented in literature often approximates to Creole and is recognized as Creole even if the language is not closely rendered and even though Anglophone Creole such as Jamaican has no official writing system. Mühleisen discusses *concepts* of Creole and traces a diachronic development in Creole writing from "representing authenticity" in the 1930s to "expressing authority" in the 1980s. She does this by examining changing functions of Creole in writing and relating this to the politics of encoding the Creole.[8] This politics of encoding Creole occupies Carolyn Cooper as she distinguishes what she describes as *chaka-chaka* spelling from *Misa Cassidy spelin* and favors the latter.[9] Creative writers, however, continue to work out their individual orthographies (*chaka chaka*), and I would argue that their selective encoding facilitates plurality of meaning. The system that better demonstrates autonomy (*Misa Cassidy*) denies the ongoing contention between discourses.

Mühleisen identifies English orthography as a particularly problematic choice, as far as Creole autonomy is concerned, for it reinforces the perception of Creole as, merely, deviant English.[10] Also, written Creole being unfamiliar, it distances the reader even though the use of the Creole signals intimacy. Thus, written Creole embodies contradiction. Because "real language" is popularly associated with a standard written form and thus with uniformity and homogeneity, written Creole conveys a contention with homogeneity. It textualizes hybridity, *especially* in utilizing English orthography. Creole use of English orthography sets up a dialectic between similarity and contrast and underscores the contention between imperial and counterdiscourse. Indeed, *chaka-chaka* does not deny Creole prestige, because a dimension of the literary empowerment of Creole is the ongoing acknowledgment of resistance conveyed in the contending linguistic systems.

Closely connected with language norms is standardization, a further index of prestige. The unstandardized condition of the Creole highlights the region's plurality—a plurality demonstrated even within the Caribbean English whose norms Allsopp documents in recording allonyms. Such regional variation, which actually characterizes every linguistic level, emerges even more definitively in literature where Creole is represented. An author needs to consider, quite deeply, a number of orthographical considerations related to the advantages of adhering to or departing from English or any other "prescribed" and uniform system of spelling.

As it happens, Creole is now represented more systematically than hitherto, which brings stability to pieces of individual writing (like the extract from Velma Pollard's *Considering Woman*, examined in chapter 2), rather than to a Creole orthography generally. Despite linguistic research and painstaking orthographical analysis, the Creole language remains uncodified—its written representation essentially a matter of choice. Creole continues to be represented rather than transcribed in creative writing, within the constraints I have outlined elsewhere.[11] Because it increasingly appears or is signaled in literature, it has also grown in prestige even without any widely utilized formal system of instrumentalization. In not only coexisting with English but also interacting with it, however, Creole language in literature challenges the very concept of linguistic superiority—it takes a hoe to the root of language prestige.

At the same time, the very stereotype of Creole as oral is exploited in literary discourse. The cultural achievements of our oral performers have been internationally recognized, contributing to the rising prestige of Creole. Reinforcing this rise in prestige, Creole participates more and more in literary discourse, but undermining all this is the fact that Creole continues to convey orality. Decades ago, in examining typical characteristics of prestige languages, Henry Kahane gathered these under two main headings—sociopolitical constellation and linguistic impact.[12] Current evaluation, however, distinguishes the overt prestige that such languages lack from the "extremely strong covert prestige" to which they owe their survival despite being highly stigmatized.[13]

In the long run, language prestige is heavily dependent not only on such criteria as distinctiveness, norms, and standardization but also on perceptions of status associated with the users of the language. While Creole has minority language status in relation to an international language, there is growing acknowledgment and insistence on the obvious fact that Creole speakers have majority status within the region. More importantly, language attitudes to Creole as a part of literary discourse are affected by how Caribbean writers themselves are perceived. Devonish has pointed out that bilingual writers who address audiences comprising both bilingual and monolingual (English) readers are the technologists of this Caribbean literary discourse and that such bilingualism has implications for the form of Creole in the literary discourse.[14] It is these bilingual writers who filter Creole marking in the discourse, and the producers of Caribbean literary discourse have overwhelmingly been writers of the scholar/artist type.

Characteristically, and perhaps inevitably, this scholar/artist type (often university professors who are linguists, literary critics, teachers of creative writing, researchers in cultural history, and so on) becomes more and more occupied with metadiscursive consideration of language as craft and with the persona of the poet as craftsman. For example, "The Carpenter's Complaint" by Edward Baugh (poet; critic; Campus Orator and professor emeritus of English, University of the West Indies, Mona) is about respect. In Creole, as represented scribally, the carpenter demands respect for his craft, and the poem is in this sense at least metaphorically metadiscursive. The poem voices the righteous indignation of a builder who is denied recognition:

But bless mi days!
Good enough to build the house that him live in,
But not good enough to make him coffin![15]

The network between members of this scholar/artist group is relatively dense, and this web of interaction reinforces a growing sense of Caribbean literary discourse as imbued with its own history, as shared by a Caribbean discourse community (even more tightly defined than the group Mühleisen envisages as a discourse community in her 2002 study).

By reference to such parameters as are discussed in chapter 2, Caribbean literary discourse can be tracked through developmental stages to its current prominence as a literature that has attracted recognition and acclaim on a global scale. At the same time, it is essential to acknowledge that, like most types of literary and linguistic periodization, the developmental phases sketched earlier in this volume are generalizations that do not link into a single or straight chain.

This is particularly true when we relate the developments in Jamaican to their regional context. We can never afford to underestimate the distinctions between national varieties and the complexity of *regional* representation. The chronological and geographical intricacies of development in representation are apparent in that curious version of the travel narrative that occurs in Naipaul's discourse where Jamaican is represented by the Trinidadian author. *The Middle Passage,* like nineteenth-century British literature set in the Caribbean, draws on limited features to signal Jamaican speech. Naipaul chooses #h- as a major representative of Jamaican Creole, in which #h- is actually associated with self-consciousness: "Whenever they was in hany real trouble I used to tell them, 'Boy, your only hope is to start bawling colour prejudice.'" Later the same character continues, "They push me hup to a place in Scotland. Not one black man in the place."[16] Another character remarks, "They have no thought for us, down in the dust and hashes."[17]

We cannot write off this limited selection of Jamaican characteristics as imprecise representation. On the contrary, the speakers are characters who are unlikely to be basilectal to begin with and who are adjusting their register to impress, as Jamaican #h often suggests. On the other hand, Naipaul gives greater coverage to characteristics of Trinidadian Creole, especially representing Trinidadian through tense/aspect:

> I wondered why he had given up his job to go to England.
>
> "Look, eh," he said. "I ask God, you hear. I went down on my two knees and ask God. And I always do what God tell me. Don't mind the

> Jamaicans gone and stink up England. I bound to get through. Morning and evening I does go down on my two knees and consult God."[18]

Even taking into account language differences associated with the construction of various characters, it appears that Naipaul more closely represents Trinidadian speech—which is hardly surprising. Caribbean writers do not appear to cross territorial boundaries with much greater ease than the ease with which British writers represent Caribbean speech—a consideration to be borne in mind when discussing regional discourse or a Caribbean discourse community. In *The Lonely Londoners,*[19] Selvon's Trindadian character, Moses, says, "You send for she?" but (in the same conversation) the Jamaican, Tolroy, says "I [not *me*] will see him tomorrow." Jamaican *me* (subject) being more basilectal that Trinidadian *she* (object), one might posit that the discourse is mesolectal in both cases. However, there are many other such contrasts, Jamaican speech being, for the most part, represented by characteristics shared with Trinidadian, as in "The boat-train come yet?" Indeed, the speech of Selvon's Jamaican characters displays Trinidadian features like Habitual *does:* "He say that I does encourage other men home."[20]

While distinctions between our regional varieties may be insignificant to non-Creole readers, Creole readers (the very ones who comprise what we might identify as the regional discourse community) readily distinguish the characteristics unfamiliar in the variety of Anglophone Creole of their own territory. As representational Creole discourse grows in quantum and accuracy, the complexities of social and regional variation increasingly problematize assessments of how close Creole representation is to Caribbean discourse. The comparison lies not only between orthography and phonology in a specific variety of Anglophone Creole but also between the orthography and phonology of its different varieties, between the orthography and phonology of codes and their intermediate varieties along the continuum in any one territory, and between approaches to representation by different writers. After all, actual Caribbean discourse must be a specific national variety further distinguished by such differences as, say, those between Trinidadian and Tobagonian, or those between Indo-Trinidadian and Afro-Trinidadian.

A dialectic of national versus regional discourse is relevant to language awareness and language attitudes in current use of Creole in literary discourse that engages increasing numbers of writers and readers. Additionally, the heterogeneous discourse in which Creole participates has developed an international readership. Vitality constitutes yet another dimension of language prestige, and vitality is associated with the number of users (in this case, both writers and readers). The vitality of our literature globally has enhanced its prestige and contributed to literary canonization. The development of the Caribbean literary canon can be argued on the basis of this literature's inclusion in the education system, and on recognition at the highest level of achievement—for example, through international awards. At the same time, interaction with English has been problematized by growing awareness of the distinctiveness of Caribbean Anglophone Creole. Increasing sensitivity to norms has intensified arguments regarding orthographical representation even as widening recognition of high-profile users of Creole has encouraged positive attitudes to its representation in Caribbean literature and increased the currency of this discourse in a global context.

With such adjustments in language attitudes, the Caribbean voice carries increasing authority; yet the importance of authenticity has intensified. I largely support Mühleisen's observation of a diachronic development in Creole in the direction of increasing authority—with one caveat. Mühleisen proposes a shift from emphasis on authenticity to emphasis on authority as motivating Creole in writing. However, the very shift in ideological perspective that relocates the Caribbean voice to the center rather than the periphery of power not only supports an increase in authority but increases the likelihood and importance of authenticity. Christian Mair notes that, with increasing global dominance, English becomes more heterogeneous and its varieties decreasingly tied to their original territories and increasingly subject to the influence of the multilingual settings in which they find themselves, viewed within the patterns of cultural flow described by Arjun Appadurai, and more specifically the global linguistic flows recognized by H. Sammy Alim et al.[21] Mary Bucholtz points out that recent frameworks from the acts of identity model of Le Page and Tabouret-Keller to the relational approach to identity put forward by Coupland move away from traditional understandings of the authentic speaker to the often unexpected identities. These identities, Bucholtz points out, emerge "from temporary and mutable interactional conditions, in negotiation and often contestation with other social actors and in relation to larger and often unyielding structures of power."[22] In the current (expansion) phase, authenticity entails accuracy in representation[23] even as a sense of the multilingual Caribbean becomes increasingly essential to authenticity. Nevertheless, such plurality in representation of the Caribbean voice does not always seem consistent with autonomy.

Central to the authentic Caribbean voice is a dissonance that reflects the complexity of Caribbean identity. Studies on identity now suggest not so much a conscious, unified individual identity (of Cartesian conception) but the mutually constituting social and individual identity discerned by Stuart Hall,[24] and, indeed, a fragmented or decentered self comprising multiple, shifting, and, at times, contradictory identities. Authenticity in Caribbean literary discourse must account for hybridity as well as for persistent plurality,[25] and plurality (consistent with autonomy or not) cannot be extricated from the politics of Caribbean discourse where identity is undergoing construction by a fractured but resilient psyche.

Because discourse is a site not only of interaction but of power struggle, Caribbean literary discourse cannot be conceived as homogeneous, as *essentially Creole,* without falling into the traditional and stereotypical view of identity as unitary and cohesive. Similarly, current concepts of identity, as multiple, fluid, collective, and even conflictual, interrogate established concepts of authenticity, autonomy, and authority. Indeed, investigations of code-switching in the emerging area of sociocultural linguistics raise issues regarding the degree to which the situation determines the linguistic choice or is itself constructed through discourse as code-switching signals changes in context.[26] Side by side with the significance of the Creole in literary discourse for identity, the ongoing role of Creole as a medium for resistance complicates the concept of autonomy and destabilizes the concept of language prestige itself even as we may try to apply it to the Creole.

Thus, ambivalence—regarding distinctiveness of code and politically fraught choices in representation—blurs the issue of autonomy. Contradiction surrounding the emergence of norms and the value of Creole in signaling resistance suggest ambivalence regarding prestige itself. Simultaneously authoritative yet disobedient, the Creole in the literary discourse both manifests and resists language prestige in conveying the multiple and dissonant dimensions of Caribbean identity.

Notes

1. The dimensions of prestige have been identified by William Stewart ("A Sociolinguistic Typology of Multilingualism," in *Readings on the Sociology of Language,* ed. Joshua Fishman [The Hague: Mouton, 1968], 531–545); and refined by C. Eersel, "Prestige in Choice of Language and Linguistic Form," in *Pidginization and Creolization of Languages,* ed. Dell Hymes (Cambridge: Cambridge University Press, 1971), 141–150; and others, notably, recently, Susanne Mühleisen, who analyzes the dimensions of language prestige in a diachronic framework. I embrace Mühleisen's understanding of prestige, which approaches language status, function, and attitudes not only as dimensions of sociocultural conditions but also as dimensions of dynamic development and catalyzing force. See Susanne Mühleisen, *Creole Discourse: Exploring Prestige Formation and Change across Caribbean English-Lexicon Creoles* (Amsterdam: John Benjamins, 2002), 25.

2. F. G. Cassidy and Robert Le Page, *Dictionary of Jamaican English,* 2nd ed.(Cambridge: Cambridge University Press, 1980).

3. Pauline Christie, "Forty Years On," in *Due Respect: Papers in English and En-*

glish Related Creoles in the Caribbean in Honour of Professor Robert Le Page, ed. Pauline Christie (Kingston, Jamaica: University of the West Indies Press, 2001), 24–36.

4. Lise Winer, "Comprehension and Resonance: English Readers and English Creole Texts," in *Creole Genesis, Attitudes and Discourse: Studies Celebrating Charlene J. Sato,* ed. John Rickford and Suzanne Romaine (Amsterdam: John Benjamins, 1999; Kingston, Jamaica: University of the West Indies Press, 1999), 393.

5. Richard Allsopp, *Dictionary of Caribbean English Usage* (Oxford: Oxford University Press, 1996), xix; Renate Bartsch, *Norms of Language: Theoretical and Practical Aspects* (London: Longman, 1987).

6. Discussion of normalization in Creole languages focuses, for example, on ways in which children have contributed to normalization in formative stages of these languages, rather than on the development of Creole normativity versus that of the official European language. See, for example, Salikoko Mufwene, "What Do Pidgins and Creoles Tell Us about the Evolution of Language?," in *The Origin and Evolution of Languages: Approaches, Models, Paradigms,* ed. Bernard Laks, Serge Cleuziou, Jean-Paul Demoule, and Pierre Encrevé (London: Equinox, 2008), 272–297.

7. James Milroy and Leslie Milroy, *Authority in Language: Investigating Language Prescription and Standardization* (London: Routledge and Kegan Paul, 1988), 36–40.

8. Mühleisen, *Creole Discourse,* 198.

9. Carolyn Cooper, "Britain no Want Join di EU fi true," *Jamaica Observer,* November 15, 1996; Carolyn Cooper and Hubert Devonish, "A Tale of Two States: Language, Lit/orature and the Two Jamaicas," in *The Pressures of the Text: Orality, Texts and the Telling of Tales,* ed. Stewart Brown, African Studies Series 4 (Birmingham, England: Center of West African Studies, 1995), 60–74.

10. Mühleisen, *Creole Discourse,* 189.

11. Barbara Lalla, "Virtual Realism and the Inscriber's Dilemma: Representing the Caribbean Voice" (Occasional Paper 32, Society for Caribbean Linguistics, University of the West Indies, St. Augustine, Trinidad and Tobago, 2005).

12. Henry Kahane, "A Typology of the Prestige Language," *Language* 62, no. 3 (September 1986): 495–508.

13. Peter Auer and Jürgen Erich Schmidt, eds., *Language and Space: An International Handbook of Linguistic Variation: Theories and Message* (Berlin: Walter de Gruyter, 2010), 443, 445.

14. Hubert Devonish, "Vernacular Languages and Writing Technology Transfer: The Jamaican Case," in *Caribbean Language Issues Old and New: Papers in Honour of Professor Mervyn Alleyne,* ed. Pauline Christie (Kingston, Jamaica: University of the West Indies Press, 1996), 101–111. Alice Wassinka's study of about the same time as Devonish's article reports ambivalent attitudes even at the end of the last century, but traces substantial change from traditional responses, "Historic Low Prestige and Seeds of Change," *Language in Society* 28 (1999): 57–92.

15. Edward Baugh, *It Was the Singing,* Toronto: Sandberry Press, 2000, 87.

16. V. S. Naipaul, *The Middle Passage* (1962; repr., Harmondsworth, Middlesex: Penguin, 1969), 245.

17. Ibid., 246.

18. Ibid., 29.

19. Samuel Selvon, *The Lonely Londoners,* Caribbean Writers Series (Burnt Mill, England: Longman, 1956), 26.

20. Ibid., 69.

21. Christian Mair, "World Non-Standard Englishes: Reflections on the Global Spread of (Some) Vernacular Varieties of English" (presentation, International Society for the Linguistics of English, College of Arts and Sciences, Boston University, Boston, Massachusetts, June 17–21, 2011); Arjun Appadurai, *Modernity at Large: Cultural Dimensions of Globalization* (Minneapolis: University of Minnesota Press, 1996); H. Sammy Alim, Awad Ibrahim, and Alastair Pennycook, eds., *Global Linguistic Flows: Hip Hop Cultures, Youth Identities, and the Politics of Language* (New York: Routledge, 2009).

22. Mary Bucholtz, "Sociolinguistic Nostalgia and the Authentification of Identity," *Journal of Sociolinguistics* 7, no. 3 (2003): 398–416; Robert B. Le Page and Andrée Tabouret-Keller, *Acts of Identity: Creole-Based Approaches to Language and Ethnicity* (Cambridge: Cambridge University Press, 1985); Nikolas Coupland, Srikant Sarangi, and Christopher N. Candlin, eds., *Sociolinguistics and Social Theory* (Harlow, England: Pearson, 2001).

23. See Lalla, "Virtual Realism."

24. Stuart Hall, D. Held, and T. McGrew, eds., *Modernity and Its Futures* (Cambridge: Polity Press, 1992), 277.

25. See Shalini Puri's interventions regarding obsessions with hybridity that marginalize surviving cultures that persist alongside the hybridized forms, *The Caribbean Post-Colonial: Social Equality, Post-Nationalism and Social Hybridity* (New York: Palgrave Macmillan, 2004).

26. See Mary Bucholtz and Kira Hall, "Identity and Interaction: A Sociocultural Linguistic Approach," *Discourse Studies* 7 (2005): 4–5; Chad Nilep, "'Code Switching' in Sociocultural Linguistics," *Colorado Research in Linguistics* 19 (2006), 1–22. Compare also Marcelo Dascal and Chris Barker, "Identities in Flux: Arabs and Jews in Israel," in *Critical Discourse Analysis: Theory and Interdisciplinarity*, ed. Gilbert Weiss and Ruth Wodak (Houndsmill, England: Palgrave, 2003), 157.

II
LANGUAGE AND AND DISCOURSE IN CARIBBEAN LITERARY TEXTS

6
Bra Rabbit Meets Peter Rabbit

Genre, Audience, and the Artistic Imagination—Problems in Writing Children's Fiction

Jean D'Costa

Every culture produces literary genres that serve culture-specific purposes. This function is a given, an obvious cliché. Genres pass from culture to culture, are modified, absorbed, and reabsorbed. Such transference is also cliché, a given. Certain kinds of transference and absorption, however, produce a unique pattern of acceptance and adaptation. In these transactions, the peculiar nature of genre to control the expectations of the audience and the audience's complementary hunger for the security of genre may precipitate insecurity, confusion, experimentation, and finally, the emergence of new-made art forms.

In the meeting of Peter Rabbit and Bra Rabbit (or his Caribbean equivalent, the spider-hero and trickster Anancy)—a meeting that is still in session—one may explore the demands genre makes of the would-be fiction writer who has listened closely to both voices. The writer's tensions echo those of the audience, which in this instance includes any Caribbean child who goes to school, who listens to the radio and watches television, and who responds to the languages of the media and of black culture. Indeed, as Graham Greene suggests, "Perhaps it is only in childhood that books have any deep influence on our lives. In later life we admire, we are entertained, we may modify some views we already hold, but we are more likely to find in books merely a confirmation of what is in our minds already. But in childhood all books are books of divination, telling us about the future, and like the fortune teller who sees a long journey in the cards or death by water they influence the future."[1]

As a writer, I have been aware of the difficulties of moving between the languages that represent the worlds of Anancy, of *Little Women*, or of the TV series *Dallas* (which ran from 1978 to 1991). It is only in recent time that the gravitational pull of genre has made me realize that, for example, a science fiction tale set in Jamaica creates conflicts between plot and characters: rockets and reggae? Rastas in space suits? The maker's imagination seems poised between two irreconcilable worlds. Yet the truth is that writer and audience make use of the genres, languages, and history of the different worlds, a living, expanding process clearly revealed in the multicultural science fiction of Nalo Hopkinson[2] and explored at length in chapter 15. Migrations and mixing create and continue these slow but endless processes. Bra Rabbit was destined to meet Peter Rabbit.

The Historical Context

The colonial migrations from Africa and Europe into the supposedly empty spaces of the Western Hemisphere produced first a seeming silence, then a division (on one hand) into the "high" culture of print and simultaneously (on the other hand) into the "low" oral tradition of an underclass. The slaves and indentured servants created a folklore that preserved forms other than those of the "high" culture, forged new types (the Jamaican Anancy story), and influenced the "high," imitative level, first decoratively and then profoundly.

During the early period of apparent silence, the colonial world produced no printed literature even where printing presses existed. Jamaica in the nineteenth century boasted several newspapers with a respectable standard of literary style. The presses turned out pamphlets and the occasional volume of prints or studies of local scenes but no novels, poems, or plays. Such texts came only from the metropolitan world. No one expected to find anything comparable to Jane Austen or Charles Dickens in a colonial capital. No one expected a Jane or a Charles to be born in such a place, but in the period of silence, our creative artists absorbed the tales told around them, the graphic, vulgar songs heard on street and back veranda, and the stories in books from abroad, that vast and mighty world to which the colonial imagination yearned—if it were literate in the language of that world.

In this group of literates we first see the meeting of "high" and "low" genres, which later produced the written literature of the new culture. Silent themselves, the literates of the nineteenth-century Sunday schools brought up a generation that rewarded its parents with earnest imitations of metropolitan literary forms: the fantasy school essay "A Day by the Seaside," satirized by Naipaul in *A House for Mr. Biswas,* finally comes true by the end of the novel when Mr. Biswas's son becomes a part of the middle-class, metropolitan world of picnic hampers and cars, in which parents are called "Daddy" and "Mummy."[3]

In the period of imitation characterized by Mr. Biswas, the reader versed in the high culture may become the aspiring writer of a new fiction. This new writer must contend with a generic conditioning that affects the narrative voice; the moral argument; the gestures and behavior of characters; the interplay of action, characters, and setting; and (most obviously) the nature of the language. Here we find the creators of such early twentieth-century works as *The White*

Witch of Rosehall and *Under the Skin,* both sensationalist romantic adventures full of derivative postures.[4]

Here, too, we find those Caribbean voices that assert the necessity of writing in Standard English, that claim the Creole languages are inadequate to express serious ideas, and that perceive only an artistic vacuum in the low culture, dismissing its depth, variety, and energy.

But the writer who succeeds the imitator suddenly seems to bend all inherited genres into new shapes: Derek Walcott fuses oral folktale, choric verse drama, and the morality play to produce *Ti Jean*. In writers such as Louise Bennett, "the comedy contains the tragedy and even overpowers it in complex forms of expression."[5] Jean Rhys takes gossip, voice, and viewpoint to extraordinary lengths to fashion a new form: the multiple first-person narratives in *Wide Sargasso Sea* that make up the account of the first Mrs. Rochester have no precedent other than the necessity of a new sensibility and imagination.

Genre as a Way of Seeing and Acting

Let us look briefly at some of the provisions a genre offers to a maker. In the oral tradition of Old English heroic verse, the maker benefits not only from the inherited accounts of tribal victory and disaster but from the "word hoard" of previous makers. The proper gestures for greeting a victorious thane, for mourning a kinsman at the funeral pyre, and for sharing drink in the mead hall stand out in the poetry of the Anglo-Saxons and form its characteristic diction and imagery. In the same way, the Anancy story offers the gestures proper to the tricking of an opponent, the wooing of a lady, and the adoption of disguise. It also offers characteristic diction and imagery: what is derogatorily described as Anancy's lisping "bungo" talk marks him as a uniquely Caribbean figure.[6]

Even the endings of the heroic poem and the Anancy tale are highly formulaic in language and in dramatic outcome: the Old English poem ends with a moral summing up of the outcome of the war play, celebrates the doomed who fell in the place of slaughter, and commends their names and deeds to the lips of those who shall come after, who shall sing their praise. The "Jack Mandora me no choose none" distances narrator and audience from Anancy's lies, tricks, and unscrupulous self-interest. His survival requires no celebration beyond the fact of itself, a Caribbean miracle. Patterns of events, gestures, moral commentaries, and character types constitute distinctive genres. It is hard to imagine what the interaction of these very different genres would be, once they have come into contact. I have chosen the examples to point up the role of genre in the history of a people as well as to show how the model of tale or heroic lay becomes a self-perpetuating force, drawing the maker's imagination toward the world it portrays.

The Making of the Writer

In the Caribbean situation, the writer deals with the demands of genre both privately, within her imagination, and publicly, within the expectations of the audience. A great change in the nature of the colonial imagination occurred when the artist began to see herself and her group as her primary audience; at this stage, the new imagination separates itself from the colonial bond. It is no accident that large metropolitan publishers have set up offices in places like Jamaica and Trinidad within the lifetime of Rhys and Walcott. It is also significant that the greatest stock-in-trade of these publishers consists of school texts and children's books. The new writer is the child of the reading audience, one who heeds the call of the low tradition while practicing the high.

The making of a writer derives from the making of a reader. In the genre of children's literature, generic influence from the literary, high culture may well be stronger, more conservative, and more pervasive in the audience than is the case in adult genres. Education and literacy exert a strong influence on the meeting of low and high literature, or, to be more exact, on the meeting of oral and printed literature in a Caribbean Creole culture. For example, a child raised on oral folktale in which the hero is a cunning, duplicitous, amoral survivor (Anancy/Bra Rabbit) meets in school and in the public library the heroes and heroines of the metropolitan, high culture: Little Red Riding Hood, Peter Rabbit, the Bobbsey twins, Lassie, Alice, and later on the heroes of Roald Dahl, Kipling, and Jack London and the heroines of L. M. Montgomery, Judy Blume, and Frances Hodgson Burnett.

The influence of the latter group (the adventure stories for the ten-to-thirteen-year-old group) tends to be more intrusive than that of the folktale because such fiction becomes part of schooling and social mobility, whereas the printed folktales (Grimm, Andersen, and Perrault) have to compete directly with the local oral tradition and may form less of a classroom staple. I did, for example, read or hear European folktales at home along with Anancy stories; my peers at primary school heard a few of the European tales in school and, typically for a small rural community, heard none at home. Instead, these friends had a wider exposure to the local oral tradition and did not meet much fiction of the high culture until later in their schooling. Moreover, European folktales adapted into the Creole cycle change so much in form that even "Mr. Bluebeard" resembles the original only in the basic plot outline.[7]

Throughout colonial times, the beginning grades of primary school drew on the European tradition, using poems, tales, riddles, and songs that contrasted sharply with the oral tradition. Jamaican individualism (which can sometimes reach the level of a social behavior) has often been identified by Jamaicans themselves with the Anancy ethic of willful self-interest. The moral of the

Little Red Hen differs critically from that of Anancy stealing Bra Alligator's eggs, yet certain moral patterns do converge.

In the European folk fairy tale, some of the same generic patterns of survival and cunning exist: Jack (with his beanstalk), Ulysses, and Puss-in-Boots all use lies, deception, and tricks to survive, to prevail against terrible odds, and to win. But at the end of the Anancy story, unlike at the end of the European folk fairy tale, the hero's great triumph usually consists in staying alive. One step ahead of his adversaries, Anancy lives, but not "happily ever after." Instead, the *conteur* disclaims responsibility for the hero's behavior: "Jack Mandora, me no choose none."

In one of the few tales in which Anancy wins a king's daughter as wife (and the kingdom as well), the *conteur* ends: "Anancy is the wickedest King ever reign. Sometime him dere, sometime him gone run 'pon him rope an tief cow fe him wife."[8] These generic actions symbolize both the literal spider and the magical spiderman: spiders get about by swinging on their webs, and Anancy gets about cunningly so as to mystify others, to rob and trick, and to enrich himself and his family.

The classic Anancy story stands indeed as a symbol for any lie, fantasy, trickery of words, or deception: "don tell me no Nancy 'tory," is a favorite command to anyone suspected of lying.

In contrast to the Anancy story, the Beatrix Potter story carries a different message expressed in different gestures. While defying human authority and power as exemplified by Mr. McGregor, Peter Rabbit lives within the authority and firm moral code of his parents. Like Anancy, the Beatrix Potter hero may act out of pure self-interest and greed; he may delight in killing and eating smaller creatures if he is Mr. Tod, and the narrator may grant him the right to do so. But the action remains framed in the safety of Edwardian middle-class childhood: being tucked in bed, having tea, going shopping, and being rescued by one's parents. All the action covertly leads toward the happy ending celebrated in Victorian children's literature passed on to the Caribbean child audience.

One need not go much farther to see that the genre represented by Anancy and that practiced by Beatrix Potter do not fit well together. Even though many of Potter's characters and plots show the triumph of the weak over the strong and the joyous amorality of gratification, her writing expresses a world that *acts* differently from that in which Anancy thrives. The worlds of Potter and of *King Lear* are essentially one. The children's writer prepares the sensibility which, at the adult stage, will comprehend M. Poirot, Lady Macbeth, and Eliza Doolittle. Writing on Beatrix Potter, Graham Greene makes the point, perceptively and deliciously, when he classifies her works under such titles as "the great comedies" and "the great near-tragedies."[9] Peter Rabbit and his cousin

Benjamin Bunny belong with the "great (paired) characters of history" such as "Quixote and Sancha." The challenge to the writer of Caribbean children's fiction lies in the creation of a world that will prepare the young Caribbean mind for Antoinette Cosway and Lady Macbeth; for J. R. Ewing and Anancy; and for Bob Marley, Dylan Thomas, and Lewis Thomas.

In large part, the differences between these genres emerge in the ability of language to summon up assumptions, moral attitudes, and cultural associations that frame any single text. The fusion of differing linguistic and generic codes thus becomes the primary challenge to the new writer.

Every literary genre belongs within a code of language usage. The narrator operates within that code, and the audience expects the code. Not to hear Jamaican Creole in an Anancy story disappoints the audience and thins the effect of the telling or reading. The hero speaks in "bungo talk," through his nose, and must do so to remain in character, just as he must also "work his head" to exploit those around him.

On the other hand, Peter Rabbit's narrator can tell the audience that "lettuce is very soporific" and get away with it. On the page facing this statement the audience sees Peter fast asleep in Mr. McGregor's garden, in great danger of capture and death. In the folktales of the Western Hemisphere, Bra Anancy and Bra Rabbit define themselves by language type as well as by language behavior: they can speak the high form if they need to, but using it forms part of their deceptions and cunning.

If every genre carries with it a unique diction, plot, narrative, and characterization, then the audience brought up on dissimilar genres and conflicting cultural assumptions must contend with the mixed signals reaching it from different sources. The old solution lay in supposedly denying the low genre in favor of the high. I say "supposedly," for Caribbean audiences have remained consistently attached to the low genres in spite of the efforts of generations of teachers and cultural missionaries. But this attachment has not prevented the "divided child" of Derek Walcott's *Another Life* from feeling a deep uncertainty when confronted with what it believed to be a choice between the high and the low.

I can make the situation plainer by referring to my own work as a divided child and a new writer. I was brought up in both traditions, and my pleasure in Anancy stories and local folktale was as acute as my appetite of English adventure stories. When I began to consider writing, my ambition focused on the pleasure and entertainment I had found in these literary worlds. I wanted to entertain and console other children of my own world: a literate and bilingual Jamaican world. But I also hoped that my work could slip into oral lore by the agency of tellers, dramatizers, and the friend who reads aloud.

To reach this audience, the tale or story would have to capture the generic expectations of an audience keyed to the voice of Anancy as well as that of Peter Rabbit. Its plot and gestures would have to reflect a Jamaican worldview, if not a Jamaican reality (the two are not the same).

How easy it would have been in the writing of *Sprat Morrison* to have lapsed into the code of the English school story. And how impossible. Sprat must live in terror of the common entrance exam, he must jostle for patties in the schoolyard, and he must carry his mother's market basket, and even though he goes to the beach for an outing, he goes as a Jamaican lower-middle-class child might: in a broken-down car patched together by his father.

As a maker of fiction, I have become very aware of how strong are the dictates of a culture in the shaping of a story. None of my novels could have come into being without the social setting that shapes them. Instead of being silenced by the existence of the high and low traditions, I rely on both to provide my material and direction. For example, Jamaican ghost stories and family lore play an important part in *Voice in the Wind*. In this novel, the plot and diction mirror the behavior and life histories of a Jamaican social type, the poor but respectable farm family of the early and mid-twentieth century. As I have been tempted by other genres, such as fantasy science fiction, I have found my imagination fired as much by the possibilities of drawing on the low tradition as by the high.

Up to recently, however, a fantasy science fiction tale might have been expected to present extreme difficulties of a purely generic kind: what technology, for example, should underlie the central conceit of such a tale? Robots and rockets have no place in Jamaican life at present. Time travel might work. A past utopia would not, unless one wished to honor the Arawaks. Although certain genres present obvious difficulties, we would be making a great mistake to assume that the world of reality and of the imagination must remain unreconciled.

For a long time, the historical novel also seemed to present insuperable generic difficulties. The past was closed, dark, frightening, and shameful. Yet Vic Reid has been able to thrill a generation of children with his re-creations of the 1831 and 1865 uprisings in Jamaica.

Perhaps the most difficult problem for me lies in the moral imperative that invades children's fiction. All societies expect a certain didacticism in children's fiction even if they allow children the right to pleasure and delight. Because of the strength of the British tradition, the moral message it carries can easily penetrate Caribbean fiction. Assumptions of class slip in, even if one overcomes those of race. Only by staring the audience in the face can one make sure that the values expressed by the new work remain true to the world for which it is intended.

Yet in spite of the contradictions and tensions that these different genres create in me as reader and as writer, I have found that they allow for a wider range of narrative; for the creation of many more voices and characters; for much irony, satire, pathos, and excitement; and ultimately, for a long and happy meeting between some of my closest friends: Bra Tiger and Mr. Tod, the rolling-calf and the Wizard of Oz, the shark hunters of Montego Bay and the cowboys of Texas, Dickon of *The Secret Garden* and Anancy himself.

If the history of the Caribbean tells us anything, it is that in dire need we can create new language forms. It tells us that the will to survive cannot be destroyed. It tells us that the imagination works on "what is past, and passing, and to come" to shape new forms. Anancy becomes Uncle Time, no simple trickster but—in Dennis Scott's vision–

> a ole, ole man . . .
> All year long 'im wash 'im foot in de sea,
> long, lazy years on de wet san'
> an' shake de coconut tree dem
> quiet-like wid 'im sea-win' laughter
> scrapin' away de lan'[10]

In Olive Senior's poem "Nansi 'Tory,"[11] he becomes "somebody's grandfather" and "Heaven's doorkeeper" whose

> atomised
> heart on a
> beach
> reassemble[s]
>
> Awaiting
> Return

Notes

1. Graham Greene, *The Lost Childhood* (New York: Viking, 1952), 13.

2. The child of a Jamaican mother and the Guyanese poet Slade Hopkinson, Nalo Hopkinson grew up in Canada. Her works include *Brown Girl in the Ring* (New York: Grand Central Publishing; Warner Books, 1998) and *Midnight Robber* (New York: Warner, 2000).

3. V. S. Naipaul. *A House for Mr Biswas* (New York: Random House, 1984), 356–357, 440, 504.

4. Herbert G. de Lisser, *The White Witch of Rosehall* (1929; repr., Basingstoke, England: Macmillan Caribbean, 2007). *Under the Skin* is untraceable at present. Said to be a novel "by a Mico College man," and published in Kingston, Jamaica, ca. 1920, it

portrays a noble African woman who, in her homeland, saves the life of a white traveler. Later enslaved in America, the heroine gives her life for her "white sister," the betrothed of the same traveler. This much I recall from reading it many times between 1945 and 1950. Despite the ridiculous plot, I was much struck by the African heroine and the world portrayed.

5. Rex Nettleford's introduction to Louise Bennett, *Jamaica Labrish* (Kingston, Jamaica: Sangster's Bookstores, 1972), 15.

6. Anancy's language is actually archaic Creole. See Barbara Lalla, *Defining Jamaican Fiction: Marronage and the Discourse of Survival* (Tuscaloosa: University of Alabama Press, 1996), 196.

7. Walter Jekyll, *Jamaican Song and Story* (Kingston, Jamaica: Sangster's Bookstore, 1966), 35–37.

8. Jekyll, "Yung-Kyum-Pyung," in *Jamaican Song and Story,* 12.

9. Greene, *Lost Childhood,* 106–111.

10. Dennis Scott, *Uncle Time* (Pittsburgh, PA: Pittsburgh University Press, 1973), 32.

11. Olive Senior, *Talking of Trees* (Kingston, Jamaica: Calabash Publishers, 1985), 28.

7
"The Dust"
A Tribute to the Folk

Velma Pollard

Comment and criticism in Anglophone Caribbean literature in the last decade or so have established the Euro-tradition and to a lesser extent the Afro-tradition as the pervasive influences on the themes and forms of Caribbean poetry. Too little attention has been paid, however, to a third and eminently valid influence, derived from both of these yet essentially different from either, the "creole" or "folk" tradition; the tradition that accounts for the lifestyle and the way of seeing things peculiar to the people who form the bulk of our Caribbean populations. It represents their reaction to and their method of coming to terms with the events and circumstances conditioning their lives on this side of the Middle Passage. This is the tradition that has evolved out of the historical social and economic hodgepodge that has been the Caribbean situation. It has assumed a unique personality and has inevitably imposed on creative activity in the area, an influence that cannot be ignored, an influence that is becoming even more pervasive as our writing describes, with increasing candor, the different realities of our societies.

This chapter will look at one Caribbean poem, the now classical "The Dust,"[1] and will comment on it as a near-perfect expression of the life, music, and philosophy of the people who have been described as the "basis of culture; people who from the centre of an oppressive system have been able to survive, adapt, recreate; have devised means of protecting what has been so gained . . . and who begin to offer to return some of this experience and vision."[2] It is not possible to put off any longer the appraisal of our more "typical" works using a frame of reference that is peculiarly our own,[3] particularly when we dare to point the way for young readers. Matter, style, and music in this particular poem have all managed to sidestep the effect of our learned responses—the whole oppressive world of school and books–and emanate entirely from within the folk tradition. The result is a song, internally whole and as deceptively simple as the lifestyle of the people it portrays.

The time is evening; perhaps one of the favorite times of the "little" people, when the prescribed money-earning masks are discarded. The place is a grocery shop, a natural center for chance congregation. It is a rural shop; if it is urban, it is one where rural habits persist, where the impersonal supermarket has not displaced the small-time shopkeeper and the credit system:

> Write two
> cake o'soap an half
> pung-a flour in Olive black balance
> book fuh me, Maisie muh dear. . . . (64)

A kind of tableau unfolds, beginning with a greeting in which everyone is identified by name each with its appropriate elaboration:

> . . . How
> you, Evie, chile?
> You tek dat Miraculous Bush
>
> fuh de trouble you tell me about?
>
> Hey Mary!
> You there?
> I int see you there
> wid you head half hide
>
> in de dark o'dat crocus bag

and with intimate concern:

> . . . How
> Darrington mule? (64)

The response to this ordinary question sparks off a discussion of the general ill-faring of things, in which Bible history and oral history are called upon for parallels to the current situation. The discussion ends with a naming one by one of the blessings that offset the dissatisfactions of life and a reiteration of the eternal unanswerable question concerning the meaning of things: the joys and sorrows of this life.

It is in the description of the present and of the comparable past that the reasoning informing the voice of the people, and the nature of that voice, come to our attention. The interpretation of fact, described firsthand or relayed to us by the main speaker, is sometimes incredible and unrealistic to the eye of sophistication.[4] But there is no imagination here. The normal response of our people to unusual phenomena is indeed as the poem illustrates it. Those who listen in country buses or in route taxis find no cause to doubt the connection between say the withering of things described as current and World War I or its connection with the eruption of the volcano in nearby St. Lucia. And in the actual discussion, narrative and description, inextricably bound together, depend for their reliability not on science or logic in the sense in which these are usually interpreted but on the actual, physical effect of phenomena on man and nature and on the rearrangement of these in the mind of each recounter, within the framework of a particular philosophy.

The description of things in terms of their concrete effects and not in abstract terms is a commonplace of folk articulation. It is part and parcel with the kind of living and growing metaphors that make ordinary folk speech a miracle of images, easily distinguishable from its educated counterpart. Here the ill-faring of things, the theme that begins and ends the discussion and the historical parallels sighted in support of its naturalness are illustrated in graphic representations characterized by this precise imagery that owes little, if anything, to the world of books and writing and everything to the world of life and speech. It is a "pestilence" they say, that is affecting both animal and vegetable alike. "Darrington mule" is:

. . . still sicky-sicky. An now
. . . de cow
gone down too . . . .
. . . .
same kind o' sickness,
like wickedness, man, dis
favour de yams. . . . (65)

The pestilence is seen as part of a natural cycle. It is one "test of the times" comparable to earlier tests. Mr. Gilkes is reported to have compared it with his experience in World War I:

. . . .when they burn out 'e balls
wid dat yellowin mustard gas. . . . (65)

It is later compared with another test, the important May Dust that Gran had described and which, presumably, other very old people remember. This event is re-created in picture terms complete with sound effects. Nature is given human and here terrible proportions:

they have a mountain near hey
that always smokin' an boilin'
like when you belly got bile . . . (66)
. . . .
whole bloody backside
o' this hill like it blow
off like they blastin' stones
in the quarry. (67)

The pictures from that faraway time are clear and down-to-earth all made from "stuff" within the experience of the listeners and, by implication, of all the readers of the poem:

Rocks big as you cow pen hois'
in the air as if they was one
set o' shingles.
. . . .
Gran say, in de broad
day light, even de white
o' she skylight went out . . . (68)

It is only Pastor who comments without the benefit of concrete examples. He bypasses the usual representation of effects and suggests rather ominously: "The Writin 'Han' pun the Wall." But the fact that his frame of reference, the Bible, is special and is in fact concerned with what gives meaning to all these tests, whenever they come, allows him the freedom to infer his examples.

The response to Mr. Gilkes's earlier-mentioned comment illustrates the kind of general comprehension Pastor can afford to take for granted. The Bible is the encyclopedia for folk reference, freely quoted by literate and illiterate alike. It is called upon to say "Amen" to Mr. Gilkes's comparison of the present with World War I and further to predict a possible World War III:

An' if you as'
me, there soon going
to be fresh wars and rumours
of wars . . . (65)

A constant current of deep religiousness symbolized by biblical quotations or by simplified Christian dogma runs through the piece. So Pastor is allowed to mention the "Writin 'Han'" and infer a reference to Belshazzar's vision with its connotations of subsequent calamity.[5] There are times, however, when the inspiration of the Bible, the kind of Christianity-inspired fatalism, intermingles freely with superstition or black people's intuition (the kind that knows that once leaves of the trumpet/congo pump/bois canot are inverted, a storm will come whether meteorologists announce it or not). At the advent of the May Dust, for instance, when the air turned gray before it turned black, Gran, one of the district elders and therefore a natural repository of wisdom, reported that:

> . . . even the fowls in the yard
> jump back pun they coops . . . . . . an' the cocks start to crow
> as if it was foreday mornin'. (68)

In the panic of the moment, no prayer to priest or leader was possible and "God gone an' darken the day." The symbols from the two kinds of inspiration are almost inseparable.

The Bible and its God-myths are consistently stronger and the biblical sounds that we know to punctuate, as a matter of course, our daily lives, are intoned over and over again throughout the varying circumstances of the narration in gratitude, trust, or awesome regard:

> we got to thank God
> fuh small mercies.
>
> Amen
>
> Evie, chile
> Amen
> Evie, chile
>
> an' agen
> *I* say is Amen.
> . . . .
> Miss Evvy, uh wants
> you to trus' me half
> pung-a flour an' two
> cake o' soap till
> Mundee come wid de will
> o' de Lord. . . . (63–64)
> . . . .
> . . . you int got to call
> the Lord name in vain
> to make me swallow
> this tale. . . . (67)

The Bible intonations with their sometimes rhythmic repetition form one kind of music throughout the poem. There are, however, other kinds of music used perhaps less self-consciously in folk situations but with equal beauty. Here they are picked up very effectively but with the same naturalness, the same deceptive effortlessness, that is maintained throughout the poem. Darrington's mule, the cows, the yams are all suffering from the same withering sickness. With no warning at all, the description of the thoroughness of the withering moves directly into a part of our musical history recalling a tea-bush seller's song known in some shape or form in all the English-speaking Caribbean territories, sometimes beginning: "Man peaba, woman peaba." We have here:

> . . . Bolinjay
> spinach, wither-face cabbage
> muh Caroline Lee an' the Six Weeks, too. (65)

And when the comparison of this test with the volcanic eruption is first made, the credibility of the story is questioned in the form of another kind of music. The Calypso rhythm is unmistakable here. The hand on the first pan is almost visible; the tune is picked out clearly while the other pans are muted in the background:

> Now how you
> know! Any-
> body live there? You
> know any-
> body from there who
> live out near here?
> Besides, where
> exactly you say this place is? (66)

The action of the volcano is described in terms that make use of a kind of onomatopoeia common to several of the more descriptive words in our "nation language," words that imitate sounds with amazing precision and become music:

> . . . One day suddenly so
> this mountain leggo one *brugg-a-lung-go.* (67)[6]

The description of the dust itself makes use of repetition for intensification[7] and repetition for rhythm together:

> But it black black black
> from that mountain back:

in yuh face, in yuh food,
in yuh eye. . . . (67–68)

In the folk milieu, every narration is an unrehearsed dramatic presentation with varying orchestration.

The beauty of the imagery and the music of the voice should not distract the attention however, from the most powerful of all the testimonies this poem gives of the importance of the folk—the underlining of their life philosophy. For in the midst of all this happening that they cannot affect but must endure, our people have always held firm a kind of fatalism and a blind gratitude that has made tolerance levels high.

And if the suggested rationale behind the inexplicable happenings reviewed in this story seems naïve, it surely is an attempt to inform irrational events with some kind of rationality, some kind of sense or plan. A cycle is made to unite science, politics, and nature—a trio at whose communal whim people seem to exist. God, the ruler of the universe, is made to oversee everything and to him is offered constant gratitude. Indeed without this philosophy, the morale of the poor would be constantly low; there would be no spiritual strength. It is perhaps in this blind gratitude, more than in anything else, that the folk have begun to offer "to return some of (their) experience and vision." The main singer of this song counts out each blessing lest we regard them as commonplace and pass over their value:

the possibility of a child for a man you love
(. . . . meet yuh man
an' if God bless yuh, beget. . . . (68)

Perhaps we understand here the uncomplimentary attitude to barrenness in the present context and the lack of cooperation with birth-control agencies: the suppleness of the body; breasts not yet shriveled up; pride and camaraderie; a piece of land small, but productive and your own; healthy children; and the unfailing progression of time with its implication of hope and faith in continuity as nature's cycle runs parallel to the human birth-cycle mentioned earlier:

. . . Dry season
follow wet season again
an' the green crop follow the rain. . . . (69)

The chronicling of all these blessings, the recital of all that hope brings us, in the sequence of the poem, back to the note of concern on which the discussion started. The response to the inevitability of an unpredictable fate leading to the eternal, frantic question when:

. . . suddenly so
widdout rhyme
widdout reason
you crops start to die . . .
. . . .
an' suddenly so, without rhyme,
without reason, all you hope gone
ev'rything look like it comin out wrong.
Why is that! What it mean? (69–70)

It would be a mistake, however, to use its sequence in the poem to interpret the cry of questioning and pain on which the piece ends, as a cry of despair. The earlier and lengthy documentation of the "small mercies" is the cue here: almost a rebuke to the sufferer for even the thought of "flying in the face of the Lord." If there is ever a message from the folk, it is one of survival in spite of misfortune, of great beauty in spite of ugliness, and of hope where despair is indicated. Their strength is in their ability to "survive, adapt, re-create," and so they construct a worthwhile existence even in the most crass circumstances. It is this strength that "The Dust" tries to illustrate with its faithful representation of some of the life-patterns of the people it portrays, in the voice of the people it celebrates.

In an earlier review of *Rights of Passage,* Edward Baugh, a poet and critic himself, recognized the poem as a new and different contribution to Caribbean creative writing. He saw it as a new dimension in dialect poetry. "One of the most satisfying sections," Baugh wrote then, "is the dust in which Bajan dialect at last finds its muse. I know of no other West Indian who has used dialect more subtly, probingly or suggestively. . . . Here he removes himself and allows the characters to be completely themselves."[8]

But "The Dust" is more than a victory of language. The very distance the poet affords himself, and that Baugh recognizes, allows the work to construct itself as a song in which voice, image, and matter are all woven from the same fabric. It is as if the integrated Caribbean musc allowed all other influence to dissolve and yielded itself completely to the spirit of the folk. The artist has picked up the essential beauty of this people and given their forms a place in the creative sun.

In Walcott's words:

. . . beauty has surrounded
Its black children and freed them of homeless ditties.[9]

The poet has called us to listen.

For Brathwaite, this is perhaps another first in Caribbean literary history.

He more than any other poet has uncovered for our benefit, much of the magic of the Afro-tradition and its nearness to our present.[10] But even while he sits at some kind of literary crossroads with his ear to the ground, interpreting the sounds from the flutes, the drums, and the bamboo-fifes, the music itself is changing. The need to record the present, which is almost already past, has never been greater. When our need and the urges of our poets meet, we give thanks.

Notes

1. Edward Brathwaite, *Rights of Passage* (London: Oxford University Press, 1967), 63–70.

2. Edward Brathwaite, *Contradictory Omens: Cultural Diversity and Integration in the Caribbean* (Kingston, Jamaica: Savacou Publications, 1974), 64.

3. Gordon Rohlehr's comment is to the point here: "But one will have to study the Caribbean people and listen to them before one can learn to make important or relevant critical statements on the new writers." "Afterthoughts," *Bim* 14, no. 56 (1973): 227–232.

4. A group of urban youth downright rejected the possibility of this kind of reasoning in the twentieth century until discussion and true-to-life examples from their colleagues convinced them.

5. See Daniel 5:27.

6. This device reaches a high point of excellence in Wordsworth McAndrew's famous "Ole Higue," where the witch is beaten to the sounds: "Whaxen, Whaxen, Pladai, Plai." See Velma Pollard, ed., *Anansesem: A Collection of Caribbean Folk Tales, Legends and Poems for Juniors* (Kingston, Jamaica: Carlong Publishers Kingston, 1985. 2nd Ed., 2002, 90–93).

7. The notion of repetition for intensification or for diminution is, by now, one of the stock phenomena of Creoles of African origin.

8. Edward Baugh, "Review, *Rights of Passage*," *Bim* 45 (1967): 66–68.

9. Derek Walcott, "As John to Patmos," *In a Green Night* (London: Cape, 1962), 12.

10. See Maureen Warner-Lewis, "Odomankoma," *Caribbean Quarterly* 19, no. 4 (1973): 51–99.

8
Collapsing Certainty and the Discourse of Re-Memberment in the Novels of Merle Hodge

Barbara Lalla

Each of the novels of Merle Hodge, *Crick Crack, Monkey* and *For the Life of Laetitia,* presents a world in which a schoolgirl is displaced from a familiar and supportive location (considered valueless to those with whom she goes to live) to an unfamiliar space in which she strives to find meaning and to construct her self.[1] In each, she encounters ambivalent values that threaten psychic fracture at a crucial point of maturation.

A first-person narrator's recollection of childhood, if it is not to be purely adult (analytic) commentary, tends to involve a reliving of the experience and a movement between retrospective discourse as the adult looks back and prospective discourse as the child moves forward—an alternating perspective that, by its very nature, spawns possibilities for alternative interpretation and evades certainty and closure. The two temporalities of the story and of the telling, which Bridgeman discusses following on Genette and others,[2] are made complex by ambiguities in the telling as the narrator withdraws and overviews or revisits and relives. In these circumstances, character development and perspectival change are inextricable. In particular, attitudinal orientation and the consequent value system are in flux.

The application of linguistic analysis to critical interpretation of Merle Hodge's novels is particularly appropriate because of this author's not only acute but also *conscious* sensitivity to linguistic detail. At the book launch for Hodge's *The Knots in English* (a grammar text),[3] Denis Solomon commented on the integration of literary, linguistic, and social activist dimensions of this author's work, an observation borne out by the approach of *Knots* that clearly distinguishes Anglophone Creole from English while conveying absolute respect for each code. The author's selection of readings for the *Knots* launch were readings (from *Crick Crack, Monkey* and *For the Life of Laetitia*) that focus on classroom scenes that portray miseducation. The writer's past and continuing engagement with language education at a variety of levels further bears out this integration of interests. Indeed, Merle Hodge may be regarded as hypersensitive to nuances of the written standard, of the oral tradition, and of code-shift and stylistic variation, and this commands careful attention to all dimensions of discourse in her novels.

In Hodge's two novels, the increasing instability of the protagonists emerges through manipulations of modality. Expanding on Roger Fowler's development of Boris Uspenskii's earlier study, Paul Simpson not only distinguishes epistemic and deontic modality but also distinguishes modal shading such as degrees of certainty in the epistemic.[4] Lubomír Doležel has since gone further to argue that it is through modal systems that convey necessity, belief, degrees of knowledge, and so on that narrative worlds are fabricated in any case.[5] In both novels by Merle Hodge, such attitudinal positioning of the central consciousness articulates in complex ways with physical shifts in time and place. Cognitive linguistics sheds light on how bodily experience (near or remote, inside or outside, and so on) affects our understanding of the world and is conveyed through deictic elements of grammar and such words as *here* and *there,* as well as through discursive strategies like metaphor. Physical, perceptual viewing positions (for example, from outside) are drawn on to convey conceptual, attitudinal points of view (for example, alienation). So the state of mind of Hodge's protagonists is conveyed not only through modality but also in terms of spatial relationships.[6]

Choice of perspective also appears to be significant in expressing a national or regional identity. Similarly, in a tale of physical, emotional, intellectual, and moral growth recounted by a narrator looking back on his or her own past, shifting perspective or point of view is an important basis for conveying personal development. In narratives where personal experience mirrors national experience, one set of perspectival shifts may run parallel to another.

Despite similarities in point of view, the novels have quite different emphases. Class confrontation intensifies cultural crises that threaten to confound personal and national maturation in *Crick Crack, Monkey,* but issues of class (while still important) are more muted in *For the Life of Laetitia,* which foregrounds gender, especially in relation to ethnicity.

Crick Crack, Monkey is a recollection of changing influences on a developing girl (Tee) who, after the death of her mother, moves from the care of a rambunctious aunt in a rural community to the more proper and sterile influence of a middle-class aunt in town. Cynthia grows away from one dimension of her identity (Tee) without being able to embrace another, offered by Aunt Beatrice. Eventually repelled by lifestyles that seem to be mutually exclusive alternatives, and guilt-ridden as a result, she looks forward to joining her father abroad. Her local environment has emptied of meaning.

For the Life of Laetitia is also a first-person recollection of a girl who shifts from one household to another in which she can never be at home. However, she begins from a position of greater strength than Tee. Laetitia, or Lacey as she is called, moves after winning a scholarship to attend school in town; and her mother is alive and working in the States. Lacey forges a close friendship with a diligent girl from a situation of extreme gender-based injustice. When this friend, Anjanee, despairs and commits suicide, Lacey is shattered but (with family support) recovers and takes up her life.

Both novels portray problems of maturation in the girl child and reflect those of the nation, through exploration of such issues as mother's absence, father's neglect, deprivation of original support systems, severing of roots, and the challenge of a prestigious, dominant, but alien way of life. Both children are propelled unsheltered and unprepared into the wilds of "civilization." Family members on whom they might be expected to depend are scattered; in each case, a parent is overseas. They move, essentially, into a vacuum, with all the gaps in experience that are to be expected of childhood. What accounts for the differing outcomes, and how are the significant differences in emotional growth portrayed?

Most narratives are framed as recollections of the past and *Crick Crack, Monkey* is not unusual in this respect. However, in *Crick Crack, Monkey,* retrospection is foregrounded. The sense of an adult looking back and reliving childhood experiences is brought to the fore through the play of tense, to establish direction in time, and through aspect, to explore the events revisited from the inside for their continuity, completion, and so forth. At the same time, the novel is an adult reflection of the society in which the author (as distinct from the narrator) developed.

Retrospective narration establishes perceptual (spatiotemporal) orientation of the implied adult looking back. Counter to this direction of retrospection, personal and national development move forward in time and in the maturation process. The novel begins with recollections of childhood experience of an inexplicable adult world in which events pertaining to issues such as death and sex can only be inferred. As the adult narrator relives the child's experience, gaps are foregrounded. The child conveys snippets of adult conversation or song without understanding.

Even as unfolding events (as the narrator relives her childhood experiences) carry us forward, the writer manipulates two planes of perspective in conveying maturation. The prospective movement following the child's development through time is *perceptual.* However, as events unfold, the child narrator experiences changes of *attitude* to these events. Alternative responses to these experiences present themselves, and these alternative responses are of varying value. In *Crick Crack, Monkey,* perspectival shifts on this ideological plane reflect the child protagonist's shifting emotional responses to those around her. In *For the Life of Laetitia,* shifts in ideological perspective convey not only alternating responses but also the child protagonist's intellectual, moral, and emotional growth. Looking back, the adult can say with some certainty what actually took place. However, the simultaneous view implied in reliving the situation provides for the wavering certainty in an immature observer.

It has already been suggested that, in each novel, developing black female consciousness mirrors a national consciousness. In each novel, the degree of maturation toward independence is reflected in relationships between the protagonist and others. The degree of successful maturation toward independence differs in these books according to the differing context of each book. I would distinguish the guardian/child relationship in *Crick Crack, Monkey* as mirroring colonial experience on the local level, from the guardian/child relationship in *For the Life of Laetitia* as mirroring postcolonial experience on the national level, although Rhonda Cobham views *Crick Crack, Monkey* as sharing "with nationalist novels of the late 1960s and 1970s a sense of postcolonial angst, even despair" while it transforms narrative conventions of which it is a part.[7] Moreover, *For the Life of Laetitia* goes further in exploring gender issues, implicating ethnic dimensions, and tracking developing black masculinity. All these have a bearing on Laetitia's maturation and affect her ultimate perspective.

Attitudes that govern routes for male development impinge on female development. Adults in *For the Life of Laetitia* differ in their approach to the education of boys and in their responses to male nonachievement. In Laetitia's maternal family, Carlyle, who gains nothing from school, must assist in the garden and home. In her paternal family, Michael's father beats him for lack of achievement in schoolwork and for rendering assistance in the house, and the father blames this involvement in household activity for his son's lack of success. Laetitia's family encourages the girl child's academic achievement, although, in the paternal household, her father expects her to demonstrate domesticity as well. The significance of ethnicity in gender roles emerges in the relayed portrayal of Anjanee's life, where feminine involvement in schoolwork is luxury and presumption. In Anjanee's situation, presuppositions about gender roles ensure that women are too busy slaving domestically to have time to better themselves.

All these indices contribute to the struggle in the maturing psyche, a struggle foregrounded through elements of the discourse that convey fluctuating certainty. Ultimately, in the juvenile negotiation of conflicting forces through which identity may be constructed or destroyed, Hodge conveys uncertainty in its most extreme form—the toss-up between life and death in the contemplation of suicide. The opening up of options to accommodate the unthinkable has much to do with collapsing certainty as the protagonist moves into unknown physical or emotional territory, particularly with regard to personal responsibility for her own existence. Lacey's initial stability has been undermined for some time before the issue of suicide arises.

In both novels, collapsing certainty is encoded in macrostructure and microstructure of the discourse. For example, at the level of *discourse structure*, parallelism allows the writer to maintain sets of unresolved options. The experiences that Tee recounts comprise a text that develops through redefinitions, negations of established positives and denials of presuppositions. She must maintain two parallel sets of parameters (as laid down by Tantie and as laid down by Aunt Beatrice)—two parallel sets of parameters for choice and inference. Tee is also redefined by others. The twisted vision of her cousins marginalizes her until the promise of translocation to paradise (she is to join her father abroad) raptures her to center stage (pariah to privilege), from "some lil relative Momma found up in the country" to our "first cousin" who "is *so* bright" (*Crick Crack, Monkey*, 109–110).

The experiences that Laetitia recounts comprise a text that contains its own (more subtly distinguished) alternatives, but the text also contains subtexts that mirror her own set of experiences—subtexts of the experiences of Laetitia's mother, the experiences of Anjanee and of Anjanee's mother. These subtexts foreshadow alternative futures open to her. This opening up of alternatives increases the potential for uncertainty.

The obvious comparison between Laetitia's and Anjanee's situations gains depth from other reflections. Laetitia's mother is the mirror image of Anjanee with the crucial difference of having no men to constrain her. She works full time; attends school afterward; arrives exhausted, often without having eaten; and sometimes falls asleep in class. She has only one friend—a woman from the outposts like herself (*For the Life of Laetitia*, 33). Her chance to succeed depends on her daughter's effort and sacrifice. She inhabits the margins of Laetitia's life and is shadowed forth in other existences, implying disembodied possibilities for success or for failure to make good. Ambivalence in the children's reasoning is conveyed through metaphors of emptiness, vanishing substance, breakage, and disembodiment. Miseducation forcibly imposes on Lacey the status of rural working-class origins as a vacuum or *hole*. The utter lack of support for Anjanee, as she fades away to transparency, locks her into future nothingness:

> "I want to come to school and pass my exam!" She had begun to speak fiercely. "And if I can't come to school and pass my exam . . . !" She stopped, staring out across the playing field, where there was nothing to be seen. (194)

> Some of us insisted on showing up by our behavior the kind of *hole* we came out of. She had to say *hole* and not *home* because people who came out of proper *homes* know how to behave. (78)

Lacey's crisis after Anjanee's suicide by poison produces sensations of dissolving insides and exploding head (201, 205).

Apart from larger structural characteristics of the discourse and the connotations produced through figurative language, *syntactic details* convey destabilization at both personal and national levels in both texts. Hodge engages with the issue of nationhood by exploding canons, and, in particular, by decanonizing the values of Europe. In *Crick Crack, Monkey,* she does this by interrogating the imagery of the canon ("what, in all creation, was a 'haystack'?" [25]). Increasing incidence of questions hints at growing uncertainty. The speaker betrays gathering confusion through lexical replacements: Miss Muffet "who for some unaccountable reason sat eating her curls away" (25), through the collapse of juncture in mindless parroting of the Lord's Prayer (27), through regurgitation of archaic (literary) forms ("Girls and Boys who went a-sleighing" [61]).

When the protagonist's control over her environment decreases, shifts occur in her role at sentence level. The first-person speaker, Tee, more frequently becomes the object of transitive verbs ("Everything was changing, unrecognisable, pushing me out" [110]). Other entities (often inanimate) become the agents of action ("A freezing dismay swarmed into my insides" [105]). Other syntactic structures also convey the speaker's diminishing understanding of her situation. For example, verbs of cognition are negated ("I had not realised" [75]). Modal verbs accumulate ("It seemed to me. . . . I decided it must be. . . . She seemed exasperated. . . . Aunt Beatrice seemed to clear her throat" [74]). These linguistic operations produce a sense of destabilization that is multidimensional. As the uprooted child mirrors the Caribbean persona in the diaspora, juvenile schizophrenia and social friction between communities reflect an internal fracture in the society.

Varying degrees of certainty are not exactly the same as varying amounts of comprehension. Children do not expect to understand everything and, indeed, in *The Life of Laetitia,* the hum of adult talk (the meaning of which is closed to her) brings Lacey security rather than insecurity. Uncertainty begins when she reaches her father's house and considers the new and ill-defined space in which she must begin to operate on the basis of unknown criteria:

> But I looked around the room and wasn't sure that I wanted to unpack anything.
>
> I wasn't sure what I would wear for home clothes. (27)

Negation of verbs of cognition conveys uncertainty; indeed, David Herman describes negation as zero degree of the speaker's "commitment to the truth of the expressed world."[8] Although Lacey arrives at her new location secure enough to absorb some amount of incertitude:

> Whether he was going to the bathroom or to complain to his mother, I did not know.
>
> I settled back into the book I was reading. (39)

But even the strong, well-grounded child is tested by uprooting and belittling forces. Miseducation contributes to the collapse of certainty in both novels.

In *For the Life of Laetitia*, Lacey's certainty begins to break down when she meets a teacher, Miss Lopez (otherwise known as the Circus-Horse), and the central consciousness evinces this uncertainty through adverbs (such as prob ably) associated with epistemic modality: "the lady did not look up. I thought to myself that she probably couldn't, what with all the weight she carried on her head" (14). Hodge also conveys the destabilizing force of miseducation through the lesson on the family. The picture of the Happy Family inspires uncertainty through the selection of modal verbs: "they seemed very pleased" (51). However, the greatest influence on Lacey's equilibrium is the value placed or not placed on human life in the community that the child inhabits. Lacey observes the lack of value placed on Anjanee's life, and Lacey's most intense anxieties relate to Anjanee and are expressed through increased use of interrogatives: "Was she too sick to come to school? Or had she really given up?" (197). Lacey's impressions are explicitly shown to be perceptions only—again, uncertainty conveyed through epistemic modality: "She did not look at all well. . . . Anjanee was beginning to seem very pale, even transparent. It was as if she was fading away" (193–194).

Lacey's strength lies in a major contrast between her situation and Anjanee's. Unlike Laetitia, Anjanee is exploited and devalued at home. She sees no hope of a future without education. Lacey has real support, but is distanced from it at the very point when she begins to display confusion about what lies ahead. As the future begins to loom grimly, "He would have nothing funny to say about these marks" (190–191), questions continue to build: "What were they going to say about my schoolwork?" (191).

For each of Hodge's protagonists, then, uncertainty accumulates to produce internal fracture. Tee invents Helen, her double. Then she corrects herself: "She was the Proper Me. And I, I was her shadow, hovering about in incompleteness" (62). As the emptiness builds in Tee, she comes to inhabit the margins of life. Laetitia, on the other hand, is the naive window into the tragedy of Anjanee and the filter that reduces Anjanee's situation to its tragic essentials. When she identifies with Anjanee, and Anjanee dies, Lacey's convictions about the value of her own life disintegrate.

Confrontation between value systems destabilizes the protagonists' perspectives in both books, and this helps to separate each growing female character from the world of the living. Tee reflects: "I observed that the sea was still offensively rolling itself backwards and forwards; no respect, no respect for anything whatsoever. Suppose I were to drown here at Canapo. Tomorrow, maybe. It was the first agreeable thought I'd had for the day" (91). As negative epistemic modality gathers (*suppose, maybe*), Tee slinks to the margins of life, as we see from spatial indicators like *out* ("crept out, stole out of the house" [91]) and eventually wishes to fade from the sight of others ("I wanted to shrink, to disappear. . . . I felt that the very sight of me was an affront to common decency. I wished that my body could shrivel up and fall away, that I could step out new and acceptable" [97]). Aunt Beatrice confirms that Tee does not belong in the world of the living. The child that died with Tee's mother in childbirth is fortunate, and Tee's mother requires divine forgiveness for having brought Tee into the world. Valuable links with the past are broken with movement from home community (paralleling diasporic movement) and with ensuing amnesia—links that can never be restored. Tee not only misses the opportunity to receive or even learn the name of her grandmother's grandmother, but she incompletely metamorphoses to Cynthia and temporarily reinvents herself as Helen. She so loses respect for the Tee-dimension of herself that she distances herself from every reminder of Tee.

Gathering uncertainty about the value of life is linked with similar issues of self-esteem in *For the Life of Laetitia*. Achievement of independent selfhood is presented as a criterion for *survival* at the individual level, which is entwined with survival of another individual in different ethnic groups. Particularly in the wider context of Caribbean society, *The Life of Laetitia* explores the complex ethnic dimension of Caribbean identity. Stuart Hall points out the development of *black experience* beyond "a single and unifying framework based on the building up of identity across ethnic and cultural difference" and positioned as the unspoken and invisible "other" of predominantly white aesthetic and cultural discourses to a more complex and heterogeneous construct that incorporates dissonances.[9] The interplay of ethnicity and gender in the balance of power is deadly for Anjanee, and these lethal effects are not contained within her one social group.

What Anjanee articulates as "I not going end up like my mother, I rather dead," Laetitia absorbs as "But if Anjanee ever had to drop out of school she would slowly shrivel up and die. She was so determined not to end up like her mother" (90). Lacey becomes less stable when, like Anjanee, she loses clarity of vision on a number of issues. In glimpsing the danger of Lacey's growing confusion, Velma comes closer to selfhood than hitherto: "'This child should go back where she belong before you really get something you didn't bargain for.' Miss Velma had stepped out of her half-dead frightened self" (186).

However, Velma's own warped perceptions are dangerous in view of her role as mother-substitute, and she is a mother-substitute both by default and by her positive intervention in details of Laetitia's personal development, such as menstruation. This role of mother-substitute makes her statements potentially influential and makes irresponsible discourse potentially damaging. For example, Velma describes Lacey as "turning [her] father into a worse beast than he was to begin with" (188), and so identifies the child as the agent of negative transformation, and locates in the child responsibility for the man's inhumanity. In this way, Velma only reinforces a growing tendency in Lacey to feel responsibility for the actions of others. She also aids a developing distortion in Lacey's vision—an inability to maintain a value distinction between life as positive and death as negative. Velma's irresponsible utterances mark as humorous a situation intrinsically marked for tragedy or pathos. "'Eh! eh! Like you drink some of what the girl drink!' Miss Velma chuckled" (202). In warping the implications of Anjanee's suicide from horror to humor, she makes way for the unthinkable in Laetitia's mind.

Unlike Tee, who can give up on the nation and region for refuge in a more impressive center, Laetitia must negotiate a position in the contradictory worldviews of the developing society. Hodge's protagonists are more complex than the type that shows what Boehmer terms the "typical nationalist quest for self-truth,"[10] the type that conveys a redefinition of everyday reality to resist images of what colonial society would define as the beautiful and normal. Tee comes to view her situation as one in which personal self-definition is impossible. She distances herself from the fractured colonial society with all its mutually confronting, opposing forces. Impelled by loss, guilt, and demolished self-esteem, Lacey actually (temporarily) lets go of life, rejects it as negative, and is attracted by death as seemingly positive. This seems the logical end to her growing confusion. The collapse of certainty has begun after her suspension from school, with the sense that she is letting everyone down. Characters with whom she has identified become indistinct in her mind, overlap and merge, and she loses her ability to evaluate the extent to which she is responsible for her own life versus that of others:

> I thought Mamma Patsy was standing over my bed, looking down at me with Miss Velma's sorrowful face. (188)
>
> Anjanee seemed to be gazing at me reproachfully, out of an older person's eyes.

> I felt as if I were going around spoiling everything. I had made an enemy of Miss Velma, and now I had let Anjanee down so badly that it did not seem as if she would ever recover. . . . (189)

It is an uncertainty conveyed through expressions of limited cognition and experience (*thought, felt as if*) and through modal verbs that qualify the truth value of the utterance (*seem*). In her own view, her life has become a site of ruin that sucks in those who care for her. Lacey becomes obsessed by anxiety about betraying her mother. Her mother merges into Anjanee ("sitting in class next to me in Anjanee's thin, faded shirt" [196]), then into Miss Velma ("standing in the middle of Miss Velma's dasheen patch . . . but when I got there it was Ma Zelline in the dasheen patch, and she threw one reproachful glance at me and fell down dead from a stroke" (197). The faces of mother include Anjanee's, preternaturally aged. Through rapidly shifting faces, the mother places a demand on the daughter, identifies the daughter's success with her own and the daughter's failure with betrayal. As the demands become overwhelming, Laetitia curses the teacher's mother, reinforcing her own guilt.

However, the major source of Laetitia's guilt is a sense of having failed Anjanee ("what Anjanee had done to herself was my fault" [201]), and she keeps reliving the reproach ("Lacey, you don't care nothing?" [189, 205]). The dialogic rather than oppositional interaction of forces gradually negotiates a composite identity but, along the way, in Lacey's confused perceptions, her life appears to have emptied of value through a web of betrayals, and the blotting out of her own existence once and for all seems the most straightforward option.

What brings Lacey back from the brink is a persistent re-establishment and realignment of values by the vitality of the family structure of which she is a part and which has been designated (according to the system of opposites taught in school) other-than-Happy, in other words, Broken. As her family close ranks around her and relationships are restored, the discourse flowing about her consistently imposes order on her thoughts. The family clusters around, talking (always) of the healthy routines of their existence, positively reinforcing life. Internally too, instinctively, she is working at getting back on track, her eyes following the lines on the *galvanize* until she can think straight and be "glad to be in the world again." They draw her into activities connotative of Life—taking nourishment, bathing children, minding chickens to sell eggs. "You *alive!*" Ma rejoices (212).

In the end, she not only reactivates her own life but perpetuates all that is healthy and positive of Anjanee's. Family support enables Laetitia to accept as a challenge the routines of traveling far to school, surviving on limited money, working while assisting with housework, and depriving herself of comfort for the sake of her mother—a state of mutual and mirroring sacrifice rather than betrayal on either side. As she weaves in the strength of varied and often conflicting influences, Lacey begins to demonstrate a maturity that mirrors social progress when she distinguishes positive from negative choices, when she refuses to relinquish her unique and independent existence: "As the reopening of school drew closer, I felt as though I was taking up her life" (213). Her ability to lay hold on life from a base in her own community demonstrates healing in the individual psyche and mirrors social and national growth in which the developing psyches of the children of different races reach to each other across apparently insurmountable dividers.

Thus the end is a birthday thanksgiving rather than another funeral. The narrative strategies at the end of *For the Life of Laetitia* proclaim feminine and postcolonial survival and rebirth in contrast to the indeterminacy of Tee's impending departure at the end of *Crick Crack, Monkey*. Tee's departure is an incomprehensible development that will take her from a situation so unbearable that the unknown is preferable. Tee's story leads to a yearning for separation from everything she knows, expressed through modal elements indicative of uncertainty, wishing, and speculation:

> Her face seemed to slump . . . for what to do?
>
> I desired with all my heart that it were next morning and a plane were lifting me off the ground. (111)

The final shift in transitivity identifies her as the helpless and passive object of rescue.

Lacey's celebration is an act of faith, and the (qualified) closure associated with her recovery does not mask the uncertainty inherent in continued existence. In the end, her observations take the form of a modest record of perception ("I felt as though . . .") rather than bold assertion of incontrovertible fact. The proposed thanksgiving looks backward and forward—a celebration of recovery and a preparation before resuming the development process. Unlike Tee's intolerable going-away party, for one opting out of local society, Lacey's thanksgiving celebrates homecoming and healing, the deictic elements (those that indicate directional relationships in the discourse) drawing other characters around her so that she can move forward with confidence: "Ma was planning . . . and a whole gang of neighbours and macommeres were going to come" (214).

Both novels explore issues of personal and national identity not in terms of an established, essential, definitive, and inherent *nature* but as a complex potential negotiated through multiple, even conflicting, histories. In her context of social disintegration, Tee misses the possibilities for synthesis, but Laetitia grasps them and moves toward a personal wholeness that the protagonist of the earlier novel could not conceive of, let alone achieve. Lacey may not take off and she may not arrive, but she sets out and begins a process of positive interaction with the contending voices.

Notes

1. Merle Hodge, *For the Life of Laetitia* (New York: Farrar, Straus, Giroux, 1993); *Crick Crack, Monkey* (London: André Deutsch, 1970).

2. Teresa Bridgeman, "Time and Space," in *The Cambridge Companion to Narrative,* ed. David Herman (Cambridge: Cambridge University Press, 2007), 52–65; Gérard Genette, *Narrative Discourse: An Essay in Method,* trans. J. E. Lewin (Ithaca, NY: Cornell University Press, 1980).

3. Merle Hodge, *The Knots in English: A Manual for Caribbean Users* (Wellesley, MA: Calaloux, 1997).

4. Roger Fowler, *Linguistic Criticism,* 2nd ed. (Oxford: Oxford University Press, 1996); Boris Uspenskii, *A Poetics of Composition,* trans. Z. Zavarin and S. Witig (Berkeley: University of California Press, 1973); Paul Simpson, *Language, Ideology and Point of View* (London: Routledge, 1993).

5. Lubomír Doležel, "Narrative Modalities," *Journal of Literary Semantics* 5 (1976): 5–14; *Heterocosmica: Fiction and Possible Worlds* (Baltimore, MD: Johns Hopkins University Press, 1998).

6. See Bridgeman, "Time and Space," 55.

7. Rhonda Cobham, "Revisioning Our Kumblas: Transforming Feminist and Nationalist Agendas in Three Caribbean Women's Texts," *Callaloo* 16, no. 1 (1993): 44–64. Compare with Simon Gikandi, who calls the voice in *Crick Crick, Monkey* "a synecdoche for the unwritten culture of the colonized," in "Narration in the Postcolonial Moment: Merle Hodge's *Crick Crack, Monkey,*" in *Past the Last Post: Theorizing Post-Colonialism and Post-Modernism,* ed. Ian Adam and Helen Tiffin (Hertfordshire, England: Harvester Wheatsheaf, 1991), 20–21.

8. David Herman, *Story Logic: Problems and Possibilities of Narrative* (Lincoln: University of Nebraska Press, 2002), 311.

9. Stuart Hall, "New Ethnicities," in *Stuart Hall: Critical Dialogues in Cultural Studies: A Reader,* ed. David Morley and Kuan Hsing Chen (London: Routledge, 1996), 141.

10. Elleke Boehmer, *Colonial and Postcolonial Literature* (Oxford: Oxford University Press, 1995), 109.

9
Cultural Connections in Paule Marshall's *Praise Song for the Widow*

Velma Pollard

Paule Marshall's *Praise Song for the Widow*[1] will probably be viewed primarily as a major addition to the growing collection of novels written by women about the conditions of women, a subject that received considerable attention during the United Nations decade for women 1975–1985. The present analysis, however, focuses on the novel more in terms of its place in the literature on the cultural connections between black people of the diaspora. And while the need for such a focus might easily be dismissed with the comment that it has all been said before, Marshall's means of involving this notion in her heroic tale, its existence as substrate consciousness in the heroine and subterranean essence in the background of the narrative (rather like an underground stream constantly refreshing the surface and spurting out at intervals to take its place in the story) introduces a new level to an old argument, one that is more convincing in the long run than more obvious attempts might be.

Marshall writes of a unity that is best described by Edward Brathwaite's phrase, used in a prose work on the Caribbean with different but related connotations, *submarine unity.*[2] In Marshall's novel, cultural unity joins the black people of the Sea Islands of the southern United States to the black people of the Caribbean and by implication to all diaspora people. The unity is the result of cultural retentions from a common ancestor, one or other of the kingdoms of the African continent from which the black populations were taken.[3]

While the claims for cultural connection between the territories of the Caribbean have been documented and have been implied with some consistency in the imaginative literature of the region, the inclusion of black people from the United States in this connection has largely[4] been the work of anthropologists[5] and of linguists who have studied Gullah,[6] the Creole language of the Sea Islands, which lie off the coast of Georgia and South Carolina. Comparisons between Gullah and the Creoles of the Caribbean have established relationships that are undoubtedly the result of similar linguistic histories. The African substrate to which all these languages are heir has come to be regarded by some linguists as the basis for most of the similarities between the Creoles, no matter to which European language their lexicon is related.[7]

While Marshall makes use of the available results of linguistic research in *Praise Song for the Widow,* her use of gross outline rather than detail and of paralinguistic more than linguistic features makes language only part of a large substrate unity of culture. This approach, because of its wholeness, is finally more convincing than exclusively linguistic comparisons have been. The very selection, however, of the linguistic environment for the significant contact in the novel—a Creole of French rather than English lexicon—is indeed a subtle claim for the relatedness of the languages. For the heroine, whose language is American English, must relate to a culture that is articulated mainly in a Creole whose lexicon is based in French.

The heroine is an aging black American widow whose youthful beauty has matured into a dignified attractiveness emphasized by good taste in clothes. The story turns on the life crisis that confronts her after a dream experience aboard ship on her annual Caribbean cruise. The experience is so powerful that she quits the cruise and moves into what the back cover of the book describes as a "harrowing Odyssey" that brings her "finally to an understanding of what she has lost—and found." Our concern here is with what the child of Sea Island ancestry lost as she matured in her social and economic rise in a northern city, what she finds in a small Caribbean island and the entity that makes them part of the same circle, despite the geographical space that separates them.

The effectiveness of Marshall's novel as a tribute to the cultural connection between people of the diaspora is largely the result of understating dissimilarity to highlight similarity. The first dilemma in which the heroine finds herself provides a clear example. She disembarks from the cruise ship at Grenada, confident that getting a flight to New York that day or the next will provide no problem at all, but discovers that even finding a taxi is a problem, not only because of a holiday on the wharf but because people do not perceive her as a stranger and so do not realize her predicament. And perhaps this is not remarkable. The woman is black and so are the people coming and going. But she is an elegantly dressed black resident of suburban New York. All this should be obvious in her dress and the "set of matching luggage at her side" (69), or so she thinks. But even when she "folded her hands in such a way that the gloves could not escape notice," people still kept smiling and waving at her in a way that was "overfriendly," even by the standards of her earlier exposure to other Caribbean islands. The ultimate experience is a hand on her elbow and a man's voice saying, "Ida, doux-doux, qu'est-ce qu'il y a? Ma'ché! Ma'ché!" (Ida, my dear, what's the matter? Hurry! Hurry!) (71) and his eventual apologetic comment, "Don't ever let anybody tell you, my lady, that you ain' got a twin in this world!" (72).

The significant comment in the text runs: "It was as if the moment they caught sight of her standing there, their eyes immediately stripped her of everything she had on and dressed her in one of the homemade cotton prints the women were wearing. . . . Their eyes also banished the six suitcases at her side and placing a small overnight bag like the ones they were carrying in her hand, they were all set to take her along wherever it was they were going" (72). When she does get a taxi, the driver explains the excessive crowd, the overfriendliness, and the language: all the people on the wharf are natives of Carriacou, an out-island off the coast of Grenada, on an annual ritual trip back to their home. He explains, "They don't miss a year. No matter how long they been living over this side, even when they's born here, come time for the excursion they gone" (73). He also explains the language—patois where she had expected English (she was, after all, on an Anglophone Caribbean island) and the bilingualism of the man, for example, who thought she was Ida: "Patois, creole, whatever you want to call it. . . . Is just some African mix-up something. You used to hear the old people 'bout here speaking it when I was a boy, but no more. Only the outislanders still bother. That's another thing about them. They can speak the King's English good as me and you, but the minute they set foot on the wharf for the excursion is only Patois crossing their lips" (75–76).

Avey Johnson, the heroine of the story, recognizes the language. She had heard it in Martinique three days earlier, and while the words were unintelligible, the cadences had reminded her, if fleetingly, of a language associated with her childhood. The vision that had hurtled her into her decision to quit the cruise had been of her great-aunt Cuney, proud resident of Tatem near Ibo Landing on one of the Gullah-speaking Sea Islands. She had heard the language and that night had dreamed of her great-aunt.

The question of why a great-aunt whose annual holiday contact had ceased half a century earlier should appear in her dream is answered by the heroine's own sense that the lilt of the language she had heard in Martinique resembled the speech of Tatem: "Sometimes the least thing seen or heard during the day or merely thought of in passing, could trigger a dream of people and events long forgotten" (67). The casual assertion that the lilt of Martiniquan French patois so resembles the lilt of the English-based Creole of the Gullah speakers as to be a possible trigger is noteworthy. For while the linguists have been looking at lexicon and more recently at syntax for the substrate that is likely to be the influence of West African languages brought by the slaves to the New World, equal academic interest cannot be said to have been taken in the sound shapes,[8] which are perhaps the most obvious part of the West African legacy. Avey Johnson makes the comparison: "There had been the same vivid, slightly atonal music underscoring the words. She had heard it and that night from out of nowhere her great aunt had stood waiting in her sleep" (67).

Whatever might have triggered it, the dream has far more significance than mere language similarity operating on the psyche. Indeed, it is the trauma of this dream that allows for the strange turn of the story. The leaving of the cruise is only the beginning of a tremendous revelation with far-reaching effects. This event, the appearance of a person already dead, is expressed in the Anglophone Caribbean by the verb *dream* used actively with the dead person as subject. "Her great aunt dream her" roughly translates the experience. Implicit in such an event is a dream message. Here, in the novel, the experience is reported as being so traumatic that it drains the heroine physically. Her great-aunt and herself had been "trading . . . blow for blow" in a fight that ended on the lawn of her suburban home in New York with all the white neighbors looking on in shock and satisfaction (44).

The struggle connected with dream or with vision is an old symbol appearing in traditional references: Jacob and the angel of the Old Testament; Hamlet and his decision making. The point of the struggle, however, its true message, only becomes clear after the next dream sequence.

The second and contrasting dream sequence begins more in reverie than in deep sleep and introduces not the great-aunt but the husband of the heroine. The struggle that lies at the core of the novel is between the influences of these two strong characters, who are both dead. They are, eventually, symbols of contrasting mores so different as to be incompatible. The appearance of the husband triggers a retrospective description of the classical journey of the black family that moves from accepting the crumbs to eating a piece of the pie that is the offering of corporate America. The physical move is from Harlem to White Plains. The contrast is between the cultural values of the black great-aunt and the target values of white America.

The story that Avey Johnson relives has been told a hundred times over in the lives of subject people who have "made it" from unfortunate circumstances. In the Caribbean, it is the story of the "hurry-come-up" (nouveau riche) family. What Marshall describes is what the new arrival sometimes loses in the super-human effort to achieve what he gains. Avey Johnson describes her husband's rejection of himself—Jerome Johnson, the man arrived, who by the time he died could speak in the third person about black people; who could not identify with his daughter's interest in the "black struggle"; who rejected physical love from his wife because he needed the time and the energy to follow through his ambition, "love like a burden he wanted to be rid of" (129); and who was a member of an exclusive lodge (a Master Mason) and the proud owner of an accounting firm in Brooklyn bearing that name, which even his wife used when she thought about him. He had become, for her, "Jerome Johnson," successful and aloof, a poor replacement for the loving, lustful, and sometimes carefree Jay she had married. Avey Johnson awakens from her second dream to a choice between the cultures represented by her late great-aunt and her late husband.

Two invocations mark the break at the end of this section of the book and the beginning of the next. One is a voodoo introit invoking Legba, a Dahomean god: "Papa Legba, ouvri barriere pou' mwê" (Papa Legba open the gateway for me!) (148). This invocation has been used elsewhere in the literature of the diaspora; for example, by Brathwaite as a cry for help at the end of a poem that seeks suitable linguistic and environmental replacements for certain aspects of colonialism. Brathwaite's note on Legba says that he is a "crucial link between men and the other gods"; that he usually presents himself as an old, lame man; and that "the celebrant possessed by Legba assumes an aged, limping form and uses a crutch."[9] The other invocation is from contemporary poetry. Here a call for physical release complements the call for psychological release implied by the earlier invocation: "Oh Bars of my . . . body, open, open, pen."[10]

In this novel, the psychological and physical realities constantly complement each other. An upset stomach hardly attributable to the meal on board ship follows the appearance of Aunt Cuney. The narrative that follows these two invocations, the waking of the heroine from the dream that relives her marriage, describes a smell to which she half-awakens, the smell of a baby who needs to be changed. She goes through motions she has not performed in thirty years, walks toward the crib in the dingy back room that is the nursery of her young womanhood. The smell is in fact her own, the result of the long, exhausting sojourn of her fully clothed body on the hotel bed: "The baby smell was nothing more than her own flesh in the slept-in clothes" (150).

An ablution follows. Avey bathes and dresses in a haphazard fashion that so contrasts with the well-dressed black woman who had entered the hotel earlier that the desk clerk cannot hide the shock on his face. The analysis of the life that has gone has removed the barriers that might prevent her entering the phase that is to come. The bath prepares her body for it.

Now with the psyche exorcised "like a slate that had been wiped clean, a *tabula rasa* upon which a whole new history could be written" (151), Avey Johnson sallies forth to meet the next and most significant "connection"—a "disagreeable old man" locking up his bar just as she stops there desperately in need of a glass of water after a long and dizzying walk along the beach.

An inner circle forms within the larger circle that is the entire narrative (beginning with a dream on a cruise ship and ending with the decision to return to the site of that dream and all the implications of that return). This man's bar is closed "for the excursion." And the taxi man's voice saying, "Come time for the excursion they gone!" (75) comes back to her, making a circle of sense in the old man's eventual concession: "Any other day you could sit as long as you wanted, oui. . . . But everybody knows that come this time of the year the place is closed. The excursion, oui. . . . It's closed for the excursion" (162). And the old man is Legba with his hipshot walk and his ancient mariner eyes. His enthusiasm so mesmerizes Avey that she agrees to cross the water and to experience what the excursion goes to celebrate. But there is much that must be learned before this decision is made. The psychocultural space newly available in her mind must be filled. The emphasis on the physical appearance, the exterior behavior of this man, makes him the Dahomean god who puts man/woman in touch with the other gods, opens an entire pantheon. It is he who brings bits and pieces of Old World/New World black history to fill the spaces in this lady's mind.

Lebert Joseph is a stoop-shouldered old man with one leg shorter than the other, but when he draws himself up with pride to clarify Avey's vague reference to Carriacou as "some place, some island—I forget the name," he looked tall enough suddenly to reach up and touch the roof of the thatch . . . 'Carriacou . . . the name of the island is Carriacou'" (162). His face is lined; he seems to be about ninety but the lines on his face are "like the scarification marks of a thousand tribes." He can be tall and he can be agile. In his excitement, he crossed the room "with a forced vigour that denied both his age and infirmity. And his hands, large, tough-skinned, sinewy, looked powerful enough to pick up Avey Johnson still clinging to the chair and deposit her outside" (161).

He speaks of a thousand tribes and tells the reasons for the "excursion," giving the most important last: "Is the Old Parents, oui. . . . The long-time People. Each year this time they does look for us to come and give them their remembrance . . . and when it comes time at the Big Drum to dance their nation for them" (165). He has to dance two "nations"—the primary Chamba for his father's people: "I's a Chamba! From my father's side of the family" and the secondary Manding for his mother: "My mother now was a Manding and when they dance her nation I does a turn or two out in the ring so she won't feel I'm slighting her" (166). Finally his "unsettling eyes" ask Avey, "'And what is you? What's your nation? . . . Arada . . .? Cromanti maybe . . .? Yarraba then . . .? Moko . . .?' All that his audience is, as her answer betrays, is 'a visitor, a tourist, just someone here for the day'" (167).

This is what the heroine of the novel tells the old man. But the reader knows better. For had not Avey's great-aunt explained to her over and over those many summers, decades earlier, why the point where the waters around the ancestral village of Tatem met the open sea had been labeled Ibo Landing? Did she not know it was the point where the Ibos, so the story went, having cast long and terrible looks at the white people who had brought them there, just "upped and walked away" into the water.[11] Had not this behavior been sanctified when to Avatara's question "How come they didn't drown Aunt Cuney?," the answer had come in the form of another question, "Did it say Jesus drowned when he went walking on the water in that Sunday School book your Moma always sends with you?" (40).

There is a coming together of Aunt Cuney of Tatem and Old Joseph of Carriacou here. The futility of the efforts of the one to save Avatara from the ignominy of forgetting her roots is obvious as the Avey Johnson that the child has become declares, "I'm from the States, New York." The depth of it is implied when the other, lowering his head in shame, confesses: "I has grands and great-grands born in that place, I has never seen! . . . Josephs who has never gone on the excursion; who has never been to a Big Drum! Who don't know nothing 'bout the nation dance!" (168). It is almost as if Aunt Cuney were here lamenting Avey and her offspring and their tacit rejection of Tatem.

Beginning with light banter describing how she came to stop at the old man's rum shop, Avey finds herself telling him her story, a kind of reversal of the Ancient Mariner role, starting with the dream she had on board ship. The old man's gaze never leaves her face: "Intense, probing, it was like a jeweler's loupe he might have fitted into his eye to get at her inner workings. There was no thought or image, no hidden turn of her mind he did not have access to. Those events of the past three days which she withheld or overlooked, the feelings she sought to mask, the meanings that were beyond her—he saw and understood them all from the look he bent on her" (171).

The reader recognizes that look, that ability to see. This half-Chamba, half-Manding shares that with the Ibos Aunt Cuney had spoken about: "Those pure-born Africans was people my gran' said could see in more ways than one. The kind can tell you 'bout things happened long before they was born and things to come along after they's dead" (38).[12] And when Avey's voice fails because she sees the intruding figure of Jerome Johnson, the new black man and his disapproval as he had appeared to her earlier, the comment is: "It didn't matter that she could not go on because the man already knew of the Gethsemane she had undergone last night, knew about it in the same detailed and anguished way as Avey Johnson, although she had not spoken a word" (175). Coconut water laced with Jack Iron (bush rum) from Carriacou not only revives a physically failing Avey but lifts the "pall over her mind." And the old man pronounces his forgiveness: "You's not the only one, oui. . . . It have quite a few like you. People who can't call their nation. For one reason or another they just don't know. Is a hard thing. I don't even like to think about it. But you comes across them all the time here in Grenada. You ask people in this place what nation they is and they look at you like you's a madman. No you's not the only one" (175). And that, he admits, is why when he kneels at the Big Drum ritual, singing the "Beg Pardon" to the ancestors, he sings not for himself alone: "Oh, no! Is for tout moun . . . I has all like you in mind." These are the people who cannot dance when the nation dances are called but must wait till the "creole dances start up later in the fete" (175).

The old man cannot believe the depth of his audience's ignorance; he feels sure there is some aspect of these things she is aware of, so just as he did in the case of the tribes, he calls out dances beginning with creole ones—"Belair," "Cariso"—and pauses at the Bongo, whose lyrics tell the sad tale of slave parents shipped one to Haiti the other to Trinidad while the children are left in Carriacou. The song is in patois but the emotion is so clear that Avey "without understanding the words . . . felt the tragic weight that underscored them pressing her down in the chair" (177). He mentions the Hallecord and the Dana and stops at the Juba when Avey shows some recognition of word at least. "Did you say Juba?" And the reader remembers here that the dreamer Avey had been surprised that Aunt Cuney's hands, long dead, were firm and not, as one might expect, fleshless bones like "clappers to be played at a Juba" (40). At this long hoped for intervention, "the man's relief . . . was so great it weakened him and he had to sit down. . . . 'So you know you remember Juba!'" (178), he says, and while his audience's mind concerns itself with the difference between the legendary city and the modern reality of a forgotten backwater, the old man repeats the question and requests, "Come show me how they dances it where you's from." "No one dances it anymore. It's only something you might hear or read about," the black woman from New York admits.

"We still dances it!" exclaims the black man from Carriacou, and he does the dance, and he sings the accompanying song in a youthful and feminine voice "his hand snapping an invisible skirt while he complains, 'A skirt! I needs a real skirt! Is the skirt in the Juba gives it beauty'" (179). His audience, in spite of herself, is actually laughing now. He invites her to join him: "I needs a partner. The Juba calls for a pair" (180).

Suddenly, the old man becomes serious and issues the larger invitation: "You must come today-self so you can see the Juba done proper" (180). The ensuing discussion—the mountains thrown up as obstacles by the New Yorker to be made molehills by the man from Carriacou—has the predictability of any comparable discussion between the native and any foreigner who is not an anthropologist. Less predictable at this point in the narrative but entirely in consonance with the cultural fatalism of the plot is the acquiescence of the heroine: "All right. I think I'd like to see the place" (184). The thrust and parry between the old man and his guest is the psychocultural struggle that runs parallel to the earlier dream struggle with Aunt Cuney (44) and leaves Avey "as exhausted as if she and the old man had been fighting—actually, physically fighting, knocking over the tables and chairs in the room as they battled with each other over the dirt floor—and that for all his appearance of frailty, he had proven the stronger of the two" (184).

This is the climax of the story. The resolution of the struggle lies in the heroine's words: "All right. I think I'd like to see the place." And the physical reaction is immediately described: "she realized that the strange discomfort in her stomach was gone and her head had stopped aching" (184). The rightness of the decision cannot now be in doubt. The widow is free in mind and body. And here the narrative might well have ended.

But the journey on the water must be made if the total cultural connection is to be achieved. It was water that broke the connections over the Middle Passage. It was water that separated the mainland and Avey's parents from Aunt Cuney's Tatem. The homecoming had to be across water. And this decision to accompany the old man *home* held no foreboding for Avatara, whom Aunt Cuney had tutored. The fearlessness here is in direct contrast to what Avey felt earlier when among the excuses for not taking the trip she had included a plan to be "home" that night in her own house. On the screen of her mind, the text reports, there was a replay of something she had seen just before Jerome Johnson had entered her reverie in the hotel. The dining room at home to which she had returned had become a "museum at the foot of Mount Pelée in the wake of the eruptions that had taken place during her absence and had reduced everything there to so many grotesque lumps of molten silver and glass" (181). It was then that the clogged bloated feeling had returned to her stomach, that feeling that imperceptibly dislodged itself when she decided to go on the out-island journey "home."

While the journey itself and the mood of the company are both worthy of comment, what is significant for our study is the symbolism of each small experience the heroine undergoes in terms of the "connections" on which this paper focuses. As she embarks, Avey remembers another boat ride—the annual trip up the Hudson on which hers and so many other black families escaped the monotony of their jobs and the dinge of Harlem to relax as they consumed large quantities of chicken and potato salad and the rice that was obligatory because her father was a Gullah black. What she remembers most, however, is the connection she used to feel then with those around her, "slender threads streaming out from her navel and from the place where her heart was, to enter those around her." The thrust of the novel, the aspect this paper wishes to represent, is encapsulated in that comment and its continuation. What the woman feels now is related to what the child felt then:

> And the threads went out not only to people she recognized from the neighbourhood but to those she didn't know well, such as the roomers

> just up from the South and the small group of West Indians whose odd accent called to mind Gullah talk and who it was said were as passionate about their rice as her father. . . .
>
> The threads streaming out from her even entered the few disreputable types who occasionally appeared in their midst from the poolrooms and bars. . . . Then it would seem to her that she had it all wrong and the threads didn't come from her, but from them, from everyone on the pier, including the rowdies, issuing out of their navels and hearts to stream into her as she stood there . . . for these moments, she became part of, indeed the center of, a huge wide confraternity. (190–191)

Aboard the *Emmanuel C* en route to Carriacou, Lebert Joseph leads her to where a group of women, the oldest women aboard, are sitting. Avey experiences a "shock of recognition" as she regards them "sitting there in their long sombre dresses, their black hands folded in their laps and their filmy eyes overseeing everything on deck. . . . They were—she could have sworn it!—the presiding mothers of Mount Olivet Baptist (her own mother's church long ago)—the Mother Caldwells and Mother Powes and Mother Greens, all those whose great age and long service to the church had earned them a title even more distinguished than 'sister.'" These the women whose "powerful 'Amens' propelled the sermon forward each Sunday," whose arms "reached out to steady those taken too violently with the spirit," and, most important for the analogy here, whose "exhortation . . . helped to bring . . . through . . . sinners and backsliders" making their way "shamefacedly" to the pulpit in response to the pastor's plea "*Come / will you come?*" (194).

The acceptance of the grandniece of Aunt Cuney by the women among whom Lebert/Legba places her is the acceptance of the backslider by the redeemed. And Avey Johnson had been a backslider in the sense that she had followed, without too much resistance, an ambitious husband to a place in the wider Euro-centered culture of corporate America and away from the narrow Afro-centered culture of her childhood summers at Tatem.

The Mount Olivet Baptist Church, the religious body providing the metaphor in the text, is one of a number of Christian groups with recognizably, non-European behaviors found throughout the Caribbean and among blacks in America. In the literature, they are referred to as black religions[13] of the New World or as black religious cults[14] and are described as lower-class movements. They are, in fact, a strong social organization within the communities in which they operate.[15] The church as a symbol joins Tatem to the northern cities—the Ring Shout of Aunt Cuney's youth is a more fundamental version of the Mount Olivet Baptist service—and both to the Caribbean.

The visual parallel between the women on the boat and the women of the church is so close that Avey begins to relive an experience of her childhood, in which the endlessness of the pastor's sermon caused a minor tragedy resulting from a stomach upset, when she could not get out of the church fast enough. The reality is that her stomach *is* upset, at the point on the water of "the channel with the two currents" (206). At the level of symbols, again there is conflict; something to be rejected, something to be kept. At the physical level, the body rejects violently all that had been eaten earlier. At every emission, the kind women support her and respond "bon" (good).

But this emission does not complete the cleansing. The boat has passed the channel; the sea is calm and silken; the stomach is clear and empty, yet Avey feels horribly ill and knows without a doubt she is about to repeat what happened at Coney Island when she was seven or eight and her younger brother refused to open the bathroom door. The heroine has sweated, she has vomited, but she must go through the last ignominy—the cleansing of her bowels. The plot requires that the metaphor of rejecting the orientation of a lifetime be played out fully. And there must be ablutions. After the sweating, she had bathed herself in the hotel room. But after this "casting" up and down, the ablutions must be done in another way at another place and by other people.

It is the house of the daughter of Lebert Joseph, the mother and grandmother of some of the children referred to earlier ("grands and greatgrands who has never gone on the excursion"). In spite of her squeamish objections, Avey is bathed by this woman and her silent handmaid. Eventually, she relaxes, and there is recognition again. It is the galvanized tub over which the woman wrings the washcloth—a replica of the one at the back of the house in Tatem, the same size and "with the same three or four grooves by way of decoration" (221). Her great-aunt would administer the weekly scrubbing as she sat up in it. And Rosalie Pavay, the daughter of Lebert Joseph, has transformed her into that child again. Afterward, Rosalie rubs her back gently with a kind of scented oil ("thou anointest my head with oil / my cup runneth over") "to see to it you skin don' dry" (222). Finally, she kneads and stretches Avey's limbs in the same way that Avey herself had treated her own children to ensure that their bones would grow straight. The sluggish flesh grown "thick and inert" from years of confinement under a long-line girdle is treated as if it were dough being made into bread or clay to be shaped and fired (223).

This is the physical remaking of the woman. It is the end of one journey and the beginning of another. The island woman has oiled and molded the body, wooing it with sweet patois sounds until eventually Avey feels in her loins and through her body "the warmth, the stinging sensation that was both pleasure and pain" (224), that sensation that had characterized her physical contact with

Jay before he became Jerome Johnson to whom love was a burden. This remaking hints at something further back than birth; it is the environment of conception; out of this something is born.

Marshall has avoided the hackneyed Christian/Western symbol of cleansing by baptism (water and blood). The rituals that are really important in the African societies are birth and death. In her state of physical and emotional alertness, the ex–New Yorker is able to accept unquestioningly "the candle and the innocent ear of corn" on the buffet—the "foods," she had been informed by Lebert/Legba in the rum shop, that the ancestors expected. Now they are as natural as the "plate of food that used to be placed beside the coffin at funerals in Tatem" (225).

What follows is again predictable. Avey attends the Big Drum ceremony, sees the dances she had been told about, including the Juba, and joins in the Carriacou tramp. Most important, she remembers as she announces her name, following the villagers' lead, her grandmother's admonition to give her whole name "Avey, short for Avatara" (251).

The new lady is to spend her retirement in Tatem where she will build a house. One of her children will understand—the youngest, the one she had tried so hard to abort, who had marched with the blacks in demonstrations (to her father's anger and shame), who had visited Nigeria and brought back films, and who knew the importance of New Yam. This one worked with poor black children. Avatara[16] would request that some of those children be sent down and every summer she would request that her grandsons be sent to her in Tatem.

The African connection has been treated before in the fiction written by black writers in America, especially since the sixties. But the connection has been a two-way connection, Africa–America, America–Africa. Paule Marshall, by including the Caribbean, Anglophone and Francophone, in her consideration, has extended this connection to show a pervasive and tenacious cultural substrate with its origins on the African continent. The unexpressed implication is that wherever slave ships went, the connection is likely to exist, worked over though it might be by the superstrate of the master culture.

This is not the first novel in which Marshall treats the coming together of cultures, nor is it the first in which she isolates communities that have retained something special and different not necessarily approved by the larger society. Bournehills, for example, the "conscious" village in *The Chosen Place, the Timeless People,*[17] a source of embarrassment to the middle class, is related in many ways to Tatem and to Carriacou, although this last is, by the standards of the plot of this novel, obviously more evolved. In the earlier novel, however, the focus is on cultural dissonance. In *Praise Song for the Widow,* the author, by shifting the focus from difference to similarity, replaces the clash with symphony.

A New Yorker of West Indian parentage,[18] Marshall is uniquely placed to assess difference as well as similarity in the cultures. The question of whether the unity described here represents reality or a personal dream is less important than the fact that the novel celebrates a triumph in the removal of layer after layer of cultural overlay to expose a being that finds an important core that she had lost.

Notes

1. Published by Virago Press (London: 1983). Further references are incorporated in the text.

2. Edward Kamau Brathwaite coins the term to describe the links that wait to be uncovered between the different cultural backgrounds of "the people who came" to the Caribbean. *Contradictory Omens: Cultural Diversity and Integration in the Caribbean* (Kingston, Jamaica: Savacou Publications, 1974).

3. There is no suggestion here of a monoculture on the African continent, but rather an acceptance of the existence of certain cultural similarities across the continent.

4. See, however, "New World A-Comin," "Tom," and "All God's Chillun," in *Rights of Passage* (9–21); and "Jah," in *Islands* (162–164) from Brathwaite's *The Arrivants: A New World Trilogy* (London: Oxford University Press, 1973).

5. Melville Herskovits must be regarded as a pioneer in this area with the publication of *The Myth of the Negro Past* (New York: Harper and Brothers, 1941).

6. Lorenzo Turner's *Africanisms in the Gullah District* (Chicago: University of Chicago Press, 1949) is among the earliest of these and has become a point of reference for later studies.

7. For details of research in this area and some perspective on it, see the introduction to Mervyn Alleyne's *Comparative Afro-American: A Historical Comparative Study of English-Based Afro-American Dialects* (Ann Arbor, MI: Karoma Publishers, 1980).

8. See, however, D. L. Lawton, "Suprasegmental Phenomena in Jamaican Creole" (PhD diss., Michigan State University, 1963); Hubert Devonish, "Tone in Guyana Creole" (presentation, Linguistics Seminar, University of the West Indies, Mona, Jamaica, May 1983); and Hazel Carter's presentations to the Society for Caribbean Linguistics Biennial Meetings 1978, 1980, 1982, and 1984. Carter's "How To Be A Tone Language" has been published in *Studies in Caribbean Language*, ed. Lawrence Carrington, in collaboration with Dennis Craig and Ramon Todd Dandaré (St. Augustine, Trinidad and Tobago: Society for Caribbean Linguistics, 1983), 90–111.

9. "Negus" in *The Arrivants*, 222–224, 273.

10. The lines are attributed to Randall Jarrell, a modern American poet.

11. This behavior has been explained elsewhere as the result of the slaves thinking they could swim back to Africa. The story from Tatem perhaps suggests this in the

comment: "And they didn't bother getting back into the small boats drawed up here—boats take too much time" (38).

12. Note that the Rastafarians of Jamaica (for whom repatriation to Africa is a goal) place great emphasis on the "eye"/"I" and the ability to see (thus RastaFARI = Rasta far-seeing eye). For more on this, see Velma Pollard, "The Social History of Dread Talk," in *Studies in Caribbean Language.*

13. See for example Leonard Barrett's *Soul-Force—African Heritage in Afro-American Religion* (New York: Doubleday, 1974).

14. See for example G. E. Simpson, *Religious Cults of the Caribbean: Trinidad, Jamaica and Haiti* (Rio Pedras: University of Puerto Rico, 1970) and J. R. Washington's *Black Sects and Cults* (New York: Doubleday, 1972), especially chapter 2, "African Roots in the Afro-American Experience."

15. For a moving comment on the quality of the church as a strengthening and cohesive force among lower-class blacks in a village in Trinidad and the fragmentation resulting from its repression, see Earl Lovelace's *The Wine of Astonishment* (London: André Deutsch, 1982).

16. *The Shorter Oxford English Dictionary* gives the meaning "descent" for Avatara (from Sanskrit) with the detail "Hindoo myth. The descent of a deity to the earth in an incarnate form."

17. For in-depth commentary on this, see Carolyn Cooper's "The Oral Witness and Scribal Document: Divergent Accounts of Slavery and the Development Process in Two Novels of Barbados," in *West Indian Literature and Its Social Context,* ed. Mark McWatt (Cave Hill, Barbados: University of the West Indies, 1985), 3–11.

18. See Marshall's almost autobiographical *Brown Girl, Brown Stones* (New York: Random House, 1959).

10

Louise Bennett's Dialect Poetry

Language Variation in a Literary Text

Jean D'Costa

Louise Bennett, Writer-Performer

In his 1966 introduction to Louise Bennett's *Jamaica Labrish,* Rex Nettleford describes her as "a poet of utterance" who, having "had the benefit of schooling," was "exposed to, in fact saturated with, models such as *Sir Patrick Spens* and *The Rime of the Ancient Mariner.*"[1] Few Caribbean writers have, however, been more original, less derivative in their art: Bennett's writing and work stand at the core of twentieth-century Jamaican cultural history, linking the 1930s to the 1980s, times of great cultural and political change.

Born in 1919, Louise Bennett helped her country move from colonial status to independence, devoting her life to the empowering of Jamaican culture. By the time of her death in 2006, her work on radio, stage, and television and in print had inspired her audience with her vivid, passionate craft. Her genius lies in bringing out and capturing essential Jamaican attitudes, characters, insights, and conflicts and in expressing them in discursive forms that are quintessentially Jamaican. Fused into her craft are the oral traditions of Jamaica, subtly enriched by the cultural heritage of her second language, metropolitan English. Her voice is characteristically Jamaican: "labrish" invites us into the gossip discourse of intimacy, humor, irony, and shared Jamaican experience.

This poet-performer made us all more aware of the gifts of our culture. A performer of "dramatic monologues," she made "the authenticity of her dialect verses speak for itself."[2] *Jamaica Labrish* spans the period beginning with the outbreak of World War II and leading to Jamaican independence in 1962. An educated, middle-class Jamaican, the only child of a baker and a dressmaker, Bennett grew up among all the language varieties of her country, and especially among the basilectal, mesolectal, and acrolectal speakers who filled her parents' daily routine. Thanks to the expected language behavior of the times, she inhabited the Standard English of the lecture room and the Jamaican Creole of the market with equal ease—or so it appeared to younger Jamaicans like myself who perceived the usage of speakers like Louise Bennett to be akin to bilingualism, yet whose shifts of usage could invoke intermediate levels between Jamaican Creole and Standard English. Critics and linguists would eventually face this issue, but it cast no shadow on Bennett's confident genius.

As the most prolific and inventive of Jamaican Creole poets, Louise Bennett faced the immensely difficult task of writing as text that she conceived in an oral language system, Jamaican Creole. No standard orthography existed for Jamaican Creole; no recognized body of writing characterized that language. Various anxieties face writers of new codes, but the first, inevitably, is that of orthography. Behind such surface problems lie more subtle issues, because shifts in discourse set off shifts in meaning and purpose. Variation rules.

Creole artists operate in a continuum. Their performance demonstrates their role in that continuum, but as they are not passive representatives of a set of speech habits, they may choose to expand and manipulate their medium using the complex choices offered them by their language culture. Their choices may be consciously artistic: At what audience do they aim? What style changes seem desirable, and for what ends? What kinds of variation and innovation can they use? Other choices may be less conscious: What forms or variants suggest or deny themselves? Which have a low frequency of usage? Which may seem acceptable variants, in free variation?

Bennett composed for performance, and her view of language was that of the oral performer rather than that of the writer confined within written conventions. She was "Jamaica's own entertainer speaking and singing in Jamaica's own language," and "the only poet who has really hit the truth about the society in its own language."[3] Even before the publication of *Jamaica Labrish* in 1966, her work appeared in newspapers where it was eagerly read, memorized, and later performed by others imitating her style.

Nettleford describes Bennett's handling of Jamaican language forms as follows: "Her belief in the people as they *are* comes out when she declared that even if the Jamaican dialect were to become a standard language in her lifetime, she would 'still write in the free expression of the people'—that is, to use her own words, 'a manner of speaking unhampered by the rules of (Standard English) grammar, a free expression, a dialect.'"[4] This passage raises questions about her attitude to language, and these are addressed at various stages in this chapter. If writing down oral poetry in a nonliterary culture presents a challenge (and Nettleford describes her as "carv[ing] designs out of the shapeless and unruly substance that is the Jamaican dialect,")[5] why should she then reject standardization of that dialect? Given her great and lasting popularity, her work (both oral and written) has been, and remains, a lasting force for normalization. Furthermore, how does one speak or write "unhampered by the rules of (Standard English) grammar" in a "free expression"?[6] If this proposition is simply a rejection of Standard English grammar, one could hardly expect any other choice from a Creole poet. Yet the statement seems to be reaching beyond that point toward a usage lacking regulation, and no language exists without a rule-bound grammar.

Bennett's words may hint at a view of language behavior in which variation is so precious in its own right that it must be preserved against standardization and protected from the sterile prescriptions of the metropolitan language. The forces creating variation become continuous shapers of the artist's view. Standardization of any kind seems to be this artist's enemy. As one who works through the entire range of Jamaican usage from Creole to Standard English, Bennett can be no mere recorder of any one code within that continuum. She acts as a conscious manipulator of different codes, appealing to her audience through their shared knowledge of Jamaica's complex language culture.

At this point, let us heed a word of warning from Derek Bickerton, whose *Dynamics of a Creole System* charted the synchronic interrelationships of variation: "The amount of variation in any given language may vary from epoch to epoch, but is always present in some degree, and continually shifts its locus; if the feature that is variable today was often invariant yesterday, it is equally often true that today's invariant was yesterday's variable. We should therefore view the development from basilect to mesolect not as the breakdown of some balanced organism, but merely as a phase in a development process that has been going on from the moment that . . . Creole or its antecedent pidgin originated, . . . only . . . unlike them, it is accessible to direct observation."[7] The crucial notions here suggest that developmental processes are continuous and that such activities do not represent the dissolution of a "balanced organism," a fixed and perfect code. Therefore, it is possible that Bennett's work may offer some insight into these processes, as it too "is accessible to direct observation."[8]

Language Variation in the Text

As an author, Bennett had inherited from nineteenth- and early twentieth century writers, such as Herbert G. de Lisser, a framework for setting down Creole on the printed page. In chapter 2 of this volume, Barbara Lalla sets out the early stages in which Creole discourse came to be set down in writing. Those scattered examples in the eighteenth and nineteenth centuries were mainly perceived as "broken" English into which strange African words were woven. Seen as ephemeral curiosities for the most part, these examples of Creole discourse suggested ways of writing Creole, but they hardly amounted to a firm, consistent, and universal model of how to write Jamaican Creole. For a creative writer whose imagination inhabited a Jamaican Creole universe, such models—shifting and changeable—challenged Bennett to find and use forms and spellings that would establish her language culture with absolute integrity.

Her moment in time is not unlike that of twelfth- and thirteenth-century English writers struggling to define and establish their suppressed, despised language culture in the hostile environment of Norman French domination; of alien rule in church, state, and land tenure; and of the social denigration of English culture.[9] In colonial Jamaica and colonial England, writers from these despised language cultures asserted their essential right to exist by acts of creative resistance. Then and now, language expressed identity, and regional dialects as well as class dialects continue to define English usage. Louise Bennett was very well aware of these aspects of English cultural history, and she did not fail to correlate them with Jamaica's situation.

Bennett's poem "Bans o' Killing" (*Jamaica Labrish,* 218–219) describes the proliferation of dialects within the English language community and emphasizes the relationship of Standard English to its contributing nonstandard varieties:

> . . . dem start fe try tun language,
> From de fourteen century,
> Five hundred years gawn an dem got
> More dialect dan we!

Historical evidence shows that Standard English "spring from dialect." Addressing "Mass Charlie," the dialect-hating character at the center of the poem, she notes that once he kills dialect, he will have to destroy wit, humor, variety, and, worst of all, "Yuh wi haffe fine a way fe kill / Originality!" To Bennett, language-making constitutes the very essence of human genius, an issue discussed in chapters 1 and 2 of this volume.

From such a writer as Bennett, one may expect some indication of how a language continuum affects artistic creation. Does her text reflect the continuum of Jamaican language usage? Does it show that "variation continually shifts its locus"?[10] What use does it make of synchronic variation? Where is it consistent, where not, and why? Finally, how does it relate to the written Standard English code so much at odds with the oral Jamaican Creole tradition, and without which Bennett's text could have had no existence on the printed page?

In order to address these questions, I must outline the strategies and limits of this chapter. As space does not permit a study of all variation in *Jamaica Labrish,* this survey is confined to an examination of twenty-five poems, the first fifteen from "City Life" (27–47), followed by seven in "War Time" (81–90), and three others chosen for their representativeness of Bennett's rhetorical experiments. These are "Hess" (94), a poem playing on the deletion of initial *h* in Jamaican usage; "Uriah Preach" (203), which mingles formal and informal styles; and a satire on Jamaican language attitudes, "Noh Lickle Twang" (209).

Because one must approach the written text of oral discourse cautiously, three phonological developments that set Jamaican Creole apart from Standard English bear examination:

1. Simplification of consonantal final clusters: SE -nd, -nt# > JC -n# (stand, want > tan, waa); SE -st# > JC -s# (first > firs); SE -kt# > JC -k# (looked > look); SE -ft# > JC -f# (soft > sof); SE -ld# > JC -l# (field > fiel); SE -pt# > JC -p# (stopped > stop).
2. Replacement of voiced and unvoiced interdental fricatives with voiced and unvoiced alveolar stops: SE ð > JC d; SE θ > JC t.
3. Deletion and addition of initial [h]: *Hess* becomes *S; up* becomes *hup.*

In the *Dictionary of Jamaican English,* F. G. Cassidy and R. B. Le Page explain the role of these features in Jamaican usage and set out allophonic variants in several cases.[11]

Two lexical items also deserve special attention. Homophones in many Jamaican idiolects, /se/ derives from English *say,* while the Creole connective /se/ used after verbs of telling, knowing, believing, and supposing is derived from Twi *sè*. Cassidy and Le Page claim that the latter "is never pronounced like English *say,* but since the meaning is close (especially in such phrases as 'tell me say') it is often taken as the same word and written so. More accurate writers of the dialect, however, spell *sey, seh,* or as here *se.*"[12] In my own and other middle-class idiolects, Standard English *say* and Jamaican Creole *se* are identical in the basilectal code: for example, /wat yu se/ "what did you say" and /mi ier se/ "I heard that." Bennett's treatment of these two items might therefore shed light on her success as an orthographer of Jamaican Creole.

Further, study of the copula in Bennett's usage should prove useful, reflecting as it does such a range of English-derived forms at the mesolectal and acrolectal levels, and powerful African-based features in the basilect. I examine the occurrence of the following five types:

1. The progressive-durative verb markers *a* and *da,* which are glossed by Nettleford as less and more intensive variants, and by Cassidy and Le Page as A_5 and DA_3, durative verb markers of which DA_3 is the "less common form."[13]
2. Predicative adjectives, such as /maŋgo raip/ *The mango(es)* is *(are) ripe* and often called the zero copula by early Creole scholars.

3. The copula *a*, defined under A_6 in Cassidy and Le Page[14] as equivalent to Standard English *be* in predicative verb slots, like /im a poliisman/ "he is a policeman."
4. The expletive or introductory *a* listed A_7 by Cassidy and Le Page[15] and equivalent to Standard English *it is, is it, there is, there are.*
5. The locative *de*, representing existence in a place of location, as in /im de a yaad/ "he is at home," and /im de ya/ "he is here." Cassidy and Le Page discuss a range of meaning under DE_2 and DE_3.[16]

Against these I have checked the incidence of English *be* forms, all of which mark the supposed—and officially proposed—relationship of Standard English to Jamaican Creole as the terminus ad quem for the reading public in the Jamaican language process. Such is the assumption regarding the use of English in Jamaica. In this process—and in Bennett's usage—it is possible that *be* forms may reflect early adaptations of Standard English or may constitute upward shifting of a deliberate kind. Still others may reflect more subtle changes outside of the conscious stylistic control of the writer-performer.

Both of these processes are interrelated, and it is often difficult to distinguish between the intrusion of a rule from another grammar (interference) and the incorporation of a feature from an alien grammar used to supply some need in the native grammar. For example, should one regard the Scandinavian *they, their,* and *them* forms as interference with Early Middle English *hi, hire,* and *hem,* or simply as regional variants? In a Creole language situation, the boundaries between levels of usage seem even subtler than do those of dialects deriving from a single, recognized mothertongue. At the same time, Creole speakers are highly sensitive to shifts and code-switches, even though certain variations seem to occur without conscious purpose or reaction. This latter tendency is akin to *drift,* the force for constant minimal change within all living languages.

Opposed to drift are *loans,* which arouse strong reactions from native speakers, as did the Latinate "inkhorn" terms of sixteenth-century England. Between these extremes lies the intermediary mixing of mesolectal language behavior where basilect and acrolect interact and create new forms not clearly derived from either. These and other problems are addressed by linguists such as Derek Bickerton and Mervyn Alleyne, but neither goes so far as to look at the semiotic and rhetorical significance of variation and interference. In chapter 3 of this volume, "The Caribbean Novelist and Language: A Search for a Literary Medium," I attempt to show that any variation implies semantic and semiotic shifting, however subtle and covert it may appear to be.

In Bennett's poems, code-switching plays an important role in tone and structure. It is an integral part of the rhetoric of "South Parade Peddler" (27),

"Candy Seller" (28), and "Uriah Preach" (203). Conscious, context-related shifting serves to create changes in tone, mood, and dramatic quality. It identifies relationships between characters and mediates between the audience and the characters in the poems. It also mediates the relationship of performer with audience. We must now see whether these conscious manipulations of language account for all the types of variation in Bennett's usage, and, if not, what may be learned from variations outside of this range.

Sound Changes and Orthographic Variation

Final Clusters

Table 10.1 sets out the items in which this feature appears. Each usage is numbered, giving the total number of occurrences within the corpus studied.

Note the high level of consistency achieved in representing Creole usage, especially in the 135 occurrences of *an,* while *and* appears only 8 times. By virtue of the high frequency of *and* forms, the /-nd/ group constitutes one of the most numerous among those studied. Of the twenty-five items listed, *and* is the only Standard English form used by Bennett. These 8 Standard English spellings represent 5.59 percent of the 143 occurrences of *and* forms, so it is worth looking at the environments in which this standard form occurs.

1. "Ackee skin and ashes is me / Dutty clothes only hope," in "Soap Vacation." (86)
2. "Up de step and dung de passage," in "Bans o' Ooman." (40)
3. "For like how so much bwoy gwan weh / And Jamaica short o' man," in "Registration." (42)
4. "Yuh fast and facety to," in "South Parade Peddlar." (27)
5. "When everybody run from shock / And lef it one fe dead," in "Earthquake Night." (32)
6. "Him frowns and sey," in "Yuh Nephew Sue." (34)
7. "Soh now de Inglish R.A.F. / Wi haffe strain dem y'eye, / Sence dem pick up 'S' aready, / Fe pick up P and Y," in "Hess." (95)
8. "Me look pon her, den look dung pon / Me han, and sey 'Teng Gad,'" in "Monday Gawn." (38)

At first glance, no apparent contextual constraints direct the poet to code-switch from Creole *an* to Standard English *and.* A closer look at the full context of each usage, however, reveals some clues.

Example 6 provides a useful hypercorrection *him frowns.* The bashful speaker, embarrassed by the formality of the meeting she is attending, is clearly code-switching upward, so a Standard English form is acceptable beside *frowns.* In

Table 10.1. Standard English -nd# in Bennett's orthography

	Jamaican Creole		Anglicized Jamaican Creole		Standard English	
Standard English term	Form	Occurrence	Form	Occurrence	Form	Occurrence
And	an	135	an'	1	and	8
Band-stand	ban-stan	1		0		0
Band	ban	4		0		0
End	en	1	en'	1		0
England	Englan	1		0		0
Find	fine	2		0		0
Finland		0	Finlan'	1		0
Friend	frien	1	frien'	1		0
Fund		0	fun'	1		0
Godsend		0	godsen'	1		0
Grand	gran	1		0		0
Grandpapa	gran-pupa	1	granpa	1		0
Ground	grung	1	groun'	1		0
Hand	han	10	han'	2		0
	han-miggle	1				
Husband	husban	2		0		0
Kind	kine	3		0		0

Standard English term	Jamaican Creole		Anglicized Jamaican Creole		Standard English	
	Form	Occurrence	Form	Occurrence	Form	Occurrence
Mind	mine	4		0		0
Round	roun	4		0		1
Sound	soun	1		0		0
Spend	spen	3		0		0
Stand	tan	10	stan	1		0
Thousand	tousen	2		0		0
Understand	undastan	2	undastan’	1		0

example 4, "Yuh fast and facety to," the line is a stanza-final climax to a series of rhetorically graded remarks by which the peddler persona approaches possible customers: "Hairnet, scissors, fine-teeth comb! / Wey de nice lady dey?" This polite English style changes to Creole with angry disappointment: "Dem torpedo yuh teet' sah or / Yuh female lick dem out?" (27–28). English permits cool detachment; Creole expresses emotion.

Given the importance of style-shifting in the rhetoric and structure of this particular poem, one might expect to find changes of mood and tone signaled by changes of usage. Formality, conscious politeness, and adjustment to upper-class boundaries are marked by Standard English usage, while Jamaican Creole marks a lessening of distance and also signals abuse, emphasis, and mockery. Therefore, it is curious to find a Standard English form in a context of angry disappointment and invective. If the *and* had occurred in the two preceding lines ("Buy someting wid de change noh sah / An meck de Lawd bless yuh!"), its usage would be contextually appropriate. Instead, the persona turns to abuse in the very next lines ("Me noh sell farden hair-curler sah! / Yuh fast and facety to"). Here, regular Creole forms denote and connote the unwelcome turn of events between persona and customer. Why then a final cry of abuse with two Standard English forms *fast and?* I return to this matter after briefly reviewing the other examples.

In example 1, the persona is complaining about a soap shortage. Here, no rhetorical constraints demand code-switches. Therefore, we might expect regular basilectal forms throughout. However, mesolectal *is* occurs adjacent to Standard English *and*: an unconscious variation may have been prompted by the proximity of *is*, even though Standard English *be* forms do not seem to exert this effect on Bennett's usage.

As for examples 2, 3, and 5, the contexts are all monosystemic Jamaican Creole and devoid of any contextual pressures to code-switch. The occurrence of *and* can thus be either an editorial error or, more significantly, it may be a feature of Bennett's usage that is no longer clearly identifiable with either extreme of the Jamaican language continuum. This possibility seems to be borne out by the presence of Standard English *her* in example 8, where mesolectal shifting is unmistakable.

I now return to example 4, "yuh fast and facety to." As I show elsewhere, Bennett is by and large at great pains to reduce English consonantal clusters in final positions. In the /-st/ group there are only three instances of Standard English forms in the corpus studied. One might hypothesize, therefore, that the co-occurrence of *fast and* reveals a deliberate shift to the standard. Far more evidence is needed to establish a rule generating these features, but such a rule might well derive from another style of reprimand used in Jamaican language behavior: the formal, lofty derogation exemplified in "thou shalt not give thy neighbours / Floolooloops to eat!" ("Uriah Preach," 203–204). If such is the case, then "yuh fast and facety to" represents a controlled code-switch in which Standard English forms are used for stylistic effect. If it is not, then it may be part of a larger mesolectal shift within Bennett's usage, one in which basilectal features are being passed through the transitional phases of variation so ably described by Bickerton.

One must also note that the past tense markers in English (-ed, -t) are absent in Creole, both because of basic sound laws and because Creole does not use these grammatical suffixes.

SE -nt, -st, -kt, -pt, -ld, -lt, -ft > JC -n, -s, -k, -p, -l, and -f

Table 10.2 presents the remaining final consonantal clusters for comparison with the /-nd/ group.

The most striking feature here is the regularity with which Jamaican Creole *kean* replaces Standard English *can't*, save for two exceptions. On the other hand, *want* occurs almost as frequently and never in other than its standard form, a far cry from Creole / wã:/ in which the final consonants have disappeared, leaving only a nasalized vowel behind. A similar rule shifts standard *won't* to Creole [wõ:], but the English spelling *won't* prevails. The other items occur in fairly closed balance, leading one to suppose that their variation may be contextually controlled.

Such clearly cannot be the case with *kean* and *want*, especially as the rhym-

Table 10.2. Standard English –nt# in Bennett's orthography

Standard English term	Jamaican Creole term		Anglicized Jamaican Creole term		Standard English term	
	Form	Occurrences	Form	Occurrences	Form	Occurrences
Ants		0		0	(rhymes with *chance*)	1
Can't	kean	16		0	can't	2
Couldn't		0	could'n	2	couldn't	1
Don't	doan	2		0	don't	3
Servant		0		0	servant	2
Want	[wã:]	0		0	want	15
Won't	[wõ:]	0	won'	2		0
Wouldn't	ooden hooden	1 1		0		0

ing of *ants* and *chance* shows Bennett's awareness of these aspects of Creole phonotactics. In "Candy Seller," the term *want* marks a dramatic moment: "Him y'eye dem a-tare out like him want / Hickmatize me candy-bole." Hypercorrection (*hickmatize* for *hypnotize*) intensifies the comic tone, marking the speaker's shift into learned language and demanding standard *want*. In the entire collection, *want* appears only six times in line-final position and never in a rhyming line. This factor suggests that it is not an easy term to rhyme in Jamaican Creole: I can find no match for it. Bennett's consistent use of *want* may thus be a regular shift toward Standard English, limited to this word, or—more probably—it may be a historical, nonphonetic spelling.

It is worth noting, however, that even in this context, Bennett goes out of her way to signal to her Jamaican audience by creating a phonetic spelling *bole:* this is a deliberate gesture to the Jamaican Creole reader to avoid the common Jamaican [baʊl] (rhyming with *prowl*), and instead to ensure a rhyme with *hole*.

Bennett is also highly consistent in her treatment of the /-st/# cluster, despite the orthographic uncertainty displayed in this and other instances by the irregular use of the apostrophe (table 10.3).

The two exceptions not yet discussed appear in the following contexts:

1. "Me meet one boonoonoonoos man / At matchis stick last night," in "Mass Wedding." (30)
2. "Beef balls noh got no taste to me," in "Rice Gawn." (85)

In example 1, the use of Standard English *at* for Creole *a* hints at mesolectal shifting, though the presence of basilectal *me* for Standard English *I* shows a contrary pull. In example 2, it is possible that the final *-t* of *taste* would be assimilated in speech to the initial *t-* of *to*. As there is no contextual reason to code-switch in either case, it may be inferred that these usages are not part of a conscious drive to introduce variation.

Table 10.4 presents the remaining consonantal clusters and again demonstrates the high level of consistency normally displayed by Bennett.

Apart from the phonetic consistency of the spellings, one is struck by the orthographic variations used to represent identical sound patterns. Such uncertainty seems characteristic of writers who labor between the oral forms of their speech communities and the conformist pressures of a written language that itself abounds with spelling variants. Like many others before her, Bennett makes use of rhyming pairs to point up the phonetic value of Jamaican Creole items while using standard orthography. As well as *ants / chance,* we find such pairs as *George / charge, stop / clap, back / lock,* and *lan / vacation*, in which the vowels of *charge, clap, back,* and *lan* are—to a Jamaican reader—cues to the rhymes and sometimes rhythm.

Yet, despite Bennett's general faithfulness to Creole sound patterns, the cases of *want* and *and* remain outstanding and troubling. In the /-nt/ group, eight other Standard English forms appear, the highest incidence of exceptions save for *and*. I now look more closely at the *don't* forms in the hope of discovering what may have prompted these variations.

1. "Dem don't even know shame," in "Wartime Grocery." (83–84)
2. "Is dat dah-meck de trouble now, / Miss Imo don't yuh see," in "Perplex." (81–82)
3. "So wen church member mel me, I / Don't answer till it reach / A rainy day wen Parson stay / Home, an Uriah preach," in "Uriah Preach." (203–204)

In example 3, we must recall that style-shifts appear earlier in this poem to express the formality of Uriah's preaching. This structural pattern might have influenced the occurrence of *don't,* save that it is Uriah, and not the speaker herself, who code-switches. Another possibility is that the context—a proud mother boasting of her son's sermons—might encourage upward code-switching. While this strategy is possible, there are too few features beyond acrolectal *I* and *don't* to make this pattern a clear rhetorical intention.

If example 3 cannot be adequately accounted for by rhetoric and context, even less clear are the rules governing examples 1 and 2. It is useful at this point to look at how all three would appear in basilectal Creole:

1. "Dem don't even know shame" becomes *Dem no know no shame.*
2. "A dat dah-meck de trouble now / Miss Imo, don't yuh see" becomes *A dat da meck de trouble now Miss Imo, yuh no see.*
3. "So wen church member mel me, I / Don't answer till it reach / A rainy day wen Parson stay / Home, an Uriah preach," becomes, *So wen chuch-memba mel me, me / No (h)answa till i reach / One rainy day wen Parson stay / Ome an Uriah-preach.*

No change in rhyme or meter arises from the use of basilectal features such as the double negative, the emphatic *da-deh,* the first person *me,* and *no* for *do not.* In the third example, strong stress and high-falling tone climax on *preach.* The basilectal versions provide an intensification of the mood and tone of each line, and, in example 3, a suggestion of intimacy with the audience replaces smugness and distance. The change is minimal, but to the Jamaican it is there. The message of each becomes subtly altered.

Here we may begin to perceive the minimal shifting toward Standard English, which Mervyn Alleyne describes in his discussion of Afro-American phonology: "From its very inception, [Creole] was involved in a relationship

Table 10.3. Standard English –st in Bennett's orthography

	Jamaican Creole		Anglicized Jamaican Creole		Standard English	
Standard English term	Form	Occurrences	Form	Occurrences	Form	Occurrences
Amongst	mongs	1		0		0
Best	bes	1		0		0
Burst	bus	2		0		0
Cast	caas	1		0		0
Fast		0		0		1
First	fus	3		0		0
Ghost		0	ghos'	1		0
Haste		0	has'e	1		0
Just	jus	7		0		0
Last	las	1	las'	1	last	1
Latest	latis	1		0		0
Lost Jamaican Creole variants [la:s], [l ɔ:s]	loss	1	las'	1		0
Most	mose	1		0		0
Must	mus	2		0		0
Must have	mussa musa	2 3		0		0

	Jamaican Creole		Anglicized Jamaican Creole		Standard English	
Standard English term	Form	Occurrences	Form	Occurrences	Form	Occurrences
Next	nex	1		0		0
Perplexed	perplex	2		0		0
Roost		0	roos'	1		0
Sweetest	sweetes	1		0		0
Taste		0		0	taste	1
Toothpaste	toot'pase	1	toot-paste	1		0
Twist	twis	1		0		0
Vexed	bex	6		0		0
Waist	wais	1		0		0
Worst	wuss	1		0		0

Table 10.4. Standard English –kt#, -pt#, -st#, -ld#, –lt#, -ft# in Bennett's orthography

Standard English consonantal clusters	Jamaican Creole		Anglicized Jamaican Creole		Standard English	
	Form	Occurrences	Form	Occurrences	Form	Occurrences
kt# >	k#					
	colleck	1	expec'	1		0
	fack	1				
	districk	1				
	negleck	1				
pt >	p#					
	cep	1		0	except	1
ld# >	d#					
	buil	1	worl'	3		0
	fole	1				
	gole	4				
	hole	1				
	ole	3				
	uphole	1				
lt# >	l#					
	sal-fish	1	sal'pork	1		0
	saal	1				
ft# >	f#					
	lif	1		0		
	liff	2				
	lef	2				
	leff	1				
	sofly	1			softly	1

with English in which the latter language must be considered the *terminus ad quem* . . . and this model was pursued to different degrees by different Afro-Americans."[17] He continues his discussion of language change by noting that "in contact situations there is always variation in language acquisition or language shift among individuals and groups," and that "considerable intra- and inter-idiolectal variation" exists in Afro-American speech communities.[18] Bennett's usage would seem to support this idea both at the conscious and unconscious levels of variation.

The presence of *don't* appears not to be an anomaly but part of an emerging pattern of variation. In three separate contexts, basilectal forms occur: *dem, dahmeck, mel* combine with intermediary mesolectal features such as the English word order of *even know;* mesolectal *is* forms a link to both Jamaican Creole *a* and Standard English *it is.* Acrolectal features such as *don't yuh see* (where only *yuh* marks nonstandard influence, together with Standard English *I* and *even*) offer possible ranges of usage all along the continuum. It is as if Bennett reaches beyond bilingual performance into an almost chaotic linguistic freedom. Such a degree of variation seemingly undetermined by context or rhetoric constitutes more than editorial error, or idiosyncrasy.

It would seem that such variation may be an integral part of Bennett's usage, a device for reaching the widest audience within the Jamaican continuum. I return to this point in the conclusion of this chapter, but here I hazard the suggestion that the occurrence of *don't* forms is not a controlled style-shift, nor is it part of a systematic intrusion of Standard English into Bennett's usage. As is often the case with *an* or *and,* the *don't* forms occur in a variety of contexts and appear to exert no pressure on the writer to alter other features. They may be taken, therefore, as satisfactory variants for *doan,* operating in that intermediary zone where basilect and acrolect may meet to form a single idiolectal grammar. As for *want,* its actual phonetic form in the performance of a Bennett poem remains at the preference of the performer. The co-occurrence of basilectal, mesolectal, and acrolectal forms leaves an open choice to the reader-performer and demonstrates something of the process by which change pursues its inevitable paths.

The interdental fricatives

In the case of Standard English /ð/, Bennett is almost completely consistent. All save six instances regularly show the Jamaican Creole voiced stop replacing the English voiced fricative. The definite article *de* occurs 145 times; English *the* appears once only. As subject pronoun and as plural marker, *dem* occurs 109 times; *them* never appears. See table 10.5.

Whether the item enjoys a high frequency of usage such as *de* or *dem,* or low (*neida* and *eida* occur once each), Bennett's spelling fulfils Jamaican Creole

Table 10.5. Standard English /ð/ > JC /d/ in Bennett's orthography

Standard English term	Jamaican Creole term	Occurrences of Jamaican Creole term	Occurrences of Standard English term
Although	aldoah	2	0
Though	doah	3	0
Bother	bada	3	0
Than	dan	2	0
That	dat	25	0
The	de	145	0
They [normally Jamaican Creole *dem*]	dey [formal Jamaican Creole]	1	0
They, their, them	dem	109	0
Themselves	demself	1	0
Then	den	12	0
There	deh	11	0
	deh-deh	2	
	dey	1	
	dere	1	
This	dis	8	0
Either	eida	1	0
Neither	neida	1	0
Farthing	farden	3	0
Father	fada	2	0
Other	oder	2	0
The other	toder	1	
Together	togedda	1	0
Rhythm	rydim	1	0
With	wid	18	0
Without	widout	2	0
Exceptions			
That's			1
The			1
Thou			2
Thy			2

sound laws. The *thy* and *thou* exceptions are highly significant, as they occur in "Uriah Preach" (203–204) and mark the formal code-switches of the sermon: "Thou shalt not give thy neighbours / Floolooloops to eat!" Biblical style and standardized language indicate a formal, ritualized speech act deeply embedded in Jamaican Creole tradition and set off by the hyper-rhetoric of Jamaican Creole *floolooloops,* a discursive style of "cutting language" created when extravagant Creole word-play juxtaposes—and mocks—metropolitan formality.

No such clarity of behavior or purpose marks the solitary occurrence of *the* in "Rough Riding Tram": "Wid all de draw yuh draw the 'tring / De tram dah-gallop still" (47). In the midst of a basilectal sentence stands this humble definite article proclaiming the metropolitan language. It is clearly not a functional code-switch: it does not belong with the Creole grammar or sound rules of the sentence, especially "'tring." If it is an editorial error, it suggests a degree of pressure from English conventions that is startling in a folk poet as determined to resist "the rules of (Standard English) grammar," as Nettleford reports.[19] Interestingly, "Rough Riding Tram" makes use of mesolectal first-person pronoun *Ah* for each of the four times that the persona addresses the tram driver; basilectal *me* occurs five times as first-person pronoun when the persona addresses her companion or makes general remarks.

The spellings *dey* for English-derived *they* and *dey* for the Jamaican Creole locative *de* contrast with Bennett's normal Creole *dem* and *deh*. These spellings indicate clear shifts toward Standard English, and, though low in occurrence, cannot be overlooked. The *they* etymon occurs in "I' Wut I'": "Dey sey mus meck we go an raise / De jooce ef it no nice!" (35). To find *dey* in an otherwise totally basilectal sentence is instructive. Clearly, it is an acceptable variant in that slot, though it has a low frequency of usage. The *dey* that represents Jamaican Creole *deh* occurs in a code-switched context, as the persuasive vendor in "South Parade Peddler" (27) moves toward Standard English while wooing a customer: "Wey de nice lady dey?" These two examples illustrate well the kinds of variation in Bennett's usage, in which the pressure to conform to Standard English seems to exert an unintended patterning in spelling and syntax.

The case for the unvoiced interdental fricative and its Creole alternative, the unvoiced alveolar stop, is less clear, as table 10.6 shows. In some instances, the variation is obviously related to controlled upward switching, as is the case with the single instance of *teeth*. This term appears as part of the persuasively polite repertoire of the vendor in "South Parade Peddler" (27). As I have already noted, this poem is constructed on shifts of mood and attitude, all presented through shifts of usage.

We should note that the polite opening stanza of "South Parade Peddler" uses *teeth* and *everything,* while the abusive fourth stanza uses *toot-brush, mout',* and *teet'*. These shifts belong within the normal range of Jamaican language

Table 10.6. Standard English /θ/ > Jamaican Creole /t/ in Bennett's orthography

	Jamaican Creole term		Anglicized Jamaican Creole term		Standard English term	
Standard English term	Form	Occurrences	Form	Occurrences	Form	Occurrences
Thank	tank tenk	2 1		0	thank	1
Thankful	tenkful (archaic Jamaican Creole)	1				
Teeth	teet	7	teet'	1		1
Theatre		0		0		2
Thick	tick	1		0		0
Thief	tief	3		0		0
Thing	ting	6		0		0
Things	tings	1		0		0
Everything	everyting	1		0		2
Nothing	nutten	3		0		0
Something	sinting	14		0		1
Think	tink	6		0		0
Thousand	tousen	2		0		0
Three	tree	1	t'ree	2		1
Threepence	tropence	1		0		0
Through		0	t'rough	1		0

Standard English term	Jamaican Creole term		Anglicized Jamaican Creole term		Standard English term	
	Form	Occurrences	Form	Occurrences	Form	Occurrences
Throat		0	t'roat	1		0
Tooth-brush	toot-brush	1		0		0
Tooth-paste		0	toot'pase	2		0
Truth		0	trut'	1		0
Authority		0		0		4
Cloth		0	clath (rhymes with *wart)*	1		0
Earthquake	eartquake	4		0		1
Forth	fort	1		0		0
Month		0	mont'	1		0
Mouth	mout	6	mout'	1		0
Oath	oat	1		0		0
Sitteth		0	sittet'	1		0
Worth	wut	3		0		0

behavior: code-switching according to situation and purpose. The same is true of the "Thank you madam" in "Yuh Nephew Sue" (34), where this and other shifts bring out the social and situational pressures on the persona attending the meeting.

The four occurrences of *authority* and the two of *theatre* may, at first glance, be accounted for by assuming that such specialized, low-frequency items might be less likely to undergo phonetic change. Certainly, context and rhetoric do not explain the retention of the "th" digraph. I am careful here to separate spelling and sound: I am not at all certain that Bennett would utter [θ] while reciting such lines as "Me kean blame de Authority" (85) or "foreign genkleman dah-come / A Ward Theatre fe sing" (35). At no point should one forget, however, that /θ/ and /ð/ are phonemes in Bennett's second language, Standard English. Phonemes exert pressure both on speech and on orthography.

Basilectal features such as first-person singular pronoun *me*, Jamaican Creole *kean* for Standard English *can't, de* for *the,* and Creole *genkleman, dah-come, a,* and *fe* make the occurrence of the "th" digraph very conspicuous. I myself find it impossible to use [θ] when reading these lines (aloud or in my mind), and I can see no code-switching rule requiring it. At the same time, such terms might tempt a *writer* to use conventional English spellings. These words belong to a more specialized and technical level of English, involving the diction of officialdom and of higher learning. Consequently, phonetic spellings of such terms may hamper readers. High-frequency, nonspecialized words such as *de* and *ting* may be more easily identified. If such is the case, the title "Jamaica Ant'em" (156) raises questions about Bennett's consistency.

Even more disturbing are the spelling of *three* in "Earthquake Night," and that of the title itself (31). The spelling *eartquake* is used for the four occurrences of this item in the poem: Why not in the title, when the less common *anthem* can be phonetically spelled as "Ant'em"? And why keep the English digraph "th" in "Me hear sey Vera baby / Three year ole Decemba gawn / Wat never cut a teet nor walk / Nor talk good from it bawn" (32)?

Equally puzzling are the occurrences of *everything* in "Mirricle" and "Overflow":

One day wen Hermitage dry up
An everything look black
Wen Mona is we ongle hope
Big Chief gwine smite de rock! ("Mirricle," 45)

Tell dem sey we yard, we pipeside
House top, kitchen, high an' low
Goatpen, pidgin coob an fowl roos'
Everything dah-overflow! ("Overflow," 46)

In each poem it is possible to make a rhetorical case for the use of upward shifts. "Mirricle" dramatizes an imaginary act of government by the chief minister, while "Overflow" claims to be a letter to the press. The *everything* of "Overflow" stands as an isolated element marking the shift, unsupported by other items. By itself, it tells the reader nothing save that an incomplete shift has taken place, or that the spelling is to be ignored and the sound change substituted to harmonize with *coob, roos',* and *dah-overflow*. In "Mirricle," we find a mingling of basilectal, mesolectal, and acrolectal elements that permit alternative readings: One might be a formal grandiose tone retaining /θ/ and /h/. Another might be a melodramatic Creole style created by ignoring the English spellings and substituting representations of Jamaican Creole pronunciations for *everything* and *hope*. Either reading is valid within the possible range of styles in Jamaican discourse. The choice of one or the other does not constitute free variation but instead leads to differing semantic goals.

Returning now to "Earthquake Night" (31), one must note that the use of Standard English "th" in that poem offers a curious shift to the Jamaican ear. It works against the tonal unity of the poem, and, if it is indeed to be pronounced, becomes an inappropriate class marker to the Jamaican audience. It is a carryover from the writer's acrolect into a context where the audience expects mesolect and basilect. Such uncontrolled variation signals either interference from Standard English, or some aspect of the linguistic insecurity characteristic of speakers within a continuum situation. It demonstrates that intra-idiolectal variation mentioned by Alleyne,[20] which he regards as having great significance: "[The] basic creole varieties . . . no longer exist, even in Jamaica as stable, consistent codes in the usage of many speakers."[21] Would Bennett have been one such speaker? Bickerton's account of the passage from basilect to mesolect is helpful here: "We may better regard the basilect as a phase through which some creole speakers pass (as the language itself has passed through it), or as something which constitutes only a part of the competence of most synchronic speakers—a very large part for some, a much smaller one for others."[22] Thus, we may interpret these variations in Bennett's usage as evidence of mesolectal language behavior, separating her idiolect definitively from what Bickerton calls the "'pure,' 'genuine' . . . creole, miraculously free from variation,"[23] a Creole that, in his view, probably never existed. At the same time, both Alleyne and Bickerton have carefully shaded their judgments: "some creole speakers" do not account for all speakers. Other speakers may retain a "pure," "genuine" Creole as yet undetected by linguists.

Finally, we must ask whether such features of Standard English usage as are listed here affect the rhetoric and tone of Bennett's writing. The answer to this question can only be affirmative. In order to accommodate such variation, we must abandon any attempt to confine her within the formula of a "'pure,' 'genuine' . . . creole" poet. Her usage clearly spans a very wide range of the Jamaican continuum, ranging from acrolect to basilect, and as is the case with other mesolectal speakers, her variations are both intended and unintended, but never without significance. She faces special challenges, however, in dealing with initial [h], and no clear solution appears in her orthography.

In the first place, the Standard English /h/ phoneme carries an exclusive phonetic, variation-bound status in Jamaican Creole. Cassidy and Le Page explain: "Initial [h] is frequently lost in unemphatic contexts and used as a hypercorrection in emphatic contexts: /aaba ~ haaba/ *arbour* and *harbour* /hanch/ *ants* /human ~ uman/ *woman* . . . /huda/ *would have*. Both the loss and the hypercorrect use are features of English dialects also."[24] Bennett, well aware of this feature of both Standard English and Jamaican Creole phonology, addresses a sarcastic warning to snobbish "Mass Charlie" in "Bans o' Killing" (219):

> An mine how yuh dah-read dem English
> Book deh pon yu shelf
> For ef yuh drop a "h" yuh mighta
> Haffe kill yuhself.

The editorial note to the poem "Hess" carries the same message more explicitly: "The Jamaican characteristically drops the aitch from the German's name and the letter 'S' (in this poem) becomes—ominously—the first letter of the word 'Spy' which Herr Hess was supposed to be."[25]

In this poem, Bennett plays constantly on the deletion of Standard English /h/ in the name "Hess": "Me mine tell me say we gwine ketch / Hitla t'rough dat Jahman 'S' . . . " and "Him sey him was Hitla right han man / But him real name is 'S'" (94). The letter *S* is used throughout the poem for *Hess,* but no other word beginning with "h" undergoes such change. Instead, all retain this feature of English spelling: *him* (twelve usages); *hear* (three usages); *how* (two usages), as well as one each of *have, haffe,* and *han*. Most of these are likely to be unstressed and without emphasis, yet the "h" spelling is deliberately used. The six occurrences of *Hitla* are all likely to be stressed, so "h" retention is less unusual.

These conventional Standard English spellings are, for the most part, characteristic of Bennett's treatment of nonphonemic [h] in her writing. Few additions or deletions occur. A single admirable pun occurs in "South Parade Peddler" (27):

> Pu dung me razor blade.
> Yuh no gat no use fe it for yuh
> Dah-suffa from Hair-raid!

The environment of plus emphasis and the nature of the pun itself make this instance a clear indication that Bennett is aware of the phonotactic rules for [h]. Yet in the twenty-five poems examined, unstressed words retain initial "h," and vowel-initial words attract no aspiration even in stressed positions.

The exceptions are very few, but their occurrence is worth noting: *ow* (three unstressed, one stressed); *'ow* (two, both unstressed); and a single unstressed *omuch.* In contrast to these forms, the Jamaican Creole *would* etymons tend to be spelled with the aspirate: one *hood;* seven *hooda;* one *hooden.* A single exception is *ooden.*

All of the *hood-hooda-hooden* forms happen to occur in positions of metrical and rhetorical stress, while the single *ooden* occurs in a position of weak stress. A few examples must suffice:

> Me hóoden háffe dróp bómb (83)
> . . . Ìt hóod be gréat! (46)
>
> Mé ben knów, whát e hóoda háppen (81)
> Quéeze-Yèye óoden séll me óne smáll tín (83)

In the last example, stress and rising-falling tone fall on "Y'éye ooden" and compel an elision, making the deletion of [h] essential.

The items to which the [h]-deletion rule might apply are so numerous that I abandoned a frequency count, preferring to concentrate on the few exceptions listed herein. Alongside Standard English words are Jamaican Creole items displaying other sound shifts, yet spelled with the Standard English initial /h/. Those items that lack the plus or minus initial [h], but which are otherwise phonetically spelled according to Jamaican Creole sound rules follow: *haffe, halla, han, han-bag, har, heaby, hebby, heng, him, Hitla, hole* (SE *hold*), *hu't ('hurt'), husban.* Standard English forms include the following: *had, haircurler, hairnet, hairpin, half, handle, hanger, happen, happy, hard, have, her, head, heap, hear, heart, heaven, here, hi, hide, high, him, hog, (nose)hole, holiday, home, hope, horse, house, how, hug, hundred, who, whole.* Many of these items enjoy high-frequency usage. In "Uriah Preach" alone, *him* occurs seventeen times (203–204). In "Po' Muffeena," *har* occurs thirteen times, while *her* appears just once (89). *Heart* occurs ten times in the poems studied, *hear* twenty-one times, and *head* fifteen times. Pronouns such as *him, her/har* usually fall in unstressed, unemphatic positions, yet Bennett consistently retains these English spellings.

Equally striking is her absolute refusal to add initial "h" to vowel-initial Standard English and Jamaican Creole items as is shown in "Bans o' Ooman" (40), where we find the following forms: *alarm, an/and, ants* (rhymes with "chance"), *at, ef, ever, every, inside, is, isle* [*sic*] for Standard English "aisle," *o'/of, ooman, oversweet, up.* The italicized items reflect Creole phonetic spellings; many of them fall in stressed, emphatic positions:

1. . . . wén sínting oversweét dem
2. Óoman quéeze me, óoman púsh me / óoman frówn
3. Is dát tíme me se de óoman dem / Líke várigáted ánts

To read *oversweet, ants,* and *ooman* in examples 1 and 2 without emphatic aspiration is possible but—to this speaker—very awkward, given the environment of *sinting, dem, queeze, dat,* and *me* as first-person singular pronoun, as well as the *chance* rhyme for *ants.* Save for elisions such as occur in example 3, unaspirated *ooman* is a most unlikely usage for the twelve occurrences of this item in this poem. Yet Bennett is a careful and deliberate orthographer in other respects, so once more, we must regard these spellings as either historical and nonphonetic, or as aspects of Bennett's actual pronunciation, or, more disturbingly, as optional features left to the reader-performer's judgment.

Vowel-initial words form a very large part of the vocabulary of the poems, ranging from low-stressed items such as *ef, if, an* to items of semantic and rhetorical importance attracting emphasis. The latter include *ackee, earring, eat,* and *ask/ax.* Jamaican Creole words that, in other respects, have been respelled to meet Creole sound rules, but lack the initial #h- that one might expect. A few items such as *ongle/only* alternate between Jamaican Creole and Standard English: *advize* (Standard English *advice*), *afta/atta, aldoah, anada, aready, eartquake, incourage, en', een/eena, evenin', everyting, expec, it/I, inclose, obeah, oat* (Standard English *oath*), *oder, off/offa, ole, ongle/only, ooman, oonoo, out/outa, ovah/over, undah, undastan, up/upa.* Bennett also makes use of regular Standard English spellings: *able, about, ackee-skin, again, airforce, alarm, all, allow, along, alphabet, always, Amy, an, and, answer, ants* (rhymes with *chance*), *anytime, arrives, as, ashes, ask/ax, at, attention, earring, earthquake, encore, enemy, engine, even, everybody, everything, exercise, exert, if, ignorance, Imo, improve, Inglish* (creolized, nonphonetic), *inside, if, into, isle* (for Standard English *aisle*), *open, or, overflow, oversweet, owe, ugly, uncle, untidy, upon.*

It is clear from the extent of these lists that no normal code-switching operates here, just as it is clear that Bennett, from her remarks in "Hess" and "Bans O' Killing" (94, 218), is quite aware of the deletion of initial [h], yet she resists adding initial [h] demanded by Creole pronunciation for stressed words beginning with a vowel. The single pun *hair-raid* and the lone contrast of *hooden/ooden* suggest that her awareness extends beyond the deletion of [h] to the addition of aspiration for emphasis. The possible significance of these unexpected standardized spellings is considered in the conclusion to this chapter.

Standard English *Say* and the Jamaican Creole Complimentizer *Se*: Conflicting Homophones

Bennett's spelling of these two items is irregular. No clear form is assigned to either; no rules of grammar, style, or context seem to determine the occurrence of *sey/say* spellings. A single "se" (for Creole *se*) appears. A study of environments produces no results, but an examination of the number of occurrences is useful (see table 10.7).

Bennett prefers nonstandard *sey* for both terms (fifty-two usages). Her difficulty may arise because the two words are homophones: "Tell dem sey I sey fe sey" ("Overflow," 46), in which the first and last "sey" are the Creole connective equivalent to *that* after verbs of knowing, feeling, and believing, while the second ("I sey") is the Creole variant of Standard English *say*. The single occurrence of the spelling *se* for Jamaican Creole *se* points up her concern to distinguish the items, but as this is her normal spelling for English *see*, it merely adds to the confusion.

One answer would be to use *say* for the Standard English verb and *sey* for the Jamaican Creole connective, but this might not adequately reveal their phonetic similarity. So, beset by pressures of phonetic accuracy and standard conventions, Bennett moves uncomfortably between variant spellings.

One last anomaly presents itself in the twenty-five poems: Bennett's use of final "h" in a number of high-functioning, monosyllabic words: English *so, no, not, where, why, away* become Creole *soh, noh, noh, weh, weh,* and *weh* (table 10.8).

This use of final "h" invites more careful study. It seems to mark the Creole vowel as short, central, and emphatic, as far from a long English vowel or diphthong as possible: [ɔ] and [o:] become [ʌ], while [ei], [ɝ:], [aɪ] become [ɛ]. Yet in any one poem, we find examples of the English spellings as well as the Creole forms: "Buy . . . fram me noh lady" and "Buy something noh me nice young man" are followed by "Yuh no gat no use fe it" ("South Parade Peddler," 27); "Mona Dam noh got no wata" ("Mirricle," 44); "So afta pickcha done," "so me goin'," "crowd so tick," "Fan look good soh tell" ("Mass Wedding," 30–

Table 10.7. Bennett's spelling of English *say* and Creole *se*

	Jamaican Creole *se*		English *say*	
Spelling style	Form	Occurrences	Form	Occurrences
Standardized	say	8	say	6
Modified Creole	sey	33	sey	19
Phonetic Creole	se	1	se	0

Table 10.8 Bennett's use of final "h" in monosyllabic function words

English	Creole
So	soh
No	noh
Not	noh
(No English equivalent)	noh (emphatic final marker) "Come, noh?"
Away	weh
Where	weh
Why	weh
You	yuh

31). Bennett's habit of rendering English *you* as Creole *yuh* carries weight here because, like *dah,* it is almost always spelled with final "h." In "Overflow," the single *you* spelling seems to hint at formality and a conscious shift to English: "Dinah, teck you pen in han" (46). In "Rough Riding Tram," however, seven *you* forms occur with a single *yuh:* making a rhetorical case for the English spellings becomes a real challenge as the speaker's invective expands. In "Noh Lickle Twang," however, language shifts illuminate the drama. The two uses of formal *you* ("Me glad fe se's you come back bwoy," and "Is soh you come" [209]) form a satiric counterpoint to the speaker's son's inability to utter any language except his native Creole and his mother's vanity in wanting him to put on "lickle language." More than any set of examples, this last poem captures the complexity of Creole's relationship to English and hints at the challenges of devising a spelling system.

The foregoing sampling of Bennett's orthography and usage demonstrates the need for a standardized spelling for Jamaican speech forms. The sampling also reveals that shifting is such an important part of Jamaican language behavior that any satisfactory orthography must accommodate rule-governed variation as well as the varying expectations of the audience.

Bennett's Use of the Copula

For durative aspect and progressive action in verb phrases, Bennett uses both basilectal *da* and mesolectal *a* as preposed markers, with a marked preference for *dah.* This is the form described under DA_3 by Cassidy and Le Page as "a less common auxiliary of durative or progressive action, present, past, or future. DA_3 + a verb is equivalent to *to be* + a present participle."[26] Typical examples from Bennett include *dah-maltreat, dah-suffa, dah-fray, dah-kin* in "Soap Vacation" (87). The related *a* form appears in "Ban Concert" (35) as *a-prims, a-walk, a-wear.* Cassidy and Le Page define this verb form under A_5: "Mi hed a hat mi / *my head is hurting me.*"[27] In *Jamaica Labrish,* Nettleford glosses *dah*[28] as an intensified variant of *a*, but the environments do not appear to bear out this interpretation. In "Him Deh Yah," we find the following: "a garden full o' song / Eena him heart a-grow," but "him dah-coax / De song out o' him heart" in the very next stanza. These examples look very much like free variation. Bennett prefers *dah* (used forty-six times) to *a,* which totals eighteen occurrences. Raw numbers seem to suggest a different interpretation.

In five of the twenty-five poems, neither form of this auxiliary verb occurs. While a further five yielded insignificant data, *da* is the preferred form in ten other poems, occurring as many as four or five times in four poems. This pattern seems at variance with Cassidy and Le Page's finding that *da* is "less common." The possible explanations may be that Bennett's usage represents an earlier stage of the interaction of these variants; that Nettleford's interpretation of *da* as an intensified form of *a* reveals another aspect of the developmental process, and that the lexicographers describe yet another stage in the flow of the continuum.

Predicative adjectives and Standard English *be* forms typically represent NP + predicative adjective,[29] save for negatives, which are not included here. There are forty sentences such as *me bex,* or *him bad* in the twenty-five poems studied. There are, as well, seventeen sentences that use an SE *be* form in place of the JC predicative adjective. In "Mass Wedding" (30), both types occur:

Predicative adjectives:
1. "Him nice and tall"
2. "crowd so tick"

Standard English *be* forms:
1. "she / Was really lookin sweet"
2. "Mary new boot was a-bun har"
3. "Diah tie ben lean"

Alleyne describes the Standard English derived *ben* of example 3 as follows: "The English morpheme *been* is the most plausible etymological antecedent for these forms: but syntactically it is obvious that *been* in English has an entirely different function."[30] Alleyne notes that the *ben* variants (Jamaican Creole *ben, en, min*) are optional, especially in contexts where time is contextually marked. Thus, *Diah tie ben lean* belongs to a level of Jamaican usage different from that of the *is/was* forms and closer to the predicative adjectives. The use of the different forms (Standard English *be* forms, Creole *ben,* and predicative adjectives) is not tied to changes of rhetoric or to contextually determined code-switches in this poem. It would appear that these variants are rhetorically permissible juxtapositions, at least in Bennett's written usage, and that while she exhibits a preference for the predicative adjective, her usage includes no strong rule excluding mesolectal *be* forms.

According to Alleyne, the sentence type of copula *a* and Standard English *be* constitutes a "subcategory of PredVb . . . represented by such English sentences as *he is a farmer* (copula)."[31] Cassidy and Le Page classify this *a* form as "A_6: *is* and other forms of the verb *to be.*"[32] Bennett provides six usages only: typically, "man a debil" and "ooman a debil mumma" (42–43). The seventeen other syntactic slots into which Creole *a* might have been fitted all display English *be* forms. Some contexts suggest intentional upward code-switching: "yuh is de bes one fe de day" in "South Parade Peddler" (27), where the vendor woos a customer. Others are ambiguous: "me an Rice is frien" in "Rice Gawn" (85), where a rule of emphatic formality might promote a shift upward. Finally, both appear side by side: "Me a po' Muffeena / Me luck is dis like mud" (89). Possible shifts of meaning and emphasis arise here, as *a* signals Muffeena's deep Jamaican identity, and English *is* stamps her bad luck with the authority of the master language. In contrast to Bennett's preference for the supposedly archaic *dah,* English-based *to be* verbs take precedence over Creole *a* in her usage.

Creole scholars such as Beryl Loftman Bailey and Mervyn Alleyne note the existence of a Creole particle that functions as a representative of place and duration.[33] In Jamaican Creole, the locative *de* carries this function. Bennett uses it as follows:

Present tense:
1. "Him Deh Yah" ("Him Deh Yah," 38)
2. "ooman deh a Tung" ("Bans o' Ooman," 40)
3. "One heaby cross deh pon me mine" ("Perplex," 81)
4. "Matty deh dung a riverside" ("Soap Vacation," 86)
5. "Which part yuh . . . winda curtain deh?" ("Bans o' Ooman," 40)

Past tense:
1. "Me wen deh a de las' mass wedden" ("Mass Wedding," 30)
2. "Me one ben deh-deh" ("Jamaica Patois," 88)
3. "Money man was deh" ("Yuh Nephew Sue," 33)

The last is a mesolectal variant of *deh-deh,* in which the first *deh* is a past-tense marker and not the locative. Bennett's usage of the locative is thus generally Creole, save for two mesolectal variations. The context of example "was deh" may have promoted this usage, as the persona of the poem is describing a very formal meeting dominated by middle-class English speakers.

With respect to Creole *a* for Standard English *it is, there is, there are,* Bennett has only two instances of the Creole form: "ef *a* noh good sinting" ("I' Wut I'," 35) and "me kean fine out / *Ah* ow me gwine get bex" ("Perplex," 81). The spelling of the second example overlaps with Bennett's normal spelling of the mesolectal first-person singular pronoun *Ah* (English *I*). Against these two usages stand twenty-six usages of mesolectal *is,* ranging from a possible style-shift in "Jamaica Patois" (87) where the persona mixes Spanish words in her affected speech ("Is hard fe intiendeh / Jamaica diniera") to a contextually and formally basilectal slot: "Is wha meck dem meck dat rule" ("Mirricle," 44). It is obvious that even if "Jamaica Patois" presents a case of contextual style-shifting, the rule creating such shifting for the *a* form constitutes no general part of Bennett's usage: she prefers mesolectal *be* forms over the Creole verb.

Conclusion

In reviewing the nature and significance of variation in these twenty-five poems from Bennett's *Jamaica Labrish,* one is struck both by her consistency and by her inconsistency, and even more by the areas of usage where these occur. Bennett is a phonetic orthographer of remarkable regularity with regard to the reduction of Standard English final consonantal clusters (especially -nd), yet unaccountably eight *and* forms appear in this group. The contrast of phonetic *kean* and Standard English *want* is sharp and troubling. The *-st* group displays considerable phonetic regularity, as do the remaining consonantal clusters in word-final position. Yet there is just sufficient variation with Standard English forms to make one question the nature of these variations, especially those unrelated to any contextual or rhetorical rule. The treatment of the interdental fricatives is also problematic. Some of the Standard English variants are clearly upward switches; others plainly are not. The regularity of English spellings for the added or deleted Creole [h] is so outstanding as to be unbelievable, particularly in the light of Bennett's statements on this feature of Jamaican Creole usage. The spellings *sey* and *say* uncover a simpler kind of variation: the uncertainty of a writer hesitating between two acceptable spellings for two homophones and making no clear etymological choice between them.

These kinds of variation open different possibilities. First, we can assert positively that Bennett regularly makes use of deliberate, rhetorically purposeful variation, and she does so with great skill and elegance as in "South Parade Peddler," "Candy Seller," "Mass Wedding," "Yuh Nephew Sue," "Mirricle," "Jamaica Patois," "Hess," and "Uriah Preach." In these and other poems, the roles of characters are developed through code-switches, and much of the rich irony and humor would be lost were these variations to pass unnoticed.

Indeed the whole structure of the poems just named would be undermined if the variations were regularized or "corrected." It is clear that Bennett reaches out to her Jamaican audience by means of variations that they will recognize and interpret correctly. Given this factor, one may now hypothesize another purpose in her use of variation. This purpose may lie in Bennett's use of Standard English forms where Jamaican Creole realizations are intended for performance. Such seems to be the case for the disappearance of initial [h-], as Bennett clearly states that Jamaicans drop the aspirate. Though she makes no statement about adding the aspirate for emphasis, the few examples of added aspirates show that this variation is known and that she places the choice of adding or deleting [h-] at the reader-performer's disposal.

I do not know if Bennett made this choice consciously; the evidence suggests otherwise. Yet given the *want/kean* contrast, and the regular standardized spellings for English /#h-/ and vowel initial words, I can only surmise that these are nonphonetic, historical spellings that disguise Creole realizations. That this may be a strong if only partly rationalized force in Bennett's mind is borne out by her rhymes. Here she often uses English spellings for pairs that actually rhyme only in Creole pronunciations, for example, *George/charge*. Thus even through the veil of standardization, Bennett sends clear messages to her audience that she desires Jamaican Creole language rules to prevail.

Occasionally, Standard English forms may be chosen over Jamaican Creole forms merely to accommodate readers: Literate Jamaicans are more familiar with English spellings because few Creole texts exist. Many Jamaican speakers translate English into Creole while reading. Into this category may fall such items as "authority" and "theatre." Thus it is possible for a Jamaican reader-performer to apply variation rules to Bennett's text without any signal from her to do so. Carol Reckord, a well-known Jamaican radio personality of the 1960s, told me that he wrote all of his scripts in English as he did not know how to write Jamaican Creole, but he was easily able to shift while performing or reading the script. Therefore, it is entirely possible that the apparent standardization of much of Bennett's spelling is misleading. Clearly, she intends variation where none is overtly indicated; she thus invites her audience, especially the reader-performer of the poems, to select certain variations at will. This invitation is crucial because it assures the reader-performer that his or her choice is part of the re-creation of the dramatic poem: without this active involvement, the writer's intentions cannot be fulfilled.

Bennett's combination of basilectal, mesolectal, and acrolectal features gives her work a broad range of audience acceptance. She is thus able to reach audiences at every level in the Jamaican continuum, certain that their own use of variation coincides at some point with her own. This instinct is probably at the root of her intuitive rejection of standardization in any form. Certainly, such a strategy demands a flexible spelling system that can accommodate variation, and to a large extent Bennett achieves this goal. However, a price must be paid. The opposite side of this strategy is the rejection by this same audience of some features of Bennett's usage. This problem will inevitably occur where her style-shifts are neither clearly related to context, nor can they be made to do so through reinterpretation. Such collisions must happen where Bennett's usage has to be taken at face value. If the audience's usage differs from hers, an interpretive problem will arise between text and audience, leading to a questioning of the writer's intentions and tone.

Such occasions do arise in *Jamaica Labrish.* They are evidence of the pressure of Standard English on a writer highly sensitized to nonstandard usage. They may also be features of usage best perceived as belonging to a time and a generation, as compromises no longer needed, because they are no longer demanded. Finally, they are clear and invaluable evidence of the complex and subtle processes by which living languages continuously transform themselves.

Notes

1. See the introduction to Louise Bennett, *Jamaica Labrish,* ed. Rex Nettleford (1966; repr., Kingston, Jamaica: Sangster's Bookstores, 1972), 16, 11.

2. Ibid., 16, 9.

3. Ibid.

4. Ibid., 9

5. Ibid.

6. Ibid.

7. Derek Bickerton, *Dynamics of a Creole System* (Cambridge: Cambridge University Press, 1975), 60.

8. Ibid.

9. F. G. Cassidy and R. B. Le Page, "Linguistic Introduction," in *Dictionary of Jamaican English,* 2nd ed. (Cambridge: Cambridge University Press, 1980), xl–xlii. See especially [h] and the reduction of consonant sounds. On the postcolonial attributes of medieval English, see Barbara Lalla, *Postcolonialisms: Caribbean Rereading of Medieval English Discourse* (Kingston, Jamaica: University of the West Indies Press, 2008).

10. Bickerton, *Dynamics of a Creole System,* 60.

11. Cassidy and Le Page, *Dictionary of Jamaican English,* xl, lxii.

12. See "se," in Cassidy and Le Page, *Dictionary of Jamaican English,* 396.

13. See Nettleford's gloss of *da,* in Bennett, *Jamaica Labrish,* 22.

14. Cassidy and Le Page, *Dictionary of Jamaican English,* 1.

15. Ibid.

16. Ibid., 144–145.

17. Mervyn Alleyne, *Comparative Afro-American: A Historical Comparative Study of English-Based Afro-American Dialects* (Ann Arbor, MI: Karoma Publishers, 1980) 75.

18. Ibid., 76.

19. Nettleford, introduction to *Jamaica Labrish,* 9.

20. Alleyne, *Comparative Afro-American,* 76.

21. Ibid., 188.

22. Bickerton, *Dynamics of a Creole System,* 60.

23. Ibid.

24. Cassidy and Le Page, *Dictionary of Jamaican English,* lxii.

25. Nettleford, notes to *Jamaica Labrish,* 94.

26. Cassidy and Le Page, *Dictionary of Jamaican English,* 141.

27. Ibid., 1.

28. Nettleford, notes to *Jamaica Labrish,* 222.

29. Beryl Loftman Bailey, *Jamaican Creole Syntax* (Cambridge: Cambridge University Press, 1966), 42–43; Alleyne, *Comparative Afro-American,* 78, 87

30. Alleyne, *Comparative Afro-American,* 85.

31. Ibid., 88.

32. Cassidy and Le Page, *Dictionary of Jamaican English,* 1.

33. Bailey, *Jamaican Creole Syntax*, 42–43; Alleyne, *Comparative Afro-American*, 78–87.

11
Conceptual Perspectives on Time and Timelessness in Martin Carter's "University of Hunger"

Barbara Lalla

Martin Carter's "University of Hunger" is about arrival and the formation of a mind—the collective mind of a people—by the circumstances of that arrival.[1] It is, therefore, a historical vision:

> They come from the distant village of the flood
> passing from middle air to middle earth
> in the common hours of nakedness. (ll. 12–14)

However, in "University of Hunger," only the last verse is Standard English past tense, with the single exception of line 20: "is they who had no voice in the emptiness." On the other hand, Caribbean English-lexicon Creole may convey reference to past time without marking past tense. Therefore, the time reference of some verbs in the poem is ambiguous. If the poem echoes with voices in both codes, it may well interweave past and present vision, and, in so doing, refocus our view of history. Thus, an important issue in interpreting this poem is its multidimensional time reference. In a phrase like *they come* (in the quotation earlier), *come* may be present or past, depending on whether the voice is English or Creole. The linguistic situation of the Caribbean enables Carter to address an international audience through the widely comprehensible code of Standard Caribbean English, but, at the same time, to counter traditional poetic discourse by intercepting standard structures in a number of ways.

"Is the university of hunger the wide waste." To begin with, if we view this first line as Standard English, we assume from the punctuation that it is a statement but from the constituent order that it is a question. If it is a statement, it is mutilated by subject deletion, and it omits a comma between complement and appositive. From the outset, then, if we assume a Standard English voice, Carter tampers with the conventions of traditional literary discourse. The fact is that the structure is more recognizable as Creole. However, he yokes the Creole sentence patterns, familiar in oral discourse, to literary diction unfamiliar in the vernacular. The tendency to frustrate reader expectations continues throughout the poem, which departs from linguistic norms not only at syntactic but at lexico-semantic levels ("The print of hunger wanders in the land" [l. 3]). However, anomaly at the lexical level creates no anxiety; it is the usual stuff of metaphor.

Apart from the first sentence (if it is read as Creole), the poem seems at first glance to make sparse use of Creole diction. The use of one feature consistently may reflect selectivity aimed at a representational effect, even in the presence of non-Creole structures such as the passive, "The huts of men are fused in misery" (l. 6). At the same time, familiar trappings of traditional Standard English literary discourse reveal their own discrepancies on examination. The second verse opens with a normal Standard English subject (*they*). However, the pronoun has no identifiable referent:

is the university of hunger the wide waste.
is the pilgrimage of man the long march.
The print of hunger wanders in the land.
The green tree bends above the long forgotten.
The plains of life rise up and fall in spasms.

The huts of men are fused in misery. (ll. 1–6)

Again and again, mechanisms that would orient the reader are suppressed or frustrated.

The limited number of Creole features is not an argument against the reality of a Creole voice. Orality in literary discourse is a function of representational features in any case. As any transcript of spoken discourse readily shows, it would be impractical for literature to mirror actual speech with its hesitations, false starts, incomplete sentences, and pauses for feedback. Moreover, literature that represents speech in a code other than the official written code usually samples features of that unofficial code. The writer selects a workable balance of features. Most should be well-enough known to be easily comprehensible, but some must contrast strongly enough with the official form to remind readers of the code they represent.

Representation can be subtle in the Caribbean. Representing the Caribbean voice need not mean producing an array of Creole features in contrast to English features. Such representation may mean exploiting features that are ambiguous in the sense of having one meaning in Creole and another in international English. This ambiguity is often lexical, but it can also be grammatical, as in *come,* where time reference depends on the code involved.

Maneuvering between past and present involves a shifting vision. So does departure from "normal" discourse—deviation from features that accurately represent the more usually selected code. Writers have adopted Creole (or their idea of Creole) for the purpose of shifting vision of the Caribbean over the past two hundred years.

Early writers, who attempted to represent Creole from little or no experience of the Creole and who were unaware of its integrity as a separate system merely sought features to indicate a shifting vision, to signal departure from the norm, the accepted, the well-formed, the civilized.[2] Current writers who are in a position to accurately represent both Creole and English speech actually sample the Creole for features that will signal a code-shift in the voice they represent or a shift from one voice to the other. Where the composite vision to be reflected is educated, highly analytic, culturally refined, sensitive to sociohistorical information available to a well-read or even erudite speaker, the shifts are subtle, mainly semantic. The shifts may play on ambiguity between Creole and English syntax.

What Carter is saying about history in the poem may well hinge on how the speaker views time and whether this vision is from behind (omniscience), from within (limited, internal), or from without (limited, external):

> They come treading on the mud floor of the year
> mingling with dark heavy waters
> and the sea sound of the eyeless flitting bat.
> O long is the march of men and long is the life
> and wide is the span. (ll. 23–27)

In terms of focalization, we might suggest that "University of Hunger" conveys a nonlocatable, indeterminate, all-seeing position of omniscience (a zero focalization), but combined with this psychological orientation is a spatial and temporal orientation, a perceptual perspective such as may be conveyed through spatiotemporal indicators such as adverbs, tense, person, and so on.[3] In "The University of Hunger," what does *they come* imply about the spatiotemporal dimensions of the speaker's perceptual orientation?

Perceptual perspective, such as what Roger Fowler compares to viewing position in the visual arts, is normally conveyed by elements of language that indicate position, in space and time, of the speaker relative to the events, characters, or situations to which the speaker refers. However, the speaker's orientation in time is conveyed both by deictic features (those that point in a direction) such as tense, and by nondeictic features such as aspect. (Aspect conveys the distribution of the action in time as complete or incomplete, as recurrent, as habitual, and so on.) Currently, narratologists often distinguish spatialization and temporality from perspective, wherein the latter is treated as encompassing wider issues of knowledge and belief about the world.[4] Manfred Jahn's treatment of focalization proposes that it creates and manipulates windows into the world of the narrative.[5] The narrator of "University of Hunger" records the new arrivals, "they come treading in the hoofmarks of the mule" (l. 7), in present tense and progressive aspect. Because the poem accommodates both Standard English and Creole, and because these codes mark tense and aspect quite differently from each other, ambiguity arises regarding the position of the speaker in time in relation to the events and situations observed.

Present-tense usage must refer to events that are current, but it may refer to events that include but extend beyond the current situation. The first two lines of "University of Hunger" appear to be timeless, to be as unlimited by particular time reference as they are by particular space reference (ll. 1–2). In fact, the dimensions of space and time are entangled by the adjective selected. The *long* march extends through both space and time—indefinitely from past, through present, into future. In these first two lines (as in many that follow), the Creole perspective identifies that which is being observed or contemplated in the *is* . . . sequences. (One is almost taunted to respond: *is the sequence of phrases the English question?*) The opening of the poem simultaneously questions and answers. Either way, it conveys stasis.

The next four lines take the reader to what may be an observation of present experience but may, also, extend indefinitely beyond the present:

> The print of hunger wanders in the land.
> The green tree bends above the long forgotten.
> The plains of life rise up and fall in spasms.
> The huts of men are fused in misery. (ll. 3–6)

First, there are two continuous situations, wide-ranging marks of hunger and the bending tree, and, again, each is linked by implication to the past by semantic components of words like *print* and *forgotten*. What is sometimes termed the *simple present* in the next action is not particularly simple in that it conveys unending, probably iterative motion, a rise and fall that extend back into the long forgotten, and continues indefinitely along the *long march*. The passive also conveys a present situation resultant from past circumstances. However, it is one from which the actor (the real subject of *fuse*) is suppressed. The line is not about "who to blame," about the agents of past misery. The line is about situation and experience, about those who inhabit the misery.

Into this sketch of a timeless, ongoing situation the observer introduces *they*, a pronoun without identifiable reference—except, perhaps (though not necessarily) to the men whose huts "are fused in misery." *They* are an ongoing unifying theme. *Come* implies movement from a point remote from the speaker and his surroundings toward the speaker and his surroundings:

> They come treading in the hoofmarks of the mule
> passing the ancient bridge. (ll. 7–8)

A series of progressives (*treading, passing*) are present if the main verb is present but past if the main verb is past. Semantic components of some words in the sentence (like *hoofmarks* and *ancient*) maintain implied reference to both present and past.

Where does *come* fit, in terms of time reference? In Standard English, *come* may be narrative present, used for recounting an event as it occurs, an event that is continuous and progressive. Recurrence of *come* in subsequent verses suggests that it is also iterative, endlessly repeated. At this point, it becomes clear that aspect has been ambiguous earlier, in lines 3 to 6. In the context of the lines that follow lines 3 to 6, it is clear that the discourse in lines 3 to 6 may be descriptive—static, timeless, continuous—or they may be narrative. *They*, the subject of *come,* could be entering the situation for the first time or for the umpteenth time. On the other hand, from a Caribbean Creole perspective, *come* is also, easily, past perfective (complete) in its reference. Finally, it could be Creole present perfect, particularly if it refers to the men whose huts are fused in misery and it accounts for their presence, tells us where they come from.

The second set of *is . . .* sequences identifies *they* further:

> is the dark ones
> the half sunken in the land.
> is they who had no voice in the emptiness
> in the unbelievable
> in the shadowless (ll. 18–22)

The first unambiguous past time reference is in line 20: "is they who had no voice." This unambiguous past tense raises, by implication, a definite contrast with the present. At the time of speaking, the *no voice* situation is presumably at an end.

Each additional *they come . . .* sequence may be a new phase in the events recounted in narrative present, or it may be a parallel set of observations to the first, merely additional information about the ongoing, progressive action. An interminable struggle forward is implied by the refrain,

> O long is the march of men and long is the life
> and wide is the span. (ll. 26–27)

Is conveys the timelessness of a generic statement. The repetition of *long* again refers both to spatial and to temporal distribution. Uncertainty about precise location in time and space is reinforced by ambiguity about the subjects of certain actions. This ambiguity of subject extends far beyond the Creole *is*. . . structures and beyond the uncertain pronoun references. Ambiguities of reference turn up in a variety of sentences. What, for example, is the subject of *mingling*?

> They come treading on the mud floor of the year
> mingling with dark heavy waters
> and the sea sound of the eyeless flitting bat. (ll. 23–25)

Is the subject *they?* Is it, by implication, the sound of the *treading*? Is it "the mudfloor of the year"? "The year"? Absence of a comma may mean little in a poem in which phrases and clauses fuse in a procession of parallel structures whose boundaries remain unmarked. Again, sentences that have *they come* as their main clause, in which time reference may be ambiguous (depending on code), frequently contain dependent participles, like *mingling,* in characteristically English sentence structures. Such participles supplement our information on action but, not being finite, they do not establish tense.

Creole structure in *is* . . . sequences and in *they come* . . . sequences is never maintained, but similarly, in the final verse, the structures of the official language are intercepted by nonstandard features:

> is they who rose early in the morning
> watching the moon die in the dawn.
> is they who heard the shell blow and the iron clang.
> is they who had no voice in the emptiness
> in the unbelievable
> in the shadowless. (ll. 41–46)

Then comes the contrast in register again, the formal, ceremonial refrain of "O long is the march." Parallelism and repetition reinforce the reader's sense of time distribution as iterative. So does the alternation between the stasis of circling *is* . . . phrases.

In the last verse, three verbs are unequivocally marked for past tense (*rose, heard, had*). However, even in the second-to-last verse, several verbs have plural subjects, are therefore unmarked (*move, fall down, stand up*), and may be Standard English or Creole. Up to this point (the end of the poem) the speaker's position in space and time, relative to what he observes, appears to be unlimited, transcending the length of the march and the width of the span.

Although most narrative is prospective in that the events tend to occur chronologically moving toward the position of the speaker; most narrative is also retrospective in that the speaker recounts events that are past at the time of narrating. However, narrative can also be simultaneous (as in a running commentary) even as events progress. In this poem, if *come* is English, the speaker recounts ongoing events that may be read as progressive or as iterative. It is in this sense that the poem can be read as a narrative, as a sequence of linked events. At the end, still observing a present situation, the speaker makes contrastive reference to past events and situations.

But what if *come* is Creole? Creole *come* (as present perfect) may refer to a specific event, a particular arrival in the past; in which case, the narrative is retrospective rather than simultaneous. Alternatively, Creole *come* (as present perfect) may account for the presence of *the dark ones*, and relate to the use of the present in the *is* . . . sequences. Perhaps the speaker tells us where the human figures on the landscape *come from*, just as *rose, heard,* and *had* in the last verse identify characteristics of the subjects in the *is* . . . phrases. *Come,* then, assigns or defines the identity of those who people the viewer's landscape. On this plane the poem is not narrative but lyrical.

The fact that finite verbs in "University of Hunger" can be read as referring to the past even while they can be read as referring to the nonpast facilitates simultaneous readings of the poem as narrative and as lyrical. This destabilizes the discourse because genres provide what Tzvetan Todorov describes as "horizons of expectation" for readers; however, expectations may be violated.[6] Heta Pyrhönen understands genre as a dynamic construct, "grounded in an interaction between three levels: the level of reader expectations, the body of texts that forms a given genre, and the rules that govern both the interpretation and the production of texts."[7] Carter's ambiguity of genre raises and manipulates parallel sets of expectations and interrogates the canonical texts and the rules of imperial literature that define such genres.

Whether the poem is read as narrative or as lyric, it conveys a perceptual perspective that is limitless, floating in space and alternating in temporal orientation. These narrative and lyrical discourses need not be independent of each other.

It is possible to distinguish multiple voices. One voice identifies the characters of the landscape and the quality of the landscape in an unrelieved series of *is* . . . phrases (ll. 1–2, 18–22, 28–31, 32–34, 41–44, and 41–46 quoted earlier). Another voice (or others) may break in to unfold origins descriptively (present perfect) or in narrative that accommodates past time reference to a series of events (Creole *they come from* . . .). At the same time, this discourse retains the immediacy of the simultaneous narrative (English *they come* . . .) and conveys identity of the characters by applying the present simple to "timeless" reference. Spatial dimensions of the poem are cosmic, in keeping with the geographical and emotional magnitude of the journey, but there is a definite and continuously reinforced sense of direction toward this speaker. One of these voices, or a new voice, or a chorus raises the refrain that links identity with history three times in the poem. At these points, the verse shifts from the spatially locatable view of the speaker who says *they come*. Whether read as narrative or lyric, the text thus accommodates an understanding of the other form (lyric or narrative) as subtext. In addition, the structures that accommodate Creole statements and Standard English questions simultaneously convey multiple voices with the right to declare and interrogate at the same time.

Therefore, this poem presents alternative perspectives or alternating perspectives. Either way, the perceptual complexity increases the angles in time from which the landscape and its inhabitants can be observed, and so enhances the vision. But there is yet another dimension of perspective that further enlarges our experience.

Psychological and spatiotemporal orientation regulate perceptual perspective, but perspective can also be conceptual and ideological—the attitudinal orientation of the speaker to the subject, event, character, situation, or setting. Features that regulate perceptual perspective can also contribute to conceptual perspective.

Like perceptual orientation, *conceptual orientation* is affected by both ambiguity of tense (present versus past/nonpresent) and ambiguity of aspect (perfective/imperfective; complete/incomplete; isolated event/iterative; bounded/nonbounded). Spatiotemporal orientation being crucial to construction of worlds in discourse, this unhooking of temporal anchors contributes to indeterminacy in the circumstances of the speaker, in the Caribbean experience conveyed. Yet even the ambiguity is inconstant. In the world Carter constructs through slippage between tense and through detachment from chronology, an objective Creole voice conveys a description that implies stasis (*is* . . . sequences), supported by gap-filling references to the provenance of the arrivants (perfect, *come from*). This lyrical description runs parallel to narrative that can be read as simultaneous and immediate (*come*, Standard English simple present), but, alternatively, the attitude to events may be more remote, retrospective (*come*, Creole past). The retrospective references accommodate a view of arrival as collective (one expanded explanation) or as divisible (innumerable arrivals that occurred parallel to each other or in series). These arrivals can only be recounted linearly, sequentially, even if they were simultaneous with each other. The flexibility in perception suggests a concept of the Caribbean situation as open-ended and dynamic. Internal change in this situation is conveyed both in expression and content.

As the poem concludes, the action gradually becomes more aggressive, more militant. At first, by context or contiguity, the *march* shares the same tempo as *pilgrimage, wanders, rise up and fall down, come treading, come in long lines.* However, at the end, again by context or contiguity, the *march* partakes of a different tempo—

The cocks of dawn stand up and crow like bugles.

is they who rose early in the morning
watching the moon die in the dawn.
is they who heard the shell blow and the iron clang (ll. 40–42)

—the tempo of "stand up and crow like bugles," "rose early," "the shell blow and the iron clang." Not only does the march quicken, but the refrain that suggests lament in the context of the opening may, at the end of the poem, imply a subtle, parting challenge. Reinforcing this possible shift in tempo and tone is another development. A number of conceptual landmarks that distinguish the discourse as Caribbean (what one might call the iconography reflected in the work) produce contrast in connotation at the beginning and end of the poem.

The vision is marked as Caribbean partly by code choice and code-shift but also by selection of content. The Caribbean is implicated by reference to common and definitive elements of Caribbean experience such as journey, poverty, twin seasons, oppression, and resistance. References to actual objects or to visual images of widespread familiarity accumulate. These are objects of immediate relevance and significance to a common, shared background and to a current condition in the region. Some (like a glimpse of the coffle) summon up the deep past of transportation from an ancestral land (the long march, the distant village). Others verbalize common impressions of past oppression and endurance (*metal brows*). Familiar images, of deep symbolic significance to the region, stud the verse: the mule, dark ones, the huts, the hoe in the ground, sea, boat, sunset, white foam on wrinkled sand, the beating drum, shell blow, iron clang—images of immediate and poignant effect. In addition to conveying a rich sequence of visual symbols, the poem echoes with sounds of equally stirring significance. The silence of despair and oppression (*no voice*) and the monotony of "treading in the hoof marks of the mule" mingle with sea sound and water melodies but are broken by the beating drum, cock crow, shell blow, and iron clang.

Visual and aural imagery of resistance accumulate at the end where dynamic and completed action (*stand up, rose, clang*) counters the stasis of repeated *is* . . . and the incomplete slow motion of *come treading*. In some Caribbean discourse, though not necessarily in all parts of the region, *shell blow* may not only refer to the sounding of the conch that marked plantation routine but it may also suggest a call to revolt. The clang of iron[8] rises louder than the friction of chains and echoes the clash of the machete. At the same time, patterns in the verb phrase change toward the end of the poem. At first, passives (*are fused*) and statives (*is*) suggest lack of participation in any action but journey (*they come*). Where verbs convey action rather than state, the verbs are often intransitives, like *come*. Only at the end does *they* occur as the subject of transitive verbs ("heard the shell blow"). At the same time, the tone throughout is one of certainty. No modal verbs suggest uncertainty about the truth of any observations in the poem. Only the orientation of speaker to subject remains unfixed and conveys plurality of meaning rather than uncertainty. Even as the verb becomes more active and increasingly transitive, an iconography of oppression (the mule) gives way to an iconography of resistance (the beating drum).

A speaker's attitudinal orientation emerges through such elements as modality, transitivity, and lexical choice that regularly mark ideological perspective. Conceptual perspective on the history of the region also emerges partly through the presence or absence of features that we have noted as marking spatial and temporal perspective. To the observer, the place from which *they come* is remote: *from, distant*. The speaker is poised at a point of time that is unspecifiable, so that the time of observation is achronal. Whether the account is timeless present, past perfective, or any other possibility of tense or aspect, and whether this account is simultaneous or retrospective, the account that constitutes this poem groups situations and events on the basis of principles that are nonchronological—a representation of events unordered by chronological sequence so much as theme or semantic association, a temporal syllepsis.[9]

In fact, "University of Hunger" approaches history in a manner that counters the familiar approach of traditional, imperial history. Imperial history recounts past events in a set of relations in which chronology is paramount. Imperial history foregrounds causal links (defined by the conceptual perspective of imperial discourse). "University of Hunger" rewrites history as unsettled, incomplete, progressive, and current—as unbounded action that perpetuates the past in the present and as iterative action ("rise up and fall in spasms," "move up and down," "returns and dies away") that unlocks closure. It also presents suffering as causeless, a range of *is*-circumstances unconnected by any term implying causal linkage. This is the big picture—vast landscape and seascape, vast movements of people over geographical space, irrational suffering of cosmic dimensions. Once, briefly, midway, and then again, at the end, this sweep of collective simultaneous history is intersected by articulation of circumstances that are decidedly past: "is they who had no voice."

For an instant, there is a glimpse of a past that is bounded, contrasting with the present. It is to this boundedness of the past that the poem returns near the end ("is they who rose," "is they who heard," "is they who had no voice") before the final echo of the refrain. So the history has time depth even in the situations that the present perpetuates. The simultaneity of collective history is one dimension of the account; the actual past of inhabitants in the timeless landscape is another. Where the past is marked in unambiguously Standard English fashion, two aspects of the past seem pertinent and entangle perceptual and conceptual perspective. The past was nonparticipatory, but, also, nonparticipation is past. The verb phrases negate participation (*had no voice in*) only for the past, then they convey the perception of action ("rose . . . watching," "heard the shell blow and the iron clang"). At this point, the energy of the sexual imagery invigorates the second-to-last verse and continues to the next (thighs, cocks, iron). The poem's view of history locates the speaker geographically at the point to which vast global movements are directed. In the temporal dimension, history is both a matter for retrospective narration and for lyrical description, where it is expressed as past—present or timeless; complete or incomplete; discrete, continuous, or iterative. History relates a current situation (stasis) to a past of eternal relevance and it presents the identity of a people as a fusion of the current situation and of the events that have produced that situation.

The effect of a fractured vision, of alternating glimpses from different angles, is a composite picture, fuller in its totality than any single perspective could have produced. Moreover, the vision matures as the poem progresses. In the context of voicelessness as past, the present contrasts and the future is open to contrast also. The refrain opens the end of the poem beyond lament over past oppression, and beyond an observation on the timeless present and illimitable endurance, and accommodates speculation on opportunity in time to come. Carter rewrites history through shifting perceptual and conceptual perspective so that the collective response to Caribbean experience is transformed between the beginning and end of the poem from lament to challenge:

> O long is the march of men and long is the life
> and wide is the span.

Notes

1. Martin Carter, *Poems of Resistance* (London: Lawrence and Wishart Ltd., 1954), 34–35.

2. Barbara Lalla, *Defining Jamaican Fiction: Marronage and the Discourse of Survival* (Tuscaloosa: University of Alabama Press, 1996).

3. Roger Fowler, *Linguistic Criticism*, 2nd ed. (Oxford: Oxford University Press,

1996). See also Gerald Prince, *Dictionary of Narratology* (Lincoln: University of Nebraska Press, 1987); Paul Simpson, *Language, Ideology and Point of View* (London: Routledge, 1993).

4. See, for example, David Herman's treatment, largely to accommodate his investigation of hypothetical focalization, in *Story Logic: Problems and Possibilities of Narrative* (Lincoln: University of Nebraska Press, 2002).

5. Manfred Jahn, "Windows of Focalization: Deconstructing and Re-Constructing a Narratological Concept," *Style* 30, no. 2 (1996): 241–267; "The Mechanics of Focalization: Extending the Narratological Toolbox," *GRAAT* 21 (1999): 85–110.

6. Tzvetan Todorov, *Genres in Discourse,* trans. Catherine Porter (Cambridge: Cambridge University Press, 1990), 18.

7. Heta Pyrhönen, "Genre," in *The Cambridge Companion to Narrative,* ed. David Herman (Cambridge: Cambridge University Press, 2007), 118.

8. Ian Robertson notes that, in Guyana, clanging a piece of metal marks stages in the routine of a work day, for example at a construction site (personal communication, St. Augustine, Trinidad and Tobago, 1998).

9. See Gérard Genette's definition, *Narrative Discourse: An Essay in Method*, trans. J. E. Lewin (Ithaca, NY: Cornell University Press, 1980), 85n119; also Ken Ireland in David Herman, Manfred Jahn, and Marie Laure-Ryan, eds., *Routledge Encyclopedia of Narrative Theory* (London: Routledge, 2005), 592.

12
Mixing Codes and Mixing Voices
Language in Earl Lovelace's *Salt*

Velma Pollard

The opening paragraph of J. Edward Chamberlin's *Come Back to Me My Language: Poetry and the West Indies* runs as follows: "Slavery shaped the West Indies. It was expensive and inconvenient, and presented considerable problems of governance; but nobody came up with an alternative, especially for the production of sugar. The desires and anxieties of the European colonizers in turn shaped slavery, through the institutions that developed for establishing civil and religious order in the region and for promoting its economic prosperity."[1] Earl Lovelace, in the first chapter of his novel *Salt*,[2] describes the very "inconvenience" to which Chamberlin makes reference and the conflict of interests that played itself out as the Europeans tried to develop systems of civil and religious order, toward curbing the natural impulses of the slave:

> And it was hard. It was hard to mould the Negro character, to stamp out his savage tendencies.
>
> They tried to make provisions for allowing him innocent amusement after Mass and until evening prayers, to see that he didn't cohabit without the benefit of matrimony, to lay out the work for him to do, pass around later to see that he do it. No really they try. . . .
>
> There was no natural subservience here. Nobody didn't bow down to nobody just so. To get a man to follow your instructions you had to pen him and beat him and cut off his ears or his foot when he run away. You had was to take away his woman from him and his child. And still that fellow stand up and oppose you. (6)

Lovelace's description might be said to provide the details for Chamberlin's general comment, and while the novel warrants appreciation for the imagination and the sensitivity with which it treats aspects of the culture-history and the politics of one Caribbean island, this chapter will restrict its comments to the language of the narrative and will try to describe with illustration the different levels of transformation that Lovelace performs on the English of which Chamberlin's writing is an example. It will also discuss the manipulation of *voice,* which is the most striking feature of the style Lovelace employs in this extraordinary novel. For just as the narrative voice shifts and slides in and out of codes, mixing Trinidad Creole and English, even so it shifts and slides in and out of voices, mixing the subject voice with the object voice, sometimes without a break, sometimes using a direct quote as a bridge from one voice to the other.

Critics concerned with theory will eventually hail Earl Lovelace as the postcolonial writer par excellence, not only because he includes in his text phenomena from all the strands that make the culture-history of his island but because he takes a summary leap in the manipulation of language. In this more than in any other of his novels, Lovelace moves beyond the traditional boundaries of the genre. The writing seems to be unselfconscious and disarming. Close scrutiny, however, reveals a complexity of style that runs parallel to the complexity of the society whose social, cultural, and political problems the novel tries to resolve.

Ashcroft et al., commenting on language in some postcolonial writing, speak of *appropriation* and define it as "the process by which the language is taken and made to 'bear the burden' of one's own cultural experience."[3] The present chapter is concerned with how Lovelace manages this appropriation.

The use of Creole languages in Anglophone Caribbean writing is not new. In fact, it is old enough to have warranted analysis by the critics quoted here. Code, however, has tended to be a feature of the identity of the speaker. So, for example, Olive Senior, Jamaican poet and novelist, in an interview with Anna Rutherford, concedes that she makes her characters "speak directly to the reader" and each tells the story in his/her mothertongue, whether it be Jamaican Creole or Jamaican English.[4] And Warner-Lewis, writing on language in Samuel Selvon's *Moses Ascending,* says that the novelist uses the "first person narrative technique" in which Moses "tells his own story" in narrative marked by swift transitions in language register, depending on context.[5]

What is different about Earl Lovelace's use of language is his exploitation of the linguistic possibilities of the Caribbean environment, the way he mixes the language of the people (Trinidad Creole) with English in the expression used not only by the various characters but by a narrative voice that may be third or first person.

Lovelace has obviously been experimenting with language for a long time. Hodge comments that "Lovelace had already displayed in his first novel (*While Gods Are Falling,* 1965) an accurate knowledge of the real language behaviour of

Creole speakers." She further notes that in *The Schoolmaster* (published in 1968), which is the focus of her paper, Lovelace creates/concocts a language that he ascribes to the people of Kumaca, the village in which the action of that novel takes place: "The fictional Kumacans' speech is a pleasant concoction made up of slightly stilted Standard English, Spanish and French mannerisms expressed in English vocabulary, the occasional Spanish or French lexical item, and Trinidadian Creole."[6] By the time Lovelace wrote *The Dragon Can't Dance* (1979), he had perfected a narrative voice that could move between English and Trinidad Creole in a way that is natural to most educated Trinidadians. Note the following from the first movement of that story: "This is the hill. Calvary Hill, where the sun set on starvation and rise on potholed roads, thrones for stray dogs that you could play banjo on their rib bones, holding garbage piled high like a cathedral spire, sparkling with flies buzzing like torpedoes. . . . Is noise whole day. Laughter is not laughter; it is a groan coming from the bosom of these houses—no—not houses, shacks that leap out of the red dirt and stone, thin like smoke, fragile like kite paper, balancing on their rickety pillars as broomsticks on the edge of a juggler's nose" (9). So he describes the major setting against which the action in the novel will be played out. The voice here signals the identity not of one individual but of a people, those who inhabit the hill. The uncompromising tone is part of the confidence that Lovelace makes this location and this people exude. The comparisons on which metaphors and similes are built are as lofty as they might have been in English, but widely accepted Creole features, notably the base form of the verb ("set," "rise"), are easily identifiable, idiomatic. Creole phrases are set side by side with English as in: "Is noise whole day. Laughter is not laughter" (9), where the switch leads the reader into a sociological and philosophical discourse on the location that is to provide the backdrop to the novel.

The method of the mixing codes becomes even more complicated in *Salt*. Note, for example, in the excerpt given earlier, that the Creole phrase is a free translation of the English phrase: "There was no natural subservience here. Nobody didn't bow down to nobody just so." The abstract "subservience" here yields to the concrete "bow down." The double negative is a Creole feature and the "just so" is idiomatic Creole.

The switching and the mixing of codes are commonplace in speech in multilingual communities. Carrington's comment on the St. Lucia situation continues to be true of most Caribbean communities: "There is a considerable amount of switching from one language to the other between speakers and within the speech of the same person during the course of a single conversation."[7] The use in writing, however, particularly of the mix exemplified in the excerpt from *Salt,* where I began, is more remarkable. In fact, it serves the additional, if serendipitous, purpose of making information accessible to both insider and outsider readerships. Code switching has been the subject of comment wherever the language of Caribbean literature has been discussed.[8]

What is performed in *Salt* is more complex than the simple switch. I want to use the term *code-mixing,* and I want to focus on the degree of the mix of Creole with English in selected chunks of narrative in a novel whose language is still predominantly English. Sometimes, several Creole features are recognizable in one chunk. Other times, the Creole flavor depends on a single word. One might reasonably compare the latter with a similar feature in some poetry from Jamaica by Lorna Goodison and by Dennis Scott, where words from the vocabulary of Dread Talk, the language of Rastafari, are used in the same way.[9]

The examples presented later show first where multiple Creole features are employed and then where one feature is selected. Early in the novel (chapter 4), Lovelace describes a religious location, a Shango palais "where they kill unspotted ramgoats and wring the neck of white and red cockerels and drink their blood and cook their flesh and eat it without salt and dance till morning to gods that drag them down into a deep deep darkness where they froth and suffocate and perspire and groan and spin until their senses leave them; my mother [1] thankful to her God that we [1] not living next door to them not by [2] those drums that would giddy [3] your head and full (3) you up with a power African and useless" (44). The narration changes from English to Creole where the sentiments of "my mother" are brought in. At that point, the following Creole features may be identified as indicated: (1) omission of verb *to be;* (2) Creole meaning of the preposition *by,* which might translate to English *near to,* (3) use of predicate adjective. It is as if the narrator wishes to conjure up the recollection of mother by an approximation to her voice.

It happens again later, at a crucial point in the narrative when Alford George, the main character of the novel, has his moment of illumination, when he knows he must change the focus of his life work, his teaching, from elitist to populist. The narrative voice moves from describing, in English, the turmoil in the head of this young exhibition class teacher who must shift his focus from preparing exhibition students to preparing the masses for life in the island, to discussing in Creole his behavior in the barber shop soon after. The description of his cogitation ends: "He realized that saving the two or three, if you could call it saving, was not enough, for his life's vocation. If he was to go on, he would have to begin afresh to prepare children for living in the island" (75). The narrative continues in a description of events that took place later that day in the unpretentious location: "That same evening Alford came to the barber shop *by* [1] Victory and *sit* down in the chair. He didn't say anything. He didn't tell me what to do or anything. He just *sit* down there *like if he* [2] *half dead and don't care anything and is only* here he could come to see if a trim could cool his brains and help him start his life again" (76). There are unmarked verbs ("sit" and "do/don't"). Again there is predication, which in Creole does not require the verb *to be* (2) and the preposition *by* with its Creole meaning (1). The idiomatic "is only here" may be compared with "is noise whole day" quoted previously. The introduction of Creole into the English narrative marks the point of the shift of location from the school, whose aspirations are elitist, to the shop where the masses converge.

One of the advantages of writing in English and in an English-related Creole is the possibility of using the same word with different meanings. There is also the possibility of using the same phrase to express similar meanings, where English would require different phrases. Compare, for example, the use of the term *not easy* in the sentences: "They wasn't easy" (7), where the intransigent nature of slaves is described in Creole, and "It was not easy" (172), where a new and difficult life of an individual is the issue articulated in English.

Lovelace's use of prepositions and prepositional phrases is particularly effective. The Creole *in front* plus noun (without *of*, which would render it English) is common and striking. Frequently, it is the only Creole feature in a chunk of uninterrupted English, giving a Creole flavor to the whole. There is, for example, an almost full-page description in English of a young woman, Vera, intent on bettering herself, attending Cosmos Business Academy, going on her way "under the unsettling gaze of taxi drivers and young police constables idling *in front* the Public Works building across from the bus stand" (37). That small inclusion immediately says something important about the girl and the setting in which she must achieve the education that might offer her the chance to leave it.

The phrase appears twice in a short space when the mother of a young narrator sees Alford George and gleefully plots her son's academic future: "Yes. He's the one to straighten you out when you get to the Exhibition class." The narrative voice takes over describing the mood of the mother: "triumphant, almost with an exultation she would replay *in front* my father who had come in from work in the forest a few moments before her and was there sitting on the bench *in front* the kitchen taking off his talltops" (50). Again the discussion is about education and is in English. The narrative contains that small touch that locates the ambition within the setting from which it hopes to lift the child.

There are other features that, like the preposition phrase just discussed, affect a whole chunk with a Creole flavor. See, for example, where the Creole possessive (two nouns juxtaposed) is used in a description of the attitude of the church, exemplified in pastor Peter Prue, to the carnival celebrations: "He wanted teachers who promoted this to be instructed to stop or to be removed from teaching *Christian people children*" (91). Those Christian people are the population at large and the inclusion of a phrase from their language conjures up the reality of "them."

Hurry is another word that serves Lovelace well. In English, it is a verb or noun, but in Creole, it becomes an adjective and part of the idiomatic *too hurry.* The attitude of Florence, who would become Alford George's lover, to Port of Spain, runs in part: "Florence had never really taken to Port of Spain, never felt quite at home there. She had been there already since she was seventeen when she ran away from Equilimado Millette, a young carpenter, a boy, really, whose mother was *too hurry* for him to marry her. She had battled her way through tough times to have a little hairdressing salon on the edge of the southern outskirts of Belmont, and a rented apartment deeper in the same Belmont district" (95). There is, in that piece, like an echo behind the English "young carpenter, a boy really," the Creole possibility: *young carpenter-boy* for those who can recognize it.

There are other phrases that Lovelace uses in this way. One example is *from small.* Part of the history of Sonan Lochan, Indian political aspirant, includes: "*From small,* Sonah was passionate about cricket, begun in the backyard with his brothers Saagar and Bal and later on with Hindu School making his debut when he was still only in third standard. When he went to Fourth he blasted the ball to every part of the ground in an innings against Government School that everybody was to recall" (228). The adverbial phrase *from small* is the Creole input in that chunk of English narrative.

An additional effect of the infusions of Creole is the indication to the reader that the succeeding chunk, though written in English, would do well to be read with a Creole rhythm. Sometimes speakers who switch between English and Anglophone Creole manipulate the phonology, the sound and the rhythm far more than they do the grammar or the lexicon of the language they use, to allow them to be comfortable in a situation that requires one or the other code. Lovelace invokes Creole rhythms by the infusions indicated herein. The transformations Lovelace performs on English to ensure the Creole presence are sometimes small but always significant. In *Salt,* he has made a fine art of code-mixing.

It is, however, in the shift and slide from voice to voice within the narrative that Lovelace's most dramatic achievement in this novel lies. It happens almost imperceptibly, making the object subject and effecting a special closeness between reader and fictive character, then moving out again, returning the character to her/his arm's length position, as in this excerpt, where "I," the young narrator, is describing his mother's relationship with husband and children:

> When my mother, anchored in the swamp of her anxiety, on this edge, believing that the world was poised and waiting for us just to make a false step to drag us down into the deep from which she struggled daily to keep us, by herself. *By myself, let me say it again and loud. Without sup-*

> *port or help from anybody except God, since your father who shoulda been the one* to *spearhead the escape and progress of his children is following his brother to dredge up a* past *that everybody gone past. Everybody seeing about theirself and their family, and he and his brother preparing to march.*
>
> When my mother, on the look out now for that limb of rescue that would heave us upwards into a brighter day worried that despite her threats and warnings, I now, the one next in line, the last hope, *Jesus! Hallelujah! Boy, like if your hearing stop up and your eyes can't see would take the opportunity that you get, this chance, luck, the prayer of a hope you have to win* a *College Exhibition and squander it.* . . . (49)

The temptation to see this as simply the omission of quotation marks must be resisted. What Lovelace is doing in shifting mother from object to subject is rejecting a choice that other writers think they have to make, and taking both alternatives, so that the reader sees the mother through her son's eyes and immediately gets her own articulated view. The reader is suddenly immersed in a double perspective announced by the change of pronoun.

Another event treated in this fashion is the one that was to change the focus of Alford George's teaching (mentioned earlier with regard to code-mixing). Mr. George confronts the boy who is too old to sit the college exhibition but who is an even keener student than his peers who will sit the exam. He reminds him that he is too old and finds that the boy *is* aware. Mr. George betrays his puzzlement and begins: "Then why . . . ?" The narrative continues:

> And even as he was saying the words, it hit him. How can a child of thirteen be too old to learn? *It was as if a light had turned on in my head. It was not the boy who should be embarrassed, it was I, me, the teacher. And as the terrible import of such thoughts hit me, I felt my entire body grow numb. I realized that I was a traitor to my own self. I had led the children astray.*
>
> "OK," he said, more to himself than to the boy. . . . (75–76)

The (possessive) pronoun qualifying *head* is *my* from *me* not the expected *his* from *he*. The single stream of narrative suddenly becomes a series of rapids engulfing the reader and as suddenly becomes a single stream again.

Later, Miss Myrtle's moment of truth, when she meets Bango, the "crazy" man she will spend her life with, is treated with the same narrative surprise. Here, however, a quotation—"Lord, what trouble . . ." (without quotation marks)—is introduced to provide the bridge mentioned earlier:

> "Good evening," he said: and at his voice the sweet trouble flashed from the earth, up from the flute of her knees and thighs and spread tingling

> through her loins and she felt, Lord! What trouble is this for me now? And she thought almost with vexation, I hope you have a house to put me and my child in; knowing, in a flash of wisdom, just from the set of his shoulders and the clear bold innocence of his eyes that such a man owned nothing but himself, that he had stumbled upon himself in her just so, with no preparation, no warning, very much as she had spied herself in him.
>
> And we stand up there, he and me, the two of us alone in the great wide world, gazing at each other with the sense of recognition and amazement and an awkward fear, exhausted by their effort to say everything by speaking nothing, and she was struck by the sudden softness of the day. . . . (136)

At the moment of deepest emotion, Lovelace hands us readers over to Miss Myrtle herself to have her speak. It is as if the storyteller should pause and say to a member of the company, "It is your story, you tell it." The third-person pronoun *she* becomes the first-person *we*. With the same speed, the same almost imperceptible sleight of pen, Lovelace hands us back to the narrator with the words: "exhausted by *their* effort," using *their* where the reader might have expected *our*. Barely ten lines later, while he continues to describe the same event, Lovelace plays the game again as the first-person *I* replaces the third-person *she*: "*She* felt herself tumbling into a new space and danger and excitement and peace with the need to hold herself from spinning and the wish to step backwards to look at him again, to *see if I could spy in him something that I mighta missed earlier, some flaw that would diminish him in my eyes, make him less invincible and vulnerable and handsome and dazzling than he appeared*" (136–137).

Merle Hodge, in the careful analysis of Lovelace's *The Schoolmaster* to which I have already referred, comments on the "shifting narrative voice" he makes use of in that novel. She sums up her commentary in this way: "Dialogue (then), extends into narration, and increasingly in Lovelace's work the role of an omniscient, external narrator will diminish, the narrative voice becoming, more often than not, one or another voice from within the action."[10]

Lovelace in *Salt* has done even better than Hodge predicted. He has, as I hope I have illustrated, merged, Anansi-like, the external narrator with the voice from within the action in a seamless web that engages the readers so totally that they first experience the sensation it creates and then have the urge to stop to find out exactly what strategy has been used to achieve the effect.

Funso Aiyejina, in the paper that launched the novel in Port of Spain, analyzes the previously illustrated feature thus: "The narrative structure of *Salt* would seem to suggest that Lovelace is of the view that both the consciousness of the subjects of a story and the consciousness of its teller are actively involved in the story-telling process. As a means of suggesting this complex relationship between the story, story-teller, and contending perceptions of history in a multi-cultural society, Lovelace adopts the use of multiple narrative voices." Later, he gives a more detailed description: "The narrative structure of *Salt* is (also) such that the subjects of the stories exercise the option to stroll into them and take over the narration from either the first person narrator or the alternate third person omniscient narrator. On such occasions . . . the inserted consciousness/voices of the subjects operate as reminders that the stories are about them and as witnesses to the veracity of both stories and their tellers." The tale as communal act, community activity in the mode of the African story-telling event, is Aiyejina's point of reference. He adds: "Through such a narrative structure Lovelace establishes that we are listening to a collective story that is collectively told through a narrative relay."[11]

Aiyejina also comments on Lovelace's underlying conviction that "every member and group . . . must be given the opportunity to tell their story such that each group will grow to know what others have been through."[12] This last is a need identified decades ago by Brathwaite, Caribbean poet and literary critic, who in *Contradictory Omens* looked forward to the expression of the interrelation between "equal subordinates" in a postcolonial Caribbean, after the "imperial dominant" has been removed.[13] Lovelace's engagement with the thought processes of political aspirants, the Negro, Alford George, and the Indian, Soonan Lochan, deals with this expression. The inclusion of the mind of the French Creole plantation owner, Adolphe Carabon, takes it somewhat beyond what Brathwaite hoped for. But this man is obviously on the way to "breaking rank" and so becomes a legitimate candidate for the "lateral creolization" that Brathwaite dreamt of.

At the beginning of this chapter, I suggested that Lovelace is using language to try to capture the complexity of the society whose social, cultural, and political problems he tries to resolve. The characters he draws are as complex as the society that engenders them and he has found the means of portraying both complexities without burdening the reader too much. Aiyejina warns the reader that *Salt* "is not a quick-read novel" and while I support that comment, I believe that the constant effortless humor and the simplicity of a complex narrative style hypnotizes readers and leads them to a reasonably quick first read and an immediate return for an intense reread.

Lovelace, in a throwaway comment in a BBC interview after the announcement that he had won the Commonwealth Literary Award 1997 for this book, says something about its being part of a process of development. Critics will agree that Lovelace has been moving toward a total "appropriation" of language, a completely Creole aesthetic, and that he has indeed achieved it in *Salt*. Let us hail him for it.

Notes

1. J. Edward Chamberlin's *Come Back to Me My Language: Poetry and the West Indies* (Toronto: McClelland & Stewart, 1993), 1.

2. Earl Lovelace, *Salt* (London: Faber & Faber, 1996). Emphasis added to quotations throughout this chapter.

3. Bill Ashcroft, Gareth Griffiths, and Helen Tiffin, *The Empire Writes Back: Theory and Practice in Post-Colonial Literatures* (London: Routledge, 1989), 38.

4. Anna Rutherford, "Olive Senior Interview," *Kunapipi* 8, no. 2 (1986): 11–20.

5. Maureen Warner-Lewis, "Samuel Selvon's Linguistic Extravaganza: *Moses Ascending*," in *Critical Issues in West Indian Literature,* ed. E. Smilowitz and R. Knowles (Parkersburgh, IA: Caribbean Books, 1984), 102.

6. Merle Hodge, "Dialogue and Narrative Voice in *The Schoolmaster*" (presentation, Sixteenth Annual Conference on West Indian Literature, Miami, FL, April 1–4, 1997), 3, 5; *Journal of West Indian Literature* 8, no. 1 (1998): 56–72. See Earl Lovelace, *While Gods Are Falling* (London: Collins, 1965; repr., Harlow, England: Longman, 1984); *The Schoolmaster* (Chicago: Regnery, 1968; repr., London: Heinemann, 1979); *The Dragon Can't Dance* (London: André Deutsch, 1979; Burnt Mill, Harlow, England: Longman, 1979).

7. Lawrence Carrington, *St. Lucian Creole: A Descriptive Analysis of Its Phonology and Syntax* (Hamburg, Germany: Buske, 1984), 27.

8. See, for example, Edward Baugh, "Goodison on the Road to Heartease," *Journal of West Indian Literature* 1, no. 1 (1986), 13–26; Barbara Lalla, *Defining Jamaican Fiction: Marronage and the Discourse of Survival* (Tuscaloosa: University of Alabama Press, 1996); Chamberlin, *Come Back to Me;* Pamela Mordecai, "Wooing with Words: Some Comments on the Poetry of Lorna Goodison," *Jamaica Journal* 45 (1981): 38–40; Maureen Warner-Lewis, "Samuel Selvon's Linguistic Extravaganza."

9. See Velma Pollard, "The Speech of Rastafari in Modern Jamaican Poetry," in *Dread Talk: The Language of Rastafari* (Kingston, Jamaica: Canoe Press, University of the West Indies, Mona, 1994; 2nd Ed., 2000), 69–85.

10. Hodge, "Dialogue and Narrative Voice in *The Schoolmaster,*" 72.

11. Funso Aiyejina, "An Intertextual Critical Approach to *Salt* by Earl Lovelace" (presentation, Book Launch of Earl Lovelace, *Salt,* Port of Spain, Martin's Miller House, December 1996), 2.

12. Aiyejina, "Intertextual Critical Approach to *Salt,*" 3.

13. Edward (Kamau) Brathwaite, *Contradictory Omens: Cultural Diversity and Integration in the Caribbean* (Kingston, Jamaica: Savacou Publications, 1974), 63.

13
Opening *Salt*
The Oral-Scribal Continuum in Caribbean Narrative

Barbara Lalla

Gordon Rohlehr refers to a continuum that "exists between a living oral tradition, and a growing scribal one in the West Indies. It relates," he continues, "to the continuum that exists between the various West Indian Creoles and Standard West Indian English."[1] In his continuing discussion, Rohlehr applies this idea mainly to the work of Louise Bennett, concluding with emphasis on "the notion that most things in the West Indies are fluid, and most people caught in a series of interlocked continua."[2]

This chapter investigates the interlocked continua of which the oral-scribal continuum partakes, in relation to the dynamics of Lovelace's opening to *Salt*. Early in *Salt*, Lovelace's narrator reflects: "That was one of the beginnings of the story that Uncle Bango sat down that year to tell."[3] Here, Bango's discourse begins with the legend of Guinea John, then is interrupted by Bango's nephew who contextualizes Bango's discourse, and then is resumed by Bango in reflection on the impossibility of unfreedom.

The present discussion assumes a shared understanding of oral expression as primal, and that this primal nature is not only clear of connotations of the "primitive" but also of attitudes of sentimentality and of values of political correctness. Another assumption is that such concepts as orality or literariness are distinguished on the basis of linguistic and discursive patterns rather than on any sense of one being more "advanced" than the other.

The scribal text is context-free in the sense that the message can be retrieved at any time, in any place, and by any reader rather than to an actual context-bound addressee, and it is on this basis that Ong describes the addressee in the written text as "fictionalized."[4] Partly because of its independence of circumstances, and because of its consequent fixity, the written text asserts authority. Ong distinguishes not only the scribal text itself but also the text-oriented mind as analytic, focused on interior rather than exterior circumstances. It is essential, in discussing orality in such discourses as *Salt*, to remain aware of the obvious fact that the oral material is inscribed and that this material is being transmitted by an author in what is now a "text-oriented tradition" (*text* being used here for "written text").

The oral-scribal relationship in Caribbean discourse, as Rohlehr points out, fits into a matrix of other concepts, but it is an uneasy fit. The most obvious of these other continua is that of the Creole continuum (itself a minefield of linguistic debate) reflected not only in dialogue but in one narrative embedded in another. "Whole night Blackpeople have they drums going,"(5) runs Bango's consciousness, without quote marks, within his nephew's memory. The association of orality with the Anglophone Creole of Trinidad and of literariness with Standard English is misleading oversimplification in an age when the Creole is increasingly versatile functionally, in which the Caribbean Diaspora has scattered versions of Creole widely, and in which global recognition of Caribbean culture has raised the prestige of both literary and oral Caribbean discourse. Susanne Mühleisen recognizes this in relating the deterritorialization of Creole not only to geographical but also to functional shifts in which the renegotiation of language prestige is ongoing.[5]

The relationship between Caribbean continua defies mapping even if each element is simplified beyond the possibilities of accuracy. According to continuum theory, which David DeCamp first articulated in 1971, speakers in a Creole continuum cannot be sorted into discrete groups socially or regionally; nor can the varieties of language be separated into clearly bounded versions; nor can the whole spectrum of language use be seen as a single entity, because the far ends of the range are so clearly distinct. At the same time, a linear order appears of varieties from one extreme of the system to the other, prompting Rickford's criteria of nondiscreteness and of unidimensionality, which others, like Peter Patrick, have correlated with social dimensions.[6] Most Creole speech is scribally represented in dilute form, and Creole narrations especially are (roughly speaking) mesolectal: "The rain decide when it going to fall."

Now a similar gradation has been suggested in connection with speech-thought transitions in narrative, and transitions between speech and thought are implicated in shifts between dialogue and narrative. Also, the connections between direct or indirect speech and the relationship of either to thought are clearly interrogated in experiments with such strategies as stream of consciousness. In the mesolectal part of the Creole continuum, that variety of Trinidadian through which the author may be representing the Creole end of the continuum, Bango's direct speech loses its quote marks. No longer identified as verbatim report, it crystallizes from the nephew's recollection into a reliving of the circumstances of unfreedom within Bango's mind—free direct thought: "Just so a yard cock will draw up his chest and crow." These direct thoughts, however, blend imperceptibly into speech that shifts unannounced between direct and indirect: "You tell a man to do something and he tell you he forget." The problem of representing speech is by no means clearly distinct from that of representing thought.

In addition to linguistic dimensions of the matrix (such as the Creole continuum) and to narrative dimensions (involving shifts between direct and indirect speech and thought), the oral-scribal continuum relates to an intercultural continuum in which variables of class and ethnicity and of conventions regarding register (such as those of propriety) contribute to discrete forms but also blend to comprise hybrid systems: "They had to ban them from walking and from raising up their dresstail and shaking their melodious backsides. They wasn't easy." In *Salt,* Lovelace's narrative scribally represents oral exchanges and the reflections of consciousnesses steeped in oral culture, but this representation is at least to some extent intercepted by scribal conventions of what has become a (written) text-oriented culture.

Such a text-oriented mindset produces narrative that is more self-conscious and, perhaps, more autonomous than a primarily oral culture. Directly (or indirectly through Bango's nephew) Bango draws together scribal and oral characteristics: "It had no brooding inscrutable consciousness here. There was no wild and passionate uproar to make people feel they is beast." Writing produces closure and enables ownership, a right version, where orature leaves the performance open and is a joint undertaking between other "authors" and in keeping with particular audiences. In Lovelace's *Salt,* especially as demonstrated by the opening pages, distinctions between oral and scribal cultures are continually subverted. The increasing permeability of boundaries between Creole and Standard English in literary discourse (a tendency that I have traced elsewhere)[7] is intimately connected in Lovelace with fluidity of voice and script: "You see! You see! That is why Blackpeople children doom*ed* to suffer." [Italics mine.]

On the first two pages, huge paragraphs conclude in a conspicuously brief sentence: "So it had to be his story." This sentence both defers responsibility for the narrative and establishes the danger that Bango might be lying in the story itself. Additionally, it unfixes the type of narrative involved, specifically a personal story, family saga, or history of a people. Such complexities present not only challenges but opportunities as linguistic plurality and hybridity increase the possibilities of multiple meanings (his story/history; uncertain referent of *it,* and so on), producing that semantic plurality that Simpson identifies as "hyperactive signification."[8] In this sense, semantic plurality or ambivalence does not violate the cooperative principle but, rather, superactivates it by enabling sliding meanings. However, part of this ambivalence (or multivalence) would easily be disambiguated by speech and the rest might never be distinguished in the swift flow of oral delivery.

Although sentence structure can reinforce a sense of the scribal through size and (associated) patterns of subordination, long sentences can also maintain a sense of the oral by highlighting paratactic elements. The second paragraph begins, "And some of them. . . ." While another sentence is balanced, "but they had eaten salt."

The paragraphs, too, are enlarged by techniques of oral performance, by accretion—a stringing together of ideas for amplification and through strategic repetition:

> They had to get people to beat people for them. . . .
> People had to get licks. . . .
> They reduced the number of lashes to twenty-five. . . .
> They tried in administering the floggings. . . .

Repetition of content effects reinforcement of an idea, strengthened by weaving together items within lexical fields (*beat, licks, lashes, floggings*). Repetition of sentence structure (parallelism) emphasizes monotony of regulation and oppressive regime. Repetition additionally provides essential redundancy in an oral culture where retention depends on memory and where storage works on a principle of "repeat or lose" the good stuff.

Accretion in incident and characterization in the second phase of Bango's introductory discourse creates an assembly of "fellars" in warrior poses, partaking of the spirit of Guinea John and his fellow ringleaders of the would-be insurrection, with whom the novel opens. They are "dangerous fellars exiled here . . . fellars who make up their minds to dead."

In an oral tradition, delivery is characterized not only by accretion but also by aggregation, which may take the form of lists, and *Salt* opens with lists of natural phenomena—burdens of Whitepeople, dances of Blackpeople, things you could tell a man to do (and he would not), things that had to happen to a country before the impossibility of captivity became clear. Aggregation works through compiling of examples, a building up of the idea rather than a breaking down through analysis—which is not to suggest that there is no analysis, but only to demonstrate the degree to which techniques of oral and scribal delivery complement each other.

Oral performance safeguards the past by creating mnemonic devices such as rhythm, balance, alliteration, assonance, and fixed sound patterns, all characteristic of oral cultures, and all diminished in written literature. The second monologue in the opening of *Salt* plays on the effects of sound, especially in recounting resistance in the environment as well as in Blackpeople. The discourse presents rain as making "a swooping sound and voops it fall down" and lists dances from the Bamboula to the Bongo, interspersed with snatches of disobedient song. Formulacity also characterizes oral delivery and is valued differently to, say, the cliché in literature, which is treated with contempt. Orature makes elegant use of formulary structures, and this characteristic fosters the embedding of particular discourse types, for example, proverbial expressions. So Guinea John warns, "but when a people begin to curse they elders, the next step they take is to curse they gods." The oral tradition transmits ancient wisdom.

Although most of the attributes identified herein are strategies for retaining the valuable through oral transmission, orature aims not only for storage of content but also at engagement. Narrators speak overtly to their audiences. Rapping, flyting, and other such types of skilled oral exchange are common in orature. Bango directly addresses his audience: "You know they could never hold people here." And sometimes a narrative voice demands a response; we have no reason to suppose all questions are rhetorical: "But what else to do?" A question repeated insistently in Bango's presentation of Whitepeople point of view. We are directly informed that Bango's story is itself an engagement on the level of the stick fight and cricket match, approached (according to the nephew-narrator) with the same "brawling parrot-toed sure-footed walk" and associated with a sense of "danger." The *story* of self-emancipation is itself a challenge.

Despite the mechanisms for retention associated with oral delivery, orature is naturally fluid, shuffling the mechanisms through which discourse is normally anchored—like point of view—in passing from episode to episode. In Lovelace's accretive story line, Bango recounts the opening episode, tracking stages of the event linearly: "mounted the cliff, put two corn cobs under his armpits and flew away to Africa." The central consciousness of the oral narrative does not take up a position outside of the event to analyze it. Bango begins the episode in medias res ("Two months after . . ."), the speaker not necessarily having worked out the order or reshuffled, in advance, the stages of his account: "[1] Two months after they [2] hanged his brother Gregoire, king of the Dreadnoughts band, and Louis and Nanton and Man Man, the other three leaders of African secret societies, who [3] Hislop the Governor claimed to be ringleaders of an insurrection that had a [4] plan, according to the [5] testimony of a mad white woman, to use the cover of the [6] festivities of Christmas Day to massacre [1]."

These stages are numbered 1 to 6 in the order in which they are recounted, but they may actually have occurred in the order 4, 5, 3, 2, 1, the location of 6 in time being uncertain. From this third-person account of Guinea John and then of those who remember him, there is a shift to first-person testimony regarding Bango and then a submergence in Bango's voice. The next chapter projects a limited third person and, later, the narrative floats into omniscience.

Still, here and there, the consciousness settles to a third-person limited account though often sliding into first-person testimony.

Such perspectival shifts reinforce the episodic structure, rather than a structure organized around a tight climactic plot. It is a structure underpinned by chronological relationships but not driven by sequential delivery. Although *Salt* moves from exterior to interior crises, and shifts between event-based focus and the articulated self, the opening to it all focuses on external events rather than on interiority and analysis.

In focusing on external events, orature is community-based, and in Bango's community, orature is itself an event. This is played out in the narrative of Guinea John. Both phases of Bango's performance constitute not only resistance but also narrative for community education, and these are pivotal and linked goals of Bango throughout. At the same time, retention of stories is influenced by the mental frameworks of recipients and the responses to Bango demonstrate that varied schemata are in place in his community. The audience orientation is consequent on the traumatic past to which he refers, to intense change underway, and to the conflictual responses (in the community) to such change. Oral narrative, however, also functions as a healing mechanism, for a re-membering after trauma. The extraordinary event with which *Salt* opens—an event of epic proportions—provides a model for self-emancipation in the oral tradition and a starting point for literary debate on the extent to which emancipation is possible or, to some, even desirable.

As celebratory of memorable events, oral narrative can have a sacral function. The Guinea John episode affirms the sacred significance of a place of origin, an owned place, a home, and affirms the mythical longing for reinstatement. These functions of cultural transmission are effected by invoking and reapplying the legend of the Flying Africans. This legend in its many versions is based on historical events associated with Igbo resistance to enslavement after transportation and angled according to the memories of survivors. The departure of the Igbos was perceived by the enslavers as suicide while the descendants of enslaved Africans regarded the resistance as self-emancipatory flight. This sacred legend, preserved through oral transmission, provides the framework for Lovelace's Bango's Guinea John's rejection of slavery and the tale that unfolds from that—of the limited success of emancipation.

Before the episode concludes, those whom Guinea John has left behind criticize him thoroughly as not only having abandoned them but as having neglected to share essential information. His return in a dream enables him to respond to the criticism. His descendants make no answer at this point in the text. In the concluding paragraphs of the novel, however, a speaker claiming to represent Africans insists that they feel "fortunate to escape the poverty and corruption in the lands from which their parents originate." This interpretation constitutes an indirect denial of complaints made by Guinea John's descendants on page 1; indeed, it demonstrates ignorance of Guinea John.[9]

The Guinea John opening thus sets up an event later to be undermined by criticism, memory loss, and denial. So from the outset, the account conforms with a tendency in orature to standardized themes and types that support the crucial mnemonic function of oral delivery in oral traditions. Guinea John himself is the heavy character familiar in oral narrative, heroic, monumental, memorable—and flatter, being unanalyzed. In the sliding between orature and literature, however, the novel that follows profoundly analyzes a variety of attempted and often abortive self-emancipatory flights. Nevertheless, orature is conveyed throughout *Salt,* a composite tale unfolding from an episode that reaffirms that everyone here is from elsewhere and left behind. The tale pulls from the diasporic consciousness of the folk fusing current and past events and concerns, condensing circumstances and peoples. Through chronological, parallel, and intersecting story lines, the narrative follows the theme of reconnection in an episodic structure and nonsequential movements rather than a distinctive plotline with intensifying suspense. Rather than dimming a main plotline, however, this movement establishes an alternative and primary structure that is accretive, through a variety of voices conveyed through a range of dialects, and a widening angle of viewing as the approach shifts between limited and omniscient narration. This composite postcolonial Caribbean voice is counterdiscursive in *Salt* in both its retellings and rewritings. The multivocal narrative reflects the cultural plurality and hybridity in the novel's setting and conveys the complexity of interaction implicated by these circumstances. *Salt* sets forth (from its opening) scribal representation of the oral as well as oral subtexts of the literary, and it interlocks oral and scribal interrogations of a constructed past.

The alternating hybrid perspective combines with the oral characteristics of the discourse to forestall closure: "That was one of the beginnings of the story that Uncle Bango sat down that year to tell." It is much later in the narrative that Bango's wife, Myrtle, points out that though he has often begun to tell her, he has never concluded, never told her the point, only marched without explanation. She was never, as his nephew was, physically present at a full performance. Alford George, for all his reading, has never been present at all, before he is eventually made audience to the full delivery. In the end, political misinterpretation of the motive to reinstatement constitutes the most tragic of losses—a complete break in transmission—what Bango's nephew identifies as "loss of the ability to feel loss."

Lovelace's achievement through the inscription of orality is that he enables both the celebration of continuity in tradition and the poignancy of breaks in transmission. Rohlehr's concept of an oral-scribal continuum, understood in a matrix of social and linguistic continua, facilitates a reading of *Salt* as a textualized debate on cultural transmission and its disruptions. This concept underscores the complexity of the language situation in which Caribbean narrative is constructed and points to the mutual relevance of close linguistic and critical analysis in opening a multivocal narrative focused on the preservation and interrogation of community.

Notes

1. In a paper delivered at a conference of the Association for Commonwealth Literature and Language Studies in 1971 and currently most accessible as "Literature and the Folk," in *My Strangled City and Other Essays* (Port-of-Spain, Trinidad and Tobago: Longman, 1992), 68.

2. Ibid., 83.

3. Earl Lovelace, *Salt* (London: Faber and Faber, 1996; repr. Persea, 1997), 3–7.

4. Walter Ong, *Orality and Literacy: The Technologizing of the Word* (London: Methuen, 1982), 102.

5. Susanne Mühleisen, *Creole Discourse: Exploring Prestige Formation and Change across Caribbean English-Lexicon Creoles* (Amsterdam: John Benjamins, 2002), 176.

6. John R. Rickford, *Dimensions of a Creole Continuum* (Stanford, CA: Stanford University Press, 1987); Peter Patrick, "Testing the Creole Continuum," Working Papers in Linguistics 6, no. 2. Selected Papers from *New Ways of Analyzing Variation* 27 (1998): 109–120.

7. On permeable boundaries between the codes, see Barbara Lalla, "Creole and Respec' in the Development of Jamaican Literary Discourse," *Journal of Pidgin and Creole Languages* 20, no. 1 (2005): 53–84.

8. Paul Simpson, *Stylistics* (New York: Routledge, 2004), 167.

9. Interestingly, in a study of indirectness in Igbo discourse, Bertram A. Okolo explores paradoxical communication, "Indirectness in Discourse: A Study in Paradoxical Communication among the Igbos," in *The Language of African Literature,* ed. Edmund L. Epstein and Roger Kole (Trenton, NJ: Africa World Press, 1998), 168–184. He explains that in indirect communication, content is not necessarily to be taken literally but must be processed at a metacommunicative level at which a shared background is essential, so that a statement may be understood to mean the opposite of what it literally says. "One of the primary uses of paradoxical speech style is to criticize," explains Okolo (180). However, he demonstrates that the speaker may go on to deny the nonliteral interpretation and claim that only the literal was intended—thus paralyzing the paradox. At the end of *Salt,* spiritual and intellectual emancipation is misrepresented as racist troublemaking and the significance of the epic flight disowned by a political orator: "They all feel they have been fortunate to escape the poverty and corruption in the lands from which their parents originate." The criticisms of Guinea John following his flight (the complaint of his neglect in passing on the secret of flight) are indirectly denied at the end of the novel, implying that translocation itself was not a subject of criticism.

14
Mothertongue Voices in the Writing of Olive Senior and Lorna Goodison

Velma Pollard

Jean D'Costa contends that West Indian writers who wish to satisfy themselves, their local audience, and their foreign audience must evolve a "literary dialect" that not only satisfies both these audiences but also is an authentic representation of the "language culture" of this community.[1] And Garth St. Omer, one of the better known of the West Indian novelists, comments on the dilemma of the postcolonial writer who must not only represent the society honestly but also must be understood by all in the society.[2] Both these writers are addressing a situation that is the context of this discussion on mothertongue. The tension between the ability to use a number of overlapping codes and the necessity to be understood not only within the society but also by the reader outside of it is a constant part of Caribbean writers' reality as they create in prose or in poetry.

This chapter looks at the language of Olive Senior's prose and of Lorna Goodison's poetry to see how this and other linguistic tensions are resolved in the writing of these two women who have achieved national and international recognition. It notes how they use the complex language situation to their advantage in the act of creating, particularly in terms of character identification.

A brief description of what D'Costa refers to as a "polydialectal continuum with a Creole base" is in order. The official language of Jamaica is Standard Jamaican English, a dialect of English as accessible to English speakers the world over as Standard American or Standard Australian English is. It is the language of the school and of all the official organizations of the society. The majority of Jamaicans, however, speak Jamaican Creole, a Creole of English lexicon that everyone in the speech community understands. Because of the lexical relationship between the two languages, most Creole speakers regard themselves as English speakers. There is, in addition, a code introduced by the Rastafari, a socioreligious group, and adopted by other speakers, particularly the young. This code, Dread Talk, has been described as an example of lexical expansion within a Creole system,[3] in this case, Jamaican Creole. The grammatical structures of the code are, with few exceptions, the same as those of Jamaican Creole. The lexical items, however, taken originally from English (the source of most Jamaican words) have been subjected to a number of word-making processes drastic enough to give some words new sounds and others new meanings.

Most educated speakers in the society switch from one to the other of the codes just described, with no difficulty at all, as the discourse situation demands. Uneducated speakers tend to speak Creole regularly and to attempt to switch to English only when they perceive the social situation to require it.

Because language and social class, in the stereotypical descriptions of these, are closely aligned, creative writers are able to use the codes to identify prototypical characters and attitudes. This is not to suggest a particular self-consciousness in the production of literary writing, for I believe that what we will look at is a reproduction of natural speech. What the artists have done is to select to write about situations requiring the use of the different codes available to speakers. It is precisely because the natural language of the people in the community is reproduced that we are able to discuss language as it functions within the speech community, using as evidence texts from the writing we are about to examine.

Olive Senior

While all the stories in Olive Senior's collections[4] might serve as a kind of laboratory for examining Jamaican speech, it might be useful to examine the speech behavior of characters presented in one story in detail, and then flesh out the comments possible with references from others. We will look at "Real Old Time T'ing," from the earlier collection, largely because the content of the tale forces the author to have characters switch from one code to the next, thus offering us good examples of how the language operates in real-life situations.

An aging father, recently made a widower, finds himself up against a social-climbing daughter who wants him to build a new house bigger than the one in which he had raised their family of nine. Patricia, the nouveau riche, is introduced by the narrator who obviously does not intend this character to be a favorite with the reader. Examine the tone of the lines that begin the piece and introduce Patricia to the reader: "Is the one name Patricia did start up bout how Papa Sterling need a new house" (54).

When Patricia eventually enters the stage, her language is immediately perceived to be different from the narrator's. Jamaican Creole is the language of the teller of the tale. Patricia attempts to speak Standard Jamaican English:

> But hear the one Patricia she—this one Sunday she did drive down with the pickney dem. The husband didnt come:

> "Poppa, this place really just too bad. The children shame to come here. We have to do something about it." (54)

The Creole plural "pickney dem" in the narrator's language is replaced in Patricia's by the Standard Jamaican English translation: "the children." Note also the Creole past tense "did drive down" (not to be confused with the emphatic *did* possible to Standard Jamaican English) where English would prefer *drove* or *had driven.* The attitude to Patricia is made clear in the idiomatic "the one Patricia she," a turn of phrase reserved for deep disdain.

Patricia considers herself a speaker of Standard English but her English retains the tell-tale signs of late or incomplete acquisition, its style typical of the speech of someone newly arrived at her current station in life. One expects "the children are ashamed to come here," for example, where Patricia uses the Jamaican Creole "the children shame."

The father in the story is a Jamaican Creole speaker who controls Standard Jamaican English well enough to use it for effect. He pretends confusion when his daughter makes the suggestion that his house is too small: "Too small? How yu mean gal? Doan is seven of you raise in this house. Plus yu mother alive then and me make nine. Nine of we live here. And now yu all gone and yu mother dead leaving me one and you telling me this house that I build with my very hands too small. Child you are speaking to me in parables" (55).

Note that the last of the sentences in the extract is in English and is in distinct contrast to what comes before. Papa has switched to English to allow the daughter to see the ridiculousness of her suggestion. He is being sarcastic. What his daughter says is quite clear. It is no parable, but it is so illogical that there must be something not immediately obvious to him. The Creole used in these passages is not pure or broad Creole, which is, in any case, an abstraction for analysis by linguists. In terms of D'Costa's description, it lies somewhere along a continuum between Jamaican Creole and Standard Jamaican English. The non-Creole speaker, while rare in the Jamaican community, is not shut out, and the foreign reader who understands English can make sense of it.

Let us look at the grammatical features of that part of the discourse that are not found in English: The verb *to be* does not always appear in Jamaican Creole where Standard Jamaican English would expect it, as in the chunk: "now yu all gone and yu mother dead." The verbs are not always marked to indicate past time where this is the time of the activity. See, for example, in "this house that I BUILD with my very hands" The subject pronoun *we* is used in the object position as in "nine of we live here."

The language with all its nuances is clear to the Jamaican reader, and the essential sense can be gleaned by the foreign reader even if some of the finer points might be missed.

Miss Myrtella, who aspires to Papa's hand, is a caricature of someone who knows the virtue of English as a status marker. She talks with her mouth "curl round the words" and is afflicted with an exaggerated case of the added *h*. Note the following report: "'Ho Cousin Orris,' she call out. Horace is Papa Sterling first name 'Oi dont know wot to do hit his so howful to be ha woman holl ho-lone hin this worl Cousin Orris'" (58). While the dropping and adding of *h* (as in "[h]am and [h]eggs") is common in Jamaican speech, the sustained adding exemplified in the preceding excerpt signals the speaker's intention to produce fine English.

Miss Myrtella has other attributes of the class Patricia wants to belong to. She wears good clothes; she knows about (green) tea (as opposed perhaps to folk drinks like mint and fever grass); and she sticks out her little finger while drinking from a cup. The two women are competitors. Miss Myrtella's arrival challenges Patricia's monopoly on these things. Patricia says maliciously that Miss Myrtella has no class and, among other things, "can't speak properly," where "properly" signifies English. The reader knows that Patricia herself has some difficulty with the language, although she has fewer problems than Miss Myrtella has. But their competition serves only to underscore the point that many Jamaicans who perceive themselves to be speakers of English are not.

While the use of language to identify character is most highly developed in this story, perhaps because its themes are class and society, it is also carefully matched with character in all the other stories. In the story "Ascot," in the same collection, the written rather than the spoken word helps the reader note the development of the hero. Compare the following letters sent home to his mother from America as Ascot moves up in the world:

> Dear Ma wel i am her in New York is big plase and they have plenty car I am going to get one yr loving son Ascot.
>
> Dear mother wel here I am in Connecticut. Connecticut is Big plais. I driveing car two year now but is not wite yr loving son Ascot.
>
> Dear Mother Chicago is Big plais I drivein wite car for a wite man but he don make me where wite is blak unform so I mite leave yr loving son Ascot. (30)

With each letter the language is more grammatically close to English and the sentences longer. (The amount of money sent home also increases with each letter.) When Ascot actually returns home on a visit, we note the change in his oral expression as well. The last record of his speech before migration runs: "Laaad Mass Jackie is nuh me do it sah," as he defends himself from the charge of banana theft. When we meet him again he greets everybody and introduces his wife, "this is my wife Anthea," language being only one of the markers of this man's social development.

Constantly language marks off territory in an unobtrusive but precise way. This continues in Senior's second collection of short stories, *The Arrival of the Snake Woman;* although the language is consistently closer to English as the characters are closer to the middle and upper levels of the society. Note, however, the broad Jamaican Creole used as the maid in "See the Tiki-Tiki Scatter" rejects the granddaughter of the house with these words: "No, no white people back yaso. . . . Go weh. Back to yu big house" (85). The word *yaso,* which translates as "here" or more precisely "in this place," signals a purer, broader level of Jamaican Creole than Senior commonly uses. The language of the helper in a household is likely to be far from English. People in the big house speak English. People in all the big houses in the stories speak English.

In another story from that collection, "Two Grandmothers," the narrator, their granddaughter in common, interacts with two women from different social worlds. Language is one of the measures of identification of these worlds. The narrator, recently back from holidaying with her father's mother, reports to her own mother: "Mummy can you believe that everyone in church remembered me? And they said: 'WAT-A-WAY-YU-GROW' and 'HOW IS YU DAADIE? AND 'HOW IS YU MAAMIE?' till I was tired." Her personal and instructive comment is: "Mummy, that is the way they talk, you know, just like Richie and the gardener next door. 'WAT-A-WAY-YU-GROW.' They dont speak properly the way we do, you know" (70).

The narrative voice in Senior's stories depends entirely on the identity of the narrator. In those instances, however, where the language is a version of Jamaican Creole, it is the turn of phrase, the idiom, more than the differences in grammar or lexicon, that signal its use. The non-Creole speaker is unlikely to have difficulty understanding the words. Note the opening gambit of perhaps the most popular story of the collection *Summer Lightning,* "Do Angels Wear Brassières?": "Beccka down on her knees ending her goodnight prayers and Cherry telling her softly, 'And ask God to bless Auntie Mary.' Beccka vex that anybody could interrupt her private conversation with God so, say loud loud, 'no. Not praying for nobody that tek weh mi best glassy eye marble'" (67). Or the righteous indignation of Aunt Mary at the kind of question Beccka chooses to ask her, whether she knew "how worms reproduce": "Yes, please. That is what the child ask me. Lightning come strike me dead if is lie I lie. In my own house. My own sister pickney. So help me I was so frighten that pickney could so impertinent that right away a headache strike me like autoclaps" (69)

Mothertongue, certainly for a writer like Senior, is a number of speech codes: the broad Jamaican Creole of the maid in "See the Tiki-Tiki Scatter," the English of the middle and upper classes, the hypercorrected forms sometimes used by the aspirants to competence in English, the barely nonstandard forms that make up the relaxed speech of many educated Jamaicans, or the mixture of all these as the educated speaker switches from one code to the other, responding to the situation or trying for effect. Because she is true to the characters she creates, and because she creates characters across the social boundaries, Senior exposes the reader to a very wide range of possibilities within the continuum between Jamaican Creole and Standard Jamaican English. Any study of this artist's language must take account of this range.

Concerning voice in her work, Senior, in an interview with Anna Rutherford, makes the following revealing statement: "To me the sound of the voice is extremely important. I try to utilize the voice a great deal in my work and more and more find that what is happening is that the voice is taking over. In other words I am more and more concerned that my characters should speak directly to the reader and therefore I am dealing almost purely in narrative, in letting people tell their own story."[5] They tell it in their own mothertongue.

Lorna Goodison

Although poetry and good prose share many features, there are several differences, not the least of which is the terseness of the poetic form. An examination of mothertongue in poetry, in this case Lorna Goodison's poetry, is qualitatively different from the exercise just performed on Senior's prose.

Pamela Mordecai and Edward Baugh have both commented on Goodison's ability to slide from one to the other code of the Jamaican speech community. Mordecai notes the significance of the effective use of code-sliding as part of the "mix-up" that is Jamaican culture.[6] Baugh's more detailed description praises her skill at, inter alia, "interweaving erudite literary allusion with the earthiness of traditional speech."[7] The idea of interweaving runs close to the present description, which uses the term *overlapping* to describe one feature of Goodison's style.

Two related features are identified here: one grammatical, the other lexical. In the one, two or three codes are made to overlap within the same line or poem; in the other, the occasional Jamaican Creole item is woven into a poem whose fabric is undoubtedly Standard Jamaican English. The fact that all the codes in the Jamaican speech community are English-related facilitates the effectiveness of Goodison's strategies. If one of the codes were French-related, as is the situation in St. Lucia, for example, the procedure would not be possible.

Baugh, in his study, looks at the poem "Poui" from the second collection *I Am Becoming My Mother*[8] and shows how by using Creole verb forms in the first and last lines ("She don't put out for just anyone / . . . and she don't even notice"), the poet gives a Jamaican Creole flavor to a poem written almost entirely in Standard Jamaican English. In Goodison's hand, the occasional Creole item is like yeast in its effect on the mass of the poem. The content is accessible to Jamaican Creole and to non-Jamaican Creole speakers alike as the language can be claimed by both.

"Shame Mi Lady," also from the series in which "Poui" appears, furnishes a good example of both grammatical and lexical overlap operating within the same three lines. To receive the force of the strategy, the reader has to be able not only to recognize but to produce Creole, because intonation is important. Let us examine the lines. The poet compares herself with the shrub whose name is the title of the poem:

> now, if I can find favour (me with my bold face)
> you bashful you shy you innocent lady
> must/bound to find absolution/grace (14)

The *you* of the second line is emphatic in English and is opposed to *I* in the preceding line. But another reading is possible. The *you* can be pronounced with a short *u* [ʊ], in which case it becomes a Creole pronoun with the accompanying predicate adjective *bashful*. The utterance "yu bashful" thus translates to English "you are bashful." The line then contains three sentences describing the lady and the sense must wait on the next line. That next line admits both Creole and Standard Jamaican English, giving the reader the choice between the Creole *must* (and) *bound* of emphatic obligation, and the English *must*. There are lexical sleights that depend only partly on intonation for their point. *Bold face,* for example, can be one Creole term, with the stress on *bold,* meaning "fearless" bordering on rude, or two English words with equal stress, the one qualifying the other. In the same line a pun on *favour* is also hinted at. The Standard Jamaican English meaning is dominant, but lurking behind it is the kind of Jamaican Creole sentence, "you face favour," for which the listener is expected to supply some response considered daring in folk parlance, *favour* being in Jamaican Creole a verb meaning "resemble."

The poem "My Will" has forty-six lines. Among them there is only one instance of linguistic overlap. But the single word does have the effect of including Jamaican Creole among the vehicles of expression. The poet is leaving in her will a number of positive attributes and behaviors she wishes on her son. Included is the following: "May you never know hungry" (19). The uninitiated may well pass that over as an error and replace *hungry* with the English *hunger*. But what it is, is the Jamaican Creole predicate adjective *hungry* in a sentence that might read "may you never hungry" and might translate to Standard Jamaican English "may you never be hungry."

Later in the same poem, Goodison, wishing for the boy none of the dangerous commodity, gold, translates the Creole *bold face* to English "its face is too bold." The initiated will immediately hear "it too bold face." Here again, Jamaican Creole and Standard Jamaican English are interwoven or overlap in the same utterance, this time only by inference. At this level, the notions depend entirely on the listener's knowledge. The national community may hear two voices and the international community, one.

The rendering of complex behaviors and the sound of complex voices in a single statement by the deft manipulation of lexicon and syntax of the different codes is, I believe, Goodison's major contribution to Caribbean literature.

Perhaps the most daring use of this strategy is in the poem "Ocho Rios II" from the earliest collection *Tamarind Season*.[9] In this poem, it is necessary to express emotions felt by all Jamaicans. Speakers of Creole, Standard Jamaican English, and the code of Rastafari are represented. The scene is set in Ocho Rios, the second largest tourist city of Jamaica. The poem begins with discourse by a Rastafarian who enters the stage soliloquizing: "Today I again I forward to the sea" (53). The form *again* recognizes both the habit of the Rasta man and the existence of an earlier poem "Ocho Rios I," analyzed in detail by Mordecai in her study "Wooing with Words: Some Comments on the Poetry of Lorna Goodison." The first-person pronoun used initially might be either Jamaican Creole or Dread Talk, but its repetition in the sentence with overtones of the first-person alternative, "I and I," available only to Dread Talk, identifies the speaker as a Rasta man. The choice of verb reinforces this interpretation, for while *forward* adequately describes the act of walking, it is not used in this way in Standard Jamaican English or in Jamaican Creole. It is, however, commonplace in Dread Talk. The first movement of the poem continues:

> to the build-up beach where a faithful few lie rigid, submit to the smite of the sun. Today I bless you from the sore chambers of my temples. (53)

These lines are written mainly in Standard English except for one area of possible grammatical overlap with Dread Talk. The reader may now recognize it in the last line. The first-person pronoun *I*, because of the repetition performed in the first line, may be identified as either Dread Talk or Standard Jamaican English. The presence of the Rasta man is maintained by the use of Dread Talk. Standard Jamaican English indicates that the sentiment expressed is shared by the larger Jamaica.

An examination of an additional stanza, once again involving the sentiments of all Jamaica, serves to reinforce the point. It is the third movement of the poem in which Jamaica blesses the tourist and apologizes to him for inclement weather:

Bless you with a benediction of green rain, no feel no way its not that the
land of the sea and the sun has failed,

is so rain stay.
You see man need rain for food to grow
so if is your tan, or my yam fi grow? is just so
P.S. thanks for coming anyway. (53)

In the first of these lines, the double negative introduces the aside that marks the switch from English to Creole, "no feel no way." In the next line the explanation "is so rain stay" is Jamaican Creole. It is the voice of the peasant farmer for whom "green rain," which ruins the tourist's tan, is a blessing. It brings green lushness and productivity to the plants that are his source of income. He apologizes for what might seem to the tourist to be a selfish preference: rain over sun. Note that Creole used here can be understood (I believe) by the English-speaking foreigner who might himself have rendered it "that is how rain is."

All the speakers identify with the sentiments of the next two lines but it is the voice of the Rasta man that articulates it. What seems to be the impersonal *man* in Standard Jamaican English is in fact the multifunction pronoun of Dread Talk sometimes represented by its variants, *the man, I-man, the I.* It is followed by the unmarked verb of Jamaican Creole and of Dread Talk. The next line continues with the voice of the peasant farmer in Creole, to be followed by the polished English of the tourist board representative thanking the disappointed tourist for choosing Jamaica for his holiday. In each case, it is language that identifies the different actors in this dramatic piece. The voices of characters identify their place in the society and the sectors of the society they represent, enhancing the word pictures that they accompany. It is in this example that Goodison's use of the languages of the society in poetry most resembles Senior's use of it in prose.

Dread Talk, the code of Rastafari, features very strongly in "Ocho Rios II." Elsewhere in Goodison, the Rasta man, through his words, is constantly acknowledged as part of the Jamaican manscape. Sometimes it is necessary to repeat an idea already expressed in Standard Jamaican English to accommodate this code. The repetition, however, is not obtrusive, because the words are different. Note, for example, the following from "Ceremony for the Banishment of the King of Swords" from the collection *Heartease,*[10] "go through this again so you can penetrate it" (53). To *penetrate* in Standard Jamaican English means to go through in a very literal sense. In Dread Talk, however, it means to *understand.* The sentence really means "go through that again so you can understand it." What is important for the purposes of this discussion is the extent to which Goodison seems to have internalized the multilingual nature of the speech community.

Another example is found in "A Rosary of Your Names" from this same collection. God is worshipped here in a litany of fine words:

> Your names are infinity
> light and possibility
> and right
> and blessed
> and upfull (58)

Upfull is a Dread Talk word whose meaning includes both "right" and "blessed." And, although it is not an English word, its sound is so much in accord with the words around it that the ear accustomed to English does not reject it.

The final example of this use is the last stanza of the poem "Heartease I," in which the poet puns on the sound of the pronoun *I* and so includes one strong symbol from the Rastafarian belief system articulated in the words of the code: the sound that is shared by the first-person pronoun mentioned before, and the organ of sight:

> Believe, believe
> and believe this
> the eye know how far
> Heartease is (33)

The-I is an alternative to *I-man* and *I-and-I.* It is the Rastafarian sound of the ego. It is also the sound that describes the organ of sight. "Seeing" is very important to the Rastafari; its opposite, "blindness," is a hallmark of nonbelievers. Again, one might easily think Goodison is employing non-Standard English and needs to correct the verb to *knows*. But the sentence is: "I know how far Heartease is." Choosing to write *eye* instead of *I* concedes that the reader will take the former for granted but needs to be pointed to the latter. Goodison is generalizing a sentiment. The narrator knows how far away from the present reality Heartease is, as do we all, especially the Rasta man who is particularly far from ease in the society in which he is the oppressed (down-pressed). Here is clever artistry that goes beyond the simple pun and describes a multiple consciousness in what seems on the surface to be a single mode of expression.

One challenge Goodison has more than adequately met is the representation of the complex Jamaican language situation within the terse form that is poetry.

Conclusion

Mothertongue, as it is traditionally defined, is one-dimensional. It is that one language the individual first acquires and learns to use in communicating with other people. To operate effectively in the Jamaican situation, however, and in situations similar to it, is to master at least two codes. Mothertongue in the Jamaican situation might usefully be thought of as "language" rather than "a language." Indeed, recent research into Caribbean language has certainly begun to consider acquisition in these terms.[11]

This brief incursion into the use of language by two creative writers points to the intricacy of the patterns people in the Jamaican and similar speech situations continually make. The exercise also responds in part to the concerns articulated by D'Costa and St. Omer and referred to at the beginning of this chapter. Both local and foreign readers are accommodated by these two artists, although admittedly, one group, for whom this complexity of codes is mothertongue, responds to each text on more levels than the other.

Notes

1. Jean D'Costa, "The West Indian Novelist and Language: A Search for a Literary Medium," in *Studies in Caribbean Language,* ed. Lawrence Carrington in collaboration with Dennis Craig and Ramon Todd Dandaré (St. Augustine, Trinidad and Tobago: Society for Caribbean Linguistics, University of the West Indies, 1983), 252–265. See also chapter 3 of this volume.

2. Garth St. Omer, *The Colonial Novel* (Ann Arbor, MI: University Microfilms, 1975).

3. For a description of this speech, see Velma Pollard, "Dread Talk: The Speech of the Rastafari of Jamaica," *Caribbean Quarterly* 26, no. 4 (1982): 32–41.

4. Oliver Senior, *Summer Lightning and Other Stories* (Harlow, England: Longman Caribbean, 1986); and *Arrival of the Snake Woman, and Other Stories* (Harlow, England: Longman, 1989). All page references in the texts are to these editions.

5. Anna Rutherford, "Olive Senior Interview," *Kunapipi* 8, no. 2 (1986), 11–20.

6. Pamela Mordecai, "Wooing with Words: Some Comments on the Poetry of Lorna Goodison," *Jamaica Journal* 45 (1981): 38–40.

7. Edward Baugh, "Goodison on the Road to Heartease," *Journal of West Indian Literature* 1, no. 1 (1986): 13–26.

8. Lorna Goodison, *I Am Becoming My Mother* (London: New Beacon Books, 1986).

9. Lorna Goodison, *Tamarind Season* (Kingston: Institute of Jamaica, 1980).

10. Lorna Goodison, *Heartease* (London: New Beacon Books, 1988).

11. See Lawrence D. Carrington, "Acquiring Language in a Creole Setting," *Papers and Reports on Child Language Development* 28 (1989). 65–71.

15
The Facetiness Factor
Theorizing Caribbean Space in Narrative

Barbara Lalla

If *poetics* refers to patterns defining a literature and its regulating laws, how should we theorize poetics for a literature that defines itself (at least in part) in terms of its contempt for regulation? This question probes a crucial discursive dimension of our literature: namely, how our writers position themselves in relation to their topics, and how they seem to negotiate their stance toward established conventions and rules. In this chapter, I propose to examine what many of us term *facetiness* as an essential attitudinal position in Caribbean literary discourse.

The Jamaican term, *facetiness,* expresses a deep-in-the-bone sense of self that vividly resists any outside inducements to conform because conformity is felt to require a denial of the self. Refusing conformity (especially metropolitan sanctities) needs forcefulness, and sometimes force. So to assert this strategic approach is to claim that Caribbean discourse operates from a position of bold impudence, of barefaced, brazen, and (if it comes to that) rude self-assertion.[1]

Perhaps because Caribbean literary discourse carries so close to the surface its lived, living, oral-aural energy and memory, and also because its voices could not be heard unless they insisted, and, most of all, because this discourse assimilates and assaults the Other metropolitan discourse in order to free itself, *facetiness* becomes a fundamental necessity—in a sense, a genetic marker.

Whether the voice is that of Louise Bennett insisting on a Creole poetics freed from all regulation, or of stylists such as Walcott who challenge metropolitan norms both from within and from without, mocking their medium while making it into a multiplicity of voices, the pressure of nonconformity thrusts at the surfaces of seeming conformity, as in Walcott's sonnets: "Poopa, da' was a fete! I mean it had / Free rum free whisky and some fellars beating / Pan . . . while he drunk quoting Shelley with "'Each / Generation has its angst.'"[2] Facetiness defies, and it subverts with mockery—most of all, through constant challenge to rules. Of mixed etymological origin, Jamaican Creole *facety* may derive partly from archaic English *face,* meaning "effrontery, cheekiness, or boldness," but it also is related to a Surinam Creole term: *fiesti* sounds exactly like the Jamaican term but means "dirty, nasty."[3] Indeed, facetiness includes an element of optional mud-slinging in its refusal to stay within prescribed limits of language or worldview. It asserts the right of the speaker to her own vision and aggressively defies any who would convert, avert, or subvert that vision. And, as we have seen, the unique vision arises in its own words: change them, and the new world dies. It is this sense in which resistance means life, and accommodation means suffocation unto death, that drives so many Caribbean voices.

Facetiness may be expressed through all sorts of behavior (in actions such as *suck-teet, backanswer,* and *butt in*), but facetiness may also infuse particular types of discourse like Robber Talk (discussed later). This dynamic has implications for our understanding of Caribbean space because facetiness entails a refusal to be contained.

For sheer facetiness, consider Nalo Hopkinson's *Brown Girl in the Ring,* which takes over Toronto and locates its villain, Rudy (what else could he be named?)[4] who "a run tings" from the CN Tower. Hopkinson follows that with *Midnight Robber,* which, in the words of Elizabeth Boyle, "projects the black Atlantic into cyberspace."[5] One is prompted to ask: What next? Or rather, *where* next? Nalo Hopkinson's speculative fiction reconceives Caribbean space in projecting the futuristic setting of her novels on an alternative world that ironically mirrors our present and our past. She appropriates and transforms space in conceiving a technology woven from our folklore and displaying a matrix of oppressive forces only too similar to those of our own world. In both novels, for the survival of her Self, the female protagonist must destroy an overwhelmingly powerful paternal exploiter who both intrudes and confines. The attitudinal orientation of characters, narrators, and author begs investigation.

Now any discourse is defined by its speakers' position in relation to what is said, whether this orientation depends on a physical or a mental viewing position, and the latter (conceptual perspective) includes attitudinal positioning.[6] It is, therefore, within a theoretical framework for considering attitudinal perspective in narrative that I propose to examine attitudes that govern some conceptions of Caribbean space, particularly by reference to Nalo Hopkinson's *Midnight Robber.*

In between a series of encouraging addresses to what turns out to be an unborn child, *Midnight Robber* unfolds the story of Tan-Tan. First, her father, Antonio, kills his wife's lover and flees the technologically advanced Toussaint planet to the prison planet of New Half Way Tree, taking along Tan-Tan as a small child. Later, after years of violent abuse by her father, the sixteen-year-old Tan-Tan kills him and escapes with the help of a douen. Subverting and expanding the role of the douen (in Trinidad folklore the wandering souls of unbaptized infants, doomed to lure others to death of soul and body),[7] Hopkinson's douens protect Tan-Tan. Hunted by Janisette, Antonio's vengeful partner, Tan-Tan takes refuge in the bush, and the douens lose their home as a result of sheltering her. Finally, haunted by guilt and by her unwanted pregnancy and stalked by Janisette, Tan-Tan nevertheless finds love, negotiates selfhood through her Robber Queen persona, and accepts and names her child.

Although spatial orientation is basically physical, and attitudinal orientation is conceptual, attitudinal orientation is often conveyed through spatial terms (as, for example, by the use of the word *orientation* itself). The attitudinal orientation that Jamaicans term *facetiness* may be described through spatial metaphor as defiance regarding boundaries laid down by the powerful. Boundaries that are impressed on the less powerful tend to be accepted—until some facety person comes along and challenges these restrictions. Challenges to power distribution occur from the opening of *Midnight Robber*: "Runners didn't respect nobody, not even their own mother-rass mayor . . ." (5). Challenge, disrespect, and both active and subversive deeds assault not only rules but the ruler itself.

Disrespect is most blatant when addressed directly to an addressee or audience, and there is a sense in which much Caribbean literary discourse tends to be dismissive of audience authority—which is not to say that it is careless of having an audience but merely that it refuses to be governed by one. Hopkinson's discourse specifically implicates such dismissal at many levels.

In Caribbean expression generally, facety dismissal of the other may be expressed through *suck-teet* or, as Trinidadians more frequently say, in *steups*–a sound of absolute dismissal, even more cutting than *cut-eye* (hard stare followed by a sweeping down and away of the eyes), through body movements (like a *rude bwai* walk) and through features of discourse including expressions like *Cho!* Linguistic analysis closely links *suck-teet* to *cho!*[8]

With regard to audience, there is a lot of *Cho!* in *Midnight Robber*. Tan-Tan, for example, positions herself in relation to her own audience: "Cho! . . . How dare the bold-face man not believe her story?" The larger narrative seems to dismiss the external audience entirely. Within its fictional world, the narratee is the unborn, the child in Tan-Tan's belly. Direct address by the prevailing raconteur is made to this audience only, excluding all else.

As far as exclusion is concerned, the facety disregard the requirements of the powerful in marking out and maintaining their space—quite aggressively, to the point of demonstrating a sort of *garrison* mentality.[9] When, for example, Tan-Tan is deprived of every physical space she might have expected to claim as her own, she marks out the space of her own body and violently refuses further contact or entry to that space. As her father proceeds to rape her yet again, she positions her blade, and he slams down on it.

In situations of extreme oppression, merely opening one's mouth or raising one's eyes amounts to impertinence. So in circumstances in which, traditionally, our tongues are not our own, it is facety to take over the discourse and regulate it on a new basis defined by ourselves. *Midnight Robber* is largely about taking over discourse, and, at its core, about the suppression, breakdown, and re-establishment of communication. The protagonist (Tan-Tan) is taken out of contact with her own world's vast electronic communication system—the Grande Nanotech Sentient and its interface, Granny Nansi's Web. So Tan-Tan must work out her story for herself. In her new location, Tan-Tan has lost the capacity to reconnect with her original discourse community and draw on its vast intelligence system, but contact is made with her unborn child. Communication resumes through the regular channels of her home planet, through the house eshu, an electronic minder. This futuristic minder is conceived on the basis of a guiding spirit (*eshu*) from traditional African belief, and much of the narrative unfolds in the eshu's discourse to the unborn. The eshu's narrative is, largely, the story of how Tan-Tan comes to tell her own tale—to "come out" through Robber Talk, the significance of which is pointed out by Findlay's poem that precedes the entire text, "I stole the torturer's tongue."[10]

A curious thing about Caribbeanness is that (despite our resentment of those who infringe our boundaries) we often demonstrate a refusal to respect boundaries established by others—a *fasness*. There is a strong element of fasness entailed in facetiness—intruding shamelessly on the space of others, not content to be disobedient in recharting one's own space, but impertinent in opening up other spaces. Indeed, this penetration of boundaries established by others is perpetrated with a sort of aggressive glee best described in Trinidadian terms: same way we does like to storm people fête, we like to push our way into their formally defined literary spaces (defined by revered writers or by practically sacred genres), and we proceed to express ourselves uninhibitedly. We rewrite Shakespeare and Bronte and relocate the sea story to the Middle Passage, but in *Midnight Robber,* we go further. We recast folktale as horror story and the story of the Middle Passage as a journey into space. We appropriate the concept of a New World and construct an alternative Caribbean on that new New World.

But we go still further. Having developed our own canon, we begin to tamper with *that*. In *Brown Girl in the Ring,* we storm Walcott's *Ti-Jean and His Brothers* and flip the relationship from a horizontal one of competition between siblings to a vertical one of violence between grandparent, parent, and child. We recast gender relations so that it is three women, Gros Jeanne, Mi-Jeanne, and Ti-Jeanne, who deal with the prospect of being consumed by a patriarchal devil. The sheer audacity of the discursive operations involved flaunts disobedience.

We have noted that facetiness is a stance for expressing self when speech is expected to be suppressed, for challenging power distribution among participants in an exchange, for dismissing authority and demonstrating lack of respect, and, quite generally, ignoring boundaries established by others. However, it not only makes inroads into the space of others, it disrupts order. In narrative, it disturbs spatiotemporal order so as to produce alternative mindscapes: in the spirit of Caribbean festival, tu'n de whole ting upside down.

In traditionally structured discourse, identifiable components (like events) relate clearly to each other, for example, chronologically or causally. *Midnight Robber* appears on the surface to follow a roughly chronological sequence of Tan-Tan's experiences, interrupted by the anxieties or recollections of some characters. What *appears* to be the governing narrative seems to be intercepted by Nancy story, some Nancy story being revised as folktale about Tan-Tan. Only, Tan-Tan is still growing up in the outer story even as the Tan-Tan folktale invokes the historic and mythical Caribbean past in which Tan-Tan the folk hero has participated.

Much discourse that we now regard as traditional (like *Wuthering Heights* or *A Tale of Two Cities*) shuffles spatiotemporal dimensions. But in *Midnight Robber,* disruptions of order are so extreme as to raise the question of where, in all of its apparently disconnected discourses, resides the governing discourse?

Curdella Forbes reminds us of Antonio Benítez-Rojo's explication of the *uncanny*, in which Benítez-Rojo points out narratives that operate as "nodes of chaos" within the larger narratives in which they are embedded and which transform these larger narratives. These "uncanny" texts, as Benítez-Rojo demonstrates, effect "violent eruptions" of the subtextual.[11] In *Midnight Robber,* the eshu's discourse disrupts the larger text through the narrator's attitude that the ultimate focus is not, in fact, Tan-Tan. Tan-Tan the protagonist exists on the outside of what is really going on, and the child's progress inside, toward the outer world, constitutes the real event. The tales of Tan-Tan's experience in the outer worlds are offered as distraction for the baby, even though, outside, they have taken over and prompt metadiscursive comment: "What a thing those Tan-Tan stories had become, oui! Canto and cariso, crick-crack Anansi back; they had grown out of her and become more than her" (299).

Alternative versions of Tan-Tan's story prompt interrogation of fixity and order in Hopkinson's plots: *Midnight Robber* not only breaks down expected order, but, in its Afrofuturism, it also revises value systems comprising social critique through the insertion of black values, experience, and speculations into science fiction. Comparable operations of discourse produce those patterns of thought that have been described as a *bacchanal aesthetics* in the writing of Earl Lovelace, as discussed by Funso Aiyejina.[12] Lovelace's challenge to traditional order produces the amorphous and ambivalent, which Sandra Pouchet-

Paquet estimates as "a thoughtful dismantling of the boundaries between self and other over the course of some 25 years."[13]

In dismantling or redefining boundaries between self and other in *Midnight Robber,* Hopkinson's accounts of Tan-Tan's settlement, dislocation, and resettlement under and beyond oppressive regimes, and her development of a discourse of resistance make up the bulk of the narrative, but it is all (by implication) embedded in the eshu's discourse, intercepted by those tales *explicitly* ascribed to the eshu.

Therefore, the events are remapped as follows. First, the eshu calms the unborn child facing its first journey and introduces Tan-Tan for the first time. Then the tale of Tan-Tan takes us through four main relocations—Toussaint, New Half Way Tree's Junjuh Village, Daddy Tree, and Bush—each carrying her further from her expectations regarding civilized habitation. Interrupting the major account of Tan-Tan are flashbacks (as in her reliving of Antonio's abuse), as well as glimpses of her future as a folk hero. However, the entire tale of Tan-Tan consists of actual past experience on which the eshu draws, in talking the child through the birth that frames the novel. So the dispersal of events in apparent disorder is achieved not only by reshuffling temporal order in narrative, but equally by interrogating a balance of emphasis between the development of Tan-Tan and of the life inside her. The sense of inversion is conveyed early in Tan-Tan's journey through the dimension veil: "it was as though her belly was turning inside out, like wearing all her insides on the outside" (73).

The *outa-order* effect is also achieved by interfering in ordered conversational form, for example, by destroying turn-taking. Many voices, speaking each at their own convenience, convey alternation, contradiction, and dissonance,[14] while shifting codes suggest shifting foci, destabilizing perspective so as to convey the fragmented, multivalent Self. Consequently, they also convey the split self. As Tan-Tan attempts to search the stories about herself for the good others see in her, the voice of her other (hateful) self whispers, "Know you is a no-good waste of space" (299). But she persists in finding a medium through which to mark out her own space.

Behind the protagonist's facetiness stands her author's disobedient discourse. Not only does the overwhelming choice of Creole in *Midnight Robber* flout old-time prescriptive rules and the intelligibility requirements of the metropolitan audience, but the Creole of *Midnight* Robber thoroughly reconstitutes actual Caribbean Creole.

The Anglophone Caribbean voice that writing represents must be that of a particular territory (Antiguan, Jamaican, Guyanese, etc.), and it must be located somewhere between the Standard English and the Creole of the particular territory. It may interface with another Creole (such as Francophone Creole) and it may be diasporic, interfacing with English outside of the Caribbean, or with the Creole or English of another Caribbean territory. Additionally, it may be an ethnic variety of any one form of the Creole spoken in a particular territory.

Most writers, in representing the Creole so as to signal the Caribbean voice, try to avoid impairing comprehension, even if they adopt a posture of not caring greatly whether they lose wider intelligibility in the bid for empowerment. Choices of representation are varied and, always, politically fraught. Even though the Creole may not be used to an extent that actually reduces wide comprehension, representation of the Creole at least signals some dismissal of the non-Creole speaker. *Representation* is itself a process through which meaning is exchanged or created by signifying systems in which a *sign* (or "signifier") refers to something quite independent of it but (as a result of this representation) comes to be conceptually linked with it.[15] Similarly, the signaling of the Caribbean rests on a signification that is really quite distinct from the voice itself.

Representing the Caribbean voice is fraught by the inapplicability but familiarity of English orthographical practices; the reality of Anglophone Caribbean voices being specific to a territory and located anywhere between the version of Standard Jamaican English or Guyanese Creole; the interplay with, say, Francophone Creoles; and the dispersal through diasporas and cusps of overlapping diasporas. The Caribbean voice is strewn along the Caribbean's intersecting continua cut here and there by a stubborn resistance to blend. So there is no actual *Caribbean voice* to represent—unless one is forward enough, like Hopkinson, to reject Caribbean linguistic reality and posit an alternative reality—a Caribbean Creole that amalgamates regional, ethnic, and other dimensions of language variety.

Finally, Caribbean expression may be located anywhere along what Gordon Rohlehr has termed an oral-scribal continuum. Scribal representation of the Creole tends to be partial, as exact representation might lose the non-Creole-speaking/-reading audience. Nevertheless, this partial representation does not necessarily lack authenticity in view of the continuum of varieties that exist along the range between Caribbean Standard English and Creole.

Hopkinson does not, however, represent writing in her construction of essentially oral communities (although she does briefly mention books as artifacts to be preserved). In *Midnight Robber,* accumulated knowledge in the web is oral, *nannysong*, rather than scribal record. So *Midnight Robber* is literature that, by implication, generally dismisses scribal tradition not only of international English but of the Caribbean, signifying orature throughout. The oral displaces the scribal as the entrenched medium of officialdom.

All this reinvention further challenges traditional boundaries: first, the representation of varied and code-shifting rather than homogeneous voices; second, the privileging of the account that not only conveys oral rather than scribal discourse but authenticates the discourse specifically by reference to its orality. Authenticity in Caribbean literary discourse must account for plurality and hybridity, neither of which may be extricated from considerations associated with power distribution where identity is undergoing construction by a fractured but resilient psyche. It is such multiplicity, fluidity, collectivity, and even conflict in the identities of Hopkinson's protagonists that challenge established concepts of authenticity, autonomy, and authority. Both Ti-Jeanne/Prince of Cemeteries and Tan-Tan/Robber Queen produce discourse that is a site not only of interaction but of power struggle and cannot be conceived of as homogeneous without falling into the traditional and stereotypical view of identity as unitary and cohesive.

Representation of the multivalent Caribbean, moreover, makes space for *backanswer* and *butt-in,* reinforcing the challenge to established order. Caribbean literary discourse answers back to institutionalized precepts and understandings, facilitating interactivity as in intertextuality and counterdiscursivity. Beyond the tentative play with *The Tempest* in the nineteenth-century *Hamel, the Obeah Man* and the bold engagement with *Jane Eyre* in Rhys's *Wide Sargasso Sea,* we have arrived at Caribbean-internal counterdiscursivity such as occurs in Hopkinson's reworking of Walcott's reworking of the *Ti Jean* folktale. No text is an island—or, if it is, there are the submarine connections to be considered. It is well known that even as western European literary canons are deeply embedded with the matter of Greece and Rome along with more indigenous material such as, for example, Celtic survivals,[16] the Caribbean canon preserves and reprocesses material from multiple sources. European literary canons intersect African and Asian traditions as well as Amerindian memories. Thus, Wilson Harris negotiates paths through multiple pasts, and Walcott reformulates Greek and Trojan confrontations in relation to Caribbean epistemes. In *Brown Girl in the Ring,* however, the rewriting of a Caribbean canonical text interrogates our own literary authorities to explore links between colonialism and gender in terms of diabolic exploitation within a framework of domestic trauma.

In producing this antiphonal relationship to male-centered discourse in other Caribbean texts, Hopkinson's fiction goes beyond appropriation or subversion of such genres as science fiction, fantasy, and so forth by the privileging regional discourse types, like Robber Talk.

In Hopkinson's fiction, Robber Talk is especially significant because of its role in Tan-Tan's self-definition. Physically, the speaker must stand forth and demand attention, so Tan-Tan's name is well suited to the Robber Queen. Now Tan-Tan is a carnival character that may be invoked in relation to Tan-Tan as folk hero, a protective older woman (familiar form of *Tantie,* or *Tants,* Trinidad "aunt," derived from French). For Tan-Tan, the developing girl, her name also echoes Jamaican *tan,* derived from English *stand* through regular initial and final consonant cluster simplification, followed by reduplication for emphasis or intensification of the idea, in this case perhaps "stand, stand against or resist, stand out."

Standing out is a requirement of Robber Talk, which arrests its audience, distinguishes the speaker's persona from the ordinary, and flaunts disobedience and refusal to observe boundaries in expression.[17] Robber Talk spins out an outrageous reality that its speaker draws up as she goes along—Anancy-like manipulation of discourse. Disconnected from the official communication system, Tan-Tan weaves her own web: "Words welled up in the somebody's mouth like water. Somebody spoke her words the way the Carnival Robber Kings wove their tales, talking as much nonsense as sense, fancy words spinning out from their mouths like thread from a spider's behind: silken shit as strong as story. Somebody's words uttered forth from Tan-Tan's tongue: 'Stop and stand forth, O Jack Sprat and his fat, fat, fat mother,' said the Robber Queen" (245).

The traditional character, the Midnight Robber from Trinidad "ole time mas," is elaborately costumed as well as elaborate in verbal performance.[18] This is an aggressive persona. The symbols of death that characteristically ornament the costume complement the operation of discourse as weapon:

> Hear this long tongue!
> Fear this long tongue! (Findlay, "Stolen")

Robber Talk is bombastic discourse, boasting of extraordinary ancestry, weaving biblical and literary references into an impossible account of exploits conveyed through exaggerated metaphor. This is a discourse type adapted in *Midnight Robber* for asserting the self in a posthuman setting: for refocusing in order to defamiliarize common ways of seeing so as to bring distortions into view and enable interrogation of such ways of seeing. It also showers contempt on referents or addressees, for accusing and denouncing. In the framework of the mutually constitutive nature of discourse and reality, Robber Talk is a particularly facety approach to construction of Self and of Other: "her cracked voice came out in two registers simultaneously. Tan-Tan the Robber Queen, the good and the bad, regarded Janisette with regal gaze and spoke" (325).

Versions of Tan-Tan's unspeakable story (the eshu's, Janisette's, and the Robber Queen's versions) speak to each other and challenge each other intertextually within the novel—in the process of which interaction, Tan-Tan reassembles her split Self. Such an act does not constitute the same as that of healing a breach between the self and the community. Facetiness inclines to brazen individualism.

Curdella Forbes points to the existence of texts that seem to refuse the very notion of community or, alternatively, predicate the emergence of the individual on the erasure of community and privilege the individual as a form of alternative unbounded universe within and of the self.[19] I am inclined to associate this individualist stance with a wider inclination of Caribbean literature to define itself as "a form of alternative unbounded universe" within and of itself.

What Hopkinson projects in *Midnight Robber* is a Caribbean that carries its essential characteristics within itself and, wherever it touches down, marks out its space so definitively as to exclude the non-Caribbean even from contemplation. Hopkinson's worlds do not include the non-Caribbean (not even the whatever-it-is that the Caribbean has displaced). And the Caribbeanness of Hopkinson's worlds is cultural, located as a conceptual space entirely outside our global accommodation *and* as an inner space entirely beyond interference. Redefining Caribbeanness from the inside has effected a perspectival shift crucial to self-formation and identity construction not as fixed, static, and waiting to be discovered but as evolving. This identity is represented not as a reflection of an independent object but as an "emotionally charged" and constructed version.[20] This construction of unfixed, evolving, emotionally charged entities operates at the core of the interactive narratives in Hopkinson's novels, through which Tan-Tan develops in outer space and the unborn in inner space.

Tan-Tan takes it upon herself to denounce falsehood and pronounce on truth, to represent the legitimate social world, and to assign names to aspects of this world, characteristics by which linguists identify the discourse of the powerful. As in the case of Ti Jeanne, the most evolved state of Tan-Tan's journey to selfhood is that in which she recognizes and names her child, which she can do only after articulating her own version of her story.

The first individual appearance of the *ole mas* character in *Midnight Robber* is accompanied by an explanation of the type:

> The Robber gestured with his guns. . . .
>
> "Arrest thou compunctively, embroiled dispoilers. Dip and fall back, and hear my sultry cry." . . .
>
> The Robber Kings' stream of consciousness speeches always told of escaping the horrors of slavery and making their way into brigandry as a way of surviving in the new and terrible white devils' land in which they'd found themselves. (56–57)

This patterning lays the ground for Tan-Tan's subsequent Robber Queen speeches. But the whole novel is itself an outrageous account of abduction and escape from oppression, of legendary descent from luminary forebears, of journey and violent resistance—arresting in the impudence of its claims, in its weaving in of disparate references and in its startling language choices. *It's all Robber Talk!*

Hopkinson challenges colonial discourse in spinning Caribbean migration and settlement in space, but she further challenges our moral complacency in portraying Caribbean colonizers exploiting indigenous species in a new New World. In *Midnight Robber,* the privileged planet, named Toussaint (evoking black statehood), is the site to which the Caribbean has relocated. Exile from this new space to another, marginalized and carceral, challenges the hope of free statehood even as it proposes a portable Caribbean, culturally rather than physically defined. Not only has the Caribbean been reconceived as center but its physical limits are endlessly deferred—except for that inner space bordered only by humanness itself. At the same time, *Midnight Robber* searchingly explores the borders of the human.

One mechanism by which authority legitimizes itself as "normal" is to represent those who differ as remote from the center, as marginal beings, departures from normalcy and wholeness, made up of fragments—including fragments of beasts. So the creating of monsters may become a strategy for marginalizing the Other or, equally, for splitting the self. It may involve inscribing repulsive or demonic features on the body of the Other, especially with reference to an unusual outer surface of body, but also to unusual size or disproportion of body parts; unstable form or shape-shifting; evil or demonic properties; remote "uninhabitable" habitation; or violent behavior. A significant attribute for defining the monster is its skin.

Monsterizing the Other is quite common in contact cultures involving inequitable distribution of power (as in medieval tales such as *Sir Gawain and the Green Knight,* which plays on the inequitable power balance between peoples in medieval Britain). In conceptualizing the posthuman or liminal, Hopkinson draws on this important Caribbean episteme—the problematic of skin.

Skin, as surface, the first thing one sees, signals a body ordered or disordered, and skin difference is fraught—from Marlon James's diseased characters in *John Crow's Devil* and Senior's Lizardy Man to the soucouyant in *Brown Girl* and nonhuman characters of *Midnight Robber*. Because skin defines immediate personal space, skin that can be shed is reptilian, snake- or lizardlike, supernatural, evil. Then color—the widespread significance of green skin as suggestive of nature and of the unnatural, poisonous, even demonic—can connote liminal states (like monstrosity) between human and beast. The douen, Chichibud, is racially alien to begin with but instantly distanced further when a green membrane frills up around his neck.

Midnight Robber includes a variety of Caribbean monsters in strange skins. Some are monsters only until one gets to know them, like Chichibud with his leathery chest and reptilian head (92, 93, 128). Other creatures on the prison planet, like Mako Jumbie (111) are too ferocious to get to know, and, at first, Rolling Calf appears to fit into this latter group with its armored hide and tusks and spikes (227, 318). Indeed Tan-Tan's sojourn with the douens, followed by her adoption and rearing of a young Rolling Calf, unsettle perceptions of her own humanity.

Outside of the Caribbean, skin metaphor is familiar enough and, like other metaphor, adjusts perspective to a new angle of viewing. Over the past two decades, following on the appearance of George Lakoff and Mark Johnson's *Metaphors We Live By*,[21] the study of metaphor has exploded beyond traditional literary discussion of figurative language to cognitive-linguistic analysis. Cognitive-linguistic analysis of conceptual metaphor has explored ways in which metaphor projects universal or culturally defined categorizations of thought, while critical discourse analysis has investigated metaphor as a cognitive mechanism for ideology and thus as culturally fraught. As Andrew Goatly points out, metaphors are cognitive filters for categorizations of thought, but "different metaphors filter different particles of truth."[22] The operation of skin metaphor in current Caribbean discourse underscores the ideological basis of metaphor posited by critical discourse analysis and reveals extensive ideological shift. Marks's adaptation of Linnaeus's notorious classification demonstrates the primary place of skin color in categorizing race.[23] Numerous analyses have explored the interlocking binaries in European literature–for example, the presence or absence of morality, or of intelligence and virtue, assigned to white and black. While a language of hybridity has by no means developed to an extent comparable to that of the black-white binary, numerous metaphors promote the idea of purity,[24] and in European discourse purity is metaphorically connoted by whiteness.

Hopkinson unmasks attitudes grounded on those value systems that mark off the Other by social and psychological boundaries, for example, when Tan-Tan asks for Chichibud to be invited to her party:

> "Nanny guard we," Janisette had said. "What you want that nasty douen in the house for?"
>
> Tan-Tan had pouted and looked at her feet. "He tell nice stories."
>
> "Is true, doux-doux," Antonio had said to Janisette. "We could have him out in the yard. He could tell 'nansi story and keep the pickney-dem entertained." (137–138)

But then, through revelations of an alternative value system (that of Chichibud and the rest of the douens), Hopkinson invalidates the prejudice-ridden hegemonic ideology of "tall-people," the futuristic Caribbean viewpoint.

Skin metaphor is subtly interrogated in Hopkinson's fiction, in connection with the most immediate of our boundaries, those of the person. The significance of skin obviously defines the combination of tales in *Skin Folk* as well as major images of *Brown Girl in the Ring* where (for example) one woman is flayed and another trapped in the role of soucouyant. For the former character, flaying is just the final stage in the destruction of her identity. In the other case, trapping Mi Jean in the role of soucouyant drains her spirit and leaves her body an emptied container. She, in turn, separated from her skin and whirling in a ball of fire, must suck the lifeblood of others to sate an excruciating appetite. In contrast to these two earlier books, however, *Midnight Robber* integrates the skin metaphor more indirectly in plotting evolving identities and working through more subtle nuance, displaying skin and skin difference participating in the definition of personal and interpersonal space. The soucouyant effect is reinterpreted, Tan-Tan becoming a shape-shifter, but her father, Antonio, transforms into the monster that fondles her skin and consumes her.

Comparisons link Tan-Tan's skin to unequivocally Caribbean foods such as molasses, cocoa-tea, and toolum, and these reverse the colonial value system in relation to *black*. Nevertheless, they maintain the gender implications of the female body as something for consumption. From Tan-Tan's earliest days, food metaphor, associated with her skin, foreshadows horrific experience to come. Moreover, because metaphoric categorizations by their very nature focus on particular characteristics rather than the whole, metaphor is inherently reductive in ways that reflect ideological underpinnings. In Antonio's value system, the relative importance of his daughter's characteristics are sorted in ways that simplify her to a tidbit.

Skin, as a boundary between inner and outer worlds, should protect against contamination, though it may be contaminated. Chichibud is Other and, therefore, nasty. The surface of the prison planet, corrupted by its inhabitants and corrupting to those who enter, is perhaps a sort of soiled and soiling skin, suggested in reference to the soil of New Half-Way-Tree (2). Then, as a skin around Toussaint, the dimension veil operates as a membrane that may be ruptured. Historical background is provided in terms of a wound made by violent destruction of innocence in the spacecraft plunging into the soil of a new world. Through implicatures of penetrated membranes, the exploration of a feminized landscape raped by technology and a new world raped by the colonizer mirrors the landscaped woman planted by man and, in the process, corrupted in his sight: "He put this baby in me like the one before. He was forever trying to plant me like I was his soil to harvest" (260).[25]

As the largest and most extensive organ of the body, the skin is a protective covering, a hide that in Tan-Tan's case thickens figuratively, a thickening that is underscored by her adoption of the baby Rolling Calf with its armor-plated skin. Skin is not only a medium for the erotic, and a boundary between inner and outer worlds, but it is also an indicator of proximity. You know they have got to you when they get *under your skin*. As a cover and protective layer, skin functions conversely as an image of vulnerability for wounds that cannot be sutured, for violent puncture or laceration.

Antonio penetrates his daughter not only physically, but in that extended psychological riding that parallels Dry Bone sucking her substance until her skin is gray (205). These abuses toughen her resistance, from the disappointed child in the alligator shoes (27) to the hardback woman (Bad Tan-Tan), and they change her into the "monster" who "kills Daddy" and continues the patricidal rampage in causing the destruction of the douen home (the Daddy Tree). She almost kills her stepmother, this Bad Tan-Tan whom Antonio *breeds*. Antonio's penetration punctures his child's soul, splits her Self (the metaphor [140]), and rends the membrane between her utopian and dystopian lives.

And he locks her up—locks her in guilty silence: "We won't even tell Janisette, all right, or she go be mad at we. You wouldn't want she to send for One-Eye to put me in the tin box, right? That would kill you poor Daddy, Tan-Tan" (141). But Tan-Tan "comes out" through Robber Talk, stunning her audience in her shameless display of Self, shedding the outer covering of Good Tan-Tan.

Skin is also a container. Inside Tan-Tan, under her skin, Antonio has embedded the baby that grows like a monster in her flesh, usurping the only space that is truly hers, eating her from inside—a thing with an attitude all its own:

> She rubbed her hands over her belly, imagining she could just dig her fingers inside and pull out the thing growing in her. (235)
>
> The monster child was taking away her wind and all. (236)
>
> Is the baby, the monster baby that was round and hard like a potato in her belly. . . . Resentfully Tan-Tan dug her fingers into her stomach. The defiant thing inhabiting her didn't yield. (255)

Tan-Tan eventually delivers her baby from the condition of a potential bolom (an unborn child, possibly aborted by its mother and consigned to limbo) and recognizes that she (herself) is not a waste of space. She comes face to face with what was protected inside her skin, even from herself—and very facety it is too: "For a second he stared right at her. He had Antonio's face, but they were her features too, *hers*. Her son was not a monster" (328). Tan-Tan recognizes that the baby is itself an embodiment of resistance, when she names him "Tubman," after that icon of liberation, Harriet Tubman, who escaped slavery then drew on a living network to rescue other slaves to freedom.[26] Thus, the outrageous tale is historicized and, perhaps, its point made clear.

What is the authorial attitude, the evaluation, suggested by all this?

Susan Hunston and Geoff Thompson discuss this dimension of attitudinal orientation (the authorial stance, viewpoint, feelings on values regarding entities or propositions being talked about), although they prefer Labov's term, *evaluation*. They point out the emphasis that Labov places on evaluation as preempting any uncertainty regarding the point of the story.[27] In *Midnight Robber,* an individual identity bounded only by her own skin is negotiated by Tan-Tan through the Caribbean genre of Robber Talk; a separate existence is affirmed in the birth and naming of a child talked-through the birth pangs, by the ancestral guide; Caribbean ways of knowing are legitimized through our own discursive operations as definitive of Caribbeanness, which is, otherwise, ultimately unbounded, always renegotiable, inevitably deferred.

Hopkinson's authorial position is at least to some extent locatable. In discussing the identity formation process in narrative, Michael Bamberg reminds us that constructing a narrative always involves revealing the self. Bamberg explains that entering a narrative as a character requires further operations but that there is (even without that involvement) always an investment of self in narrating, the act itself lodging claims about the speaker's sense of self.[28] Bamberg's view throws light on identity formation in the unborn, in Tan-Tan, in Hopkinson's Caribbean. Moreover, he tells us that in narratives-in-interaction (such as those in *Midnight Robber*), evaluation functions not as a predetermined position but as one that is negotiated through the interaction. The evaluative stances of the eshu, of the Robber Queen and (who knows) perhaps of Hopkinson actually seem to develop through interaction and even through challenges to the narrator's position—challenges that may well provoke one to facetiness.

A major challenge is douen wisdom surfacing repeatedly in Tan-Tan's struggle for Self, to prompt her consciousness of obligation to the world of living things, and to argue against her dispensing with the life of even a monster baby:

> "I can't give birth to this thing, Abitefa. Is a monster. I rip one of the brutes out of me once, I could do it twice."
>
> Abitefa's arms were more like wingflaps now, feathered and longer. The feathers puffed out in shock. "Why? You make egg, you must lay it; is a gift from the daddy tree."
>
> Gift. That squeezed another bitter laugh from Tan-Tan's lips. "We don't lay," she corrected Abitefa. "We does push out our babies live and screaming. And this ain't no gift, is a curse."
>
> "No egg? Oho," Abitefa said, peering at Tan-Tan's stomach. "So is that why I can't see no egg. . . skin round the baby." (233)

From the angle of Abitefa's view of the bolom, skin folk may be Other. The douens of Trinidad folklore are aborted children, stuck in limbo, but in *Mid-*

night Robber, they are a race (combining reptilian and birdlike traits) that are marginalized and displaced by "tall-people," but who manifest an alternative wisdom that challenges Tan-Tan to evolve, just as the defiant thing inside her refuses to abort despite Tan-Tan's best efforts.

And this alternative perspective is itself embedded in another. The eshu, the futuristic electronic minder extrapolated from the African guide, a mischievous and ambivalent teller, is consistently inconsistent, turning the whole thing upside down and inside out.

I have argued that Caribbeanness in literary discourse is at least in part defined by a conceptual orientation that is conveyed through spatial metaphor; that defiant attitudes to one's place and boundaries (such as we term *facetiness*) may be expressed through poetic stances, narrative operations, and genres that parallel facety Caribbean behaviors (responses and positionings like *suck-teet, backanswer,* and *fasness*) through which one marks off one's space, dismisses the boundaries set by others, flaunts Self, and disses Other. In similarly impertinent ways, Caribbean narrative such as Hopkinson's marks out or opens up invented outer and inner spaces through a variety of discursive strategies. To project alternative mindscapes, the discourse subverts traditional requirements for established form and devices for meaning. Through interventions in structure and perspective and manipulations of meaning (as in the interrogation of skin metaphor), the discourse conveys its impudent refusal to be contained, as well as its defiant reconfiguration of the Caribbean as, ultimately, timeless and unbounded, and as essentially defined in terms of inner space.

Notes

1. "Impudent, bold, rude, overbearing," F. G. Cassidy and R. B. Le Page, *Dictionary of Jamaican English,* 2nd ed. (Cambridge: Cambridge University Press, 1980); "bold, bare-faced, brazen, impudent," Richard Allsopp, *Dictionary of Caribbean English Usage* (Oxford: Oxford University Press, 1996).

2. Derek Walcott, "Tales of the Islands, Chapter VI." *Collected Poems 1948–1984* (New York: Farrar, Straus, 1986), 24–25.

3. Cassidy and Le Page, *Dictionary of Jamaican English,* 172.

4. Nalo Hopkinson, *Brown Girl in the Ring* (New York: Warner Books, Grand Central Publishing, 1998). Note *rudy, rudie,* short for *rude boy* [ru:d bwai]. In Jamaican, *rude* carries more intense reference to objectionable behavior than it does in Standard English. It suggests even violent defiance as well as sexual excess. See Cassidy and Le Page, *Dictionary of Jamaican English, rude.*

5. Nalo Hopkinson, *Midnight Robber* (New York: Warner Books, 2000); Elizabeth Boyle, "Vanishing Bodies: 'Race' and Technology in Nalo Hopkinson's *Midnight Robber,*" *African Identities* 7, no. 2 (May 2009): 177–191.

6. Paul Simpson addresses this in *Language, Ideology and Point of View* (London: Routledge, 1993).

7. *Douen* or *dwen* derives from Spanish *duende*, or goblin, and Efik *dwen*, spirit of the dead. See Lise Winer, *Dictionary of the English/Creole of Trinidad and Tobago* (Montreal: McGill-Queen's University Press, 2009), 311–312. A full description of these ghost-children appears in Winer.

8. John Rickford and Angela Rickford, "Cut-Eye and Suck-Teeth: African Words and Gestures in New World Guise," *Journal of American Folklore* 89, no. 353 (1976): 194–309; Peter Patrick and Ester Figeroa, "Kiss-Teeth," *American Speech* 77, no. 4 (2002): 483–497.

9. A stronghold controlled by a don; a community in which borders are violently maintained, operating as political enclave.

10. The poem prefaces the novel and was written by her partner, David Findlay, according to Hopkinson in an interview by Paul Jarvey, *Canadian Science Fiction Review* 1, no. 3 (2011). http://aescifi.ca/index.php/non-fiction/34-interviews/471-nalo-hopkinson.

11. In Benítez-Rojo, *The Repeating Island (*Durham, NC: Duke University Press, 1996), 88; and see Curdella Forbes, "Fracturing Subjectivities: International Space and the Discourse of Individualism in Colin Channer's *Waiting in Vain* and Jamaica Kincaid's *Mr. Potter*," *Small Axe* 25 (2008): 16–37.

12. See Funso Aiyejina, ed., "Introduction: Finding the Darkness in Which to Grow: The Journey towards Bacchanal Aesthetics," *Growing in the Dark: Selected Essays,* by Earl Lovelace (San Juan, Trinidad: Lexicon, 2003), v–xx.

13. This characterization includes such maneuvers as his adopting the mask of violent revolutionary on an intellectual level. Compare Sandra Pouchet-Paquet, "The Vulnerable Observer: Self-Fashioning of Earl Lovelace's *Growing in the Dark* (Selected Essays)," *Anthurium: A Caribbean Studies Journal* 4, no. 2 (2006): 1–26, http://scholarlyrepository.miami.edu/anthurium/vol4/iss2/7WEB.

14. Stuart Hall, D. Held, and T. McGrew, eds., *Modernity and Its Futures* (Cambridge: Polity Press, 1992), 277.

15. See Stuart Hall's version, which adjusts Saussure's usage, in *Representation: Cultural Representations and Signifying Practices*, Cultures, Media and Identities Series (Milton Keynes, England: Open University, 1997), 13–74.

16. This cultural collision is extensively discussed throughout Barbara Lalla's *Postcolonialisms: Caribbean Rereading of Medieval English Discourse* (Kingston, Jamaica: University of the West Indies Press, 2008).

17. Lise Winer, *Dictionary of the English/Creole of Trinidad and Tobago:* "1n. The formal verse speech of a Robber Mas character, specifically a Midnight Robber, spoken in very commanding tones, referring to the robber's supernatural powers, boasting and threatening others with destruction." "2n. Any overdone threatening kind of language esp. by or in reference to authority; a style without much substance" (764).

18. The costume includes a hat with a huge fringed brim decorated with ominous symbols, a similarly elaborate decorated cloak, and so on.

19. Curdella Forbes, "Fracturing Subjectivities," 18.

20. Chris Barker and Dariusz Galasinsky, *Cultural Studies and Discourse Analysis: A Dialogue on Language and Identity* (London: Sage, 2001), 28.

21. George Lakoff and Mark Johnson's *Metaphors We Live By* (1986; repr., Chicago: University of Chicago Press, 1991).

22. Andrew Goatly, *Washing the Brain: Metaphor and Hidden Ideology* (Amsterdam: John Benjamins, 2007), 25, see also p. 3.

23. Linnaeus's *Systema Naturae* [1798] is quoted in J. Marks, *What It Means to Be 98% Chimpanzee* (Berkeley: University of California Press, 2002), 57; and see Goatly, *Washing the Brain,* 45.

24. See Goatly, *Washing the Brain,* 49.

25. See also Giselle Lisa Anatole, "Maternal Discourses in Nalo Hopkinson's *Midnight Robber,*" *African American Review* 40, no. 1 (2006): 111–124.

26. Other subtle intertextual links are relevant. When Harriet Tubman was very young, a blow from an overseer left her subject to bouts of severe pain and to visions, which she came to believe were divinely sent.

27. Susan Hunston and Geoff Thompson, *Evaluation in Text: Authorial Stance and the Construction of Discourse* (Oxford: Oxford University Press, 1996), 213–238.

28. Bamberg, "Narrative Discourse and Identities," in *Narratology beyond Literary Criticism,* ed. Jan Christoph Meister, T. Kindt, W. Schernus, and M. Stein (Berlin: Walter de Gruyter, 2006), 224.

Bibliography

Aberdeen, Athene. "The Oral and Written English of a Group of First Year University Students: a Study in Variation." MA diss., University of the West Indies, St. Augustine, 1976.

Aiyejina, Funso. "An Intertextual Critical Approach to *Salt* by Earl Lovelace." Presentation at the Book Launch of Earl Lovelace, *Salt,* Port-of-Spain, Martin's Miller House, December 1966.

——— ed. "Introduction: Finding the Darkness in Which to Grow: The Journey towards Bacchanal Aesthetics." In *Growing in the Dark: Selected Essays.* By Earl Lovelace, v–xx. San Juan, Trinidad: Lexicon, 2003.

Alim, H. Sammy, Awad Ibrahim, and Alastair Pennycook, eds. *Global Linguistic Flows: Hip Hop Cultures, Youth Identities, and the Politics of Language.* New York: Routledge, 2009.

Allen, Carolyn. "Creole: The Problem of Definition." In *Questioning Creole: Creole Discourses in Caribbean Culture.* Edited by Verene Shepherd and Glen Richards, 47–63. Kingston, Jamaica: Ian Randle, 2002; Oxford: James Curry, 2002.

Alleyne, Mervyn C. *Comparative Afro-American: A Historical Comparative Study of English-Based Afro-American Dialects.* Ann Arbor, MI: Karoma Publishers, 1980.

Allsopp, Richard. *Dictionary of Caribbean English Usage.* Oxford: Oxford University Press, 1996.

———. "The Problem of Acceptability in Caribbean Creolised English." Presentation at the Conference on Creole Languages and Educational Development, University of the West Indies, St. Augustine, 1972.

Anatole, Giselle Lisa. "Maternal Discourses in Nalo Hopkinson's *Midnight Robber.*" *African American Review* 40, no. 1 (2006): 111–124.

Anderson, Benedict. *Imagined Communities: Reflections on the Origins and Spread of Nationalism.* London: Verso, 1991.

Appadurai, Arjun. *Modernity at Large: Cultural Dimensions of Globalization.* Minneapolis: University of Minnesota Press, 1996.

Arnold, Matthew. *Lyric, Dramatic and Elegiac Poems.* Oxford: Hall and Stacy, 1881.

Ashcroft, Bill, Gareth Griffiths, and Helen Tiffin. *The Empire Writes Back: Theory and Practice in Post-Colonial Literatures.* London: Routledge, 1989.

Atkins, John. *A Voyage to Guinea, Brasil, and the West Indies*. London: Cesar Ward and Richard Chandler, 1736.

Auer, Peter, and Jürgen Erich Schmidt, eds. *Language and Space: An International Handbook of Linguistic Variation: Theories and Message*. Berlin: Walter de Gruyter, 2010.

Bailey, Beryl Loftman. *Jamaican Creole Syntax: A Transformational Approach*. Cambridge: Cambridge University Press, 1966.

Bamberg, Michael. "Narrative Discourse and Identities." In *Narratology beyond Literary Criticism*. Edited by Jan Christoph Meister, T. Kindt, W. Schernus, and M. Stein, 213–238. Berlin: Walter de Gruyter, 2006.

Barker, Chris, and Dariusz Galasinski. *Cultural Studies and Discourse Analysis: A Dialogue on Language and Identity*. London: Sage, 2001.

Barrett, Leonard. *Soul-Force—African Heritage in Afro-American Religion*. New York: Doubleday, 1974.

Barthes, Roland. *Writing Degree Zero*. Translated by Annette Lavers and Colin Smith. 1953. Reprint, New York: Hill and Wang, 1968.

Bartsch, Renate. *Norms of Language: Theoretical and Practical Aspects*. London: Longman, 1987.

Baugh, Edward. "Goodison on the Road to Heartease." *Journal of West Indian Literature* 1, no. 1 (1986), 13–26.

———. *It Was the Singing*. Toronto, Canada: Sandberry Press, 2000.

———. "Review, *Rights of Passage*." *Bim* 45 (1967): 66–68.

Bennett, Louise. *Aunty Roachy Seh*. Edited by Mervyn Morris. Kingston: Sangster's Bookstores, 1993.

———. *Jamaica Labrish*. Edited by Rex Nettleford. Kingston, Jamaica: Sangster's Bookstores, 1966. Reprint, 1972.

———. *Selected Poems*. Edited by Mervyn Morris. Kingston: Sangster's Bookstores, 1983.

Bickerton, Derek. *Dynamics of a Creole System*. Cambridge: Cambridge University Press, 1975.

———. "How to Acquire Language without Positive Evidence." In *Language Creation and Language Change: Creolisation, Diachrony and Development*. Edited by M. DeGraff, 49–74. Cambridge, MA: MIT Press, 1999.

———. "On the Nature of a Creole Continuum." *Language* 49, no. 3 (1973): 640–669.

Bobb, June D. *Beating a Restless Drum: The Poetics of Kamau Brathwaite and Derek Walcott*. Trenton, NJ: Africa World Press, 1998.

Boehmer, Elleke. *Colonial and Postcolonial Literature*. Oxford: Oxford University Press, 1995.

Booker, M. Keith, and Dubravka Juraga. *The Caribbean Novel in English: An Introduction*. London: Heinemann, 2001.

Boyle, Elizabeth. "Vanishing Bodies: 'Race' and Technology in Nalo Hopkinson's *Midnight Robber*." *African Identities* 7, no. 2 (May 2009): 177–191.

Bradford, Richard. *A Linguistic History of English Poetry*. London: Routledge, 1993.

Brathwaite, Edward Kamau. *The Arrivants: A New World Trilogy*. London: Oxford University Press, 1973.

———. *Contradictory Omens: Cultural Diversity and Integration in the Caribbean*. Kingston, Jamaica: Savacou Publications, 1974.

———. *History of the Voice: The Development of Nation Language in Anglophone Caribbean Poetry*. London: New Beacon, 1984.

———. *Rights of Passage*. London: Oxford University Press, 1967.

Bridgeman, Teresa. "Time and Space." In *The Cambridge Companion to Narrative*. Edited by David Herman, 52–65. Cambridge: Cambridge University Press, 2007.

Brodber, Erna. *Jane and Louisa Will Soon Come Home*. London: New Beacon Press, 1980.

Bucholtz, Mary. "Sociolinguistic Nostalgia and the Authentification of Identity." *Journal of Sociolinguistics* 7, no. 3 (2003): 398–416.

Bucholtz, Mary, and Kira Hall. "Identity and Interaction: A Sociocultural Linguistic Approach." *Discourse Studies* 7 (2005): 4–5.

Carrington, Lawrence. "Acquiring Language in a Creole Setting." *Papers and Reports on Child Language Development* 28 (1989): 65–71.

———. *St. Lucian Creole: A Descriptive Analysis of Its Phonology and Syntax*. Hamburg, Germany: Buske, 1984.

———. "The Status of Creole in the Caribbean." In *Due Respect: Papers on English and English Related Creoles in the Caribbean in Honour of Professor Robert Le Page*. Edited by Pauline Christie, 24–36. Kingston, Jamaica: University of the West Indies Press, 2001.

Carrington, Sean, Henry Fraser, and John Gilmore, eds. *A–Z of Barbadian Heritage*. Kingston, Jamaica: Heinemann Caribbean, 1990. Republished, Oxford: MacMillan Caribbean, 2004.

Carter, Hazel. "How To Be A Tone Language." In *Studies in Caribbean Language*. Edited by Lawrence Carrington, in collaboration with Dennis Craig and Ramon Todd Dandaré, 90–111. St. Augustine, Trinidad and Tobago: Society for Caribbean Linguistics, 1983.

Carter, Martin. *Poems of Resistance*. London: Lawrence and Wishart Ltd., 1954.

Cassidy, F. G. *Jamaica Talk*. London: MacMillan, 1971.

Cassidy, F. G., and R. B. Le Page. *Dictionary of Jamaican English*. Cambridge: Cambridge University Press, 1967; 2nd ed., 1980.

Chamberlin, J. Edward. *Come Back to Me My Language: Poetry and the West Indies*. Toronto: McClelland and Stewart, 1993.

Chatman, Seymour. *Story and Discourse: Narrative Structure in Fiction and Film*. Ithaca, NY: Cornell University Press, 1978.

Christie, Pauline. "Forty Years On." In *Due Respect: Papers in English and English-Related Creoles in the Caribbean in Honour of Professor Robert Le Page*. Edited by Pauline Christie, 24–36. Kingston, Jamaica: University of the West Indies Press, 2001.

Cobham, Rhonda. "Revisioning Our Kumblas: Transforming Feminist and Nationalist Agendas in Three Caribbean Women's Texts." *Callaloo* 16, no. 1 (1993): 44–64.

Condé, Maryse. "On the Apparent Carnivalization of Literature from the French Caribbean." In *Representations of Blackness and the Performance of Identities*. Edited by Jean Muteba Rahier, 91–97. Westport, CT: Bergin and Garvey, 1999.

Cooper, Carolyn. "Britain no Want Join di EU fi True." *Jamaica Observer*, November 15, 1996.

———. *Noises in the Blood: Orality, Gender and the "Vulgar" Body of Jamaican Popular Culture*. London: Macmillan, 1993.

———. "The Oral Witness and Scribal Document: Divergent Accounts of Slavery and the Development Process in Two Novels of Barbados." In *West Indian Literature and Its Social Context.* Edited by Mark McWatt, 3–11. Cave Hill, Barbados: University of the West Indies, 1985.

Cooper, Carolyn, and Hubert Devonish. "A Tale of Two States: Language, Lit/orature and the Two Jamaicas." In *The Pressures of the Text: Orality, Texts and the Telling of Tales.* Edited by Stewart Brown, 60–74. African Studies Series 4. Birmingham, England: Center of West African Studies, 1995.

Coupland, Nikolas, Srikant Sarangi, and Christopher N. Candlin, eds. *Sociolinguistics and Social Theory.* Harlow, England: Pearson, 2001.

Craig, Dennis R. Interview with D'Costa on reading performance of Jamaican children. University of the West Indies, Kingston. 1980.

———. "Language-Education Research in the Commonwealth Caribbean." *Caribbean Journal of Education* 1, no. 1 (1975): 23–36.

———. "Some Developments in Language Teaching in the West Indies." *Caribbean Quarterly* 12, no. 1 (1966): 25–34.

Craton, Michael. *Searching for the Invisible Man: Slaves and Plantation Life in Jamaica.* Cambridge: Harvard University Press, 1978.

Creary, Jean C. (now D' Costa). "Mathematics for Children Speaking Jamaican Creole." *Caribbean Quarterly* 2 (1965): 85–94.

Crowe, Captain Hugh. *Memoirs.* London: Longman, Rees, Orme, Brown and Green, 1830.

Crystal, David. *A Dictionary of Linguistics and Phonetics.* Oxford: Blackwell, 1985, 2008.

Culler, Jonathan. *Structuralist Poetics: Structuralism, Linguistics and the Study of Literature.* London: Routledge and Kegan Paul, 1975.

Dahlstrom, Michael F. "The Role of Causality in Information Acceptance of Narratives: An Example from Science Communication." *Communication Research* 37 (2010): 857–875. http://crx.sagepub.com/content/37/6/857.

Dance, Daryl Cumber. *Fifty Caribbean Writers.* Westport, CT: Greenwood Press, 1986.

———. *Folklore from Contemporary Jamaicans.* Knoxville: University of Tennessee Press, 1980.

Dascal, Marcelo, and Chris Barker. "Identities in Flux: Arabs and Jews in Israel." In *Critical Discourse Analysis: Theory and Interdisciplinarity.* Edited by Gilbert Weiss and Ruth Wodak, 150–166. Houndsmill, England: Palgrave, 2003.

D'Costa, Jean C. *Escape to Last Man Peak.* Harlow, England: Longman, Blue Mountain Library Series, 1975. Reprint, London: Longman, Horizon Series, 1980.

———. "Expression and Communication: Literary Challenges to the Caribbean Polydialectal Writer." *Journal of Commonwealth Literature* 19, no. 1 (1984): 123–141.

———. "Language and Dialect in Jamaica." *Jamaica Journal* 2 (March 1968): 71–74.

———. "Louise Bennett's Dialect Poetry: Problems of Variation along a Creole Continuum in a Literary Text." In *Studies in Language Ecology.* Edited by Werner Enninger and Lilith Haynes, 135–158. Wiesbaden, Germany: Franz Steiner Verlag GMBH, 1984.

———. "Oral Literature, Formal Literature: The Formation of Genre in Eighteenth Century Jamaica." *Eighteenth-Century Studies* 27, no. 4 (1994): 663–676.

———. *Sprat Morrison*. Kingston, Jamaica: Ministry of Education and Collins-Sangster, 1972. Reprint, London: Longman, 1990.

———. *Voice in the Wind*. London: Longman, 1978.

———. "The West Indian Novelist and Language: A Search for a Literary Medium." In *Studies in Caribbean Language*. Edited by Lawrence D. Carrington in collaboration with Dennis Craig and Ramon Todd Dandaré, 252–265. St. Augustine, Trinidad and Tobago: Society for Caribbean Linguistics, University of the West Indies, 1983.

D'Costa, Jean, and Barbara Lalla, eds. *Voices in Exile: Jamaican Texts of the 18th and 19th Centuries*. Tuscaloosa: University of Alabama Press, 1989.

DeCamp, David. "Social and Geographical Factors in Jamaican Dialect." In *Creole Language Studies*. Vol. 2. Edited by Robert B. Le Page, 61–84. London: Macmillan, 1961.

———. "Towards a Generative Analysis of a Post-Creole Speech Continuum." In *Pidginization and Creolization of Languages*. Edited by Dell Hymes, 349–370. Cambridge: Cambridge University Press, 1971.

de Lisser, Herbert G. *Jane's Career: A Story of Jamaica*. London: Methuen, 1914. Reprinted, London: Heinemann, 1972.

———. *The White Witch of Rosehall*. 1929. Reprint, Basingstoke, England: Macmillan Caribbean, 2007.

DeLoughrey, Elizabeth, George Handley, and Renee Gosson. *Caribbean Literature and the Environment: Between Nature and Culture*. Charlottesville: University of Virginia Press, 2005.

Devonish, Hubert. "Tone in Guyana Creole." Presentation at the Linguistics Seminar, University of the West Indies, Mona, Jamaica, May 1983.

———. "Vernacular Languages and Writing Technology Transfer: The Jamaican Case." In *Caribbean Language Issues Old and New: Papers in Honour of Professor Mervyn Alleyne*. Edited by Pauline Christie, 101–111. Kingston, Jamaica: University of the West Indies Press, 1996.

Dissanayake, Wimal, and Carmen Wickramagamage. *Self and Colonial Desire: Travel Writings of V. S. Naipaul*. New York: Lang, 1993.

Doležel, Lubomír. *Heterocosmica: Fiction and Possible Worlds*. Baltimore, MD: Johns Hopkins University Press, 1998.

———. "Narrative Modalities." *Journal of Literary Semantics* 5 (1976): 5–14.

Eco, Umberto. *A Theory of Semiotics*. Bloomington: Indiana University Press, 1976.

Eersel, C. "Prestige in Choice of Language and Linguistic Form." In *Pidginization and Creolization of Languages*. Edited by Dell Hymes, 141–150. Cambridge: Cambridge University Press, 1971.

Ellis, J. M. "Linguistics, Literature, and the Concept of Style." *Word* 26, no. 1 (April 1970): 65–78.

Emmott, Catherine. *Narrative Comprehension: A Discourse Perspective*. Oxford: Oxford University Press, 1997.

Equiano, Olaudah. *The Interesting Narrative of the Life of Olaudah Equiano, or Gustavus Vassa, the African*. London: n.p., 1789.

Fabb, Nigel. *Linguistics and Literature: Language in the Verbal Arts of the World*. Oxford: Blackwell, 1997.

Fairclough, Norman. *Discourse and Social Change*. Cambridge: Polity, 1992.

Fasold, Ralph. *Sociolinguistics of Language*. Oxford: Blackwell, 1990.

———. *The Sociolinguistics of Society*. Oxford: Blackwell, 1984.

Ferro, Marc. *Colonization: A Global History*. London: Routledge, 1997.

Findlay, David. "Stolen." 1997. Epigraphic poem in Hopkinson, Nalo. *Midnight Robber*. New York: Warner Books, 2000.

Fishman, Joshua A. *Advances in the Sociology of Language I*. Edited by Joshua A. Fishman. The Hague: Mouton, 1972.

———. *Language and Nationalism*. Rowley, MA: Newbury House, 1972.

———. *The Sociology of Language: An Interdisciplinary Social Science Approach to Language in Society*. Rowley, MA: Newbury House, 1972.

Fleischman, Suzanne. *Tense and Narrativity*. Austin: University of Texas Press, 1990.

Floyd, Jean Laurie. "Reading in the Lives of Jamaican Teenagers." Master's thesis, University of the West Indies, Mona, 1974.

Forbes, Curdella. "Fracturing Subjectivities: International Space and the Discourse of Individualism in Colin Channer's *Waiting in Vain* and Jamaica Kincaid's *Mr Potter*." *Small Axe* 25 (February 2008): 16–37.

Fowler, Roger. *Language in the News: Discourse and Ideology in the Press*. London: Routledge, 1994.

———. *Linguistic Criticism*. 2nd ed. Oxford: Oxford University Press, 1996.

Genette, Gérard. *Narrative Discourse: An Essay in Method*. Translated by J. E. Lewin. Ithaca, NY: Cornell University Press, 1980.

Gikandi, Simon. "Narration in the Postcolonial Moment: Merle Hodge's *Crick Crack, Monkey*." In *Past the Last Post: Theorizing Post-Colonialism and Post-Modernism*. Edited by Ian Adam and Helen Tiffin, 13–22. Hertfordshire, England: Harvester Wheatsheaf, 1991.

Gilroy, Paul. *The Black Atlantic: Modernity and the Double Consciousness*. Cambridge: Harvard University Press, 1993.

Glissant, Édouard. *Caribbean Discourse: Selected Essays*. Translated and introduced by J. Michael Dash. Charlottesville: University Press of Virginia, 1992.

Goatly, Andrew. *Washing the Brain: Metaphor and Hidden Identity*. Amsterdam: John Benjamins, 2007.

Goodison, Lorna. *I Am Becoming My Mother*. London: New Beacon Books, 1986.

———. *Heartease*. London: New Beacon Books, 1988.

———. *Selected Poems*. Ann Arbor: University of Michigan Press, 1992.

———. *Tamarind Season*. Kingston: Institute of Jamaica, 1980.

———. *To Us, All Flowers Are Roses*. Urbana: University of Illinois Press, 1995.

Graddol, David, Dick Leith, and Joan Swann. *English: History, Diversity and Change*. London: Routledge, 1996.

Greene, Graham. *The Lost Childhood*. New York: Viking, 1952.

Gregory, Michael, and Suzanne Carroll. *Language and Situation*. London: Routledge and Kegan Paul, 1978.

Grice, H. P. "Further Notes on Logic and Conversation." In *Syntax and Semantics*. Vol. 9. Edited by P. Cole and J. Morgan, 113–127. New York: Academic Press, 1978.

———. "Logic and Conversation." In *Syntax and Semantics*. Vol. 3. Edited by P. Cole and J. Morgan, 41–58. New York: Academic Press, 1975.

Grimes, Joseph E. "Dialects as Optimal Communications Networks." *Language* 50, no. 2 (1974): 260–269.

Gunst, Laurie. *Born fi' Dead: A Journey through the Jamaican Posse Underworld*. New York: Holt, 1995.

Hall, Stuart D., "New Ethnicities," in *Stuart Hall: Critical Dialogues in Cultural Studies: A Reader*, ed. David Morley and Kuan Hsing Chen (London: Routledge, 1996), 141–49.

———. *Representation: Cultural Representations and Signifying Practices*. Cultures, Media and Identities Series. Milton Keynes, England: The Open University, 1997.

Hall, Stuart, D. Held, and T. McGrew, eds. *Modernity and Its Futures*. Cambridge: Polity Press, 1992.

———. "What Is This 'Black' in Black Popular Culture?" In *Stuart Hall: Critical Dialogues in Cultural Studies: A Reader*. Edited by David Morley and Kuan Hsing Chen, 465–475. London: Routledge, 1996.

Halliday, M. A. K. *Language as Social Semiotic: The Social Interpretation of Language and Meaning*. London: Edward Arnold, 1978.

Hamley, Col. William G. *Captain Clutterbuck's Champagne: A West Indian Reminiscence*. 4 vols. Edinburgh: Blackwood, 1862.

Harney, Stefano. *Nationalism and Identity: Culture and the Imagination in a Caribbean Diaspora*. Kingston, Jamaica: University of the West Indies Press, 1996. London: Zed, 1996.

Herman, David. *Story Logic: Problems and Possibilities of Narrative*. Lincoln: University of Nebraska Press, 2002.

Herman, David, Manfred Jahn, and Marie Laure-Ryan, eds. *Routledge Encyclopedia of Narrative Theory*. London: Routledge, 2005.

Herskovits, Melville. *The Myth of the Negro Past*. New York: Harper and Brothers, 1941.

Hickey, Raymond, ed. *Varieties of English in Writing: The Written Word as Linguistic Evidence*. Amsterdam: Benjamins, 2010.

Higden, Ranulph. "*Polychronicon Ranulphi Higden, Monachi Cestrensis*," *Together with the English Translations of John of Trevisa and an Unknown Writer of the Fifteenth Century*. Edited by Churchill Babington and Joseph Rawson Lumby. Rolls Series 41. 9 vols. London: Longman, Roberts, and Green, 1865–1886.

Hockett, Charles Francis. *Refurbishing Our Foundations: Elementary Linguistics from an Advanced Point of View*. Amsterdam: John Benjamins, 1987.

Hodge, Merle. *Crick Crack, Monkey*. London: André Deutsch, 1970.

———. "Dialogue and Narrative Voice in *The Schoolmaster*." *Journal of West Indian Literature* 8, no. 1 (1998): 56–72.

———. "Dialogue and Narrative Voice in *The Schoolmaster*." Presentation at the Sixteenth Annual Conference on West Indian Literature, Miami, FL, April 1–4, 1997.

———. *For the Life of Laetitia*. New York: Farrar, Straus, Giroux, 1993.

———. *The Knots in English: A Manual for Caribbean Users*. Wellesley, MA: Calaloux, 1997.

———. "A Study of Language in Trinidad and Tobago Prose Fiction of the Twentieth Century with Special Reference to the Works of Earl Lovelace." PhD diss., University of the West Indies, St. Augustine, 2007.

Hopkinson, Nalo. *Brown Girl in the Ring*. New York: Warner Books, Grand Central Publishing, 1998.

———. *Midnight Robber*. New York: Warner Books, 2000.

Hunston, Susan, and Geoff Thompson. *Evaluation in Text: Authorial Stance and the Construction of Discourse*. Oxford: Oxford University Press, 1996.

Hymes, Dell. "On Communicative Competence." *In Sociolinguistics: Selected Readings*. Edited by J. B. Pride and Janet Holmes, 269–293. 1971. Reprint, Harmondsworth, England: Penguin, 1972.

The Importance of Jamaica to Great Britain Consider'd in a Letter to a Gentleman. London: Dodd, 1740.

Jahn, Manfred. "The Mechanics of Focalization: Extending the Narratological Toolbox." *GRAAT* 21 (1999): 85–110.

———. "Windows of Focalization: Deconstructing and Re-Constructing a Narratological Concept." *Style* 30, no. 2 (1996): 241–267.

Jakobson, Roman. "Linguistics and Poetics." In *Roman Jakobson, Selected Writings*. Vol. 3. Edited by Richard and Fernande De George. Garden City, NJ: Doubleday, 1972. 85–122.

Jarvey, Paul. "Interview: Nalo Hopkinson." *Canadian Science Fiction Review* 1, no. 3 (2011). http://aescifi.ca/index.php/non-fiction/34-interviews/471-nalo-hopkinson.

Jay, Paul. "Hybridity, Identity and Cultural Commerce in Claude McKay's *Banana Bottom*." *Callaloo* 22, no. 1 (1999): 176–194.

Jekyll, Walter, ed. *Jamaican Song and Story*. 1907. Reprint, New York: Dover, 1966; Kingston: Sangster's Bookstore, 1966.

Jenkins, Lee M. *The Language of Caribbean Poetry: Boundaries of Expression*. Gainesville: University Press of Florida, 2004.

Joseph, E. L. *Warner Arundell: Adventures of a Creole*. Edited by Lise Winer, Bridget Brereton, Rhonda Cobham, and Mary Rimmer. 1838. Reprint, Kingston, Jamaica: University of the West Indies Press, 2001.

Kahane, Henry. "A Typology of the Prestige Language." *Language* 62, no. 3 (September 1986): 495–508.

Kaplan, Robert. "Concluding Essay: On Applied Linguistics and Discourse Analysis." In *Annual Review of Applied Linguistics 11*. Edited by Robert Kaplan, 199–204. Cambridge: Cambridge University Press, 1990.

Kihm, Alain. "Creoles, Markedness and Default Settings: An Appraisal." In *The Handbook of Pidgin and Creole Studies*. Edited by Silvia Kouwenberg and John Victor Singler, 411–439. Oxford: John Wiley and Sons, 2009.

Lakoff, George, and Mark Johnson. *Metaphors We Live By*. 1986. Reprint, Chicago: University of Chicago Press, 1991.

Lalla, Barbara. "Conceptual Perspectives on Time and Timelessness in Martin Carter's 'University of Hunger.'" In *All Are Involved: The Art of Martin Carter*. Edited by Stewart Brown, 106–115. Leeds, England: Peepal Tree, 2000.

———. "Creole and Respec' in the Development of Jamaican Literary Discourse." *Journal of Pidgin and Creole Languages* 20, no. 1 (2005): 53–84.

———. "Creole Dimensions of Development in Caribbean Literary Discourse." Presentation at the Conference of the Society for Pidgin and Creole Linguistics, University of Hawaii, Honolulu, 2003.

———. "Creole Representation in Literary Discourse: Issues of Linguistics and Discourse Analysis." Presentation at the Conference of the Society for Caribbean Linguistics, St. Lucia, 1998.

———. *Defining Jamaican Fiction: Marronage and the Discourse of Survival.* Tuscaloosa: University of Alabama Press, 1996.

———. "Nation Language and Caribbean Discourse." Presentation at the Conference of the Society for Caribbean Linguistics at The University of the West Indies, Mona, Jamaica, August 2000.

———. "Possible Caribbeans: Assembling the Fictional Voice." In *Reassembling the Fragments: Voice and Identity in Caribbean Literary Discourse.* Kingston, Jamaica: University of the West Indies Press, forthcoming.

———. *Postcolonialisms: Caribbean Rereading of Medieval English Discourse.* Kingston, Jamaica: University of the West Indies Press, 2008.

———. "Registering Woman: Senior's Zigzag Discourse and Code-Switching in Jamaican Narrative." *Review of International English Literature* 29, no. 4 (1998): 83–98.

———. "A Sociolinguistic Approach to Critical Analysis in the Caribbean." In *Studies in Caribbean Language 2.* Edited by Pauline Christie, Barbara Lalla, Velma Pollard, and Lawrence Carrington, 112–127. St. Augustine, Trinidad and Tobago: Society for Caribbean Linguistics, 1999.

———. "Virtual Realism and the Inscriber's Dilemma: Representing the Caribbean Voice." Occasional Paper 32, Society for Caribbean Linguistics, University of the West Indies, St. Augustine, Trinidad and Tobago, 2005.

Lalla, Barbara, and Jean D'Costa. *Language in Exile: Three Hundred Years of Jamaican Creole.* Tuscaloosa: The University of Alabama Press, 1990. Reprinted paperback, 2009.

Laure-Ryan, Marie. *Possible Worlds, Artificial Intelligence and Narrative Theory.* Bloomington: Indiana University Press, 1991.

Lawton, D. L. "Suprasegmental Phenomena in Jamaican Creole." PhD diss., Michigan State University, 1963.

Le Page, Robert B. "Dialect in West Indian Literature." *Journal of Commonwealth Literature* 7 (1969): 1–7.

Le Page, Robert B., and David DeCamp. *Jamaican Creole.* London: MacMillan, 1960.

Le Page, Robert B., and Andrée Tabouret-Keller. *Acts of Identity: Creole-Based Approaches to Language and Ethnicity.* Cambridge: Cambridge University Press, 1985.

Lewin, Olive. *Rock It Come Over: The Folk Music of Jamaica.* Kingston, Jamaica: University of the West Indies Press, 2000.

Lewis, Matthew G. *Journal of a West India Proprietor.* London: Murray, 1834.

Long, Edward. *The History of Jamaica.* 3 vols. London: T. Lowndes, 1774.

Lovelace, Earl. *The Dragon Can't Dance.* London: André Deutsch, 1979. Burnt Mill, Harlow, England: Longman, 1979.

———. *Salt.* London: Faber and Faber, 1996; New York: Persea Books, 1997.

———. *The Schoolmaster.* Chicago: Regnery, 1968. Reprinted, London: Heinemann, 1979.

———. *While Gods Are Falling*. London: Collins, 1965. Reprinted, Harlow, England: Longman, 1984.

———. *The Wine of Astonishment*. London: André Deutsch, 1982.

Mair, Christian. "World Non-Standard Englishes: Reflections on the Global Spread of (Some) Vernacular Varieties of English." Presentation at the International Society for the Linguistics of English, College of Arts and Sciences, Boston University, June 17–21, 2011.

Mais, Roger. *Brother Man*. London: Cape, 1954. Reprinted, London: Heinemann, 1974.

Manley, Edna, ed. *Focus: An Anthology of Contemporary Jamaican Writing*. Kingston, Jamaica: City Printery, 1960.

Marks, J. *What It Means to Be 98% Chimpanzee*. Berkeley: University of California Press, 2002.

Marly, or, the Life of a Planter in Jamaica. 2d ed. Glasgow: Printed for R. Griffin, 1828. Republished. Edited by Karina Williamson. Oxford: Macmillan Caribbean, 2005.

Marshall, Paule. *Brown Girl, Brown Stones*. New York: Random House, 1959.

———. *Praise Song for the Widow*. London: Virago Press, 1983.

McKay, Claude. *Banana Bottom*. 1933. Reprint, London: Pluto, 1986. New York: Harper, 1961.

———. *Songs of Jamaica*. Kingston, Jamaica: A. W. Gardner and Co., 1912.

Mendes, Alfred. *The Wages of Sin and Other Poems*. Port-of-Spain, Trinidad: Yuille's Printer, 1925.

Milroy, James, and Leslie Milroy. *Authority in Language: Investigating Language Prescription and Standardization*. London: Routledge and Kegan Paul, 1988.

Mordecai, Pamela. *de Man*. Toronto: Sister Vision, 1996.

———. "Wooing with Words: Some Comments on the Poetry of Lorna Goodison." *Jamaica Journal* 45 (1981): 38–40.

Mordecai, Pamela, and Betty Wilson, eds. *Her True True Name*. Kingston, Jamaica: Heinemann Caribbean, 1989.

Moreton, J. B. *West India Customs and Manners*. 1790. Reprint, London: Parsons, 1793.

Morris, Mervyn. *"Is English We Speaking" and Other Essays*. Kingston, Jamaica: Ian Randle, 1999.

Mufwene, Salikoko. "What Do Pidgins and Creoles Tell Us about the Evolution of Language?" In *The Origin and Evolution of Languages: Approaches, Models, Paradigms*. Edited by Bernard Laks, Serge Cleuziou, Jean-Paul Demoule, and Pierre Encrevé, 272–297. London: Equinox, 2008.

Mühleisen, Susanne. *Creole Discourse: Exploring Prestige Formation and Change across Caribbean English-lexicon Creoles*. Amsterdam: John Benjamins, 2002.

———. "Introduction—Creole Languages in Creole Literatures: Status and Standardization." Special issue, *Journal of Pidgin and Creole Languages* 20 (2005).

Mukarovsky, Jan. "Standard Language and Poetic Language." In *Linguistics and Literary Style*. Edited by Donald C. Freeman. Translated by Paul L. Garvin, 40–56. New York: Holt, Rinehart, and Winston, 1970.

Murray, Henry Garland. *Manners and Customs of the Country a Generation Ago: Tom Kittle's Wake*. Kingston, Jamaica: Jordan, 1877.

Naipaul, V. S. *A House for Mr Biswas*. New York: Vintage, 1961; New York: Random House, 1984.

———. *The Middle Passage*. 1962. Reprint, Harmondsworth, Middlesex: Penguin, 1969.

———. *Reading and Writing: A Personal Account*. New York: NYREV, 2000.

Nettleford, Rex. Introduction to *Jamaica Labrish,* by Louise Bennett. Notes by Rex Nettleford. Kingston, Jamaica: Sangster's Bookstores, 1972.

Nilep, Chad. "'Code Switching' in Sociocultural Linguistics." *Colorado Research in Linguistics* 19 (2006): 1–22.

Noel, Keith, ed. *Caribbean Plays for Schools*. Portsmouth, NH: Heinemann Educational Books Ltd., 1985.

Nugent, Lady Maria. *Lady Nugent's Journal of Her Residence in Jamaica, from 1801 to 1805*. Edited by Philip Wright. Kingston, Jamaica: Institute of Jamaica, 1966.

O'Callaghan, Evelyn. *Woman Version: Theoretical Approaches to West Indian Fiction by Women*. London: Macmillan Caribbean, 1993.

Okolo, Bertram A. "Indirectness in Discourse: A Study in Paradoxical Communication among the Igbos." In *The Language of African Literature*. Edited by Edmund L. Epstein and Roger Kole, 168–184. Trenton, NJ: Africa World Press, 1998.

Ong, Walter. *Orality and Literacy: The Technologizing of the Word*. London: Methuen, 1982.

Patrick, Peter. "Testing the Creole Continuum." Working Papers in Linguistics 6, no. 2. Selected Papers from *New Ways of Analyzing Variation* 27 (1998): 109–120.

Patrick, Peter, and Ester Figeroa. "Kiss-Teeth." *American Speech* 77, no. 4 (2002): 483–497.

Patterson, H. Orlando. *The Sociology of Slavery*. London: MacGibbon and Kee, 1967. Reprinted as *The Sociology of Slavery: An Analysis of the Origins, Development and Structure of Negro Slave Society in Jamaica*. Kingston, Jamaica: Sangster's Bookstores, 1973.

Perkins, Cyrus Francis. *Busha's Mistress, or Catherine the Fugitive: A Stirring Romance of the Days of Slavery in Jamaica*. 1911. Edited by Paul E. Lovejoy, Verene A. Shepherd, and David V. Trotman. Reprint, Kingston, Jamaica: Ian Randle, 2003.

Phillipson, Robert. *Linguistic Imperialism*. Oxford: Oxford University Press, 1992.

Pollard, Velma, ed. *Anansesem: A Collection of Caribbean Folk Tales, Legends and Poems for Juniors*. Kingston, Jamaica: Carlong Publishers Kingston, 1985. 2nd Ed., 2002.

———. "Code-Switching in Jamaica Creole: Some Educational Implications." *Caribbean Journal of Education* 5, nos. 1 and 2 (1978): 16–31.

———. *Considering Woman*. London: Woman's Press, 1989.

———. "Dread Talk: The Speech of the Rastafari of Jamaica." *Caribbean Quarterly* 26, no. 4 (1982): 32–41.

———. "Mothertongue Voices in the Writing of Olive Senior and Lorna Goodison." In *Motherlands: An Anthology of Critical Writing on Black Women Writers from Africa, the Caribbean, South Asia, Great Britain*. Edited by S. Nasta, 239–245. London: Women's Press, 1991.

———. "The Social History of Dread Talk." In *Studies in Caribbean Language*. Edited by Lawrence Carrington, in collaboration with Dennis Craig and Ramon Todd Dandare, 46–72. St. Augustine, Trinidad and Tobago: Society for Caribbean Linguistics, University of the West Indies, 1983.

———. "The Speech of Rastafari in Modern Jamaican Poetry." In *Dread Talk: The Language of Rastafari*. Kingston, Jamaica: Canoe Press, University of the West Indies, Mona, 1994. 2nd Ed., 2000, 69–85.

———. "*To Us, All Flowers Are Roses:* Writing Ourselves into the Literature of the Caribbean." In *Centre of Remembrance: Memory and Caribbean Women's Literature*. Edited by Joan Anim-Addo, 164–74. London: Mango Publishing, 2002.

Pouchet-Paquet, Sandra. "The Vulnerable Observer: Self-Fashioning of Earl Lovelace's *Growing in the Dark* (Selected Essays)." *Anthurium: A Caribbean Studies Journal* 4, no. 2 (2006): 1–26. http://scholarlyrepository.miami.edu/anthurium/vol4/iss2/7WEB.

Pratt, Mary Louise. "Scratches in the Face of the Country: What Mr Burrow Saw in the Land of the Bushmen." In *Race, Writing and Difference*. Edited Henry Louis Gates Jr., 138–162. Chicago: University of Chicago Press, 1985.

Prince, Gerald. *Dictionary of Narratology*. Lincoln: University of Nebraska Press, 1987.

———. *Narratology: The Form and Functioning of Discourse*. Berlin: Mouton, 1982.

Puri, Shalini. *The Caribbean Post-Colonial: Social Equality, Post-Nationalism and Social Hybridity*. New York: Palgrave Macmillan, 2004.

Pyrhönen, Heta. "Genre." In *The Cambridge Companion to Narrative*. Edited by David Herman, 109–123. Cambridge: Cambridge University Press, 2007.

Rahim, Jennifer. "From Archaeology to Iconography: The Tropics in Senior's *Gardening in the Tropics* and Goodison's *To Us, All Flowers Are Roses*." *Journal of West Indian Literature* 8, no. 2 (1999): 68–72.

Rampini, Charles. *Letters from Jamaica, the Land of Wood and Streams*. Edinburgh: Edmonston and Douglas, 1873.

Reid, Capt. Mayne. *The Maroon*. 3 vols. London: Hurst and Blackett, 1862.

Reid, Vic. *The Jamaicans*. 1976. Reprint, Kingston: Institute of Jamaica, 1978.

———. *New Day*. 1949. Reprinted. Caribbean Writers Series 4. London: Heinemann, 1973.

Rhys, Jean. *Letters 1931–1966*. Edited by Francis Wyndham and Diana Melly. London: André Deutsch, 1984.

———. *Smile Please: An Unfinished Autobiography*. New York: Harper and Row, 1979.

———. *Tigers Are Better-Looking*. New York: Popular Library, 1976.

———. *Wide Sargasso Sea*. Harmondsworth, England: Penguin, 1980.

Rickford, John R. *Dimensions of a Creole Continuum*. Stanford, CA: Stanford University Press, 1987.

Rickford, John, and Angela Rickford. "Cut-Eye and Suck-Teeth: African Words and Gestures in New World Guise." *Journal of American Folklore* 89, no. 353 (1976): 194–309.

Roberts, Ian. "Verb Movement and Markedness." In *Language Creation and Language Change: Creolisation, Diachrony and Development*. Edited by Michel DeGraff, 304–307. Cambridge, MA: MIT Press, 1999.

Roberts, Peter. *From Oral to Literate Culture: Colonial Experience in the English West Indies*. Kingston, Jamaica: University of the West Indies Press, 1997.

Rohlehr, Gordon. "Afterthoughts." *Bim* 14, no. 56 (1973): 227–232.

———. *My Strangled City and Other Essays*. Port-of-Spain, Trinidad and Tobago: Longman, 1992.

Rojo-Benítez, Antonio. *The Repeating Island.* Durham, NC: Duke University Press, 1996.

Russell, Thomas. *The Etymology of Jamaican Grammar, by a Young Gentleman.* Kingston, Jamaica: M. De Cordova, MacDougall, 1868.

Rutherford, Anna. "Olive Senior Interview." *Kunapipi* 8, no. 2 (1986): 11–20.

Saakana, Amon Saba. *Colonisation and the Destruction of the Mind: Psychological Issues of Race, Class, Religion and Sexuality.* London: Karnak House, 1996.

Schilling-Estes, Natalie. "Investigating 'Self-Conscious' Speech: The Performance Register in Ocracoke English." *Language in Society* 27 (1998): 53–83.

Schneider, Edgar W. "Investigating Variation and Change in Written Documents." In *The Handbook of Language Variation and Change.* Edited by J. K. Chambers, Peter Trudgill and Natalie Schilling-Estes, 67–96. Oxford: Blackwell, 2002.

Schneider, Edgar W., and Christian Wagner. "The Variability of Literary Dialect in Jamaican Creole: Thelwell's *The Harder They Come.*" *Journal of Pidgin and Creole Languages* 21, no. 1 (2006): 45–96.

Scott, Dennis. *Uncle Time.* Pittsburgh, PA: Pittsburgh University Press, 1973.

Scott, Michael. *Tom Cringle's Log.* 1833. 2 vols. Reprint, Edinburgh: Blackwood, 1834; London: Gibbings, 1894. Republished, London: Picador, 1999.

Selvon, Samuel. *The Lonely Londoners.* Caribbean Writers Series. Burnt Mill, England: Longman, 1956.

Senior, Olive. *Arrival of the Snake Woman, and Other Stories.* Harlow, England: Longman, 1989.

———. *Discerner of Hearts.* Toronto: McLelland and Stewart, 1995.

———. *Encyclopedia of Jamaican Heritage.* Kingston, Jamaica: Twin Guinep, 2003.

———. *Gardening in the Tropics.* Toronto: McClelland and Stewart, 1994.

———. *Summer Lightning and Other Stories.* Harlow, England: Longman Caribbean, 1986.

———. *Talking of Trees.* Kingston, Jamaica: Calabash Publishers, 1985.

Shepherd, Verene. "The Ranking Game: Discourses of Belonging in Jamaican History." Professorial Inaugural Lecture. University of the West Indies, Mona, Jamaica, April 12, 2002.

A Short Journey to the West Indies. 2 vols. London: Murray and Forbes, 1790.

Simpson, G. E. *Religious Cults of the Caribbean: Trinidad, Jamaica and Haiti.* Rio Pedras: University of Puerto Rico, 1970.

Simpson, Paul. *Language, Ideology and Point of View.* London: Routledge, 1993.

———. *Stylistics.* New York: Routledge, 2004.

Sisam, Kenneth, ed. *Fourteenth Century Verse and Prose.* Oxford: Clarendon Press, 1955.

Sistren, with Honor Ford-Smith. *Lionheart Gal: Life Stories of Jamaican Women.* London: Women's Press, 1986.

Sloane, Sir Hans. *A Voyage to the Islands Madera, Barbados, Nieves, S. Christophers and Jamaica: With the Natural History . . . of the Last of Those Islands; to Which Is Prefix'd an Introduction, wherein Is an Account of the Inhabitants, Air, Waters, Diseases, Trade, &c. . . . Illustrated with the Figures of the Things Describ'd.* 2 vols. London: British Museum for the Author, 1707–1725.

Smith, Faith. *Creole Recitations: John Jacob Thomas and Colonial Formation in the Late Nineteenth-Century Caribbean*. Charlottesville: University of Virginia Press, 2002.

St. Omer, Garth. *The Colonial Novel*. Ann Arbor, MI: University Microfilms, 1975.

Stewart, William. "An Outline of Linguistic Typology for Describing Multilingualism." In *Study of the Role of Second Languages in Asia, Africa and Latin America*. Edited by F. A. Rice, 15–25. Washington: Center for Applied Linguistics, 1962.

———. "A Sociolinguistic Typology of Multilingualism." In *Readings in the Sociology of Language*. Edited by Joshua Fishman, 531–545. The Hague: Mouton, 1968.

Tanna, Laura. *Jamaican Folk Tales and Oral Histories*. Kingston, Jamaica: Institute of Jamaica, 1984.

Tannen, Deborah. *Spoken and Written Language*. Norwood, NJ: Ablex, 1982.

Thomas, J. J. *The Theory and Practice of Creole Grammar*. Port of Spain, Trinidad and Tobago: Chronicle Publishing Office, 1869; London: New Beacon Books, 1969.

Thompson, J. Downing. "The Novel before 1950." In *A History of Literature in the Caribbean: English- and Dutch-Speaking Caribbean*. Vol. 2. Edited by Albert James Arnold, 115–126. Amsterdam: John Benjamins, 2001.

Todorov, Tzvetan. *Genres in Discourse*. Translated by Catherine Porter. Cambridge: Cambridge University Press, 1990.

Torres-Saillant, Silvio. *Caribbean Poetics: Toward an Aesthetic of West Indian Literature*. Cambridge: Cambridge University Press, 1997.

Turner, Lorenzo. *Africanisms in the Gullah District*. Chicago: University of Chicago Press, 1949.

Uspenskii, Boris. *A Poetics of Composition*. Translated by Z. Zavarin and S. Witig. Berkeley: University of California Press, 1973.

Walcott, Derek. *Another Life*. London: Jonathan Cape, 1972.

———. *Collected Poems 1948–1984*. New York: Farrar, Straus, 1986.

———. *Dream on Monkey Mountain and Other Plays*. New York: Farrar, Straus, and Giroux, 1970.

———. *In a Green Night*. London: Cape, 1962.

[Ward, Edward]. *A Trip to Jamaica, with a True Character of the People and the Island*. London: n.p., 1698. (Bodleian Library ref. Mason 1.1. 147).

Wardhaugh, Ronald. *Languages in Competition: Dominance, Diversity, and Decline*. Oxford: Blackwell, 1987.

Warner-Lewis, Maureen. "Odomankoma." *Caribbean Quarterly* 19, no. 4 (1973): 51–99.

———. "Samuel Selvon's Linguistic Extravaganza: *Moses Ascending*." In *Critical Issues in West Indian Literature*. Edited by E. Smilowitz and R. Knowles, 101–111. Parkersburgh, IA: Caribbean Books, 1984.

———. "Samuel Selvon's Linguistic Extravaganza: *Moses Ascending*." In *Something Rich and Strange: Selected Essays on Sam Selvon*. Edited by Martin Zehnder, 65–76. Leeds, England: Peepal Tree Press, 2003.

———. "Trinidad Yoruba: Its Theoretical Implications for Creolisation Processes." *Caribbean Quarterly* 44, nos. 1 and 2 (1998): 50–59.

Washington, J. R. *Black Sects and Cults*. New York: Doubleday, 1972.

Wassinka, Alice. "Historic Low Prestige and Seeds of Change." *Language in Society* 28 (1999): 57–92.

Williams, Cynric. *A Tour through the Island of Jamaica from the Western to the Eastern End, in the Year 1823*. London: Hunt and Clarke, 1826.

Wilson-Tagoe, Nana. *Historical Thought and Literary Representation in West Indian Literature*. Gainesville: University of Florida Press, 1998. Kingston, Jamaica: University of the West Indies Press, 1998. Oxford: James Currey, 1998.

Winer, Lise. "Comprehension and Resonance: English Readers and English Creole Texts." In *Creole Genesis, Attitudes and Discourse: Studies Celebrating Charlene J. Sato*. Edited by John Rickford and Suzanne Romaine, 391–406. Amsterdam: John Benjamins, 1999. Kingston, Jamaica: University of the West Indies Press, 1999.

———. *Dictionary of the English/Creole of Trinidad and Tobago*. Montreal: McGill-Queen's University Press, 2009.

Youssef, Valerie. "Varilingualism: A Discrete Sub-Type of Language Competence." *Journal of Multilingual Communication Disorders* 3, no. 3 (November 2005): 216–226.

———. "Working Out Conversational Roles through Questioning Strategies." In *Due Respect: Papers on English and English-Related Creoles in the Caribbean in Honour of Professor Robert Le Page*. Edited by Pauline Christie, 219–246. Kingston, Jamaica: University of the West Indies Press, 2001.

Index

Tables are indicated with an added t. Page references containing "n" refer to notes; for example, "39n9" refers to note number 9 on page 39.